Diagnosis and Treatment Planning in Counseling

Second Edition

Diagnosis and Treatment Planning in Counseling

Second Edition

Linda Seligman
George Mason University
and Center for Counseling and Consultation
Fairfax, Virginia

Plenum Press • New York and London

Library of Congress Cataloging-in-Publication Data

Seligman, Linda.
    Diagnosis and treatment planning in counseling / Linda Seligman. -
- 2nd ed.
        p.   cm.
    Includes bibliographical references and index.
    ISBN 0-306-45351-7 (hardback). -- ISBN 0-306-45352-5 (pbk.)
    1. Mental health counseling. 2. Counseling.   I. Title.
    [DNLM: 1. Counseling--methods. 2. Mental Disorders--diagnosis.
3. Patient Care Planning.   WM 55 S465d 1996]
    RC466.S45 1996
    616.89--dc20
    DNLM/DLC
    for Library of Congress   96-29020
                                                              CIP

ISBN 0-306-45351-7 (Hardbound)
ISBN 0-306-45352-5 (Paperback)

© 1996 Plenum Press, New York
A Division of Plenum Publishing Corporation
233 Spring Street, New York, N. Y. 10013

10 9 8 7 6 5 4 3 2 1

The first edition of this book was published by Human Sciences Press, Inc., New York, 1986

Printed in the United States of America

Preface

Mental health counseling and diagnosis and treatment planning have grown enormously in importance since the 1986 publication of the first edition of this book. Licensure or certification for counselors is now available in all but a handful of states. Training in diagnosis and treatment planning is provided by nearly all graduate programs in Counselor Education. I have traveled throughout the United States and Canada, providing hundreds of workshops and courses that trained thousands of clinicians in the *Diagnostic and Statistical Manual of Mental Disorders* (DSM) and in effective treatment planning.

In the preface to the first edition of this book, I wrote, "To date, little of value to counselors has been written on diagnosis and treatment planning." That statement is no longer true; many articles and some books have been written since that time on the use of diagnosis and treatment planning by counselors. However, the field of mental health counseling is still young; more research and writing is needed to establish a sound theoretical base for the profession and to teach the skills of diagnosis and treatment planning. The purpose of the second edition of this book is to help counselors and other mental health professionals to acquire up-to-date information on diagnosis and treatment planning and to develop related clinical skills that are essential to their effectiveness.

Chapter 1, The Changing Role of the Counselor, reviews efforts to develop a definition of mental health counseling. An overview of the history of the counseling profession is provided, as well as information on the expanding role of the counselor, professional associations, credentialing for both counselors and counselor education programs, and the current impact of managed care on the profession. This chapter concludes with a review of important competencies of the mental health counselor.

New roles for mental health counselors are the focus of chapter 2, Opportunities for the Mental Health Counselor. This chapter looks at new and growing client groups, employment settings, and problem areas of relevance to the mental health counselor. The chapter also discusses the types of mental health professionals and the mental health treatment team.

The *Diagnostic and Statistical Manual of Mental Disorders* is the focus of chapter 3, Diagnostic Systems and Their Use. This chapter provides an overview of the benefits and pitfalls of diagnosis and of its history. The chapter also reviews the diagnoses in the current edition of the DSM.

The Use of Assessment in Diagnosis, chapter 4, discusses tools for qualitative and quantitative assessment that can enhance the process of diagnosis and treatment planning. The chapter also provides information on planning an assessment and on interpreting client information.

Chapter 5, Intake Interviews, reviews the nature and importance of the intake interview and provides an outline for an extended intake interview. Also included in this chapter are a transcript of an intake interview and written reports of both brief and lengthy intake interviews. In addition, ways to conduct a mental status examination are described.

Chapter 6, The Nature and Importance of Treatment Planning, presents the DO A CLIENT MAP, a structured format for treatment planning.

In chapter 7, Theories and Techniques of Individual Counseling, information on the major theories of individual counseling is presented, including important concepts, key interventions, and appropriate use. Examples illustrate the information presented in both chapters 6 and 7.

Diagnosis and Treatment Planning for Families, chapter 8, provides guidelines and tools for assessing family functioning. The important approaches to family counseling are discussed, including their appropriate use. An example of an assessment and treatment plan for a family is provided as well as cases for discussion.

Chapter 9, Assessment and Treatment Planning for Groups and Organizations, encompasses ways to describe and diagnose the needs of groups, as well as discussing counselor roles in group treatment and important approaches to group counseling. An example of the assessment and planning of a counseling group is provided.

Writing and Record Keeping in Counseling, chapter 10, discusses the importance of these activities in counseling. It provides models for progress notes, interim reports, assessment reports, professional disclosure statements, safe-keeping contracts, and other reports prepared by counselors.

Future Trends and Projections, chapter 11, reviews the predictions made in the first edition of this book and discusses their current status. In addition, predictions are made about the counseling profession, based primarily on trends and issues discussed throughout this book.

Acknowledgments

I would like to express my appreciation to some of the people who contributed to the writing of this book. Many thanks to:

- My husband, Dr. Robert Zeskind, for your love and support.
- My friend, Bettie MacLennan Young, for your friendship, good advice, and understanding.
- Bonnie Moore, Director of Educational Counseling Services, Office of Adult and Community Education, Fairfax County Public Schools, and doctoral student at George Mason University, for your contribution to this book.
- Stephanie Hardenburg, doctoral student at George Mason University, for your help with this manuscript.
- My colleagues at George Mason University, especially Dean Gustavo A. Mellander, Associate Dean Martin Ford, and Assistant Dean Clark Dobson, for your encouragement of my writing and research.
- My clients, who helped me really to understand diagnosis and treatment planning.
- The participants in my courses and workshops on diagnosis and treatment planning, who contributed greatly to my knowledge.

Contents

Linda Seligman and Bonita Marcus Moore

The Changing Role of the Counselor

THE EVOLUTION OF THE COUNSELING PROFESSION

The counseling profession is nearly 100 years old. For most of those years, "counselor" usually meant school or career counselor. However, since the early 1980s, the counseling profession has undergone dramatic changes, evidenced most strongly in the emergence and rapid growth of the specialization of mental health or community agency counseling (West, Hosie, & Mackey, 1987) as well as the decline, during the 1980s, of opportunities for school counselors (Ritchie, Piazza, & Lewton, 1991). By the early 1990s, graduate programs to train mental health counselors, including community agency counselors and marriage and family counselors, outnumbered programs to train school counselors (Cowger, Hinkle, DeRidder, & Erk, 1991). In fact, Fong (1990) proposed that all counseling should be described as mental health counseling because that, in fact, is its focus. This book will also take a broad view of mental health counseling.

Many social, political, and economic trends have contributed to the growth of mental health counseling. Nugent (1990) viewed the most important of these as increased social, economic, and cultural stress; growing awareness of the proliferation and impact of dysfunctional families; and an overall increase in opportunities and stressors. Other trends that contributed to this growth include greater understanding of the relationship between the mind and the body; increased media attention to such pervasive problems as substance abuse and physical and sexual abuse; and an expanding acceptance of the value of counseling. Opportunities for counselors emerged not only in a broad range of mental health settings but also in business and industry. Counselor education programs responded by training increasing numbers of mental health counselors.

DEFINITIONS OF COUNSELING

Many writers have struggled to define counseling and to clarify what distinguishes counseling from the other mental health professions, such as social work and psychology. Numerous efforts also have been made to explain how mental health counseling differs from counseling in general.

Ivey (1989, pp. 28–29) advanced a definition of mental health counseling that is broad enough to encompass the work of all counselors: "Mental health counseling is a profession which conducts its developmental practice with both the severely distressed and those facing normal developmental tasks. This developmental practice exists within a multicultural awareness and seeks to address clients and the systems in which they live." According to Ivey, counseling and development interventions should help individuals and systems (families, groups, and organizations) to fulfill their potential, effect positive change, and grow, regardless of the severity of their concerns. He believed that "Mental health counseling recognizes that individual change may not be possible unless family, school, community and sociocultural systems are also in place. Mental health counseling, then, does not focus narrowly on individual change, but on a careful assessment of both individual and environment and then acts on or treats both personal and systemic variables."

Fong's (1990, p.108) definition of mental health counseling also is broad. She viewed mental health counseling as encompassing a "...continuum of services that is developmental, environmental, and ecological, as well as remedial." It emphasizes interventions that "focus on competencies, strengths, coping, resources, negotiating life transitions, and managing stressors."

Spruill and Fong (1990, p. 21) provided further understanding of mental health counseling in the following definition: "Mental health counseling, a core mental health care profession, is the aggregate of the specific educational, scientific, and professional contributions of the disciplines of education, psychology, and counseling, focused on promotion and maintenance of mental health, the prevention and treatment of mental illness, the identification and modification of etiologic, diagnostic, and systems correlates of mental health, mental illness, and related dysfunction, and the improvement of the mental health service delivery system."

Mental health counseling, then, is characterized by:

- taking a holistic, systemic, and developmental view of people, their families, their environments, and their interrelationships
- using approaches that are preventive, remedial, rehabilitative, and enhancing
- advocating an understanding of pathology and dysfunction, but maintaining an emphasis on health, wellness and growth

- enabling people to identify and build on their strengths so that they can help themselves
- stressing the need for an awareness of and sensitivity to individual, gender, cultural, and other differences
- taking place in a wide range of settings with a great variety of people
- being multifaceted and interdisciplinary, encompassing a broad range of theories, techniques, and interventions, that can be adapted to meet the needs of a particular client or group

Despite the apparent consistency in these definitions, professional identity continues to be a paramount issue for mental health counselors (Weikel & Palmo, 1989), still striving to establish a clear and positive image of themselves in the minds of the general public and in relation to other mental health professions. The purpose of this book is to present some of a counselor's important roles and tools and to contribute to enhancing and clarifying the counselor's identity and image.

EARLY HISTORY OF THE COUNSELING PROFESSION

At its inception in the early 1900s, the field of counseling was a relatively well-defined and circumscribed one. The primary task of the counselor was to help people make occupational choices by seeking a good match between person and job. The guiding theory was what has been called the trait-and-factor approach advanced by Frank Parsons in his 1909 book *Choosing a Vocation*. Vocational or career counseling, then, was the counselor's primary role for more than 30 years. This was reflected by the first national professional organization for counselors, the National Vocational Guidance Association (NVGA) founded in 1913.

COUNSELING IN THE 1940s, 1950s, AND 1960s

The role of the counselor changed and expanded through the 1940s and 1950s. World War II and the Korean War led to a need for counselors to facilitate the readjustment and rehabilitation of veterans. In 1944, the Veterans Administration established a nationwide network of guidance services. In that same year, the United States Employment Service was initiated, eventually establishing a total of 1500 offices (Rockwell, 1991). Counselors began to realize they could best meet people's needs by considering their emotional development as well as their physical concerns and occupational aspirations. They became increasingly interested in helping healthy people deal with transitions and developmental concerns.

Carl Rogers contributed to the shift in the counselor's role with the 1942 publication of *Counseling and Psychotherapy* and his theory of what was called non-directive or client-centered counseling. Rogers' writing encouraged counselors to define their goals in terms of people's needs and to adopt a broader and more flexible array of skills as well as to pay attention to the counseling relationship.

In 1951, the Personnel and Guidance Association (PGA) was founded, the organization that would evolve into today's American Counseling Association. At its inception, the PGA had four divisions reflecting the primary roles of counselors at that time: the American College Personnel Association; the National Association of Guidance Supervisors and College Trainers, forerunner of the modern Association for Counselor Education and Supervision (ACES); the National Vocational Guidance Association; and the Student Personnel Association for Teacher Education. The American School Counselors Association (ASCA) soon became a fifth division and in 1957 the American Rehabilitation Counseling Association became division six. In the 1960s, the Association for Measurement and Evaluation in Guidance and the National Employment Counselors Association became additional divisions of what was then called the American Personnel and Guidance Association.

Professional associations for other helping professionals also were initiated during these years, reflecting the growth in those professions as well as in the counseling field. The American Association of Marriage and Family Therapists was established in 1945, and in 1955 the National Association of Social Workers was founded (Nugent, 1990).

During the 1950s and 1960s, Erik H. Erikson (*Childhood and Society*), Rollo May (*Man's Search for Himself*), Fritz Perls (*Gestalt Therapy*), Leona Tyler (*The Work of the Counselor*), Robert J. Havighurst (*Human Development and Education*), and Albert Bandura (*Principles of Behavior Modification*) all published influential texts that focused counselors' attention on people's developmental needs. Counselors began to attend to prevention and to the personal growth of their clients as well as to remediation of difficulties. Humanistic psychology gained interest and was called the third force in psychology, along with behaviorism and psychoanalysis (Nugent, 1990).

The 1960s was a transitional period in which politicians as well as the general public recognized that large segments of the population were dissatisfied and had emotional and physical needs that were not being met. Civil rights issues, campus unrest, increasing drug abuse, and antiwar demonstrations contributed to a growing national feeling of discontent. That feeling was especially strong among the poor, who typically had not been well served by traditional helping agencies. Many programs were developed during the 1960s in response to this dissatisfaction. Among them were the Peace Corps, VISTA, the War on Poverty, and Operation Headstart. In addition, strong special interest groups were formed to promote racial equality and women's rights.

Those movements had a strong effect on the role of the counselor. They brought increasing recognition to the importance of the community or environment in a person's emotional development. People were less often thought of as abnormal or troubled and more often as unable to cope successfully with a stressful or destructive environment.

That recognition led to the realization that mental health professionals were reaching only a small fraction of people in need of help. The medical model, emphasizing one-to-one contact with troubled people who actively sought help, increasingly seemed outmoded and ineffective. Changes had to be accomplished in communities as well as in individuals before progress could be made in reducing the number of people with emotional difficulties.

In 1963, the Community Mental Health Centers Act was passed, providing a great impetus to the redefinition of the field of counseling. That act mandated establishment of a nationwide network of approximately 2000 community mental health centers (CMHCs), designed to be multifaceted and comprehensive agencies offering a broad range of readily accessible services. The goal of the CMHCs was to both prevent and ameliorate emotional difficulties by enabling communities and their people to expand upon and share their abilities and strengths and to develop skills needed to cope with their problems. Preventive approaches were emphasized as mental health workers became change agents in the community.

The importance of CMHCs was accelerated by a move toward deinstitutionalization, an effort to curtail the length of inpatient treatment for people with serious mental illness, and a shift toward outpatient care of the chronically mentally ill. This effort was facilitated by the development of more effective psychotropic medications to treat schizophrenia and other mental disorders. Although deinstitutionalization was cost effective in the short run and certainly helped many people regain independence they had lost unnecessarily, it complicated the treatment process and some people did not receive the treatment they needed because of difficulty in accessing services.

At the outset, CMHCs were controlled largely by the well-established helping professionals, the psychiatrists and doctoral level psychologists. In order to fulfill the mission of the CMHCs, however, community psychology, a new area of specialization, soon evolved. As defined by Zax and Specter (1974, p. 3), "Community psychology is regarded as an approach to human behavior problems that emphasizes contributions made to their development by environmental forces as well as the potential contributions to be made toward their alleviation by the use of these forces." The growth in CMHCs as well as their community focus led to the hiring of masters-level helping professionals (counselors, psychologists, and social workers) as well as paraprofessionals to meet staffing needs and provide workers who might have common backgrounds with catchment area residents.

Counselor education programs, responding to growth in employment of school and mental health counselors, began to expand and diversify. In the early 1960s, the National Institutes for Mental Health provided funds for pilot training programs for mental health counselors (Magoon, Golann, & Freeman, 1969). National Defense Education Act Institutes, initiated in 1958 primarily for school counselors, also lent credibility and refinement of skills to the profession as the Federal government sought to train counselors who would identify talented youth who could help the United States compete with the Soviet Union.

Counseling became well established in colleges and universities, as it was in secondary schools and mental health centers. By the early 1960s, most colleges and universities offered free counseling to their students. Legislation at that time also contributed to an expansion of the numbers and responsibilities of counselors in elementary schools.

COUNSELING IN THE 1970s AND 1980s

Between 1964 and 1976, the number of counselor education programs increased by about 35% (Shertzer & Stone, 1980). Important ideas and writings by C. Gilbert Wrenn (*The Counselor in a Changing World*), Albert Ellis (*Reason and Emotion in Psychotherapy*), John Krumboltz (behavioral counseling), Robert Carkhuff and C. B. Truax (facilitative conditions), and Norman Kagan (Interpersonal Process Recall) further expanded the counselors' repertoire of skills and promoted diversification and a sense of growth in the profession.

The 1970s was a time of reorientation for the profession. Counseling was maturing and the influx of counselors into mental health facilities continued. However, the declining birthrate, coupled with nationwide financial constraints on state and local budgets, led to a decline in the employment of school counselors. In 1976, the ratio of trained school counselors to available positions was 2.4 to 1, although counselor-student ratios had increased by 50% (Shertzer & Stone, 1980). At the same time, however, counselor education programs, many only recently initiated, were being forced to increase enrollments due to universities' financial concerns.

Clearly, then, the way to meet the needs of people who wanted to counsel and of programs that needed to grow was in a redefinition of the counselor's role and the expansion of the field of mental health counseling. This trend has been evident on many fronts over the past two decades.

The events of the 1970s also shaped the role of the counselor. The men and women returning from the Vietnam war brought problems of adjustment, family conflict, and Posttraumatic Stress Disorder (PTSD) to the counselors' offices. Drug abuse became a growing problem, spreading into the middle classes and necessitating additional treatment programs for substance abuse. In addition, the Human Potential Movement, spearheaded by a group of well-known therapists including Fritz Perls, Virginia Satir, Bill Schutz, and others, expanded the repertoire of counselors' skills and experimented with marathon therapy sessions, confrontation groups and other innovative approaches. Important theorists in counseling, including Ivey and Carkhuff, focused particularly on the identification and teaching of effective counseling and communication skills.

Interest grew in multicultural counseling and in group counseling, particularly effective in treating substance use, PTSD, and other disorders that gained attention during the 1970s. These interests were reflected in the addition of more divisions to APGA, including the Association for Non-white Concerns in Personnel and Guidance (forerunner of the Association for Multicultural Counseling and Development), the Association for Specialists in Group Work, the Association for Religious and Value Issues in Counseling, (forerunner of the Association for Spiritual, Ethical and Religious Values in Counseling), and the American Mental Health Counselors Association.

Other important changes in the field of counseling during the 1980s included a growing emphasis on brief, active, and structured approaches to counseling. Aaron Beck promoted cognitive therapy, and Jay Haley, Cloé Madanes, Steve deShazer, and others developed strategic and brief models of counseling. As mental health settings increasingly employed counselors, the need for counselors to develop expertise in diagnosis and treatment planning grew. I was the first to offer nationwide training for counselors on these topics through the American Counseling Association. The first edition of this book, published in 1986, was the first volume on that subject directed specifically toward counselors and one of the first books published that focused on the work of the mental health counselor.

In 1980, 552 counselor education programs were identified in the United States and its territories (Wantz, Scherman, & Hollis, 1982). Between 1978 and 1980, nearly all of the programs expanded and added an average of 2.76 new courses, typically in areas such as (in order of frequency) family counseling, consultation, geriatric counseling, career and life planning, and women's studies. Specializations in mental health counseling were being offered under a variety of names: agency, social agency, community agency, or clinical counseling; human development; marriage and family counseling; corrections counseling;

pastoral counseling; personal counseling; and rehabilitation counseling. Although most of the programs were housed in schools or colleges of education, the term "counselor" was no longer synonymous with "school counselor"; mental health counselors were being graduated in numbers equal to if not greater than school counselors (Wantz & Scherman, 1982). By 1986, 90% of the graduate training programs in counseling offered a specialization in community agency counseling (Spruill & Fong, 1990). Other changes in counselor preparation included a stronger emphasis on developmental rather than preventive or remedial counseling, an increase in field experience requirements, a focus on integrating and applying existing counseling modalities rather than searching for new approaches, and contact with a broad range of client groups.

These changes were reflected in the counselors' primary professional organization, the American Personnel and Guidance Association (APGA), now the American Counseling Association (ACA). That organization had grown rapidly since its inception and had over 42,000 members in 1984 as well as state and local divisions throughout the United States. At that time, after years of debate, APGA changed its name to the American Association for Counseling and Development (AACD), reflecting the altered and broadened role of the counselor of the 1980s. In that same year, the *Occupational Outlook Handbook* included listings for both general counselors and mental health counselors, providing further national recognition of the establishment of the counseling profession (Glosoff, 1992). A few years later, in 1988, the Civilian Health and Medical Program of the Uniformed Services (CHAMPUS) included mental health counselors as approved service providers.

Changes in the counseling profession also were mirrored in the establishment of the American Mental Health Counselors Association (AMHCA), founded in 1976 by Nancy Spisso and James Messina as an independent professional organization for community mental health counselors and allied professionals. AMHCA clearly met a need and its membership grew rapidly. In 1978, it became the thirteenth division of APGA. Throughout the 1980s and into the 1990s, the number of mental health counselors grew as did membership in AMHCA. By the 1990s, AMHCA had over 12,000 members and for many years has vied with the American School Counselors Association for the distinction of the largest division of ACA.

During the 1980s, a trend emerged for mental health counselors to define their clinical interests and specialties more specifically. Interest grew in such areas as family counseling, counseling of adults, and treatment of substance use disorders. Several new divisions, including the Association for Adult Development and Aging, were added to the American Counseling Association.

In 1989, the International Association of Marriage and Family Counselors (IAMFC), developed by Robert Smith, Jon Carlson, Don Dinkmeyer, and other leaders in the counseling field who had a particular interest in family counseling, became an affiliate of ACA. Within one year, it had 2800 members and attained the status of one of the fastest growing divisions of ACA.

Graduate students in counseling got their own organization in 1985 with the establishment of Chi Sigma Iota, a national honorary society for counselor education. By the 1990s, it had over 90 chapters and over 3000 members, including students, faculty, and practitioners in counseling.

Several changes during the 1980s, along with the expansion of credentialing discussed later in this chapter, led to growth in opportunities for counselors as well as some changes in their roles and approaches. By the late 1980s, many states mandated that counselors be available in the elementary schools. This led not only to an increasing demand for counselors with training in working with children but also promoted early identification of troubled children. This in turn seems to have led to increasing attention to the problems of abuse and dysfunction in families and to greater collaboration between schools and community mental health agencies.

DEVELOPMENT OF THE COUNSELING PROFESSION IN THE 1990s

The training of mental health counselors has become an increasingly important component of counselor education programs. By the early 1990s, the number of programs to train school counselors and the number of programs to train community agency counselors was approximately equal (Cowger et al., 1991). The area of mental health or community agency counseling was becoming refined and specialties such as marriage and family counseling, adult development and aging, substance abuse counseling, and child counseling were becoming popular. The 30-credit masters' degree of the 1970s was rare and most programs required at least 45 credits, with a requirement of 60 credits for a masters degree in counseling becoming increasingly common.

The American Counseling Association (ACA) continued to struggle with problems of name recognition and identity, culminating in another name change. In 1992, the American Association for Counseling and Development assumed its current name, the American Counseling Association. In 1994, the name of the association's newsletter also was changed; *Guidepost* would now be called *Counseling Today*. The advocates of the association's name change believed that the simple and straightforward new name would promote better public recognition and understanding. The new name also paralleled the names of other organizations for mental health professionals, the American Psychological Association and the American Psychiatric Association, representing ACA's goal of parity with those organizations. Membership in ACA continued to grow, despite a decline in membership in some years. ACA also lost one division and was threatened by the possible withdrawal of AMHCA and ASCA. However, by the mid-1990s, ACA had well over 50,000 members.

The Orlando Model Project

Assessment of qualifications, credentialing, and accountability continue to be areas of emphasis for counselors. An important program to promote improvement in the quality of services provided by mental health counselors is the Orlando Model Project, designed to identify competency based training standards for counselors at preprofessional, internship, residency, and practitioner levels. In 1994, AMHCA approved the formation of the National Commission for Mental Health Counseling with a 12 member board of governors to oversee the Orlando Project, to promote information sharing and networking, to develop publications and an annual conference on mental health counselor competency, and to promote employment and quality education for mental health counselors (Altekruse & Sexton, 1995a). A collaborative venture of AMHCA and ACES, the Orlando Project has set as minimal standards for mental health counselors 60 graduate hours of coursework, 1000 hours of internship, two full years of residency or postgraduate supervised experience, and 20 hours a year of continuing education (Messina, 1995). Further clarification of competencies required for effective counseling is underway. A major goal of this project is addressing the discrepancy many have reported between the needs of practicing mental health counselors and their formal training; education that is more relevant and timely should result from the recommendations of the Orlando Model Project.

Impact of Managed Care

Perhaps the biggest impact on the role of counselors in the 1990s has come from changes in health insurance and the way that health care is being provided. A nationwide movement to provide all people access to treatment for physical and emotional problems gained considerable attention during the Clinton administration. The value of a preventive approach to health maintenance also has been recognized. At the same time, the escalation of health care costs has led health insurance companies to seek more economical methods of providing health care. New approaches to approving and providing services have resulted from those potentially conflicting thrusts.

The most widespread of these are health maintenance organizations (HMOs), providing managed health care. In 1970, three million people were serviced by 33 HMOs, most of them emphasizing preventive approaches and treatment of the whole person. The number of HMOs has continued to grow, with the numbers peaking in 1987 when there were 707 HMOs (DeLeon & Vanden-Bos, 1991). As of 1994, over 53 million people were enrolled in HMOs. HMO subscribers typically pay a predetermined monthly or annual fee regardless of the frequency or nature of their health problems. Services are then provided by the HMOs at little or no additional cost. Most of these have a gatekeeper model, in which participants have a primary care physician who determines whether counseling and other specialized services should be authorized for a particular person.

A related model for delivery of health care services is Preferred Provider Organizations (PPOs) or Individual Practice Associations (IPAs), groups of independent health care providers who offer reduced-rate services to subscribers of insurance plans with whom the providers have contracts. Over 75% of HMOs contract with private practitioners (DeLeon & VandenBos, 1991). In turn, these practitioners in PPOs or IPAs acquire an increased and more stable client load and reliable payment. Subscribers who choose providers recommended by their insurance company also benefit; generally their co-payment, the part of the cost paid by the person, is reduced or eliminated.

The extensive network of HMOs has changed the nature of counseling, especially for counselors in private practice. The need for counselors to provide services has increased, as has their opportunity to treat people with a broad range of mental disorders. However, many HMOs and third-party payers require pre-authorization of treatment. Before receiving approval for a series of sessions, then, counselors typically must prepare a diagnosis and treatment plan for a client and submit that to the HMO for a utilization review, usually by other mental health service providers. Approvals for mental health services rarely are open-ended; generally they authorize a specific number of sessions. If more sessions are needed as counseling proceeds, additional requests and information must be submitted to the HMO, but limits imposed by such policies as capitated reimbursement or predetermined fees for various diagnosis-related groups can severely curtail the number of sessions.

Treatment of mental disorders currently costs 15–25% of the money spent on health care (Johnsen, 1994). Because most third-party payers are trying to contain the escalating cost of health care, they typically encourage a brief therapy model. DeLeon and VandenBos (1991) found that 63% of people who received outpatient mental health services through HMOs were seen for fewer than ten sessions. Inpatient treatment of serious mental disorders also emphasized short-term treatment with 80% being hospitalized less than two weeks. By the mid-90s, this model of brief therapy, with mental health service providers taking an active and directive role, permeated the field.

Considerable concern has been expressed over the impact of managed care on the availability and delivery of mental health services. Foos, Ottens, and Hill

(1991, p. 332) described managed care as being "…driven more by costs than by client needs" and encouraging minimalist treatment goals. To deal with managed care successfully, counselors need to market their services aggressively and demonstrate their success. They need to develop expertise in such areas as treatment of drug and alcohol problems, relapse prevention, treatment of dual diagnoses, crisis intervention, use of community resources, and pain and stress management. Flexibility and breadth in skills, the ability to match technique to disorder, and involvement in a multidisciplinary group practice also are viewed as desirable in the managed care arena.

At present, the counselors' role in managed care is an evolving one. Many counselors have not become preferred providers or applied for third-party payments, sometimes because they are not aware that they would qualify. However, a study in Ohio (Zimpfer, 1995) found that 87% of insurance carriers reimbursed licensed professional clinical counselors in that state and that 78% of claims that counselors submitted had been paid. Zimpfer concluded, "…mental health carriers are accepting the master's degree as an appropriate level of training for counselors" (p. 110).

Although managed care may limit the freedom of the counselor and make the provision of long-term counseling services difficult or impossible, it may well lead to greater recognition and opportunities for counselors and to more affordable, available, and effective services for most people. Although it has limitations, short-term counseling can have a powerful impact. Hill (1990), for example, reported that as few as six visits to a counselor were associated with a reduction in medical bills by as much as 75% over five years. Managed care also makes an important contribution by promoting accountability, early identification and treatment of emotional difficulties, and maximization of clinical effectiveness. Managed care can prompt counselors to find better and more efficient ways to help people, as long as the counselors remain proactive in their relationships with managed care.

THE MENTAL HEALTH COUNSELOR TODAY

In 1986, the Board of Directors of the American Mental Health Counselors Association, in their Standards for the Clinical Practice of Mental Health Counseling, (1994, p.II.D-1) adopted the following definition: "Clinical mental health counseling is the provision of professional counseling services involving the application of principles of psychotherapy, human development, learning theory, group dynamics, and the etiology of mental illness and dysfunctional behavior to individuals, couples, families and groups, for the purposes of promoting optimal mental health, dealing with normal problems of living and treating psychopathology. The practice of clinical mental health counseling includes, but is not limited to, diagnosis and treatment of mental and emotional disorders, psychoeducational techniques aimed at the prevention of mental and emotional disorders, consultations to individuals, couples, families, groups, organizations and communities and clinical research into more effective psychotherapeutic treatment modalities." That broad definition captures the essence of mental health counseling although, as Ginter (1991, p.187) concluded, "The mental health counseling profession has experienced dramatic growth and development in a relatively brief period of time."

The mental health field of today is a broad and diverse one which calls for counselors who are flexible and knowledgeable generalists who can draw on a wide range of skills and approaches to meet the multifaceted needs of their clients. It calls for people who can discard the security and prestige of conducting long-term individual counseling sessions in isolated offices and who can become involved with and make good use of community resources, managed care, consulting, program development, and collaboration with other mental health service providers. It calls for counselors who can assess and deal sensitively with developmental, cultural, gender, and family contexts; who are skilled in diagnosis and treatment planning; who can develop effective and innovative preventive and remedial approaches; and who can provide good role models and supervision to students and other counselors.

Counselors need to have a high tolerance for ambiguity and change and a low need for power and immediate gratification; their rewards often come from developing the strengths of the community and the individual and fostering self-help, mobilizing people's resources, and increasing opportunities for growth, rather than from displaying their own ability to heal others. Counselors need to be self-motivated, focusing on strengths rather than weakness or illness. They need to relate successfully to people who may seem different from themselves and learn to prize and foster the individuality of those people. Counselors have to be able to deal with resistance by demonstrating quickly and effectively that they do have something to offer and are capable of meeting client needs. They have to be politically aware and assertive and assume the role of being their clients' advocates, often focusing on issues and groups rather than on individuals. They need to be familiar with legal and ethical standards that may have an impact on their work and on their clients and must practice in accord with those guidelines.

Counselors will have to accept and establish a true partnership with their colleagues, their clients, and their communities. In order to accomplish this, counselors need to develop a broad range of skills, to participate actively in their professional associations and in advocacy for their profession, to obtain state and national credentials, to know and deal effectively with advances in technology and in the profession, and to promote the counseling profession by exemplifying ethical behavior and a high level of skills.

The primary roles of nearly all counselors include management and treatment of clients and conducting intake interviews for assessment and diagnosis (West et al., 1987). Testing, to provide further information on people's abilities, interests, values, and personalities, is another essential role of the counselor. Nearly all counselors conduct individual, group, and family therapy sessions while most are involved in consultation and education, planning and conducting community services, supervision, and evaluation of services.

Counselors are increasingly adopting a brief model of counseling that is problem-focused, based on a knowledgeable assessment and diagnosis, and rooted in a clear understanding of a client's family, cultural, and other systems and world views. Rather than advocating a single model of change or intervention, mental health counselors are seeking to individualize treatment approaches in eclectic, integrative, and creative ways (Kelly, 1991). The personality and natural style of the counselor are important, and counselors should consider carefully and make good use of the part they play in their clients' lives as circularity in counseling relationships gains in importance.

THE GROWTH OF CREDENTIALING

As the field of mental health counseling grew, so did the need to develop credentials that would establish and maintain standards for the profession as well as advance its reputation. Credentialing of counselors and counselor education programs has become increasingly important during the 1980s and 1990s.

Credentials for counselors are of two types, licensure or certification issued by the state in which the counselor practices, and certification, generally issued by a national professional organization. Both credentials indicate that counselors have achieved specified levels of training, experience, and knowledge. These credentials are important to the counselor as well as to the general public. They safeguard the consumer from unqualified practitioners, protect counselors' right to practice, increase the likelihood of third party payments and privileged communication, and generally promote the prestige, importance, and familiarity of the profession (Alberding, Lauver, & Patnoe, 1993).

National Certification for Counselors

Emphasis on well-defined standards, reflected in credentials, has been one of the greatest contributions of AMHCA leaders to the counseling field and was a hallmark of the development of the counseling profession during the 1980s. In

1979, leaders of AMHCA established the National Academy for Certified Clinical Mental Health Counselors (NACCMHC) with James Messina as its first chair. NACCMHC determined criteria for certification as a mental health counselor and awarded that credential to applicants who met those requirements and passed a rigorous screening process, including a written examination and submission of work samples.

NACCMHC initiated an emphasis on national certification for counselors that has continued up to the present. Recognizing that not only mental health counselors needed certification, ACA established the National Board of Certified Counselors (NBCC) in 1982 to certify generic counselors as National Certified Counselors or NCCs. The two national bodies to certify counselors, NACCMHC and NBCC, coexisted for over 10 years, creating considerable confusion in the minds of many counselors as to their differences as well as their respective benefits. Finally, in 1993, NBCC merged with what was then called the Academy of Clinical Mental Health Counselors and all those who had been certified as mental health counselors (CMHCs) also became NCCs.

Certification by professional associations is an important credential for counselors, although it is less restrictive and less powerful than state licensure. Certification standards sometimes are more relevant because they have been developed by counselors rather than legislators. Certification promotes visibility and accountability. NBCC and other certifying bodies maintain and disseminate registries, listing people they have credentialed. These directories facilitate networking as well as referral to people with particular areas of expertise. Certification is required by many employers and is another way to demonstrate competence and support the counseling profession. Certifying bodies also encourage professional development by requiring continuing education in order to maintain one's certification.

The National Board of Certified Counselors offers a general credential for all counselors, the designation of NCC (National Certified Counselor), thus far awarded to well over 20,000 counselors. Requirements for the NCC include a master's degree in counseling with a minimum of 48 semester hours. Coursework must cover eight of the following ten areas, with the first two areas required: counseling theory; supervised counseling; human growth and development; social/cultural and family foundations; the helping relationship; group dynamics, processing, and counseling; lifestyle and career development; appraisal of individuals; research and evaluation; and professional orientation. Also required are at least 20 hours a week of post-master's counseling experience for two years, satisfactory performance on the National Counselor Examination, and two professional references. Maintenance of the NCC credential requires at least ten continuing education units (CEUs) or 100 hours of professional development (e.g., coursework, workshops) every five years.

In addition to the NCC, the NBCC offers the following specialty certificates: Certified Clinical Mental Health Counselor (CCMHC), Master Addictions Counselor (MAC), National Certified School Counselor (NCSC), National Certified Gerontological Counselor (NCGC), and National Certified Career Counselor (NCCC). These certifications all require the NCC plus specialized experience and training. Other certifications available to counselors include Certified Family Therapist (CFT) and Certified Rehabilitation Counselor (CRC).

State Licensure and Certification for Counselors

When "counselor" meant "school counselor," credentialing counselors in the states where they were employed followed procedures established for credentialing teachers and attracted little attention or controversy. Counselors' coursework and experience were reviewed by state education agencies, and, if they qualified, counselors were endorsed, certified, or licensed to serve as school counselors.

However, when counselors joined the staffs of mental health agencies and established private practices, another sort of credential was needed to give counselors credibility and autonomy, to help the public identify qualified practitioners, and to enhance professional identity so counselors could achieve the status of the other nonmedical credentialed mental health practitioners (social workers and psychologists). In 1972, in Weldon vs. the Board of Psychological Examiners, the Virginia Supreme Court found that "the profession of personnel and guidance counseling is a separate profession from psychology and should be so recognized" (Seiler & Messina, 1979, p. 4). This paved the way for Virginia to become, in 1976, the first state to license counselors. By 1995, a total of 43 states and jurisdictions had adopted credentialing procedures for counselors. Twelve of those also had separate credentials for mental health counselors (Messina, 1995). Most of the remaining states had licensure laws pending or in preparation. State credentialing of counselors currently includes both licensure and certification, although licensure is the more common and stronger credential.

State credentials are necessary for independent practice. In addition, with the spread of credentialing for counselors, the state license is increasingly required for employment beyond the entry level. Even when that credential is not required, licensed counselors usually seem to have a competitive edge in the employment market.

Although licensure requirements vary from state to state, most states require a master's degree in counseling with 45–60 semester hours of graduate coursework, at least 3000 hours of clinical experience, at least 100 hours of direct face-to-face supervision, and an examination, usually that given by NBCC (Brooks & Gerstein, 1990). The examination is waived by most states for people who already have the NCC credential (Weinrach & Thomas, 1993).

State legislation also establishes the scope of the counselors' practice. Most states grant or permit by implication the diagnosis and treatment of mental disorders by counselors (Throckmorton, 1992). Ohio is one of the few states that has two levels of licensure, generic and clinical licensure. In that state, only counselors with the clinical license can diagnose and treat mental and emotional disorders. In states that have laws regulating the profession of counseling, no unlicensed people can legally call themselves counselors or perform the work of counselors, except while under approved supervision or employed by certain types of agencies.

Credentialing of counselors also facilitated counselors' efforts to receive third-party payments. As of 1995, ten states had so-called Freedom of Choice legislation that required health insurance companies based in those states to provide third party payments for the services of all licensed mental health professionals in those states.

Accreditation of Counselor Education Programs

The credentialing procedure for counselor education programs also underwent modification during the 1980s. For many years, most counselor education programs had been reviewed for approval by the National Council for the Accreditation of Teacher Education (NCATE). At the time when counselor preparation focused primarily on school counselors, the well-established NCATE was an appropriate evaluator for such programs. However, with the expansion of counselor education into mental health counseling, a credentialing body was needed that was familiar with and had criteria for evaluating the increasing range of counseling specialties. In 1981, ACA led the development of the Council for Accreditation of Counseling and Related Educational Programs (CACREP) to establish more uniform and rigorous standards for counselor preparation and further enhance the reputation of the profession. As of the mid-1990s, CACREP had accredited 235 programs at a total of 87 institutions, most of those programs focused on training school counselors (Hollis & Wantz, 1994). The council on Rehabilitation Education, Inc. (CORE) had accredited 81 programs and the American Association of Pastoral Counselors had accredited 36. While these numbers comprised fewer than half of the existing counselor education programs, this number is increasing steadily. However, only a small fraction (approximately 5%) of the programs to train mental health counselors were CACREP approved (Hollis & Wantz, 1994). CACREP presently accredits two areas of specialization for mental health counselors, community counseling and mental health counseling. The definition of and distinction between these two areas seem unclear and they have considerable overlap (Cowger et al., 1991). Changes in CACREP standards may be needed before CACREP can fully meet the accreditation needs of training programs for mental health counselors.

THE EDUCATION OF THE MENTAL HEALTH COUNSELOR

The early 1990s witnessed a considerable increase in training programs for counselors. As of 1993, well over 1000 programs at the master's level and approximately 200 programs at the doctoral level had been identified (Hollis & Wantz, 1994).

The Master's Degree in Counseling

Between 1990 and 1993, the number of programs to train school counselors increased 32% from 263 to 348 while the number of programs in mental health and community agency counseling increased 81% from 160 to 289 (Hollis & Wantz, 1994). The number of programs to train marriage and family counselors showed the most rapid growth, increasing 240% from 30 to 102. Increases also were found in programs to train rehabilitation counselors and student affairs counselors.

During the 1990s, nearly all programs added new faculty and courses and increased their admission requirements (Hollis & Wantz, 1994). Programs typically required an undergraduate grade point average of approximately 3.0. About half required courses in psychology as a prerequisite for admission. Fewer than half of the existing programs required prior relevant employment or volunteer experience, an interview, or a standardized admissions test.

Programs to train mental health counselors vary considerably but generally entail the equivalent of two years of full-time academic study and 45 or more semester hours of course work (Cowger et al., 1991). They require approximately 200 hours of practicum and nearly 500 hours of internship (Hollis & Wantz, 1994) and may award the M.A., M.S., or M.Ed. degree.

Common areas of specialization for students in mental health or community counseling included, in descending order of popularity, marriage and family counseling, adult development and aging, general mental health counseling, substance abuse counseling, career development, and child counseling (Cowger et al., 1991). Courses added to programs, in descending order of frequency (with the last three being added at the same rate), included substance abuse counseling, marriage and family counseling, legal/ethical issues, supervision, gerontological counseling, consultation, play therapy, human sexuality, computer and related technology, mental health classification, and multicultural counseling (Hollis & Wantz, 1994). Self-instructional training and other alternative models of teaching are beginning to be incorporated into counselor education programs.

The Doctoral Degree in Counseling

Many more people receive the master's degree in mental health counseling than receive the doctorate in counseling. Approximately 8000 people enter the profession each year with a master's degree in mental health counseling. Over 1000 people each year receive doctorates in counseling (Zimpfer & DeTrude, 1990). Doctoral students in counseling commonly are embarking on a second or modified career and have a mean age of 36.7 at graduation. Most have master's degrees in counseling or related areas and had been employed in the human services field. In recent years, the interest of these students in independent practice has increased while their interest in university teaching has decreased. Counselor education programs at the doctoral level require an average of 96 semester hours and approximately 1100 hours of clinical experience (Hollis & Wantz, 1994).

PROFESSIONAL ASSOCIATIONS FOR MENTAL HEALTH COUNSELORS

Membership and active participation in professional associations is important for counselors, for many reasons:

1. Conferences, newsletters, journals, books, home-study programs, and continuing education workshops produced by professional associations help counselors to develop good knowledge and skills in their field.
2. The conferences and publications offer counselors a forum for disseminating their own research and ideas.
3. Networking, employment, and identification of colleagues with similar interests or important areas of expertise is facilitated by membership in a professional association.
4. The professional associations have made great strides over the years in promoting the field of counseling, in obtaining state licensure for counselors, and obtaining parity for counselors with other mental health service providers in managed care, privileged communication, and other areas. By supporting professional associations through

service and dues, counselors are contributing to the advancement of their profession.

The primary professional association for counselors is the American Counseling Association (ACA). Membership in this association is approaching 60,000. The Three-year Strategic Plan (1992, p. 22) of ACA states, "The American Counseling Association (ACA) is an organization of counseling professionals who work in educational, health care, residential, private practice, community agency, government, and business and industry settings." Its mission is "...to enhance human development throughout the life span and to promote the counseling profession." Important values of the association include caring for self and others, facilitating positive change, acquiring and using knowledge, promoting leadership, and encouraging networking. The fundamental purposes of ACA include human development, human rights, interprofessional and international collaboration, organization and management, professional development, professionalization, public awareness and support, public policy and legislation, and research and knowledge.

ACA presently includes thirteen divisions and three organizational affiliates. The largest division specifically for mental health counselors is the American Mental Health Counselors Association (AMHCA). Included among over 12,000 members of AMHCA are more than 4600 counselors in private practice and 1800 working in public mental health agencies (Messina, 1995). Other divisions and affiliates of particular interest to mental health counselors include the Association for Adult Development and Aging, the Association for Counselors and Educators in Government, the Association for Multicultural Counseling and Development, the American Rehabilitation Counseling Association, the Association for Specialists in Group Work, the International Association of Addiction and Offender Counselors, the International Association of Marriage and Family Counselors, the National Career Development Association, and the National Employment Counseling Association. Additional divisions and affiliates of ACA include the Association for Assessment in Counseling, the American College Counseling Association, the Association for Counselor Education and Supervision, the Association for Humanistic Education and Development, the American School Counselor Association (the largest division of ACA), and the Association for Spiritual, Ethical, and Religious Values in Counseling. Members of ACA are required to join at least one division, but many people belong to multiple divisions. In addition, each state has a branch of ACA as well as statewide divisions, paralleling some of those in ACA. Regional chapters that facilitate networking as well as professional development and involvement by counselors who are geographically close to each other also are available.

COMPETENCIES OF THE MENTAL HEALTH COUNSELOR

In the 1990s, counselors became increasingly aware of the importance of demonstrating their competence and accountability to other mental health service providers, consumers, and managed care groups. This accelerated interest in the development of standards of practice. In 1994, AMHCA advanced the Standards for the Clinical Practice of Mental Health Counseling. According to that document, mental health counselors should have a minimum of 60 graduate semester hours of coursework, including 12 hours in mental health counseling, as well as a clinical counseling practicum and internship. They should have at least 3000 hours of supervised postgraduate clinical experience over at least two years and at least 200 hours of supervision. Clinical experience is specifically defined as the delivery of counseling to people who have been diagnosed as having a mental disorder, generally according to the standards in the current edition of the *Diagnostic and Statistical Manual of Mental Disorders* (discussed in chapter 3 of this book). Mental health counselors should comply with the regulations governing their practice as well as with the code of ethics for mental health counselors. Mental health counselors are expected to monitor and ensure their competence by evaluating the effectiveness of their services and through involvement in supervision and peer consultation. They are expected to have knowledge and competence in the following areas:

1. Counseling theory, including the counseling process, theories of psychotherapy, and couples and family counseling.
2. Human growth and development including abnormal psychology, life span development, and personality development.
3. Social and cultural foundations, including multicultural issues, sociological and anthropological principles, and human sexuality.
4. Helping relationships, including techniques of counseling and consultation.
5. Group dynamics, process, development, and counseling.
6. Lifestyle and career development and counseling.
7. Appraisal, including testing and assessment.
8. Research and evaluation.
9. Professional orientation, including ethics.
10. Foundations of mental health counseling.
11. Diagnosis of mental disorders.
12. Clinical services in mental health counseling, including assessment and treatment procedures, collaboration and referral, and knowledge of psychopathology, psychopharmacology, abuse, and addictions.

The profile of the skilled mental health counselor is further clarified by a survey conducted by the National Commission for Mental Health Counseling. Clinical Mental Health Counselors throughout the country received a survey on their perceptions of important competencies, skills, attitudes/styles, and traits. When the survey results were compared to available research, the common areas reflected a profile of the competent mental health counselor (Sexton, 1995). The results of this survey, as well as a review of the literature on current course offerings in counselor education and on the functions of the mental health counselor, suggest that the training of counselors should include the following areas of preparation and competence:

A. Helping Relationship

   1. Knows the developmental stages of the helping relationship.
   2. Knows the desirable and recognized therapeutic conditions most likely to facilitate development and positive change.
   3. Is familiar with common reactions to a helping relationship (e.g., defense mechanisms, transference, modeling and identification, culturally related responses, change, and verbal and nonverbal responses).

B. Communication Skills

   1. Possesses and can model good oral and interpersonal communication skills.
   2. Can write clearly and correctly and can prepare well-written reports, letters, and other communications.
   3. Can generally hear and respond appropriately to both overt and covert, verbal and nonverbal client messages.
   4. Can communicate empathy, positive regard, genuineness, and acceptance and can use constructive confrontation and other essential listening behaviors needed in intervention.
   5. Can teach communication skills to individuals or groups and promote improved interpersonal relations.
   6. Can communicate to people the nature of the counseling process and help them to understand both its value and its limitations.
   7. Can effectively conduct an interview or discussion with people from various educational, cultural, and socioeconomic backgrounds.

C. Human Growth and Development

   1. Understands the processes and principles of normal human development and the typical concerns of various age groups including

neonatal, childhood, adolescent, and adult development as well as concepts of aging and dying.
2. Can discriminate between healthy and disturbed development and has knowledge of abnormal psychology.
3. Is familiar with the common personality types and patterns.
4. Understands cognitive development.
5. Understands sexual development and behavior.
6. Can take a holistic view of clients.
7. Can enable others to gain understanding of their own development.
8. Can use crisis counseling, brief psychotherapy, educational programs, and other appropriate techniques to promote positive human development.

D. Assessment and Appraisal Procedures

1. Knows the indications and contraindications for an assessment or appraisal procedure.
2. Can conduct psychosocial histories, assessments, intake interviews, and mental status examinations.
3. Knows when to refer people for physical and neurological examinations.
4. Is familiar with the appropriate use, interpretation, strengths, and limitations of instruments that are widely used in assessing development, intelligence, abilities, interests, values, and personality.
5. Can use assessment to facilitate diagnosis, treatment planning, and provision of mental health treatment.

E. Techniques and Theories of Counseling

1. Knows the general principles and practices for the promotion of optimal mental health.
2. Is familiar with and able to use a broad range of cognitive, behavioral, and affective counseling models and techniques.
3. Is skilled in crisis intervention, problem solving, and other brief, action-based methods of intervention.
4. Is familiar with social models of intervention including therapeutic use of self, milieu therapy, and therapeutic communities.
5. Can teach coping and interpersonal skills including decision-making, assertiveness, and nonjudgmental listening.
6. Knows the kinds of situations for which the various theories and techniques of intervention are especially useful.
7. Can provide a theoretical rationale for approaches to treatment.

8. Is able to engage effectively in many levels of counseling (e.g., individual, family, group, organization, community).
9. Can assess people's needs and can develop both preventive and remedial treatment plans which effectively address those needs.
10. Can help people to set viable long- and short-range goals.
11. Can promote client motivation and deal effectively with resistance.

F. Clinical Skills and Services

1. Knows the principles and practices of diagnosis, treatment, and prevention of mental and emotional disorders and dysfunctional behavior.
2. Is familiar with the specific models and methods for assessing mental status and identifying abnormal, deviant, or dysfunctional behavior, affect, or cognition.
3. Is knowledgeable about the nature and use of the *Diagnostic and Statistical Manual of Mental Disorders.*
4. Knows the indications and contraindications for mental health intervention.
5. Can develop sound and comprehensive treatment plans.

G. Group Counseling

1. Possesses understanding of group development, process, and dynamics.
2. Can help others to understand and modify group process.
3. Can work effectively with both small and large groups, homogeneous and heterogeneous groups.
4. Knows the strengths and limitations of group counseling and can determine when and how it is likely to be helpful.
5. Has competence in theories and techniques of group counseling and can assist groups in overcoming obstacles.
6. Understands the goals and procedures of different types of small groups (e.g., growth, problem solving, support, education).
7. Is knowledgeable about member selection and member and leadership roles in groups.
8. Is familiar with intervention strategies to be used in groups for special populations (e.g., children, parents, physically ill, chronically mentally ill).

H. Career Counseling

1. Understands the changing patterns and meaning of work in modern society.

    2. Understands the lifelong process of career development and the broad scope of career counseling.

    3. Is familiar with sources of career information and knows how to help people acquire and use that information.

    4. Is familiar with a broad range of inventories designed to assess interests, abilities, and values and can use those instruments effectively as a part of career counseling.

    5. Can promote improved life/work planning via client self-exploration, values clarification, development of alternatives, decision-making, reality testing, pre-retirement planning, leisure counseling, and other appropriate techniques.

    6. Can help people develop the skills needed for effective job seeking (e.g., interview skills, resumé writing).

I. Family (Couples) Counseling

    1. Has understanding of patterns of family dynamics and of the family life cycle.

    2. Can determine when family/couples counseling would be an effective treatment modality.

    3. Is familiar with and able to use the major approaches to family and couples counseling.

    4. Can use methods to promote positive parent/child interaction.

J. Behavioral Medicine

    1. Has a basic understanding of neurophysiology.

    2. Has knowledge of theories and techniques of relaxation, exercise, nutrition, stress management, holistic health, and their appropriate uses.

    3. Understands the application of behavioral approaches to such problems as smoking, eating disorders, and drug/alcohol abuse.

K. Therapeutic and Mood Altering Chemicals

    1. Is aware of the most frequently abused chemical agents, their classification, and physical effects.

    2. Understands the signs and stages of chemical dependence and abuse.

    3. Knows what to do in the event of undesired effects of chemical agents.

    4. Is familiar with commonly used psychotropic medications.

    5. Knows when and how to make a referral for a medication evaluation.

L. Consultation

1. Understands the roles and responsibilities of the consultant.
2. Understands organizational development.
3. Can function independently and define own goals and those of clientele with little structure or supervision.
4. Can attend to and balance organizational and individual needs.
5. Can promote problem-solving and conflict resolution.
6. Can facilitate communication and change in organizations in a way that fosters self-help and increased competence.

M. Training, Supervision and Program Development

1. Can develop programs that reach large numbers of people and promote mastery and shared learning.
2. Is comfortable in a teaching role and can integrate teaching and counseling skills.
3. Can conduct in-service training programs.
4. Is aware of a variety of models of and approaches to supervision.
5. Can supervise, train, and work effectively with indigenous, professional, and paraprofessional workers.
6. Possesses administrative skills.
7. Can coordinate and collaborate effectively with other human service workers.
8. Can plan and execute outreach programs and approaches to bring services to communities.

N. Social Systems and Community Organization

1. Understands the place of mental health counseling in the larger context of society, including human services, politics, and economics.
2. Understands and can use the principles of social change, social systems analysis, community intervention, public education, community planning, and organization.
3. Can understand issues as well as individual and community needs.
4. Can identify and work effectively with both community strengths and growth-inhibiting and stressful aspects of the community and can assess the need for community change.
5. Can take a multifaceted approach to helping others.
6. Can assume the roles of advocate, change agent, and political activist when appropriate.
7. Can build coalitions and collaborate with others to help people.

8. Is familiar with and can make effective use of community and other resources via referral, linkage, advocacy, and consultation in order to provide a comprehensive and continuous system of services.
9. Can facilitate the strengthening of socially devalued groups.
10. Can involve the community in program planning and develop and draw on community leadership.
11. Has knowledge of causes and dynamics of major social problems (e.g., substance abuse, child abuse, rape, delinquency), their legal ramifications, and ways to prevent and treat them.
12. Has a broad range of approaches to help others develop their life skills and their abilities to help themselves (e.g., parent effectiveness training, assertiveness training, sex education).
13. Is familiar with the concepts of outreach and prevention in mental health.

O. Special Populations

1. Is aware of and appreciates individual, life style, and cultural differences.
2. Can interact well with people of all ages and backgrounds, functioning at various intellectual and emotional levels, and can understand their points of view.
3. Can take account of the effect that a cultural and environmental background has had on a person's development.
4. Can help people who represent special populations to become aware of their needs and set their own priorities and goals and can accept the validity of their wants.
5. Can help people develop and make use of appropriate support systems.

P. Research

1. Understands the principles of assessment and evaluation.
2. Is conversant with important research in the field of counseling.
3. Can understand, plan, and conduct research studies.
4. Appreciates the importance of evaluating the impact of one's efforts and the need for accountability.
5. Can develop and execute valid evaluation procedures.

Q. Self-Growth and Awareness

1. Has the conviction that individuals, families, groups, and communities can change and improve.
2. Is openminded and emotionally stable.

3. Has tolerance and respect for all people and their values.
4. Is aware of and can deal with own prejudices and stereotypes as well as those of clients.
5. Is flexible and able to cope with constant change.
6. Can function effectively as leader, team member, and autonomous helper.
7. Has good overall awareness of own strengths and weaknesses, likes and dislikes.
8. Is committed to lifelong learning and professional development.
9. Understands the ethical standards of counselors and behaves in a way that is consistent with those standards.

The overall competence of mental health counselors should be advanced by the plans of the National Commission for Mental Health Counseling. The National Commission intends to establish Regional Centers for Excellence in Mental Health Counselor Training that will promote the Orlando model competency based standards of training and practice. This book, too, will focus on the important skills of the mental health counselor. The growing breadth of the role of the mental health counselor and the diverse range of employment opportunities open to counselors suggest that the most effective and employable counselors will be those who have acquired these skills.

Opportunities for the Mental Health Counselor

Today's mental health counselor has a wide range of roles and employment opportunities. For example, counselors can be diagnosticians and treatment planners, psychotherapists, teachers and trainers, community organizers, case managers, consultants, human relations specialists, workshop leaders, grant writers, coordinators and program developers, referral agents, researchers, evaluation specialists, report writers, and supervisors. Additional roles for counselors continue to evolve.

Upon receiving the master's degree in mental health counseling, about half of recent graduates found employment in public agencies (Hollis & Wantz, 1994). Approximately 25% found employment in private agencies or private practices, 12% entered advanced graduate programs, 8% worked in managed care settings, and the remaining 7% made other choices. Counselors with experience and credentials beyond the master's degree are even more likely to be in private practice, although they, too, are found in a broad range of employment settings.

In a survey of members of the American Counseling Association who reported community counseling as their speciality, Bubenzer, Zimpfer, and Mahrle (1990) found that 58.3% identified private practice as their primary work setting. Other frequently reported work settings included community mental health centers, medical or psychiatric hospitals, employment and career counseling agencies, correctional institutions, business and industry, military programs, and rehabilitation facilities. Of those surveyed, 92.7% counseled adults, 63.9% counseled families, 63.7% counseled adolescents, and 37.2% counseled children.

Counselors' roles may be described in terms of the client population and issues they address, work settings, and responsibilities. This chapter will look at mental health counselors from all three perspectives.

CLIENT ISSUES OF SPECIAL INTEREST TO MENTAL HEALTH COUNSELORS

Mental health counselors are encountering increased diversity and severity of client problems in their work. Although diversity now has a broad meaning, its importance in counseling initially stemmed from the increasingly multicultural nature of counselors' work.

Multicultural Counseling

By the year 2000, more than one-third of the population of the United States will be racial and ethnic minorities as will be 45% of students in public schools (Sue, Arredondo, & McDavis, 1992). By 2010, the term "minorities" will be a misnomer, when so-called racial and ethnic minorities will comprise 50% of the population. Even now, the term "visible racial/ethnic groups" (VREGs), suggested by Thompson and Atkinson (1991), perhaps is more appropriate. Two trends are primarily responsible for this growth: immigration patterns and relatively high birth rates among many visible racial and ethnic groups. Pedersen (1990, p. 93) wrote, "Just as humanism became a third force to supplement the psychodynamic and behavioral perspectives, multiculturalism is becoming a 'fourth force' in its influence on the field of mental health counseling."

The number of people in the United States from Asian or Latino backgrounds is growing particularly fast. The diverse attitudes toward counseling and seeking help typical of people from these groups reflects the challenges inherent in multicultural counseling. People from a Latino background usually turn to family members for help while those from an Asian background are more likely to seek information to address their concerns. Counselors need to understand these differences and modify their interventions appropriately. Building credibility with clients, when counselor and client come from very different backgrounds, may be challenging and slow, but it is essential to effective counseling.

Successfully counseling people from diverse backgrounds calls for three areas of competence (Pedersen, 1990; Sue et al., 1992):

1. Developing awareness of one's own assumptions, values, and biases.
2. Understanding, both cognitively and emotionally, the worldview of culturally different people, including ethnographic variables (ethnicity, nationality, religion, language), demographic variables (age, gender, place of residence), status variables (social, economic, and educational factors), and affiliations in order to view people's behaviors, beliefs, and responses in context and grasp their meaning and importance.

3. Having appropriate skills, intervention strategies, and techniques for working with these clients, as well as the ability to develop treatment plans that are based on cultural understanding.

Gender Issues

Just as culture shapes personality and behavior, so does gender. Attention has been paid to the special needs of women in counseling since the 1970s, with a particular emphasis on women's strong interpersonal values, problems in self-esteem, and restricted opportunities. The 1990s witnessed a growing interest in the common problems of women in mid-life and the later years, including gynecological cancers, menopause, responsibility for elderly parents, and widowhood.

Unfortunately, increased sensitivity to women's difficulties has sometimes led to a view of men as their oppressors. This attitude clearly has been changing during the 1990s with the recognition that men, too, have been shaped and often limited by gender stereotypes. Men now are receiving special attention in counseling, with particular attention being paid to encouraging men to build on their strengths and abilities, to celebrate and affirm their assets, and to develop closer relationships with other men, especially their fathers (Kelly & Hall, 1992). These efforts are dispelling the myth of the inexpressive male and helping people see that men and women both value relationships but typically prefer different ways of achieving closeness (Twohey & Ewing, 1995). Men typically develop closeness by doing, engaging in side-by-side interactions, while women usually seek conversation and self-disclosure as the path to intimacy.

Two useful perspectives on gender issues have been suggested. Social constructionism locates the gender differences in the context in which development and relationships occur, while the essentialist point of view suggests that men and women are fundamentally different (Twohey & Ewing, 1995). Both approaches seem to have merit and probably need to be considered together to explain gender differences.

Issues of Sexual Orientation

Gender issues may be compounded by issues of sexual orientation for the large number of people with a homosexual orientation. House (1991) estimated that approximately 20–25 million people in the United States are gay or lesbian. Issues that are particularly prevalent in this population include acknowledging their sexual orientation to themselves and others, developing an integrated and valued sense of themselves, achieving intimacy and commitment in relationships, and finding their place in society, as well as parenting, religious issues, drug and alcohol abuse, guilt, loneliness and depression, and AIDS. Under-standing cultural values and messages is important with these clients, too. Their difficulties often are exacerbated by homophobia (fear or hatred of those who define themselves as gay or lesbian) and heterosexism (the assumption that heterosexuality is the normal and superior orientation) in their environment. Although the notion that homosexuality is a mental disorder was officially discarded by the American Psychiatric Association in 1980, the special problems of people who are homosexual still warrant special attention and understanding in counseling.

Trauma

The aftermath of the Vietnam War provided counselors with much greater understanding of trauma. Its impact is usually profound and often delayed, complicating diagnosis and treatment. Between 500,000 and 850,000 Vietnam veterans continue to experience a wide range of stress-related symptoms, includ-ing issues of safety, trust, power, self-esteem, intimacy, and withdrawal, as a result of their war experiences (Lawson, 1995). Similar symptoms of Posttrau-matic Stress Disorder (PTSD) can be observed in people who have been abused and people who have been exposed to accidents or natural disasters as well as people who have faced other traumatic experiences.

Critical Incident Response Teams (CIRT) are being specially trained to prevent the development of the symptoms of PTSD in people who have been exposed to trauma or violence, including police and firefighters. Morrissey (1994) reported that there are more than 300 of these teams in the United States. They provide rapid intervention (within no more than 48 hours), usually includ-ing the following seven phases: introductions are made and guidelines are provided; participants describe the facts of the experience; participants describe their thoughts about the experience; they discuss their emotional reactions to the incident and the impact it has had on them; specific symptoms are identified and normalized; stress reduction, thought stopping, image replacement, and other relaxation and coping techniques are taught and mobilized; and re-entry is facilitated, with continuing opportunity to obtain help.

Sexual and Physical Abuse

One of the most challenging and troubling problems counselors address and one that often has a traumatic impact is sexual and physical abuse. Although these problems have probably always been present, public awareness of the prevalence of these problems is relatively recent. Many authorities agree that approximately one-third to one-half of women and at least 10% of men seen for counseling have a history of physical or sexual abuse. In the general population, as many as 20% of women may have experienced sexual abuse by a family member (Courtois, 1988).

This increased awareness and attention to sexual and physical abuse has led counselors to address several related problem areas. Mental disorders such as Dissociative Identity Disorder, Borderline Personality Disorder, and Posttraumatic Stress Disorder are especially prevalent among people who have been physically or sexually abused and may require long-term intensive treatment. Memories of early abuse may have been partially or completely repressed, surfacing years later in confusing and upsetting ways. Helping people deal with and make sense of these memories is an important and difficult aspect of counseling, complicated by questions that have been raised about the veracity of these memories, the so-called false memory syndrome. Even counselors who focus their work on current and developmental concerns such as career or relationship issues must be attuned to the possibility that a longstanding issue such as abuse is contributing to the present concern and must be addressed. Counselors specializing in helping people who have been abused have had to acquire new tools such as hypnotherapy and eye movement desensitization and reprocessing to work effectively.

The perpetrators of sexual abuse sometimes can be described as having a sexual addiction, another new area of focus for counselors. This dysfunctional behavior pattern seems more likely to develop in people who have experienced abuse. Counselors should be alert to the possibility of sexual addiction and abuse in their clients and should have ways of addressing those behavioral patterns.

Sexual harassment is another issue that has been gaining attention, and may be associated with sexual addiction or a need for control and dominance. Counselors in business and industry as well as those providing career counseling are particularly likely to encounter clients who are either the perpetrators or the recipients of sexual harassment.

Substance Abuse

Physical and sexual abuse often is accompanied by substance abuse, another very prevalent problem. At some point in their lives, nearly 20% of all people in the United States will have a Substance-Related Disorder (Maxmen & Ward, 1995). Most of these people have a coexisting mental disorder such as depression, Antisocial Personality Disorder, or an Impulse Control Disorder. These dually diagnosed people are another growing segment of the counselor's work. Their diagnosis and treatment is difficult because of the interaction of the disorders, and relapse is a great concern, as it is with most people with Substance-Related Disorders. Even the federal government has acknowledged the prevalence and severity of these disorders with the establishment, in 1992, of the Substance

Abuse and Mental Health Services Administration, focused on understanding and developing effective ways to treat problems related to addictive or mental disorders.

Counselors encounter Substance-Related Disorders, as they do problems of abuse, in nearly all settings from elementary schools to nursing homes and often find that substance-related problems underlie people's presenting concerns, particularly in employee assistance counseling. Experience with these disorders has led counselors to broaden their repertoire of interventions; they have had to become knowledgeable about the physical and psychological impact of chemical abuse, detoxification, inpatient and outpatient treatment, twelve step programs (e.g., Alcoholics Anonymous, Narcotics Anonymous), correctional systems, and interventions to overcome resistance.

Family Issues

The importance of viewing problems such as Substance-Related Disorders and physical and sexual abuse in their family context has contributed to the increasing attention that has been paid in recent years to the family. Family counseling is the fastest growing specialization within mental health counseling, reflecting its importance in treating nearly all problems. For example, substance abuse counselors focus on issues of co-dependency and adult children of alcoholics; those who focus on physical and sexual abuse consider issues of intergenerational transmission; and counselors who address gender issues consider family role models and gender-related norms. Helping people with family issues also necessitates understanding of nontraditional families. Single-parent and remarriage families comprise nearly 45% of all families and have special characteristics (Hayes & Hayes, 1988), as do families with adopted children, gay and lesbian family members, and people with serious mental or physical disabilities. Chapter 8 of this book provides additional information on theories and techniques of family counseling as well as ways to understand family dynamics.

Age- and Stage-Related Issues

Involvement in family counseling has led counselors to learn more about the problems and interventions associated with particular roles and stages in life. Counselors working with children have had to learn about play therapy, effective parenting, consultation with school counselors and teachers, and the prevalent disorders of children and adolescence, including Attention-Deficit/Hyperactivity Disorder and Conduct Disorder.

Counselors also are paying more attention to the needs of the elderly and their care givers. According to Myers (1990, p. 245), "Mental health counseling with older persons is an emerging specialty, stimulated by changing demograph-ics and dramatic increases in the numbers of older persons during this century." By 2000, 35 million people in the United States will be age 65 and older (Gross & Capuzzi, 1991). One-third of these will need care and supportive services to remain in their communities, although 80% of people in this age group are able to live independently and are in good health. The percentage needing care is likely to grow since people 85 and older represent the fastest growing segment of the population (Myers, 1989). Usually this care is provided by adult children, most often daughters between the ages of 40 and 70 who typically must balance many responsibilities (Schwiebert & Myers, 1994).

Common issues of older people include losing their work role; seeking intimacy and identity; coping with change and loss; establishing new goals; declining independence; experiencing depression, loneliness, and chronic medi-cal problems; and adjusting to the finiteness of life. They must contend with the often negative and devaluing perceptions of their society and sometimes even with bias from their therapists who may not appreciate the great abilities and continued need for challenge and growth in older clients (Myers, 1990).

Counselors working with older people typically use approaches that enhance their dignity, worth, and independence; take account of their culture, environment, historical context, and physical capacities; improve socialization and relationships; reduce anxiety and depression; and address difficulties in a problem-focused way (Gross & Capuzzi, 1991). In order to work effectively with this population, counselors have had to learn some specialized techniques, including remotivation therapy, reminiscing groups, milieu therapy, and life review. They also need to become familiar with physical and emotional disorders that are especially common in this group, such as arthritis, heart disease, cancer, and the Cognitive Mental Disorders, especially Dementia of the Alzheimer's Type.

Some of the problems of the later years can be prevented through counseling during mid-life. The mental health counseling literature has been paying more attention to the years between 40 and 60 (Sundel & Bernstein, 1995). For most, these are years of increased freedom and self-confidence as well as of introspection and pursuit of goals as yet unrealized. People can use this time to anticipate the future, taking stock of their lives and addressing practical matters such as estate planning and wills. Counselors can help people to make the most of this time in their lives and develop plans and skills that will help them as they grow older.

Career Concerns

An important area of focus for people in mid-life is their careers. Common mid-life career-related concerns include dissatisfaction, interpersonal conflict, coping with technological changes, stress and competition, relocation, downward mobility and job loss, and shifting personal values (Aubrey & D'Andrea, 1988). Skills such as assessment, values clarification, knowledge of transferability of skills, stress management, team building, and conflict resolution are important to counselors helping people with career-related concerns.

Conflict Resolution

Conflict resolution is a particularly important skill that has been growing in use in a variety of settings, including schools, family counseling, and the military as well as in business and industry. Using such skills as mediation, role reversal, and negotiation and encouraging empathy and active listening, counselors help people clarify their concerns and conflicts and reach mutually agreeable solutions based on cooperation rather than competition (McFarland, 1992).

Issues Related to Medical Conditions, Health, and Wellness

Researchers such as Kobasa (1979), who studied the relationship between personal attributes and physical health, David Spiegel (1990), who found a connection between emotional support and the life span of women with advanced cancer, and others have demonstrated the existence of a strong connection between emotional and physical health. Counselors are increasingly helping people cope with chronic and life-threatening medical conditions such as AIDS, cancer, heart disease, asthma, and arthritis and are finding that counseling can not only promote adjustment to the condition but also can reduce the severity of the symptoms and improve prognosis for many conditions. Hill (1990) reported that as few as six sessions of psychotherapy could reduce medical bills by as much as 75% over five years. Techniques such as visual imagery and relaxation, creative therapies such as drawing and writing, and other cognitive and behavioral interventions are useful in counseling people with chronic and life-threatening illnesses.

Counseling also is assuming an important role in helping people without significant medical conditions maintain or improve their health. In 1989, the American Counseling Association passed a resolution entitled The Counseling Profession as Advocates for Optimum Health and Wellness that endorsed goals of promoting wellness and health development and preventing mental and physical illness (Myers, 1992). O'Donnell (1988, p. 369) stated, "Up to 90% of the patients seeking medical help are estimated to suffer from disorders well within the range of self-healing."

Behavioral medicine, a growing specialization for counselors, includes such areas as weight management, smoking cessation, the promotion of nutrition and exercise, stress management, and pain management. It usually entails psychoeducation, direct clinical service, family counseling, and consultation with medical personnel and takes a holistic and comprehensive approach, whatever its immediate focus. Hettler (1984), for example, advanced the SOSPIE model of wellness that addressed social, occupational/career, spiritual, physical, intellectual, and emotional areas of a person's life.

Chronic or Severe Mental Disorders

Counselors are assuming new roles in working with people who have chronic and serious mental disorders such as Schizophrenia, Dementia, and recurrent Mood Disorders. While these people may benefit from both medication and traditional counseling, they often also need case management and advocacy services in which the counselor integrates and oversees the various services being provided and helps people to negotiate the health care delivery system so they can receive the services they need.

Other Issues

This section of the chapter has highlighted new and growing areas of attention for counselors. Counselors continue to help people with a broad range of other issues, including depression and anxiety, behavioral concerns, social skill deficits, loss and change, decision-making, goals and direction, and interpersonal concerns, discussed further in the next two chapters.

EMPLOYMENT SETTINGS FOR MENTAL HEALTH COUNSELORS

Clearly, mental health counselors are providing services to a challenging and diverse array of people, are addressing a wide variety of concerns, and are using a complex and innovative range of techniques and interventions. Correspondingly, counselors have an extensive and expanding array of employment options in mental health settings.

Community Mental Health Centers

The movements of the 1950s and 1960s to reduce the psychiatric inpatient population (deinstitutionalization) and increase readily available mental health services led to a rapid growth in community mental health centers (CMHCs) and an accompanying growth in employment of mental health counselors. Offering preventive as well as clinical services and treating people of all ages and economic circumstances, CMHCs and the mental health workers they employ typically provide 10 essential services: inpatient treatment, outpatient treatment, emergency service, partial hospitalization, consultation and education, diagnostic services, rehabilitation, pre- and after-care, training, and research and evaluation (Bloom, 1983). CMHCs offer counselors a challenging and diverse client population and a broad range of opportunities for collaboration and intervention. These agencies are a particularly good place of employment for beginning counselors who want supervision, role models, and breadth of experience as they determine their particular areas of interest and specialization.

Marriage and Family Counseling Agencies

The past twenty-five years have witnessed the rapid growth of the field of family counseling. National attention has been paid to issues such as the high divorce rate; spouse and child abuse; blended, single-parent, and other nontraditional families; and the important part that family dynamics can play in the course of Schizophrenia, Attention-Deficit Disorders, and many other emotional and physical difficulties. Mental health agencies that specialize in family-related concerns are numerous, reflecting the belief that problems linked to family interaction respond best to treatment that involves the family as well as the person presenting the problem. Some agencies that emphasize family counseling prefer their employees to have specialized training (e.g., mediation, brief family therapy), but others provide employment to entry-level counselors.

Rehabilitation Counseling Agencies

Rehabilitation counselors work with people who have physical disabilities, people with mental retardation, people with substance-related (drug or alcohol) problems, people who have been incarcerated, or people with severe or chronic emotional disorders. These counselors typically focus on behavioral change; promoting self-esteem, independence, and feelings of competence; and addressing the adjustment and career-related needs of their clients.

Originally, most rehabilitation counselors were employed in large governmental agencies where they had a large case load comprised primarily of people with medical conditions that limited their occupational opportunities. Now, however, rehabilitation and mental health counselors have many options.

Counseling for People with Physical Disabilities

A large number of people have some type of physical impairment that limits their choices. Livneh (1991) reported that 2 million Americans are blind, 15–16 million have a hearing impairment, 150,000 have spinal cord injuries, and as many as 5 million have epilepsy. Each year, one million people are diagnosed with cancer and 500,000 people incur traumatic head injuries. Rehabilitation counselors usually have specialized training in the medical aspects of their clients' disorders. The focus of the counseling, then, is on both physical and psychosocial variables to facilitate a rewarding involvement in the community and the labor force. Counselors help their clients to obtain appropriate training and employment, provide follow-up, and make referrals for additional help as needed in order to improve the quality of their clients' lives (Livneh, 1991).

Corrections and the Court System

Counselors with a special interest in corrections may find employment in prisons, in pre-release programs, or in parole settings. Sometimes counselors employed in corrections fill both counseling and authoritative roles, a difficult combination. Counselors in corrections usually have the opportunity for both group and individual counseling and often deal with challenging and resistant clients.

Counselors also may become involved with the court system by providing assessment and testimony in child custody cases; through employment with juvenile and family courts; via agencies that specialize in treating people with behaviors that may lead to their arrest (e.g., partner abuse, pedophilia); and in serving as expert witnesses. These counselors not only need to be skilled in group and individual behavioral counseling, they also need to understand the legal system and the privileges and constraints it imposes on counselors.

Substance Abuse Treatment Programs

Substance abuse treatment facilities have been a major employer of mental health counselors for many years. Counselors interested in helping people with drug or alcohol problems are engaged primarily in providing group treatment, but also may have an opportunity for individual and family counseling, organizing interventions for people who are resistant to treatment, and providing education and information. These counselors need to be knowledgeable about drug- and alcohol-related problems, their signs and negative effects; support groups such as Alcoholics Anonymous and Rational Recovery; and community resources that can help their clients with job training and placement, public assistance, and continued treatment. Counselors specializing in the treatment of Substance-Related Disorders may be employed in inpatient settings where they will work intensively with people who usually are spending up to four weeks in detoxification or initial treatment, or they may work in outpatient facilities where treatment is less intensive but broader and longer, seeking both to stop the substance use and to prevent relapse.

Treatment Programs for the Chronically Mentally Ill

An area of increasing opportunity for counselors is programs designed to help people with serious and chronic mental disorders such as Schizophrenia or severe Personality Disorders. Such programs often are affiliated with CMHCs and are funded by the government and third-party payments. The counselors' primary role usually is that of case manager, a multifaceted role that involves overseeing and coordinating clients' services, making referrals and collaborating with other professionals, providing some counseling to promote adjustment, and perhaps making home visits.

Career Counseling or Employment Agencies

Increasing social acceptance of the lifelong nature of career development and the increasing frequency of midlife career change have led to the growth of career counseling services. Such agencies may serve a general clientele or an identified group (e.g., women reentering the work force, high school students, military retirees). Career counselors also may serve as consultants to business, industry, and governmental agencies that are reducing the size of their staffs and need counselors to facilitate outplacement and retirement as well as help in maintaining organizational morale. Employment agencies, too, hire career counselors, but their focus tends to be more on matching clients to job opportunities listed with the agencies than on providing a broad range of services.

Agencies focused on career counseling typically offer a combination of services: counseling; assessment using computerized and paper and pencil inventories of interests, values, and abilities; information-giving; training in job-seeking skills such as networking, interviewing, and résumé writing; and placement. They also may offer support groups for job seekers.

Employee Assistance Programs

One of the fastest growing areas of employment for counselors, employee assistance programs (EAPs), are generally affiliated with or retained by businesses, industries, or governmental organizations to provide counseling to employees. Approximately 5000 employee assistance programs have been established in the United States. People with master's degrees in counseling comprise approximately one-third of their professional staff (Hosie, West, & Mackey, 1993). Employers generally provide this service in order to maximize employee productivity, retain capable employees, and reduce absenteeism and accidents by ameliorating personal or job-related problems that are leading to impairment. Clients may be self-referred or supervisor-referred, although confidentiality is almost always guaranteed unless clients' continued employment depends on their cooperation with counseling. Common concerns presented to EAP counselors are substance use, family difficulties, and employee-supervisor conflict. Counseling usually is brief and crisis- or problem-focused, with referrals made if extended counseling is needed. Counselors in EAPs not only are engaged in individual or family counseling but also provide workshops and seminars on such topics as stress management and career planning, conduct assessments, consult with supervisors and administrators, and market and evaluate their services. Prevention and referral are at least as important in their work as is remediation. Counselors in health maintenance organizations (HMOs) perform similar roles, but typically are less involved with supervisory and employee issues and more involved with the formalities of managed care.

New opportunities developing for counselors in business and industry include executive coaching, team building, conflict resolution, mediation, organizational development, and leadership development (Lewis & Hayes, 1988; Morrissey, 1995). In addition, counselors in these settings may assume some of the responsibilities of career counselors, including promoting career advancement, administering interest inventories, and facilitating relocation, retirement, and outplacement.

Schools

Typical school counselors have large case loads, often over 250 students, and a variety of responsibilities such as scheduling, assessment, and program development, along with individual and group counseling and consultation with parents and teachers. Their role generally does not allow them to provide extensive counseling to students with serious emotional difficulties. However, when they encourage parents to seek outside help for their children, the referral often is ignored or dismissed as too costly or time-consuming.

To address this problem, many schools are forming partnerships with community agencies in which the agency, often a CMHC, will place mental health counselors in schools for part of their work week. The increased availability of mental health counselors, trained to diagnose and treat serious mental disorders, is increasing the availability of counseling to children and adolescents. Through early identification and treatment, the development of more serious problems later may be avoided. Mental health counselors in schools work closely with teachers and school counselors and need to be skilled in the diagnosis and treatment of mental disorders that are common in children and adolescents as well as in techniques such as play therapy that are especially helpful to children.

Hospitals

Because of their traditional focus on developmental concerns rather than pathology, counselors have been less likely to be employed in inpatient or psychiatric hospital settings than have other helping professionals. Now, however, mental health counselors have the diagnostic and intervention skills they need to work effectively in these settings and are increasingly finding employment in working with a seriously disturbed or physically ill population. Often, in such settings a team approach is used, with counselors promoting adjustment and providing family counseling while medication and other medical treatments are provided by physicians or psychiatrists. Counselors also play a rehabilitative role in working with people who are hospitalized for potentially life-threatening illnesses or surgery that has caused an alteration in appearance and functioning.

Other Medical Services/Settings

Counselors have been working with medical personnel in outpatient settings in response to the growing awareness that attending to both physical and emotional concerns can facilitate decisions, adjustment, and recovery. Such settings may include programs to help people with problem pregnancies or infertility; programs for people with cancer, designed to help them reduce side-effects of their treatment and promote a fighting spirit; hospice programs to provide support and resources to people who are dying and their families; and genetic counseling facilities designed to provide information on genetically transmitted disorders to prospective parents, enabling them to make informed decisions.

Counselors also are finding employment in hospital emergency facilities. Counselors in those settings must make a rapid assessment and diagnosis of people who present with severe emotional symptoms and make recommendations on hospitalization or other treatment options.

Nursing homes and continuing care facilities are other medically related facilities that employ counselors. These residential programs provide care to people with serious mental or physical disorders, such as Alzheimer's disease, head trauma, or advanced neurological disorders, who are not able to care for themselves. A large percentage of people in these facilities are older adults, but younger people also may be found in these settings. Family counseling as well as consultation with medical personnel are important aspects of the counselors' role in these settings, although group and individual therapy to promote adjustment and improve functioning also are important.

Residential Facilities

Residential facilities, such as group homes for troubled adolescents, apartments for mentally retarded adults, and halfway houses for people with Substance-Related Disorders or a recent history of incarceration, employ counselors. In such settings, counselors usually have small caseloads but work closely with their clients in flexible ways, perhaps teaching them to cook, promoting socialization, or helping them to locate housing. Work hours also tend to be flexible.

Day Treatment Programs

These programs are established for people who are not currently capable of total independence and who need a supervised and therapeutic daytime program. Day treatment programs have been available for many years for older people and for people who are chronically mentally ill. In recent years, day treatment programs for troubled children and adolescents have proliferated, partly in response to the high costs of inpatient treatment and partly in response to the growing number of young people who present with dangerous conditions such as Eating Disorders, Conduct Disorders, and Substance Use Disorders. Counselors in these settings provide education, group and individual treatment, therapeutic activities, and family counseling. These programs typically are designed to simulate a community; they are very structured and emphasize behavior modification and a system for earning rewards and penalties.

Crisis Intervention Settings

Counselors engaged in crisis intervention may focus on suicide prevention, accompany the police to deal with reports of domestic violence, serve as intake workers in a hospital or CMHC, work in victim assistance programs, or staff a hot line, offering counseling over the telephone. Such counseling tends to be short-term, perhaps only one contact, and typically calls for the counselor to make rapid decisions, intervene quickly, and have knowledge of and make use of referral sources.

Military and Government Settings

Counselors are employed by a broad range of military and governmental agencies, in roles in addition to that of employee assistance counselor discussed earlier. Counselors affiliated with governmental agencies might work with people who are receiving public assistance, who are involved in foster care, or who are in funded programs to help people develop job skills. These counselors typically have a large case load, see their clients on an irregular and as needed basis, and are involved with case management, referral, and administrative responsibilities.

Counselors also may be employed to help firefighters, police, and others in stressful public service jobs. Critical incident response teams are especially useful in those settings. The military, too, employs counselors. They are involved in addressing special problems among military personnel such as abuse, facilitating relocation of families and employment of spouses, providing assessment and career counseling, working in schools for military dependents in the United States and overseas, and providing a broad range of services at inpatient and outpatient treatment facilities on military bases or connected with the Veterans Administration. Counselors in these settings need to be familiar with the diagnosis and treatment of the common problems found in these settings such as Posttraumatic Stress Disorder, partner abuse, substance-related problems, marital conflict, and Adjustment Disorders.

Religious/Spiritual Counseling Settings

Churches and other religious and spiritual settings increasingly are hiring counselors to supplement the work of the clergy who may not have the time or expertise to offer mental health services. Counselors in these settings need to understand the beliefs and values of their clients and emphasize spiritual issues. However, most of their work is not much different from that of a general mental health counselor and primarily involves helping people with a broad range of interpersonal and adjustment problems.

Wellness and Prevention Settings

The preventive and developmental skills that counselors have are being put to especially good use in a variety of health and wellness settings. Counselors have found employment in fitness centers; smoking cessation, weight control and other behavioral change programs; programs that teach relaxation, imagery, meditation, and other wellness skills; and programs that reach out to high-risk populations (e.g., children from lower socioeconomic families) in an effort to help them develop the skills and resources they need to cope with difficulties they are likely to encounter.

Specific Focus Agencies

A broad range of mental health agencies can be identified that specialize in treating a specific disorder, problem, or type of person. These agencies can be categorized according to the age group served (e.g., children, people over 65), the special population or problem addressed (e.g., people who recently have been bereaved, people going through marital separation and divorce, survivors of rape and abuse, people with eating problems, recent immigrants, Vietnam veterans), or the approach to treatment espoused (e.g., rational emotive behavior therapy, biofeedback, hypnotherapy). Counselors with special areas of interest or training may seek employment in such settings. This may help them to develop strong skills in an area of specialization but usually will not provide them experience in counseling people with a broad range of disorders or concerns.

Consulting Settings

Counselors may be self-employed or employed by agencies to engage in the process of consulting, one of several roles for counselors that focus on effecting change in systems. Approximately 90% of master's degree programs in counseling currently offer course work in consultation (Stoltenberg, 1993). Consultation typically involves a triadic relationship, including the consultant who is the expert or specialist, the consultee who is requesting help, and the client system that is the focus of the change efforts. Dougherty (1995) described the following four types of mental health consultation:

1. Client-centered case consultation—helping consultees assess and address client problems (e.g., conferring with another counselor about a client in crisis).
2. Consultee-centered case consultation—addressing the consultees' lack of knowledge and skills, as well as their difficulties.
3. Program-centered administrative consultation—advising others on how to set up programs or deal with programmatic problems.
4. Consultee-centered administrative consultation—focusing on difficulties in the consultees that are limiting the effectiveness of programs (e.g., helping counselors deal with the introduction of a new system of record keeping).

Typically, the counselor-consultant is hired by several different agencies on a short-term, fee-for-service contract to provide expertise in a specified area. Consultants might conduct assessments for a rehabilitation firm, provide training in communication skills for supervisors in business or government, offer stress management workshops for members of a professional association, or provide training for other mental health professionals in a particular skill or theory. Consultation may involve mental health counselors with their colleagues; with parents, teachers, and administrators in school settings; with the administrators of mental health organizations; and with employees in a range of other settings that have an influence over clients. The consultant role typically is an active, directive, and facilitative one, requiring skills and knowledge in needs assessment, collaboration, organizational development, interpersonal relationships and communication, and formative and summative evaluation (Splete, 1988). While consulting may be an unpredictable and potentially stressful endeavor, many counselors enjoy part-time consulting in addition to full-time employment.

Private Practice

The advent, in the 1970s, of state licensure and certification for counselors has led counselors to enter private practice in increasing numbers. Private practice is the most common work site for members of the American Mental Health Counselors Association, with over 4600 of its 12,000 members in private practice (Messina, 1995). Private practices take many forms: they may be full-time or part-time, often in addition to teaching or another counseling position; they may be solo or group practices; and they may be general or specialized practices.

Private practice clearly is a viable option for counselors; state licensure allows them to practice independently and they are generally recognized by health insurance companies. Private practice has many rewards: counselors can set their own hours, they can choose the clients or issues they want to deal with, and they have the potential to do well financially. On the other hand, counselors in private practice, particularly those who practice alone, must be prepared to assume full responsibility for the diagnosis and treatment planning for their clients, they often experience isolation, their income is uncertain and does not continue when they take vacations or sick days, and they must be actively involved in marketing, billing, and completing applications forms for managed care (Beck, 1994). Although there probably always will be a place for counselors in private practice, the appeal and availability of private practice may have peaked, and establishing a successful practice is becoming increasingly difficult with the continued expansion of managed care and cost containment.

Overview of Opportunities

Clearly, counselors have a broad range of employment settings open to them. Beginning counselors should choose their work settings carefully, starting with their internships. With each work experience, skills will be developed and opportunities will be expanded. However, other opportunities will become less available as counselors narrow their focus. A clear view of the path they hope their careers will take can help counselors to develop the competencies they need while still maximizing their marketability.

THE MENTAL HEALTH SERVICE PROVIDERS

Counselors increasingly are working collaboratively with other providers of mental health services. The counselor may be part of a treatment team, working with several others, or may consult with another provider to determine the best treatment for a client. To maximize the effectiveness of the collaboration as well as maintain their own roles, counselors need to be familiar with the other helping professionals as well as knowledgeable about how their own roles and responsibilities both differ from and resemble those of other helping professionals.

The Mental Health Treatment Team

The diversity of training and areas of specialization of mental health professionals employed in CMHCs and other multiservice mental health facilities has led to the evolution of the mental health team. In this generic model of staffing, a mental health team is composed of two or more treatment providers with different areas of specialization. Such a team might include a psychiatrist, a psychologist, and a counselor or social worker. Depending upon the nature of the treatment facility, the team also might include recreation therapists, psychiatric nurses, paraprofessionals, and other specialists. Members of a team will have some roles or duties they all perform, such as individual counseling or psychotherapy, and some that are assigned only to certain members of the group, based on their training or expertise. For example, the psychiatrist determines whether people need medication as part of their treatment, the social worker may specialize in family therapy, and the counselor may focus on promoting behavioral change. Generally, the team will meet as a unit to develop treatment plans and will evaluate them at regular intervals. One member of the team may serve as the case manager or primary therapist, ensuring that team members collaborate smoothly and that clients' needs are addressed.

In some agencies, the treatment team is formed at the time of the intake interview. The counselor may gather information on a person's background and presenting concerns, the social worker interviews the client's family, the psychologist conducts an assessment through projective tests and other inventories, and the psychiatrist performs a medical assessment. When the intake procedures have been completed, all four mental health workers meet to share their findings and develop a diagnosis and treatment plan.

In other settings, the team will develop on an as needed basis. For example, a counselor who conducts an intake interview of a confused person, age 63, with a previous diagnosis of Alcohol Dependence and a family history of Dementia, may ask a psychiatrist or a psychologist to evaluate the person to determine whether a Cognitive Mental Disorder, a Substance-Induced Disorder, or a Psychotic Disorder is present.

The team approach offers many advantages. It allows mental health treatment providers to become experts in some areas while drawing on the knowledge and talents of others to supplement their skills. The collaboration afforded by the team approach can yield considerable information and insights about people and often promotes sounder diagnoses and treatment plans. In addition, this model can contribute to cost containment and increased availability of services. In many regions of the country, psychiatrists, typically the highest paid mental health professionals, are in short supply. The team approach can circumvent this problem by using psychiatrists primarily for their unique skills such as prescribing medication and by using more available and less costly mental health treatment providers to perform tasks in areas of shared expertise (e.g., individual and family psychotherapy).

Counselors, especially those in private practice, often develop their own informal treatment teams to reduce their isolation and increase the range of services they have available. For example, a counselor may meet with other counselors for weekly peer supervision, may refer people whose disorders commonly benefit from medication to a psychiatrist in whom the counselor has confidence, may suggest that clients with suspected Learning Disorders or Attention-Deficit Disorders see a psychologist for testing, and may consult with a social worker to obtain information on subsidized housing and other social service programs. This sort of networking can help mental health counselors to provide the best possible treatment to their clients and have confidence that they understand and are dealing effectively with their clients' difficulties.

Although collaboration with other providers offers many benefits, it also may present challenges. Issues of competition, distribution of power, and manipulation by clients may arise (Seligman & Ceo, 1986). To maximize the likelihood of a smooth and productive collaboration, counselors should confer with their colleagues frequently; be sure they have compatible theoretical orientations, mutual understanding and appreciation of each other's skills; and a cooperative orientation.

The Mental Health Treatment Specialists

The diversity of treatment providers can be confusing to clients as well as to helping professionals themselves. Counselors need to understand the differences and similarities among the various mental health professionals to know whom to consult when help is needed and how to facilitate productive communication and collaboration. At present, four groups of mental health professionals (psychiatrists, psychologists, social workers, and psychiatric nurses) are viewed as core providers by many organizations. Mental health counselors have been actively seeking to be included as core providers and this recognition is anticipated soon. The following section provides brief descriptions of core and other mental health treatment providers.

Psychiatrists

Psychiatrists are unique among the mental health treatment providers in that they have a medical degree, generally an M.D., and are qualified to assess physical conditions, diagnose medical problems, and prescribe medication. They typically have the most extensive education of the mental health professionals, including four years of medical school and at least several years of residency. However, the training that psychiatrists receive in psychotherapy varies; some have completed advanced training programs and additional residencies and may have considerable expertise in psychotherapy while others concentrate on the biochemical treatment of mental disorders and may have relatively brief training and experience in psychotherapy. Counselors actually have more expertise in human development and psychotherapy than do some psychiatrists.

Although counselors, of course, cannot diagnose physical complaints or prescribe medication, they are often the first to hear of clients' medical complaints or of undesirable side effects or lack of effectiveness of prescribed medication. Consequently, counselors need to stay informed about their clients' medications and physical conditions and understand which mental disorders and symptoms benefit from medication so that they can refer clients to a psychiatrist when a medical evaluation seems warranted.

Psychologists–Doctoral Level

Doctoral level psychologists can be categorized by their areas of specialization and their degrees. Most will have a Ph.D. degree (Doctor of Philosophy), but some will have an Ed.D. (Doctor of Education) and others will have a Psy.D. (Doctor of Psychology). The Psy.D. is generally granted by programs focused on preparing practitioners rather researchers, the Ph.D. typically has emphasized research as well as practice, and the Ed.D. has been most strongly associated with an interest in teaching or employment in educational settings. However, considerable overlap exists among the requirements and course offerings for the three degrees.

Psychologists may specialize in such areas as clinical, counseling, developmental, experimental, or industrial/organizational psychology. Psychologists employed in mental health settings are most likely to be clinical or counseling psychologists. Although here, too, considerable overlap exists, clinical psychologists are typically more interested in abnormal behavior and severe emotional disturbance and their remediation while counseling psychologists tend to be more interested in normal development, prevention, and problems of adjustment.

Most practicing psychologists have completed three to four years of post-baccalaureate study, a one-year internship, a thesis or dissertation, and two years of supervised post-doctoral experience. They are licensed by the states in which they practice. Doctoral-level psychologists are trained in psychotherapy and typically have considerable expertise in psychological testing, including the use of projective techniques (e.g., Rorschach Test, Thematic Apperception Test).

Psychologists–Master's Degree Level

Master's degree level psychologists typically have received specialized training in a particular area of psychology (e.g. testing, counseling, or industrial and school psychology). They are often employed as psychometricians or school psychologists where their primary function is assessment. Psychologists without a doctorate generally cannot be licensed or certified to practice independently as psychologists (although some states allow school psychologists to have independent practices that focus on educational psychology). Consequently, the role of the psychologist without a doctorate is limited. Some psychologists are circumventing this by taking extra course work and seeking credentialing as counselors.

Counselors who work with children and families often will collaborate with school psychologists. They specialize in assessment of learning problems, developmental disorders, and other difficulties that may prevent children from performing well at school. School psychologists work closely with school counselors to determine children's special needs and develop individualized educational plans to address them. Testing is emphasized in their work, although counseling is increasingly becoming part of the role of the school psychologist. Most school psychologists are employed in schools, although some are moving into the private sector.

Social Workers

Practicing social workers typically have the master's degree (MSW) and credentials from state (LCSW) and national (ACSW) credentialing bodies. Requirements for state credentialing of social workers are comparable to those for licensed counselors: approximately 60 semester hours of graduate credit including field work and two years of supervised post-master's experience. However, social workers have a longer history in the mental health field. Initially, social workers often collaborated with psychiatrists, seeing the families of troubled clients. Over the years, they have acquired considerable independence and credibility. Consequently, the general public seems to have more awareness of the field of social work than of the newer field of mental health counseling. While considerable overlap exists between the interests and training of clinical or psychiatric social workers and mental health counselors, social workers tend to be more knowledgeable about public policy and organizational issues. However, they generally do not have counselors' expertise in testing and in dealing with educational or career-related concerns. Social workers are particularly likely to be found in medical and social service settings, although like mental health counselors they often work in private practices, family counseling, CMHCs, and other mental health treatment programs.

Psychiatric Nurses

Psychiatric nurses, sometimes known as clinical nurse specialists, generally have a master's degree in their field, with supervised experience in mental health settings. They have training in counseling and human development as well as in medical diagnosis and treatment. Their work often emphasizes prevention, community health, and wellness. They frequently are part of a treatment team in hospital settings and in settings involving people with physical or medical concerns (e.g., detoxification programs, rehabilitation programs), but also may be found in private practice, CMHCs, and other mental health settings.

Pastoral Counselors

Credentialed pastoral counselors generally have the same training and experience as other mental health counselors with additional or previous training in theology and an interest in spiritual issues. The best-qualified pastoral counselors follow accepted principles of effective counseling, such as offering advice sparingly and attempting to maintain objectivity.

Marriage and Family Therapists

National certification is available for marriage and family therapists through the American Association of Marriage and Family Therapy and through the International Association of Marriage and Family Counselors, affiliated with the American Counseling Association. Some states also offer credentials for marriage and family therapists. These specific credentials are not required for marriage and family therapy as long as counselors have state licensure or certification in counseling.

Marriage and family therapists may have had their training in programs especially for family therapists or may be mental health counselors, social workers, or other helping professionals with particular interest and special training in family counseling. They may be found in a broad range of mental health settings including private practice but, of course, are likely to specialize in marriage and family therapy.

Certified Addictions Counselor

Certified addictions counselors (CACs) typically have less education and training than other mental health professionals but more direct experience. Many CACs are recovering from their own addictions and want to use their experience to help others. The CAC credential requires a two-year college degree with extensive coursework and experience in addictions and other mental health areas. As members of a treatment team, CACs may be able to establish rapport rapidly with clients and can offer special insights and information.

In recent years, the CAC credential has become very marketable because of the great need for therapists to have expertise in addictions. Consequently, many licensed mental health counselors have also received the specialized training they need be become CACs, a particularly valuable combination of credentials.

Expressive Therapists

Expressive therapists specialize in the use of creative arts in counseling. They may focus on art therapy, music therapy, dance therapy, or other creative therapies. They often have credentials as counselors or other helping professionals and use traditional counseling approaches as well as creative ones in their work. They can be especially helpful to people who have difficulty verbalizing their feelings, have physical concerns, seem to have repressed memories, or are severely disturbed.

Psychoanalysts

The term "psychoanalyst" describes people who have received extensive specialized post-graduate training in the field of psychoanalysis and who have generally undergone personal analysis. Nearly all are either psychiatrists or doctoral level psychologists. "Psychoanalyst," however, does not indicate a degree received but, rather, the nature of a person's training and practice (e.g., using the ideas and techniques of Freud and his followers and seeing clients five times a week for several years or more).

Psychotherapists

"Psychotherapist" is a general term that describes anyone who practices counseling or psychotherapy. It does not provide information about education, training, or techniques, but does imply an interest in treating people with mental disorders, rather than focusing on providing help to people with problems of adjustment or life circumstance.

Counselors

Definitions of mental health counselors have been provided earlier in this book. Mental health counselors often collaborate with each other and may interact with school counselors and counselors in higher education settings.

Considerable overlap and commonality exists between mental health counselors and other helping professionals. A study by Falvey (1992) of 128 clinicians representing six mental health professions found that the clinicians were very similar in terms of the assessment criteria they used, the categories they addressed in their history taking, their treatment planning, and the goals they established for clients. Only their interventions showed much variability. Similarly, West, Hosie, and Mackey (1987) found no significant differences in employment of people with master's degrees in counseling, social work, and psychology.

Mental health counselors, however, are particularly well-trained to use a wide range of techniques and approaches to help people with developmental, social, emotional, family, and career-related concerns; to conduct assessments, using interviews and standardized, objective tests; and to make use of community resources and support systems to help people. They are involved in individual, group, and family counseling; diagnosis and treatment planning, supervision; program development and evaluation; training; consultation; staff development; community education and organization; referral; administration; fund raising and grant writing; and case management. The work of mental health counselors also typically has a few clear limits; they cannot evaluate physical concerns, prescribe medication, or use projective tests. Despite these few limitations, the roles and skills of mental health counselors are broad, enabling them to effectively diagnose and treat a wide range of clients and disorders. The rest of this book will provide information on those essential skills of the mental health counselor.

Diagnostic Systems and Their Use

"At the foundation of effective mental health care is the establishment of a valid psychodiagnosis" (Hinkle, 1994b, p. 174). The American Counseling Association Code of Ethics and Standards of Practice (1995, p. 36) states, "Counselors take special care to provide proper diagnosis of mental disorders." Diagnosis is an essential tool of the mental health counselor. As of 1990, nearly 80% of students in counseling were taught to make diagnoses (Ritchie et al., 1991).

Conservative estimates indicate that 40–50 million Americans have mental and addictive disorders (Maxmen & Ward, 1995). Knowledge of and skill in the use of diagnosis can enhance the counseling process and help the counselor in many ways (Seligman, 1991):

1. A diagnostic system provides a consistent framework as well as a set of criteria for naming and describing mental disorders.
2. Knowing a client's diagnosis can help counselors to anticipate the typical course of the disorder and develop a clearer understanding of the person's symptoms.
3. Probably the most important benefit of diagnosis is that it enables counselors to develop treatment plans that have a high probability of success.
4. The process of diagnosis employs a common language, used by all other mental health disciplines, thereby facilitating parity, credibility, communication, and collaboration.
5. Diagnoses are linked to several standardized inventories (e.g., the Minnesota Multiphasic Personality Inventory, the Millon Clinical Multiaxial Inventory), enabling counselors to make use of these in-

ventories to facilitate diagnosis and treatment planning as well as gain insight into clients.

6. Counselors are less vulnerable to malpractice suits if they have made a diagnosis and treatment plan according to an accepted system.

7. Using a standardized system of diagnosis is required in order for counselors to receive third-party payments for their services, thereby making counseling more affordable.

8. Sharing diagnoses with clients, when appropriate, can help them to understand themselves better.

9. Knowing that others have experienced similar symptoms and that information is available about their conditions can also reassure people.

10. Explaining to people that they have a mental disorder can unbalance previously established views of their difficulties, can reduce their tendency to erroneously blame others or blame themselves for their problems, and can increase receptivity to treatment and change.

11. If a person relocates or transfers from one counselor to another, the use of a shared diagnostic language can promote continuity of service.

12. Records kept of diagnoses, treatment interventions, and outcomes enable clinicians and agencies to determine needed services, assess and refine the quality of their interventions, demonstrate accountability, and justify the work of the agency or clinician.

13. Making accurate diagnoses helps counselors to determine those people they have the skills and training to work with as well as those clients who need a referral for medication or other services that counselors do not provide.

Controversies and Limitations

Despite the many benefits inherent in the process of diagnosis, some counselors still question whether diagnosis of mental disorders is an appropriate skill for counselors. As Johnson (1993, p. 236) wrote of this debate, "The field of mental health counseling is currently wrestling with at least two orientations toward carving out its unique role among the mental health professions. One orientation might be best described as placing an emphasis on a developmental-psychoeducational model....A competing orientation suggests that, to take our place as another core mental health profession, we must engage in the practice of clinical diagnosis and treatment of mental and emotional disorders....[T]hese orientations...are not mutually exclusive." In fact, according to Hinkle (1994a, p. 34), "Just as mental health counselors 'cannot not communicate,' 'cannot not influence,' and 'cannot not behave,' they cannot not diagnose or plan as part of the [counseling] context." Only if they know whether or not a person has a mental disorder and understands that mental disorder, if one is present, can counselors determine whether and what developmental, psychoeducational, or clinical interventions are likely to be effective.

Counselors can make the best use of the diagnostic process and avoid its pitfalls if they keep the following risks in mind (Seligman, 1991):

1. Attaching a diagnostic label to someone can be stigmatizing; can lead to negative perceptions of that person at school, work, or in the family; and can limit one's ability to obtain insurance.

2. In some cases, knowing the diagnostic term for a person's symptoms can be more discouraging and threatening than viewing the problem in lay terms. For example, parents may be more comfortable dealing with a child they view as having high energy than with one who has an Attention-Deficit Disorder.

3. Diagnosis can lead to identifying people with their mental disorders (e.g., a Borderline, a Depressive) rather than as people with a particular set of concerns, and can promote a focus on pathology rather than on health.

4. Although the linear process of diagnosis can facilitate information gathering and treatment planning, it can make it more difficult to think about people in developmental and systemic terms and to take a holistic view of clients and their difficulties.

5. Similarly, attaching a diagnostic label to one person may put the focus of treatment on that person rather than on a family or social system. This can reinforce a perception of that person as the problem and can make it more difficult for a family to work together on shared issues and concerns.

6. In addition, the widely used *Diagnostic and Statistical Manual of Mental Disorders* (DSM) has been based primarily on disorders and conditions found in the United States and may have limited relevance to people from other cultures.

Maximizing the Benefits of Diagnoses

Research has shown that a high degree of agreement on diagnoses can be obtained from experienced clinicians (American Psychiatric Association, 1994; Blocher & Biggs, 1983). Mental health professionals agree on a given diagnosis 80% of the time (Pfeiffer, 1995). In order to make an accurate diagnosis, counselors must gather information on people's presenting concerns, their backgrounds and history, and their current situations. Data gathered are then organized and analyzed by the counselors. The *Diagnostic and Statistical Manual of Mental Disorders* provides descriptive data, information on the *what*; other sources are needed to determine *why* and *what now* of mental disorders (Maxmen and Ward, 1995). Detailed information on the process of intake interviews, assessment, and treatment planning, all part of the diagnostic process, are provided later in this book. The following guidelines should help counselors to make accurate and useful diagnoses and minimize the shortcomings of the diagnostic process:

1. View people in context, considering cultural, social, gender, and other factors. Keep in mind that mental disorders should be diagnosed only if thoughts and behaviors are aberrant for the person's culture.

2. Be aware that the symptoms people present may change rapidly, depending on the time of day, their immediate stressors, the progression of the disorder, or the characteristics of and questions posed by the interviewer. Diagnosis is not an exact science and often takes considerable time and many samples of behavior as well as information from records and other people before an accurate diagnosis can be made.

3. Do not be tempted to overdiagnose to maximize third-party payments or to underdiagnose to avoid labeling a person. Both are unethical and may be illegal. Overdiagnosis can jeopardize the client's future insurance coverage and may prevent employment in some jobs; underdiagnosis may suggest that the counselor failed to appreciate the severity of a person's difficulties.

4. Finally, always consider the whole person, with diagnosis being only one important piece of information about that person.

DIAGNOSTIC SYSTEMS

Two diagnostic systems are widely used. The *Diagnostic and Statistical Manual of Mental Disorders*, now in its fourth edition (DSM-IV, American Psychiatric Association, 1994), is the accepted diagnostic system in the United States. In other countries, however, the *International Statistical Classification of Mental and Behavioural Disorders*, (ICD-10, World Health Organization, 1992) may be the diagnostic system of choice. The DSM-IV and the ICD-10 have a common numbering system and many similarities. Although the parallels between the two are outlined in Appendix H of the DSM-IV, clinicians in the United States usually only need to be familiar with the DSM-IV.

DEVELOPMENT OF THE *DIAGNOSTIC AND STATISTICAL MANUAL OF MENTAL DISORDERS*

The first edition of the *Diagnostic and Statistical Manual of Mental Disorders*, containing 108 categories of mental disorder (Hohenshil, 1993), was published in 1952. It was developed primarily by and for psychiatrists and presented a psychobiological view of emotional disorders. The DSM-II, published in 1968 and containing 185 categories of mental disorder, was strongly influenced by Freud and psychoanalytic theory. The DSM-III, published in 1980, with 265 categories of mental disorder, can be viewed as the first of the modern generation of diagnostic manuals. A collaborative venture of the American Psychiatric Association and the American Psychological Association, the DSM-III was in preparation for several years and was field-tested by over 500 clinicians before it was published. A revision of the DSM-III, the DSM-III-R, was published in 1987 and contained 290 categories. In 1994, the DSM-IV was published, describing over 300 categories of mental disorder. The DSM-IV, like the DSM-III, was deliberately atheoretical; it sought to describe mental disorders in a way that was useful to clinicians of all theoretical orientations. Although the DSM-IV does not provide information on treatment of these disorders, this manual is the stepping-stone to determining effective treatment strategies. According to Hinkle (1994b, p.182), "An understanding of this diagnostic system and its vast implications in counseling will be imperative to the effective and ethical delivery of professional mental health counseling services."

For each disorder, the DSM generally provides information on:

1. Diagnostic criteria for the class of disorders and all disorders it encompasses
2. Subtypes and specifiers relevant to the disorder
3. Recording procedures
4. Associated features and disorders
5. Specific age, culture, familial, and gender-related features
6. Prevalence
7. Typical course of the disorder
8. Information on differential diagnosis or the differences between that disorder and similar ones.

Three criteria have guided recent revisions of the DSM. The primary justification for change was compelling empirical support. Extensive literature reviews, clinical trials, and drafts with invited feedback provided the information to determine whether support was available for a suggested change. Clinical utility and compatibility with the ICD were other criteria for change.

DEFINITION OF A MENTAL DISORDER

The DSM-IV defines a mental disorder as "…a clinically significant behavioral or psychological syndrome or pattern that occurs in an individual" (p. xxi) and is associated with distress, impairment and/or significant risk (American Psychiatric Association, 1994). Responses that are expectable or culturally sanctioned are not considered mental disorders.

MULTIAXIAL ASSESSMENT

Multiaxial assessment using the DSM-IV involves the use of five axes or ways of viewing people. Multiaxial assessment is an approach to diagnosis that encourages clinicians to take a holistic view of their clients. Axis I, *Clinical Disorders and Other Conditions That May Be a Focus of Clinical Attention*, and Axis II, *Personality Disorders and Mental Retardation*, are the axes where mental disorders as well as other conditions are listed. The only two diagnostic groups included on Axis II, encompassing long-standing and deeply ingrained disorders, are all of the Personality Disorders and Mental Retardation (including Borderline Intellectual Functioning). Defense mechanisms and personality traits may also be listed on Axis II. All other disorders are coded on Axis I.

Axis III is termed *General Medical Conditions*. Physical disorders that may be relevant to a person's emotional condition are listed on this axis. Although clinicians may informally list signs and symptoms on Axis III in their own notes, an official multiaxial assessment should include on Axis III only medically verified physical conditions.

On Axis IV clinicians list *Psychosocial and Environmental Problems* that may be causing a person difficulty. These typically include external processes or events, such as living in poverty, getting divorced, or being incarcerated, that have occurred within the past year. Clinicians can simply list the stressors in their own words and organize them into the categories in the DSM to facilitate record-keeping procedures.

Axis V, the *Global Assessment of Functioning* (GAF) scale, is a 1–100 scale on which clinicians rate a person's current level of functioning. Higher numbers reflect better functioning and numbers below 50 indicate people with severe symptoms. Most people seen in outpatient settings, presenting such concerns as Mood Disorders, Anxiety Disorders, and Personality Disorders, will be rated with numbers in the 50–70 range.

The DSM-IV assumes that a person's principal diagnosis is the first listed on Axis I. Only if another diagnosis is viewed as principal does that need to be specified. The DSM-IV offers the optional use of the descriptor Reason for Visit, to be used if a presenting concern was listed but was not viewed by the clinician as the principal diagnosis. For example, a person who sought counseling for a Sleep Disorder (Reason for Visit) was found to have a Mood Disorder (Principal Diagnosis) that seemed to be contributing to the sleep disorder.

Clinicians using the DSM generally should specify the severity of a person's mental disorders, with the terms "Mild," "Moderate," and "Severe" being the most likely choices. For a descriptor of "Mild," a person must meet at least the minimum criteria for a particular disorder and manifest impairment that is minimal relative to that disorder. The terms "Moderate" and "Severe" suggest greater impairment and more symptoms. The descriptor "In Partial Remission" characterizes a mental disorder that once was present but now is manifested in more limited ways that do not meet the diagnostic criteria for the disorder. "In Full Remission" describes the presentation of disorders that are clinically relevant but whose symptoms no longer are evident, perhaps because the person is receiving medication for the disorder. Another descriptor, "Prior History," allows disorders to be listed that may have been absent or in remission for years but that are noteworthy, perhaps because they have a tendency to recur under stress.

-- EXAMPLE OF A MULTIAXIAL ASSESSMENT

The following diagnosis of the difficulties of Cathy, a 47-year-old woman, is an example of a multiaxial assessment.

Axis I.   296.23 Major Depressive Disorder, single
           episode, severe, without psychotic features
           300.23 Social Phobia, moderate
Axis II.   301.6 Dependent Personality Disorder
Axis III. 714.0 Arthritis, rheumatoid
Axis IV.   Marital separation, change in residence
Axis V.   GAF = 50

The Principal Diagnosis for Cathy is Major Depressive Disorder. Specifiers indicate this is the first time she has had this disorder and that her symptoms are severe, although she is not out of touch with reality. In addition to presenting symptoms of incapacitating depression, loss of appetite, and difficulty sleeping, Cathy reported that throughout her life she had been uncomfortable in social situations that involved meeting new people in large groups and that, much to her regret, she had avoided attending her children's school programs and her husband's office parties because of that fear. These symptoms suggested her second Axis I diagnosis, Social Phobia.

Cathy also reported that she had always had low self-esteem and had tried her best to please others. She lived with her parents until she was 27 and then married a man chosen for her by her father. She has spent the last twenty years caring for her home, her husband, and her children; although she sometimes found that rewarding, she often had been bored and unfulfilled by her life but felt that she was not capable of holding a job and should always be available to meet the needs of her family. She reported great difficulty in decision-making and generally let her husband make all family decisions. Cathy also stated that she felt very frightened and almost desperate when she was alone. These symptoms suggest a diagnosis of a Dependent Personality Disorder.

The diagnosis of arthritis on Axis III was made by Cathy's physician. Painful and sometimes disabling arthritis contributed to Cathy's fears and self-doubts.

Axis IV indicates the stressors in Cathy's life during the past year. Cathy's husband has asked for a divorce. They have sold their home, and Cathy and her two children have moved in with her parents.

The rating of 50 on Axis V reflects Cathy's severe depression and some fleeting suicidal thoughts. Close monitoring of her progress is needed in light of this GAF score.

This multiaxial assessment describes Cathy's present situation and provides a basis for understanding her difficulties. Counselors now could readily begin to plan Cathy's treatment.

THE 17 DIAGNOSTIC CATEGORIES

The DSM-IV includes 17 broad categories, with multiple diagnoses included in each category. This section will present an overview of these diagnoses. Information on the treatment of these disorders will be provided in subsequent chapters.

DISORDERS USUALLY FIRST DIAGNOSED IN INFANCY, CHILDHOOD, OR ADOLESCENCE

The first category in the DSM is the most extensive and diverse. It includes those disorders that typically begin before the age of 18 but often continue into adulthood. The following reflects the subcategories and their most important characteristics:

1. *Mental Retardation*—This category is typified by an I. Q. score below 70 along with impairment in adaptive functioning. By definition, this disorder begins before age 18. It is listed on Axis II.

2. *Learning Disorders*—These disorders describe the phenomenon in which a person's achievement in a specific area such as reading or mathematics is substantially below what would be expected, based on age and intellectual level, and interferes with academic or other functioning. Problems of self-esteem and adjustment often are associated with these disorders.

3. *Motor Skills Disorder*—Developmental Coordination Disorder in this section is characterized by motor coordination that is substantially below what would be expected, based on age and intellectual factors, and is severe enough to interfere with functioning.

4. *Communication Disorders*—This grouping includes Expressive Language Disorder, typified by a marked deficit in verbal skills (e.g., limited vocabulary, errors in tense); Mixed Receptive/Expressive Language Disorder, a diagnosis describing someone who has difficulty with both comprehension and expressive language; Phonological Disorder or failure to use appropriate speech sounds; and Stuttering.

5. *Pervasive Developmental Disorders*—This section includes four disorders: Autistic Disorder, Rett's Disorder, Childhood Disintegrative Disorder, and Asperger's Disorder. All are characterized by impairment in one or more of the following areas: social interaction, communication, and behavior (usually restricted or stereotyped). These disorders begin in childhood and cause considerable impairment in functioning. Autistic Disorder begins before age 3 and involves impairment in all three of the above areas. It often is accompanied by mental retardation. Rett's Disorder, reported only in females, also involves pervasive impairment but is distinguished by a later onset (usually between 5 and 30 months following a period of normal development) and by a deceleration in head growth. Childhood Disintegrative Disorder is evident between 2 and 10 years of age and involves impairment in at least two of the three areas (social interaction, communication, and behavior). Asperger's Disorder typically does not entail severe impairment in language, thinking, or self-help skills; problems focus on social interaction and behavior.

6. *Attention-Deficit Disorder* (ADD)—ADD may manifest itself primarily with inattention (e.g., forgetfulness, carelessness, difficulty sustaining attention, distractibility), primarily with hyperactivity-impulsivity (e.g., impatience, fidgeting, excessive talking, high level of

motor activity), or with a combination of these symptoms. In order for these diagnoses to be justified, the attention deficit must be observed in at least two settings (e.g., school and home) and the onset must be before age 7. Conduct Disorder or Oppositional Defiant Disorder frequently accompanies this diagnosis, which is more common in males than in females and often continues into adulthood.

7. *Conduct Disorder*—This disorder, also more common in boys, entails a persistent and pervasive pattern of violating rules and the rights of others, including in the past 12 months at least three incidents of behaviors such as aggression toward people and animals, destruction of property, violations of rules, or theft. Types of this disorder include Childhood Onset, beginning before age 10, and Adolescent Onset, with a later onset. An early onset usually is associated with a poorer prognosis. If the symptoms of this disorder begin before age 15 and persist beyond the age of 18, the diagnosis usually is changed to Antisocial Personality Disorder, listed on Axis II.

8. *Oppositional Defiant Disorder*—This disorder is characterized by at least six months of negativistic, defiant, disobedient, and hostile behavior. Oppositional Defiant Disorder seems to have a better prognosis than Conduct Disorder but it, too, can cause considerable impairment in family relationships and functioning at school.

9. *Feeding and Eating Disorders of Infancy or Early Childhood*—This grouping includes Pica, repeated eating of a nonnutritive substance such as paint, crayons, or paste; Rumination Disorder, involving persistent regurgitation and rechewing of food; and Feeding Disorder of Infancy and Early Childhood, a diagnosis that is characterized by a refusal to eat adequately.

10. *Tic Disorders*—These disorders entail sudden, rapid, and recurrent involuntary motor movements or vocalizations that typically worsen under stress. Tourette's Disorder, a particularly severe tic disorder, involves multiple motor and vocal tics, sometimes including coprolalia or expression of unacceptable words, such as obscenities or racial slurs.

11. *Elimination Disorders*—This section lists disorders that entail repeated problems with bowel control (Encopresis) or bladder control (Enuresis). Encopresis is more common in boys and may stem from anxious or oppositional attitudes, while Enuresis is more likely to be biologically-based (Maxmen & Ward, 1995).

12. *Other Disorders of Infancy, Childhood, or Adolescence*—This section includes the remaining diagnoses in this category. *Separation Anxiety Disorder* is usually characterized by difficulty separating from home

or significant adults and can involve refusal to go to school or to be alone, as well as nightmares and multiple fears. The primary symptom of *Selective Mutism* is a failure to speak in certain situations where speech is expected, despite speaking in other situations. Usually people with this disorder speak at home but not in other settings. The symptoms of *Reactive Attachment Disorder* begin before age 5 and involve problems in attachment or relatedness, often stemming from a history of neglect or poor care. The Inhibited Type of this disorder is characterized by avoidance and ambivalence in interactions, while the Disinhibited Type is characterized by indiscriminate familiarity with others. *Stereotypic Movement Disorder*, the final diagnosis in this category, is typified by repetitive and apparently driven motor behavior such as rocking or head banging that causes impairment and even self-injury. This disorder often is associated with mental retardation or physical disabilities such as blindness.

DELIRIUM, DEMENTIA, AMNESTIC, AND OTHER COGNITIVE DISORDERS

Disorders in this section, all due to brain damage or dysfunction, are referred to as Cognitive Disorders. Psychiatrists or neurologists generally are the primary therapists for people with these disorders. Counselors do need to be able to recognize the signs of Cognitive Disorders so they can make appropriate referrals, but most will not need the detailed information on these disorders that would be necessary if they were making the diagnosis or planning the treatment. Common symptoms of these disorders include memory impairment, confusion, poor judgment, and decline in intellectual functioning. These disorders are more common in later life and frequently have an identified medical cause.

The Cognitive Disorders include the following diagnostic groups:

1. *Delirium*—This is characterized by rapid development of disorientation and memory impairment.
2. *Dementias*—Multiple cognitive deficits, with significant impairment in functioning, typify these disorders. Changes in personality and impulse control also are often reported. Common causes include Alzheimer's disease, strokes (Vascular Dementia), and other medical conditions such as HIV disease and head trauma.
3. *Amnestic Disorders*—Amnestic Disorders are cognitive disorders in which memory impairment is the primary symptom.

MENTAL DISORDERS DUE TO A GENERAL MEDICAL CONDITION ───────

This section of the DSM-IV includes the following disorders, caused by physiological or medical conditions: Catatonic Disorder Due to a General Medical Condition (such as encephalitis), Personality Change Due to a General Medical Condition (such as temporal lobe epilepsy), and Mental Disorder Not Otherwise Specified (NOS) Due to a General Medical Condition. The medical cause of all these disorders should be listed on Axis III, while the mental disorder is listed on Axis I. These disorders, like the Cognitive Disorders, will be diagnosed and treated primarily by physicians, although counselors may work collaboratively with them to promote clients' adjustment.

SUBSTANCE-RELATED DISORDERS ───────────

This section includes both the induced or physiological disorders resulting from drug or alcohol use such as Intoxication, Tolerance, and Substance-Induced Mood Disorder and the psychological or behavioral disorders associated with substance use (Substance Abuse and Substance Dependence). Substance Dependence almost always is more severe than Substance Abuse and is characterized by significant impairment, resulting from drug or alcohol use, including at least three prominent symptoms such as tolerance, withdrawal, unsuccessful efforts to control the substance use, reduction in occupational or leisure activities, and continued use despite recognition of one's substance related problems, occurring at any time during a 12-month period. The following specifiers can be used to describe the diagnosis of Substance Dependence: With or Without Physiological Dependence, In Remission, On Agonist Therapy (such as Antabuse or Methadone), and In a Controlled Environment (such as a prison or half-way house).

The diagnosis of Substance Abuse also entails significant impairment and at least one of the following criteria due to drug or alcohol use: continued use despite interpersonal problems related to the substance, failure to fulfill professional or interpersonal obligations, recurrent substance use in hazardous situations (e.g., while operating machinery), or recurrent substance-related legal difficulties (e.g., charges of driving while intoxicated).

The Substance-Related Disorders are listed alphabetically by substance in the DSM and include disorders stemming from use of alcohol; amphetamines; caffeine; cannabis; cocaine; hallucinogens; inhalants; nicotine; opioids; phencyclidine; sedatives, hypnotics, or anxiolytics; and others (such as steroids). Polysubstance dependence involves the use of at least three groups of substances with no one substance predominating.

SCHIZOPHRENIA AND OTHER PSYCHOTIC DISORDERS

The following psychotic disorders not caused by a medical condition are included in this section of the DSM:

1. *Schizophrenia*—This disorder is characterized by severe, pervasive loss of contact with reality, causing significant impairment and extending over at least six months. Common symptoms are hallucinations (usually auditory), disorganized speech or behavior, and delusions. Subtypes of Schizophrenia include Paranoid Type, Disorganized Type, Catatonic Type (usually characterized by agitation or motoric immobility), Undifferentiated Type, and Residual Type. This disorder tends to run in families and usually has a gradual onset, typically in early adulthood.

2. *Schizophreniform Disorder*—This disorder is similar to Schizophrenia, except in duration. It has a minimum duration of one month and a maximum duration of six months. The specifier, With or Without Good Prognostic Features, including good premorbid functioning, rapid onset, perplexity regarding the symptoms, and an absence of flat affect, provides information on the probable course of this disorder. About half of the people with this disorder recover while half develop Schizophrenia (Maxmen & Ward, 1995).

3. *Schizoaffective Disorder*—This can be thought of as a hybrid diagnosis, including symptoms of Schizophrenia along with those of a Mood Disorder. Specifiers indicate whether the Mood Disorder resembles a Bipolar Disorder or a Major Depressive Disorder.

4. *Delusional Disorder*—This disorder is characterized by nonbizarre delusions of at least one month duration. The delusions tend to be egosyntonic and focus on an area of stress or dissatisfaction. This disorder usually is less pervasive and incapacitating than the psychotic disorders discussed above. Types of Delusional Disorder include Erotomanic Type, Grandiose Type, Jealous Type, Persecutory Type, Somatic Type, Mixed Type, and Unspecified Type.

5. *Brief Psychotic Disorder*—This disorder encompasses symptoms of either Schizophrenia or Delusional Disorder, but with a briefer duration (at least one day but no more than one month) and a better prognosis. This disorder also has specifiers, With or Without Marked Stressors or With Postpartum Onset, characterizing a psychotic disorder beginning within 4 weeks postpartum.

6. *Shared Psychotic Disorder*—This disorder involves the development of delusions in one person in a close relationship with another person who already has a delusion.

MOOD DISORDERS

These common disorders are characterized by a depressed mood and/or an elevated mood. Like Schizophrenia, the Mood Disorders usually begin in late adolescence or early adulthood and often run in families. The following specifiers are available to clarify a person's experience of a Mood Disorder:

- *Melancholic Features*—characterized by loss of pleasure in almost all activities and loss of reactivity
- *Atypical Features*—includes mood reactivity, excessive sleeping and eating, and rejection sensitivity
- *Catatonic Features*—motoric immobility or excessive activity
- *Rapid Cycling*—at least four episodes of mood disturbance in a Bipolar Disorder, during a 12-month period
- *Seasonal Pattern*—characterized by a temporal relationship between mood disorder and season, usually winter depression
- *Postpartum Onset*—within four weeks postpartum
- *With or Without Interepisode Recovery*—recovery between episodes is associated with a better prognosis and the possibility of a seasonal pattern

Included in the section on Mood Disorders are the following:

1. *Major Depressive Disorder*—Significant depression of at least two weeks' duration characterizes this disorder. Suicidal ideation and unreasonable guilt may be present as well as changes in appetite, weight, sleep patterns, and libido.
2. *Dysthymic Disorder*—This disorder is characterized by prolonged depression of moderate severity. It has a minimum duration of one year in children and adolescents and two years in adults.
3. *Bipolar Disorders*—These disorders involve mood fluctuations and include the following three diagnoses:

   a. *Bipolar I Disorder*—This includes at least one manic episode and may also include depressive and hypomanic episodes. Manic episodes usually entail such symptoms as a diminished need for sleep, unpredictable behavior, rapid speech, loss of inhibitions, poor judgment, and risk-taking behavior. Hypomanic episodes are similar to manic episodes but are less severe and incapacitating.
   b. *Bipolar II Disorder*—This disorder is similar to Bipolar I but involves only hypomanic and depressive episodes; the person with this disorder has never had a manic episode.

  c. *Cyclothymic Disorder*—This disorder is characterized by numerous episodes of hypomania and mild-to-moderate depression within a period of at least two years for adults and one year for children and adolescents.

ANXIETY DISORDERS

Physical and emotional symptoms of anxiety characterize all the disorders in this section including:

1. *Panic Disorder With or Without Agoraphobia*—Hallmarks of these disorders are recurrent brief attacks of unexpected panic (usually as brief as five minutes and rarely longer than 30 minutes) and at least one month of concern about these attacks. People with Panic Disorders often develop Agoraphobia, in an effort to avoid situations that they believe are likely to trigger a panic attack.

2. *Agoraphobia*—Fear of crowded or other places from which escape might be difficult characterizes this disorder. People with severe forms of this disorder may not have left their homes for years.

3. *Specific Phobia*—This disorder involves a persistent and excessive fear of such stimuli as heights, flying, thunder, blood, or snakes that markedly interferes with daily activities.

4. *Social Phobia*—This disorder is characterized by a persistent and excessive fear of certain social situations such as public speaking or attending parties. If the manifestation of this disorder extends to nearly all social activities, it is described as Generalized Type.

5. *Obsessive-Compulsive Disorder*—This disorder is characterized by recurrent unwanted thoughts (obsessions) and/or repetitive unwanted behaviors (compulsions) that cause distress or impairment. Washing and checking are particularly common compulsions, while obsessions typically focus on violence, sinfulness, and contamination. People with this disorder usually are aware that their thoughts and behaviors are excessive or illogical and may try to change them.

6. *Posttraumatic Stress Disorder* (PTSD)—This disorder, with a minimum duration of one month, is triggered by an event that involves threatened death or injury and is characterized by reexperiencing of the event, withdrawal, and increased arousal. Symptoms may be immediate or can be delayed for long periods of time. People with PTSD have undergone such experiences as war, rape, a serious accident, or a natural disaster. PTSD also can be found in police, firefight-

ers, and others who deal with life-threatening experiences and their aftermath.

7. *Acute Stress Disorder*—This diagnosis can be viewed as a brief PTSD with rapid onset. Acute Stress Disorder begins within four weeks of a traumatic event; it has a minimum duration of two days and a maximum duration of four weeks. This diagnosis describes reactions that do not persist as long as PTSD.

8. *Generalized Anxiety Disorder*—This disorder is characterized by at least six months of excessive worry about several events and activities as well as by free-floating anxiety and physical symptoms of anxiety.

SOMATOFORM DISORDERS

People with Somatoform Disorders believe they have medical or physical conditions; however, their complaints do not receive medical verification. Somatoform Disorders have been known as psychosomatic disorders. People with Somatoform Disorders seem to use their bodies as their vehicle for self-expression and often benefit from the secondary gains of their symptoms. The following diagnoses are included in this section:

1. *Somatization Disorder*—People with this disorder have a long history of multiple unverified physical complaints. Criteria require a minimum of four pain symptoms, three gastrointestinal symptoms, one sexual symptom, and one neurological symptom.

2. *Undifferentiated Somatoform Disorder*—This disorder, characterized by at least six months of distress or impairment in response to one or more medically unverified physical complaints, probably is more frequently used than the above diagnosis. The primary focus of both Somatization and Undifferentiated Somatoform Disorders generally is on the experience of the symptoms, not on the fear of disease.

3. *Conversion Disorder*—This disorder typically is manifested by a prominent motor or neurological symptom or deficit such as paralysis of a limb, inability to see, or seizures, without medical cause.

4. *Pain Disorder*—This disorder has two subtypes, With Psychological Factors and With Both Psychological Factors and a General Medical Condition. The disorder is characterized by a report of pain that either has no medical basis or is in excess of what would be expected, based on the existing medical problem.

5. *Hypochondriasis*—Hallmarks of this disorder include fears of having a serious disease and overinterpretation of physical symptoms. The specifier, With Poor Insight, characterizes a variety of this disorder that is likely to be difficult to treat.

6. *Body Dysmorphic Disorder*—This disorder involves preoccupation with an imagined or exaggerated defect in appearance. People with this disorder may have undergone many cosmetic surgeries; however, because their real difficulty is emotional rather than physical, they are unlikely to feel much happier after the surgeries.

FACTITIOUS DISORDERS

Factitious Disorders are different from Somatoform Disorders in that the former involve intentional feigning of symptoms in order to assume the role of an ill person. This diagnosis has three subtypes, With Predominantly Psychological Signs and Symptoms, Physical Signs and Symptoms, or Combined Type. Sometimes the person with this disorder produces symptoms in or attributes symptoms to someone under their care, usually a child, in order to vicariously receive the attention given to the sick person. This is known as Factitious Disorder by Proxy.

DISSOCIATIVE DISORDERS

All the Dissociative Disorders involve an alteration in memory, identity, or awareness that is not caused by a medical or cognitive disorder.

1. *Dissociative Amnesia*—This disorder involves inability to recall important information about one's identity or past, leading to significant distress or impairment. Usually the forgotten information is stressful or traumatic.

2. *Dissociative Fugue*—Sudden travel away from home, along with confusion or memory loss related to one's identity, characterizes this disorder.

3. *Dissociative Identity Disorder* (DID)—This new name for Multiple Personality Disorder is a more accurate term to describe those people whose personalities have dissociated or fragmented. They may report having a range of diverse personalities. This disorder, too, usually entails inability to remember important information and can cause considerable distress and impairment. A history of abuse is common in people with this disorder.

4. *Depersonalization Disorder*—This disorder involves persistent, distressing experiences of feeling detached, as though one is outside one's body observing oneself.

SEXUAL AND GENDER IDENTITY DISORDERS

This category includes three groups of disorders: Sexual Dysfunctions, Paraphilias, and Gender Identity Disorders.

1. *Sexual Dysfunctions*—Disorders in this section describe difficulties in sexual desire, arousal, comfort, and functioning that are due to psychological factors or to a combination of psychological and medical conditions. Specifiers indicate whether the symptoms are Lifelong or Acquired, Generalized or Situational.
2. *Paraphilias*—Disorders in this section all involve a period of at least six months in which a person has an unusual primary source of sexual arousal that typically causes interpersonal difficulties. Examples of Paraphilias are Exhibitionism, Pedophilia, and Voyeurism.
3. *Gender Identity Disorders*—This section includes Gender Identity Disorder in Children and Gender Identity Disorder in Adolescents and Adults. Both of these are characterized by significant distress or impairment related to discomfort with one's anatomical gender.

EATING DISORDERS

The two most prevalent eating disorders are included in this section. Both are most often found in adolescent and young adult women. Anorexia Nervosa is characterized by a body weight that is 85% or less than what is expected and often is accompanied by a fear of becoming fat, a distorted body image, and perfectionism. Specifiers for this disorder include Restricting Type if the low weight is due to limited eating and Binge-Eating/Purging Type if it is due to a pattern of excessive eating and purging.

Bulimia Nervosa is a disorder that entails recurrent binge-eating. Here, too, specifiers are included: Purging Type if compensatory behaviors such as self-induced vomiting or excessive use of laxatives are part of the disorder, Nonpurging Type if those behaviors are not manifested. Bulimia Nervosa is more common than Anorexia Nervosa and often is associated with depression (Maxmen & Ward, 1995).

SLEEP DISORDERS

In diagnosing Sleep Disorders, clinicians must determine whether other disorders are related to the sleeping difficulties. Sleep Disorders that stand alone are called Primary Sleep Disorders while those related to other diagnoses are classified under Sleep Disorders Related to Another Mental Disorder or Sleep Disorders Due to a General Medical Condition.

The DSM-IV includes the following types of Sleep Disorders:

1. *Insomnia*—This disorder is characterized by difficulty initiating or maintaining sleep for at least one month and often is associated with depression.
2. *Hypersomnia*—Excessive sleepiness and difficulty awakening, with symptoms extending over at least one month, are the hallmarks of this disorder.
3. *Narcolepsy*—This diagnosis is characterized by uncontrollable attacks of sleep. The attacks are most likely to occur under conditions of high arousal or boredom.
4. *Breathing-Related Sleep Disorder*—This disorder, reportedly more common in men, involves a breathing condition that interferes with restful sleep and can lead to serious physical problems. Loud, sudden snoring can signal the presence of this disorder.
5. *Circadian Rhythm Sleep Disorder*—This diagnosis involves a mismatch between a person's natural sleep cycle and the person's life style. Types include Delayed Sleep Phase Type, Jet Lag Type, Shift Work Type, and Unspecified Type.
6. *Nightmare Disorder*—The hallmark of this disorder is frightening dreams during the second half of sleep, usually recalled upon awakening.
7. *Sleep Terror Disorder*—This disorder also involves frightening dreams, but these typically occur during the first third of a major sleep period, causing a person to awaken feeling terrified and disoriented.
8. *Sleepwalking Disorder*—Repeated walking while asleep characterizes this logically named disorder.

IMPULSE-CONTROL DISORDERS NOT ELSEWHERE CLASSIFIED

This section encompasses the following disorders, all characterized by episodes of failure to resist dysfunctional impulses. Typically, people with these disorders experience a buildup of tension that is released through impulsive behavior and is followed by a sense of relief and sometimes subsequent regret.

1. *Intermittent Explosive Disorder*—This disorder is characterized by episodes of violent and aggressive behavior such as assault or destruction of property. Substance-Related Disorders and Mood Disorders often accompany this disorder.
2. *Kleptomania*—Impulsive theft of objects that are not needed is the hallmark of this disorder. It, too, is usually accompanied by other disorders.
3. *Pyromania*—Recurrent fire setting out of a fascination with fire and fire-fighting is the primary symptom of this disorder, which is more prevalent in males.
4. *Pathological Gambling*—Persistent and self-destructive gambling characterizes this disorder, also more common in men, particularly those with difficult childhoods.
5. *Trichotillomania*—This disorder involves pulling out the hairs on one's own head or body. It is more common in females and often is associated with Mood, Anxiety, or other Impulse Control Disorders.

ADJUSTMENT DISORDERS

Adjustment Disorders entail mild to moderate distress or impairment that develops within three months of a stressor (e.g., divorce, serious illness, relocation, school problems, retirement, job loss). This diagnosis can be maintained for a maximum of six months after the end of a stressor and its consequences. This affords clinicians some flexibility in their use of this diagnosis. Subtypes of this disorder include With Depressed Mood, With Anxiety, With Mixed Anxiety and Depressed Mood, With Disturbance of Conduct, With Mixed Disturbance of Emotions and Conduct, and Unspecified. This disorder is described as Acute if the symptoms persist less than six months or Chronic if the symptoms persist longer.

PERSONALITY DISORDERS

Personality Disorders all involve deeply ingrained, pervasive, and maladaptive behaviors. People with these disorders typically have poor social skills, difficulty with impulse control, inflexibility, and impairment and distress in all areas of their lives. Personality Disorders are listed on Axis II in the multiaxial assessment and are prevalent, found in approximately 15% of the general population and 30–50% of a clinical population (Gunderson, 1988).

The following list includes the 10 Personality Disorders, divided into three groups, along with their primary characteristics:

Cluster A—characterized by odd, eccentric, and guarded behavior:

1. *Paranoid Personality Disorder*—Pervasive distrust and suspiciousness characterize this disorder. It is described as Premorbid if criteria are met prior to the onset of Schizophrenia.
2. *Schizoid Personality Disorder*—Indifference to other people, detachment, involvement with solitary and non-people oriented activities are all typical of people with this disorder.
3. *Schizotypal Personality Disorder*—Impaired social skills and poor awareness of reality reflected in symptoms such as ideas of reference, magical thinking, and restricted affect are hallmarks of this disorder.

Cluster B—characterized by emotional, unpredictable, and egocentric behavior:

4. *Antisocial Personality Disorder*—Disregard for the laws and the rights of others, impulsivity, irresponsibility, and manipulativeness characterize this disorder, which begins as Conduct Disorder before the age of 15. A large percentage of people who are incarcerated have this disorder, which is more common in men.
5. *Borderline Personality Disorder*—Low self-esteem, self-destructive behavior, problems with impulse control, dependence on others, and depression are primary features of this disorder. It is more common in females and often is associated with a history of abuse.
6. *Histrionic Personality Disorder*—High emotionality, attention seeking, excessive focus on intimate relationships, egocentrism, and materialism are characteristic of people with this disorder, also more common in females.
7. *Narcissistic Personality Disorder*—Egocentrism, high need for power and admiration, and a sense of entitlement are features of this disorder. People with this disorder are more likely to be male and often appear arrogant and grandiose.

Cluster C—characterized by anxiety, fearfulness, and self-doubts:

8. *Avoidant Personality Disorder*—Social discomfort and avoidance, low self-esteem, and hypersensitivity characterize people with this disorder. They may want to have more social contact but are fearful and inhibited about socializing.
9. *Dependent Personality Disorder*—Lack of initiative, deference to the wishes of others, and overinvestment in relationships are typical of people with this disorder. Although it seems to be more common in

women than in men, care should be taken not to use this diagnosis inappropriately for women who follow traditional paths but do not manifest the pathology associated with this disorder.

10. *Obsessive-Compulsive Personality Disorder*—Perfectionism, inflexibility, self-righteousness, and a tendency to be controlling characterize people with this disorder who often have some occupational success but typically have considerable difficulty as partners, parents, and supervisors.

Personality Traits—These are milder than personality disorders, perhaps less pervasive, enduring, or disruptive. Personality Traits come in the same varieties as Personality Disorders (e.g., Dependent Personality Traits, Avoidant Personality Traits). Although they have no code numbers and are not considered mental disorders, they may be listed on Axis II and can provide useful descriptive information about a person's patterns of behavior and thinking.

OTHER CONDITIONS THAT MAY BE A FOCUS OF CLINICAL ATTENTION

The terms in this section identify areas that may be a focus of attention in counseling but are not considered to be mental disorders. These terms may stand alone if they are used to describe a person who does not have a mental disorder or they may be used along with one or more mental disorders on a multiaxial assessment to indicate essential issues to be addressed in treatment.

This section is comprised of the following conditions:

1. *Psychological Factors Affecting Medical Condition*—This condition is reflected by the presence of a personality, behavioral, or emotional condition that is having a negative impact on a medically diagnosed condition, as when anxiety worsens high blood pressure. The medical condition would be listed on Axis III.

2. *Medication-Induced Movement Disorders*—This section contains conditions that describe the adverse physiological effects of neuroleptic or other medication, such as Neuroleptic-Induced Tardive Dyskinesia or Medication-Induced Postural Tremor.

3. *Relational Problems*—Categories in this section include Relational Problem Related to a Mental Disorder or General Medical Condition, Parent–Child Relational Problem, Partner Relational Problem, Sibling Relational Problem, and Relational Problem Not Otherwise Specified.

4. *Problems Related to Abuse or Neglect*—This section includes descriptors for neglect or physical or sexual abuse in children or adults who are either victims or perpetrators of abuse.
5. *Additional Conditions That May Be a Focus of Clinical Attention*—Included in this final group of miscellaneous conditions are the following:

   a. *Noncompliance with Treatment.*
   b. *Malingering* or deliberately feigning or exaggerating symptoms, perhaps to obtain financial gain, prescriptions for drugs, or diminishment of responsibilities.
   c. *Adult, Adolescent, or Childhood Antisocial Behavior*—This condition encompasses antisocial behavior not due to a mental disorder. Usually it is manifested by isolated acts rather than persistent patterns.
   d. *Borderline Intellectual Functioning*—This condition, listed on Axis II, is characterized by an IQ between 71 and 84.
   e. *Age-Related Cognitive Decline*—This condition includes memory impairment that is within normal limits.
   f. *Bereavement*—This condition encompasses normal reactions to death of a loved one.
   g. *Academic Problem, Occupational Problem, Identity Problem, Religious or Spiritual Problem, and Acculturation Problem*—These conditions can be used to describe distress or difficulty at any age about issues related to such areas as academic achievement, career development, sense of self, religious beliefs and affiliation, and adjustment to cultural change.
   h. *Phase of Life Problem*—Examples of this condition include problems related to graduation from school and to career, marital, and parenting changes.

ADDITIONAL CODES

Of course, not all people have a mental disorder or condition listed on Axis I and Axis II. When a diagnosis is not appropriate, the phrases No Diagnosis or Condition on Axis I and No Diagnosis on Axis II can be used. Diagnosis or Condition Deferred or Unspecified Mental Disorder also can be written on either axis to indicate diagnostic uncertainty. In addition, at the end of each major category in the DSM is a Not Otherwise Specified or NOS diagnosis (e.g., Sexual Disorder Not Otherwise Specified, Mood Disorder Not Otherwise Specified).

The NOS diagnoses are sometimes useful in labelling symptoms that do not exactly match a specific diagnosis but clearly represent a mental disorder.

MAKING A DIAGNOSIS

When symptoms are prominent and clinicians are astute, diagnoses sometimes are immediately apparent. At other times, clinicians benefit from using some tools to help them make their diagnoses.

Decision Trees

Appendix A of the DSM-IV includes the following six decision trees to facilitate the process of diagnostic discrimination. Each tree consists of a series of boxes that contain yes-or-no questions. To use these tools, the clinician begins at the upper left box in each tree and then follows the arrows determined by responses to the questions in the boxes until the clinician arrives at a diagnosis.

1. *Mental Disorders Due to a General Medical Condition*—This tree lists mental disorders that are caused by a medical illness or condition.
2. *Substance-Induced Disorders*—This tree includes disorders that are a direct consequence of drug or alcohol use such as Substance-Induced Sexual Dysfunction and Substance Withdrawal. It does not include Substance Dependence or Substance Abuse.
3. *Psychotic Disorders*—Schizophrenia, Delusional Disorders, and other disorders that entail loss of contact with reality are included in this tree.
4. *Mood Disorders*—This tree encompasses Bipolar Disorder, Dysthymic Disorder, Major Depressive Disorder, and Cyclothymic Disorder, all characterized by depression, irritability, expansiveness and/or elevated mood.
5. *Anxiety Disorders*—Panic Disorder, Phobias, Generalized Anxiety Disorder, Posttraumatic Stress Disorder, Obsessive-Compulsive Disorder, and other disorders with anxiety, fear, increased arousal, and avoidance as their hallmarks are included in this tree.
6. *Somatoform Disorders*—Disorders characterized primarily by physical complaints that do not have a verified medical explanation are listed in this tree. This includes all the Somatoform Disorders (e.g., Conversion Disorder, Pain Disorder, Hypochondriasis), the Factitious Disorders, Psychological Factors Affecting Medical Condition, and other disorders and conditions. Although physical complaints may

produce anxiety, when the physical complaints are the person's primary concern, this tree, rather than the Anxiety Disorders tree, should be consulted.

Key Questions for Diagnosis

Although the decision trees are very useful, they do not include all mental disorders. A more comprehensive approach is the use of four key questions:

1. *What are the primary symptoms?*—This question should be answered in non-technical terms, with typical symptoms including anxiety, depression, acting out, excessive consumption of alcohol, medically unverified physical pain, or pervasive dysfunction.
2. *What is the approximate duration of the disorder?*—Responses might include days, weeks, months, years, or of indefinite and long-standing duration.
3. *How severe are the symptoms?*—Adjustment Disorders typically are mild. Disorders of moderate severity include many of the Personality Disorders and most of the Mood and Anxiety Disorders. Disorders that cause great impairment and loss of contact with reality, such as most of the Psychotic and Cognitive Disorders, are severe.
4. Has a specific cause or *precipitant* for the symptoms been identified?—This yes-or-no question often provides important diagnostic information.

Application of the Key Questions

Appendix A provides a series of tables illustrating the application of the key questions to the most common mental disorders. Counselors are encouraged to use those tables in conjunction with the DSM to facilitate the diagnostic process.

The following example illustrates the use of the key questions:

Case: A 24-year old single female lawyer sought counseling two weeks after she discovered that the man she had been dating and hoping to marry was already married. She reacted with bouts of sadness and crying, diminished performance at work, and some withdrawal from friends and leisure activities, although she maintained a demanding work schedule and reported no suicidal ideation. She stated that she had not experienced similar feelings in the past. She was optimistic that, with some help, she could put this disappointment behind her and resume an active social life.

Primary symptoms: Sadness, crying, some impairment in functioning.

Duration: Brief/several weeks.
Severity: Mild.
Precipitant: Yes.

This is a relatively mild and brief disorder with an identified precipitant. These characteristics suggest it is an Adjustment Disorder, with the primary symptoms reflecting the type (With Depressed Mood).

SUPPLEMENTS TO THE DSM

Several worthwhile resources have been developed to help people refine their diagnostic skills. The *DSM-IV Casebook* (Spitzer, Gibbon, Skodol, & Williams, 1994) is a compendium of interesting case vignettes with their appropriate diagnoses. Other books available to provide further clarification of the DSM include *DSM-IV Made Easy* (Morrison, 1995), the four-volume *DSM-IV Sourcebook*, published by the American Psychiatric Association, and *Study Guide to DSM-IV* (Fauman, 1994). An audiotaped home study program on the DSM-IV is also available (Seligman, 1995).

CASES FOR DIAGNOSIS

Assess your diagnostic abilities. Do a multiaxial assessment for the following five cases.

Case 1. June is a 25-year-old elementary school teacher. Several months ago, while watching her students in the playground, she became extremely anxious; she felt her heart pounding and thought she might faint. Although she recovered within 20 minutes, she experienced these same symptoms a few weeks later in the school cafeteria and not long after, while teaching her class. June has now become apprehensive and is fearful about going to work each day. She has been taking so many sick days because of this fear that her job is now in jeopardy.

June's life over the past year has been difficult. Her mother died, and she has been caring for her father with whom she lives. She has tried to maintain an active social life but has found that difficult because of work and family demands. In addition, she has been diagnosed with endometriosis. Before this year, she functioned well, had several friends, and was involved in many activities. She had received high ratings at work.

Case 2. Fred is a seven-year-old boy who was brought in for counseling by his mother. Fred's parents divorced about two years ago, and Fred has seen little of his father since then. Although Fred seemed to adjust well to the divorce, when regular contact with his father ceased he became sad and listless, eating little but sleeping a great deal, and losing interest in friends and other activities. Although he went to school regularly and generally was cooperative and obedient, the life seemed to have gone out of him. Fred was in a special class because of his below normal intellectual level (I.Q. score in the 70–75 range). Fred's mother also reported some specific symptoms. Fred had never been fully toilet trained and continued to wet the bed at least twice a week. In addition, over the past few months, his teacher reported that Fred frequently was found eating crayons and wads of paper.

Case 3. Marcy, age 14, was brought to counseling by her parents. They reported that for the past year or so Marcy had been difficult; she had a quick temper and was hostile and argumentative, she disobeyed her parents repeatedly to meet her boyfriend at a local shopping mall, she blamed her teachers for her poor grades in some subjects but would not ask them for help, and she had even been teasing her 4-year-old sister whom she used to adore. Although Marcy had never been a strong student because of the great difficulty she has in writing, she was a bright girl who found ways to compensate for her writing difficulty. Now, however, her attitude had changed, and family as well as teachers reported that she was difficult and uncooperative, but could not provide an explanation for the change. A physical examination revealed no medical problems.

Cases 4 and 5. Peter and Doris came for counseling at the urging of Doris's oncologist. Peter and Doris, both age 44, have been married for twenty-two years and have three children, aged 17, 14, and 9. Doris had always focused all her energies on her family, cooking, cleaning, and sewing for long hours each day. She had few friends or outside interests but seemed contented, if not happy, with her life. Recently, she had a hysterectomy because of a cancerous tumor. Her recovery has progressed slowly, partly because Doris insists on doing more than she should, although her physician has advised her to rest and recuperate over the next month. Doris expresses great guilt about her illness and blames herself because the house is not spotless. She also is very worried about her surgery and fears that Peter will no longer think she is desirable.

In fact, Peter has hinted that if Doris is not back to normal soon, he will have to look elsewhere for gratification. Peter blames Doris for her medical condition, insisting that she should have seen a physician earlier, and expresses the belief that Doris is enjoying being ill because she is "getting a free ride" and "doesn't have to do anything around the house." This attitude is typical of Peter's behavior both at home and at work, where he often suspects that others are taking advantage of him and are untrustworthy. He has had longstanding grudges against several of his co-workers and has been referred to the employee assistance program at work several times because of conflicts with others. When asked about these difficulties, Peter reports that his only problem is a medical one; he thinks that he has had stomach cancer for several years and cannot understand why Doris is getting so much attention when he is even sicker. He has consulted several physicians, but they could find no medical explanation for his intestinal discomfort.

Case 6. Susan was referred to a counselor at her college after physically attacking her roommate. Susan stated that her roommate's father, a television producer, was in love with her and only the roommate stood in the way of their happiness. The roommate stated that her father and Susan had only met once and Susan's belief that the father was in love with her was a figment of Susan's imagination. Although Susan agreed they had met only once, she indicated that the father sent frequent gifts to the girls for use in their apartment as evidence of his feeling for her. Susan functioned well academically but had few friends or leisure activities. Most of her time was spent in studying or exercise, and in the past year she had lost 25 pounds, now weighing 80 pounds.

DIAGNOSES OF CASES

Case 1
Axis I.   300.21 Panic Disorder with Agoraphobia, moderate
            V62.89 Phase of Life Problem
Axis II.   V71.09 No mental disorder on Axis II
Axis III.   617.9 Endometriosis
Axis IV.   Death of mother, caretaking of father
Axis V.   60

Case 2
Axis I.   300.4 Dysthymic Disorder, moderate, early onset
            307.6 Enuresis, nocturnal only
            307.52 Pica, moderate
Axis II.   V62.89 Borderline Intellectual Functioning
Axis III.   None
Axis IV.   Little contact with father
Axis V.   55

Case 3

Axis I.   313.81 Oppositional Defiant Disorder, moderate
          315.2 Disorder of Written Expression, mild
Axis II.   V71.09 No diagnosis on Axis II
Axis III. None
Axis IV.   Family conflict, academic difficulties
Axis V.   55

Case 4 (Peter)

Axis I.   300.7 Hypochondriasis, with Poor Insight, moderate
Axis II.   301.0 Paranoid Personality Disorder
Axis III. Deferred—reports intestinal discomfort
Axis IV.   Wife diagnosed with cancer, conflict at work, intestinal discomfort
Axis V.   55

Case 5 (Doris)

Axis I.   309.24 Adjustment Disorder with Mixed Anxiety and Depressed Mood
Axis II.   301.6 Dependent Personality Disorder
Axis III. 183.0 Neoplasm, malignant, uterus, primary
Axis IV.   Diagnosis and treatment of cancer, conflict with husband
Axis V.   55

Case 6

Axis I.   297.1 Delusional Disorder, Erotomanic Type
          307.1 Anorexia Nervosa, Restricting Type, severe
Axis II.   V71.09 No diagnosis on Axis II
Axis III. None reported
Axis IV.   Conflict with roommate
Axis V.   30

An earlier version of this chapter was published in the *Virginia Counselors Journal*. Seligman, L. (1995). Mastering the *DSM-IV*. *Virginia Counselors Journal*, *23* (1), 3–19.

4

The Use of Assessment in Diagnosis

"The meaning of diagnosis is 'to know' the client in terms of both internal and external perspectives" (Blocher & Biggs, 1983, p. 186). Chapter 3 presented an approach to diagnosis that primarily involved the determination and classification of people's symptoms and personality patterns, culminating in the naming or labeling of their emotional disorders. Viewed only in this way, the process of diagnosis can seem dehumanizing and can detract from the establishment of a collaborative counselor–client relationship. However, as the quotation opening this chapter suggests, the process of diagnosis can be approached in a comprehensive way that enables counselors to develop a good understanding of people and their environments and, through the process of assessment, formulate a diagnosis and treatment plan as well as enhance the counseling relationship.

Most people in counseling are in pain and are eager for help. Consequently, they generally respond well to a genuine and sensitive counselor who wants to get to know them better in order to help them. The assessment process should be a way of recognizing the importance and uniqueness of each person, a way of saying to the person, "You are special and I want to get to know you and understand why you are the way you are." This attitude can help people feel optimistic and committed to the counseling process. The assessment process is, ideally, a collaboration between counselor and client in which both gain in knowledge and understanding while their working relationship is developed and helpful interventions are identified and implemented.

The assessment process can occur at several points in a counseling relationship. Some sort of assessment almost always will occur at the outset of the counseling process. Typically, an intake interview will be conducted, perhaps accompanied by psychological testing, so that an initial diagnosis and treatment plan can be developed. Chapter 5 discusses the intake process in detail.

Structured assessment also can occur during the middle stages of counseling. It can be occasioned by the counselor's or client's wanting to measure the progress that has been made in counseling or recognizing that new issues and dynamics have come to light, calling for a reconceptualization of the original diagnosis and treatment plan. Such an assessment, or progress report and review, also can be requested by the client's health insurance company or the mental health agency where treatment is taking place. Such mid-counseling assessments may be global, a way to provide an overview of the client's development and level of functioning, or they may be specific, seeking to clarify a particular aspect of the person's life (e.g., career development, intellectual ability, substance use). Assessments also may be conducted toward the end of a counseling relationship as a way of measuring progress and determining the appropriateness of termination. In addition, counselors engage in informal and on-going assessment throughout the therapeutic process to insure treatment effectiveness.

According to Shertzer and Linden (1979), assessment has four overriding purposes: classification, evaluation, selection, and prediction. All four may be involved in diagnosis and treatment planning. Evaluation and classification generally are most important as the counselor seeks to explore the cognitive, behavioral, emotional, interpersonal, and environmental aspects of a person and classify the findings according to some framework (e.g., the DSM, developmental stages, or levels of intellectual ability). Assessment, as part of treatment planning, may be used to select people for certain therapeutic programs (e.g., counseling groups, day treatment centers). Predicting the likelihood of such events as a person's succeeding in a particular educational program or engaging in violent or suicidal behavior can also play an important part in treatment planning.

Assessment can enhance the counseling process in the following ways (Seligman, 1994):

1. Streamline the information-gathering process
2. Enable counselors to make an accurate diagnosis
3. Facilitate development of a treatment plan that is likely to be effective
4. Determine a person's suitability for a particular program or treatment
5. Simplify goal-setting and measurement of progress
6. Promote insight into a person's personality and clarify self-concept
7. Assess environment or context
8. Promote more relevant and focused counseling and discussion
9. Indicate the likelihood that certain events will happen, such as success in occupational or academic endeavors
10. Promote the translation of interests, abilities, and personality dimensions into occupational terms

11. Generate options and alternatives
12. Facilitate planning and decision-making

<hr>

Areas of Assessment

The assessment process may focus on any or all of the following areas:

1. *Cognitive attributes*—thinking and learning style, intellectual abilities, academic and creative potential, thought patterns, problem solving abilities, values and beliefs, awareness of reality.
2. *Behaviors*—overall behavioral patterns as well as behavior in specific areas such as eating, sleeping, substance use, attention, violence, assertiveness, and others.
3. *Affect*—emotional states and traits such as depression and anxiety, fears and phobias, appropriateness and lability of emotions, ability to manage and express feelings.
4. *Interpersonal relationships and context*—family background and dynamics, relationship patterns, interpersonal conflicts and strengths, culture- and gender-related attitudes and behaviors.
5. *Physical attributes*—appearance, size and shape, physical abilities and disabilities.

<hr>

Conducting an Effective Assessment

The assessment process is an integral part of the counseling process. It should be planned and conducted with the same care as the overall counseling process. According to the American Counseling Associations's ethical standards (1995, June, p. 36), "Counselors promote the welfare and best interests of the client in the development, publication, and utilization of educational and psychological assessment techniques." Increasingly, mental health professionals are recognizing that the counselor, not the test, is the key ingredient in effective assessment. As Anastasi (1992, p. 610) stated, "A conspicuous development in psychological testing during the 1980s and 1990s is the increasing recognition of the key role of the test user. Most popular criticisms of tests are clearly identifiable as criticisms of test use (or misuse), rather than criticisms of the tests themselves. Tests are essentially tools. Whether any tool is an instrument of good or harm depends on how the tool is used."

Assessment should contribute to the development of rapport, advance the goals of counseling, and take account of the client's preferences and areas of difficulty. Both counselor and client should understand the purpose and nature of the assessment process and should be involved in its planning and implementation. Results should be shared in a timely and helpful way. Assessment may be formal or informal, on-going or time-limited, and use any of a broad range of quantitative or qualitative tools. The rest of this chapter will discuss the assessment process as well as the many approaches that are available to conducting an assessment.

TOOLS OF ASSESSMENT

Assessment tools can be qualitative or quantitative. Qualitative tools tend to be more subjective in nature; their interpretation, more ambiguous and challenging. They yield information that may have limited reliability and validity but can provide important insights that perhaps cannot be obtained in any other way. Quantitative tools, on the other hand, yield numerical data on people, thereby facilitating comparisons and providing a useful measure of change. Generally, both qualitative and quantitative approaches to assessment are used with a client to provide a picture that has depth and richness as well as adequate reliability. Selection of the best approaches to the assessment of a particular person will be discussed later in this chapter.

Qualitative Approaches

Interviews probably are the most important qualitative approach to assessment. They are nearly always part of the process of diagnosis and treatment planning and tend to be the first method used to get acquainted and build rapport with a client. The primary goal for the interviewer is to have a clear purpose and direction in mind and conduct an interview that will achieve that purpose. However, interviews, as well as other forms of qualitative data, are prone to being affected by interviewer bias, client resistance, and other factors. Interviews are discussed further in chapter 5.

Counselor-made questionnaires often are combined with intake interviews and also can be useful in gathering information. Most mental health agencies use questionnaires as a way of gathering demographic and background information on clients. Counselors may want to supplement those with either general or individualized questionnaires on people's concerns or on particular aspects of their development (e.g., marital adjustment, career development, social history). Providing written rather than oral responses is easier for some people and can promote self-disclosure.

Observational data provide another source of qualitative information and may be gathered in systematic or informal ways. In *systematic* observation, the person is observed during a predetermined period or event. For example, a student with an Attention-Deficit Disorder might be observed for the first fifteen minutes of school every day in order to assess frequency of disruptive and inattentive behaviors. Systematic observation often involves counting behaviors, making the observation a quantitative as well as a qualitative measure. *Informal* observations are conducted in casual and unobtrusive ways. Data obtained will typically be anecdotal rather than numerical. Counselors might gather such data by observing a person in the waiting room, making a home visit to a client, or observing a person engaged in play. Of course, throughout the counseling process, clinicians also are gathering observational information in informal ways. Teachers and school counselors sometimes keep *anecdotal records* on students as a way of observing patterns and changes in behavior (Vacc & Loesch, 1987).

Observations provide insight into people's environments and can help counselors understand how people behave outside of the counseling setting. They also provide essential base line information that facilitates assessment of subsequent change. In structuring observations and collecting observational data, however, damage may be done to the counseling relationship if deception or embarrassment is involved. Observations should be carefully planned to ensure that they are beneficial for clients as well as counselors.

Secondhand reports or information are another source of qualitative data. These might be provided to counselors by clients' teachers, employers, friends, or family members as well as by other mental health professionals. Sometimes counselors will seek out such data. For example, counselors working with young children will almost always interview the parents and perhaps also the children's teachers. Information on previous diagnoses and treatment of someone who has a longstanding or prior mental disorder is essential to sound treatment planning. However, at other times, secondhand reports will be unsolicited and even unwelcome when they are offered. For example, the counselor may want to minimize contact with the overprotective parents of a 25-year-old man who is trying to establish his independence, although the parents seek contact with the counselor to share their perception of their son's difficulties. In interpreting and evaluating secondhand reports, counselors should take into account the possible bias and personal needs of the observer. Such sources can, however, provide important and otherwise unavailable material.

Autobiographies or life histories, written by clients, can be useful in providing information, especially in the case of people who are not comfortable with discussion. Autobiographies also can be used to promote self-exploration. People may be given little or no direction in writing the narrative (e.g., "Write an overview of your life in no more than 10 pages") or the person may be given guidelines or questions to direct the development of the autobiography. A comparison of interview and autobiographical data can be a fruitful source of information; the counselor can take note of similarities and differences in content, the items included, and the tone, emphasis, and organization. Errors and distortions may come to light as well as areas of consistency and repetition.

Products made by a person can be another valuable source of information as well as a way of promoting discussion with a withdrawn or hostile client. These might include drawings, poems, photographs, crafts projects, letters, essays, songs, and other items that have importance to the person and reflect an investment of time and energy. Suggested products also can be useful in resolving impasses or conflicts in treatment. For example, a client was asked to write a letter to her deceased father who had sexually abused her; a client who was enraged because his counselor had been out of town when he had a crisis was asked to draw a picture of his anger; and a client who was a skilled weaver was asked to create a wall hanging that reflected her relationship with her mother. Discussion of the creation of these items and the meaning they have for the person can reveal much about values, experiences, feelings, and abilities.

Time lines are yet another way of obtaining information. A line can be drawn, representing a person's life to date as well as his or her future. Ages might be indicated on the time line to provide guidance. The client then is asked to indicate on the time line developmental milestones or significant events, writing them next to the age at which they occurred. Projections also can be made of future happenings or realization of goals. Discussion of this information can give counselor and client a good sense of the person's history and objectives.

Daydreams and fantasies are other sources of qualitative information that can provide insight. These can be elicited through imagery and can give a perspective on people that is quite different than what might be elicited in more structured ways.

Nonstandardized Quantitative Approaches

Nonstandardized quantitative approaches to acquiring information yield a number, score, or rating but do not have established validity and reliability. Consequently, such instruments do not allow predictions to be made with any confidence nor do they permit a meaningful comparison of one person to another. However, they do provide a common frame of reference and a convenient method of obtaining data. These approaches can be useful for measuring changes in the behavior, thoughts, or feelings of a person; for clarifying areas needing further exploration; and for promoting discussion between client and counselor. This information can be gathered via commercially available questionnaires or rating scales or through informal tools developed by the counselor.

Checklists present an array of problems or concerns; people mark those that affect them. This can provide a useful starting point for an intake interview and can be especially valuable in couples or family counseling, with family members independently completing the checklist and then comparing their self-reports. Like checklists, the *semantic differential* is a common format for inventories that may have only face or content validity. These typically consist of pairs of items placed on a bipolar, seven-point continuum that can measure potency (strong–weak), activity (fast–slow), or quality (good–bad). An example is:

Cheerful   1   2   3   4   5   6   7   Depressed

People indicate where on the scale they would place themselves or some aspect of their lives. Counselor-made semantic differential scales can be useful in assessing client self-images and attitudes. Several administrations of the same scales over time can provide an indication of change.

Rating scales are useful not only for an initial assessment but for setting goals and measuring progress. Once difficulties have been identified, people can be asked to indicate the severity of their difficulty on a 1-10 scale (e.g., how troubled are you by the conflict you are having with your sister? how fearful are you of dogs?) The person can then set a goal, using the rating scale (e.g., what number on the scale would you like to reflect your comfort with dogs?) Progress can be tracked by regularly asking people to rate the level of their difficulties. Despite the imprecise nature of this scale, most people seem to have little difficulty providing meaningful ratings.

Numerical rating scales can be made more specific by providing five to seven graduated descriptions for the rater's use. A common format describes frequency of behavior:

I am able to assert myself with authority figures

5—almost always
4—usually
3—often
2—sometimes
1—rarely

A similar rating tool is the *visual or linear analog*. People are presented with a series of lines of a consistent length (10 centimeters is common) with descriptive statements at each end. They are asked to make a mark on each line to describe themselves. An example would be:

Not at all tired ——————————————————————— Extremely tired

Measurement of the distance between the left end of the line and the mark a person has made on the line provides a baseline and allows comparison with subsequent administrations of this tool.

Card sorts are another tool that can be developed or adapted to meet the needs of a particular client. The client is presented with a set of cards containing descriptors, pictures, statements, or other stimuli such as occupations written on each card. The person then is asked to divide the cards into a predetermined number of stacks, according to their relative standing on a particular criterion (e.g., importance, interest). The number of cards to be sorted into each pile usually is specified. This can promote self-awareness and facilitate decision-making.

Rank-ordering can serve similar purposes. In this approach, people are asked to organize a list of variables (e.g., goals, tasks, losses, interests) in a hierarchical way according to a guiding principle such as importance or urgency.

Frequency logs are used to assess how often events occur as well as their nature. People might be asked to keep daily logs of drug or alcohol consumption, dysfunctional eating behaviors, suicidal thoughts, or aggressive impulses. Affect can be tracked by asking people to rate their levels of depression or anxiety at one-hour intervals. Concurrent behaviors, thoughts, or life events also can be listed in the log to facilitate understanding of precipitants of dysfunctional behaviors.

All of the formats described in this section (checklists, semantic differentials, numerical rating scales, rank-orders, linear analogs, card sorts, and frequency logs) have been used both for standardized inventories with high reliability and validity and for experimental, unstandardized, or counselor-made inventories used for exploration and discussion.

Validated Quantitative Approaches

Inventories that have been standardized and have been shown to have a satisfactory degree of validity and reliability can enhance the counseling process by providing an objective source of data, allowing comparison of the client with others, facilitating the uncertain process of prediction, and providing access to information that might otherwise be unavailable. The process of administering and interpreting standardized tests and inventories requires counselors to develop some relevant skills and knowledge. The counselor should become familiar with the types of tests that are available and should become comfortable using *Mental Measurements Yearbooks*, *Tests in Print,* and other references designed to simplify test selection. Some knowledge of the statistical aspects of assessment also is needed when counselors evaluate the appropriateness and worth of a standardized inventory and when counselors are interpreting people's inventoried scores. In addition, counselors should be aware of optimal procedures for test administration and should become accustomed to observing people's test-taking behaviors, another source of information on their adjustment, attitudes, motivation, and work habits.

TYPES OF INVENTORIES

A survey of members of the American Counseling Association who focused on community-based counseling indicated that over 50% used standardized testing in their work (Bubenzer et al., 1990). Most used two or three instruments on a regular basis and tested primarily to assess personality, intelligence, and career-related interests. The inventories most often used, in order of frequency reported, included the Minnesota Multiphasic Personality Inventory, the Strong Interest Inventory, the Wechsler Adult Intelligence Scale, the Myers-Briggs Type Indicator, the Weschler Intelligence Scale for Children, the 16 Personality Factor, the Thematic Apperception Test, the Bender-Gestalt Visual-Motor Test, the Wide Range Achievement Test, and the Millon Clinical Multiaxial Inventory.

Standardized and established inventories can be divided into three categories, depending on whether they are to measure ability, interests, or personality. Although it is beyond the scope of this book to provide detailed information on specific inventories or on the statistical aspects of test evaluation and interpretation, an overview of the categories of available inventories is provided to help counselors determine when testing is in order and what types of inventories might be most useful.

Measures of Ability

Ability tests measure a combination of innate capacities and learning acquired through formal and informal education. These tests can be threatening to some people because they raise the possibility of poor performance; the impact of such instruments on the client–counselor relationship should, consequently, be considered carefully before they are administered. In addition, charges of gender as well as racial bias have been levied against measures of ability, necessitating extreme care in their selection and interpretation. Inventories should be viewed as only one of many sources of information on a person's abilities; the data they yield should be combined with other information about a person to yield the most meaningful and accurate knowledge. With proper use, however, such tests can provide important information on people's abilities, their academic needs, and their suitability for particular educational or occupational endeavors.

Achievement, intelligence, and aptitude tests all are measures of ability. The three types of tests may appear indistinguishable, consisting of a series of questions or tasks with predetermined correct answers. However, the development, scoring systems, and normative samples of the inventories usually differ, enabling them to serve three different, though related, purposes.

Achievement tests are designed to measure previously attained mastery or ability in a particular area. These tests generally are used to assess the impact of academic experiences, to indicate academic strengths and weaknesses, to provide an objective measure of learning, and to indicate the relative standing of a person's level of learning in a sample or normative group (class, school, nationwide sample).

Achievement tests typically are of limited interest to most mental health counselors but are of considerable interest to school, employment, and career counselors. However, students' records may include data on achievement tests such as the Iowa Test of Basic Skills (Riverside) and the Comprehensive Test of Basic Skills (Macmillan) that will need to be understood and interpreted by the mental health counselor. Many high schools require satisfactory performance on proficiency or achievement tests as a prerequisite for graduation, and counselors dealing with adolescents may consequently become involved in the process of assessing achievement. Moreover, counselors may make use of a comprehensive achievement test such as the Wide Range Achievement Test (WRAT), published by Jastak Associates, as part of a test battery. The WRAT, which evaluates achievement in spelling, arithmetic, and reading, is a much-used inventory, designed to measure the basic academic skills of young people and adults. Both the Scholastic Aptitude Tests and the Graduate Record Examination, published by Educational Testing Service, include achievement tests in selected subject areas.

Intelligence tests are more likely than achievement tests to become part of the diagnostician's repertoire. Many years of debate have addressed the as-yet unresolved question of exactly what intelligence is. A survey of psychologists found that most viewed intelligence as a combination of abstract thinking or reasoning, problem-solving ability, and the capacity to acquire knowledge (Snyderman & Rothman, 1987). Level of inventoried intelligence can and usually does change throughout the life of most people.

Group and individual tests of intelligence are available. The individual tests generally are more valid and informative as well as more time-consuming and complicated to administer. Counselors are qualified to administer group tests of intelligence such as the Otis-Lennon School Ability Test, published by Psychological Corporation. Some counselors also have the specialized training needed to administer individual intelligence tests such as the Stanford-Binet Intelligence Scale (Riverside) and the Wechsler intelligence scales (the Wechsler Preschool and Primary Scale of Intelligence, the Wechsler Intelligence Scale for Children, and the Wechsler Adult Intelligence Scale published by Psychological Corporation). Counselors without this specialized training will need to make a referral to a psychologist when a highly reliable measure of a person's intellectual functioning must be obtained. This is most likely to occur when a diagnosis of mental retardation is suspected and needs to be confirmed or disconfirmed by an individual intelligence test. Intelligence tests also might be used when counselors suspect that a person's academic experiences have not provided an accurate reflection of his or her academic achievement (i.e., the person is what often is described as an underachiever) or when career and educational counseling is part of the treatment plan.

Aptitude tests are designed to evaluate a person's potential for learning or profiting from a given educational experience or the probability of that person succeeding in a particular occupation or course of study. Two types of aptitudes have been identified, *simple or specific aptitudes* and *complex aptitudes*. Tests have been developed to measure each type. Specific aptitudes often measured include motor abilities, clerical ability, and language ability. A specific aptitude such as clerical speed is readily defined and measured and bears an obvious relationship to success in certain occupations. Complex aptitudes commonly are measured by using a multi-aptitude battery that consists of a group of tests of specific aptitudes that may be given either singly or in combination. An overall measure of aptitude can be derived by combining scores from a group of tests in the battery. The Differential Aptitude Tests (Psychological Corporation), the Armed Services Vocational Aptitude Battery (U.S. Department of Defense), the Tests of Adult Basic Education (CTB/Macmillan), the Scholastic Aptitude Tests and the Graduate Record Examination (Educational Testing Service) are examples of widely used multi-aptitude test batteries. Many counselors took the Graduate Record Examination or the Miller Analogies Test (Psychological Corporation) to demonstrate their aptitude for graduate school. A complex aptitude tends to be difficult to define. An aptitude for law school is a complex aptitude, for example, although a test has been developed to measure it (the Law School Aptitude Test). Aptitude test scores tend to be highly correlated with school grades and scores on other inventories of ability. Therefore, counselors often can infer information on people's aptitudes without administering these inventories.

However, counselors do need to understand aptitude test scores included in a person's record and may decide to include an inventory of aptitudes as part of a battery of tests administered to a person contemplating a career change or experiencing academic difficulties. Aptitude, as well as achievement and intelligence, tests also can be important aids in the diagnosis of developmental and learning disorders.

Interest Inventories

Interests may be defined as constellations of likes and dislikes and are manifested through the activities people pursue, the objects they value, and their patterns of behavior. Information on people's interests may be gathered through discussion (expressed interests), an examination of behaviors and activities (manifest interests), and scores on questionnaires (inventoried interests). Interests typically are the primary determinant of both college major and occupational choices (Betz & Hackett, 1981), and congruence of interests and career choice is significantly correlated with enjoyment of and persistence in an occupation (Betz, Fitzgerald, & Hill, 1989). Identification of interests is important not only in career or rehabilitation counseling but also in counseling focused on such problems as Somatoform Disorders, depression, anxiety, and dysfunctional relationships. Often, people with difficulties in these areas have withdrawn, have a low activity level, and may have a lifestyle that does not mesh well with their interests. Planning activities and experiences that are likely to be pleasurable and to give a feeling of accomplishment and competence can contribute to improvement in mood, coping skills, and interpersonal relationships. In addition, a comparison of a person's inventoried and expressed interests with their manifest interests or how they spend their time can provide insight into sources of dissatisfaction.

A large variety of interest inventories are available. They range from self-administered and self-scored inventories such as the Self-Directed Search (Psychological Assessment Resources) to extensive questionnaires that provide a computer-scored measure of people's interest in more than 200 occupational areas (the Strong Interest Inventory, published by Consulting Psychologists Press). Other widely used interest inventories include the Kuder Occupational Interest Survey (Science Research Associates) which relates interest patterns to both occupations and college majors, the Harrington O'Shea Career Decision-Making System (AGS), and the Career Assessment Inventory (National Computer Systems) that is available in both professional and vocational versions. Comprehensive assessment tools such as the COPSystem Career Guidance Program (EdITS) and the Differential Aptitude Test Career Planning Program (Psychological Corporation) include measures of interests as well as measures of aptitude and values.

Although a great deal of information can be obtained from exploring people's expressed and manifest interests, counselors involved in career assessment, leisure counseling, or preretirement counseling as well as those counseling people who have few expressed or manifest interests may obtain additional useful information by administering interest inventories. These instruments, which have no right or wrong answers, typically are less threatening to people than are tests of ability. However, scores on interest inventories, like their answers, also tend to be less clear-cut and more difficult to interpret than those of ability tests. A high interest score in the occupation of musician, for example, should not immediately be interpreted to mean that the person should become a musician. Exploration is needed to determine the person's preparation for and talent in the field, the degree of congruence between the lifestyle of a musician and the person's preferred lifestyle, and what it is about that occupation that appeals to the person. Related occupations that involve music, creativity, and the experience of performing also should be explored as well as the option of satisfying the person's interests through leisure rather than occupational activities. Client–counselor dialogue, then, is critical to the effective interpretation of interest inventories.

Personality Inventories

Personality inventories may be global in scope and designed to provide an overall picture of a person's emotional style or they may be specific, focusing on particular aspects of personality (e.g., self-concept, career maturity, values, interpersonal skills, depression, or anxiety). Measures of personality can be very helpful to counselors involved in diagnosis and treatment planning. The measures can provide a clear and well-organized picture of a person's personality, highlight strengths and weaknesses, and obtain information a person may be unwilling or unable to provide directly. Those personality inventories that measure states, or short-term changes, rather than traits, or underlying personality dimensions, can be useful in assessing progress during counseling. Personality inventories also can be helpful in career and family counseling.

Types of Personality Inventories

Inventories of personality can be divided into projective and objective measures. A wide range of objective or standardized personality inventories are available for use by counselors. These generally consist of a series of descriptive statements; respondents are asked to indicate whether the items are true of them or which of several items best describes them. Scoring is standardized and numerical values, related to predetermined aspects of personality, are provided when the inventory is scored. Little skill is involved in the administration and scoring of these inventories. However, their interpretation can require considerable skill and knowledge of behavior and personality.

Standardized personality inventories can be divided into *general personality inventories*, *clinical personality inventories*, and *specialized personality inventories*. General personality inventories are designed to provide a broad-based picture of the personalities of people who are not assumed to have significant emotional difficulties. Well-established general personality inventories that are available for counselor use include:

1. *Adjective Checklist* (ACL)—This inventory, published by Consulting Psychologists Press, consists of 300 adjectives. People can indicate on this inventory how they perceive their real selves and their ideal selves, and how they believe they are perceived by others.
2. *California Psychological Inventory* (CPI)—The CPI, also published by Consulting Psychologists Press, consists of true/false items that yield scores on 20 basic aspects of personality and four lifestyles (alpha—dependable, enterprising, outgoing; beta—reserved, responsible, moderate; gamma—adventurous, pleasure seeking, restless; and delta—private, withdrawn, disaffected). Special scales provide information on managerial potential, work orientation, leadership, and creativity. The CPI is useful for assessing personal style, goals, motivation, and drive of both adolescents and adults.
3. *Myers-Briggs Type Indicator* (MBTI)—The MBTI, published by Consulting Psychologists Press and based on Carl Jung's theory of personality, is one of the most widely used inventories for normal populations (McCaulley, 1990). It is useful in promoting personal growth, self-awareness, leadership skills, team building, and career development, and in enhancing interpersonal skills. Important to its appeal is its assumption that all personality preferences are equally valuable. The MBTI yields scores on four bipolar dimensions: introversion-extroversion, sensing-intuition, thinking-feeling, and judging-perceiving. Combinations of these scores describe 16 personality types. The MBTI can be computer analyzed to provide information on the interaction of the personality types of two people, useful in couples counseling. A children's version of the MBTI, the Murphy-Meisgeier Type Indicator for Children, is available for use in grades 2 through 8.
4. *Sixteen Personality Factor* (16PF). The 16PF measures 16 basic bipolar dimensions of personality (e.g., reserved/outgoing, affected by feelings/emotionally stable). Versions of this inventory also are available to measure the personalities of young people (High School Personality Questionnaire, Children's Personality Questionnaire, and the Early School Personality Questionnaire).

Several clinical personality inventories are available. These provide information on the diagnosis and treatment of mental disorders and are of great use to mental health counselors. The two most widely used broad-based and standardized clinical personality inventories are:

1. *Minnesota Multiphasic Personality Inventory* (MMPI)—First published in 1942 and revised in 1989, the MMPI is the most widely used and

researched personality inventory (Hood & Johnson, 1991). Consisting of 567 true-false items designed to identify symptoms and diagnose pathology, the MMPI scales reflect such areas as level of depression, potential for addiction, adjustment, psychosis, and physical complaints. Many special scales have been developed, making the MMPI an extremely flexible and useful inventory. Its interpretation is complex, however, and requires special training and experience.

2. *Millon Clinical Multiaxial Inventory* (MCMI)—Published by NCS as is the MMPI, the MCMI was developed by Theodore Millon who specializes in the study and treatment of personality disorders. The MCMI is linked to the *DSM* and provides information on the diagnosis and treatment of personality and other mental disorders. It is a lengthy inventory that is best scored by machine. A version of this inventory for adolescents is also available.

3. *Profile of Mood States* (POMS)—The POMS, published by EdITS, consists of 65 rating scales on which respondents indicate the extent to which they have experienced specified feelings during the past week. Completion of the inventory yields scores on six mood states (Tension-Anxiety, Depression-Dejection, Anger-Hostility, Vigor-Activity, Fatigue-Inertia, and Confusion-Bewilderment) as well as a total mood disturbance score. This inventory yields information on states rather than traits, is easy to administer and score, and can be used repeatedly to assess change in mood (McNair, Lorr, & Droppleman, 1992).

Specialized personality inventories also can be useful in mental health counseling to assess a particular variable and to track progress. The following list includes major types of these inventories:

1. *Specialized Clinical Inventories*—A broad range of specialized inventories has been developed to assess specific emotional or behavioral difficulties. These are very important to counselors involved in diagnosis and treatment planning. Even if counselors believe they have made an accurate diagnosis, an inventory can serve as a double-check on the counselors' conclusions. These inventories also quantify and provide descriptive information on symptoms, thereby facilitating treatment planning, goal setting, and assessment of progress. Widely used examples of these inventories include the Beck Depression and Anxiety Inventories (Psychological Corporation), the Eating Inventory (Psychological Corporation), and the Maslach Burnout Inventory (Consulting Psychologists Press).

2. *Values Inventories*—These inventories probably are used most by career counselors but also can be used by other mental health counselors to promote client self-awareness, to facilitate decisions and transitions, and to help people with religious or spiritual concerns. Examples of values inventories include the Salience Inventory and the Values Scale, based on the research of career-development pioneer Donald Super and published by Consulting Psychologists Press, and the Hall Occupational Orientation Inventory (Scholastic Testing Service).

3. *Inventories of Self-Esteem*—Although these inventories generally have not been shown to have high reliability or validity, they can be useful in promoting discussion, self-exploration, and insight. Examples include the Coopersmith Self-Esteem Inventories (Consulting Psychologists Press), the Piers-Harris Children's Self-Concept Scale, and the Tennessee Self-Concept Scale, both published by Western Psychological Services.

4. *Wellness and Leisure Inventories*—These inventories, too, can promote self-awareness and help people make their lifestyles healthier and more rewarding. The Lifestyle Coping Inventory, published by the National Wellness Institute, is typical of these and yields information on the following 10 dimensions: physical fitness, nutrition, self-care, drugs and driving, social-environmental, emotional awareness, emotional control, intellectual, occupational, and spiritual.

5. *Other Inventories*—Inventories are available to assess thinking, learning, and decision-making style (e.g., the Decision-Making Inventory, Marathon Consulting Press); marital satisfaction and adjustment (e.g., The Marital Satisfaction Inventory, Western Psychological Services); and career maturity and development (e.g., Assessment of Career Decision Making, Western Psychological Services). Counselors can use the catalogues of test publishers as well as books such as *Tests in Print* and *Mental Measurements Yearbook* to locate inventories that meet their specific needs.

Projective Tests

A projective test has been described as, "A relatively unstructured personality test in which an examinee responds to materials such as ink blots, ambiguous pictures, and other objects by telling what he sees, making up stories, or constructing and arranging objects. Theoretically, since the material is fairly unstructured, whatever structure the examinee imposes on it will be a projection of his own personality" (Aiken, 1976, p. 328). The administration and interpretation of projective personality tests require specialized training and supervised experience. Such training generally is not a part of counselor education programs, and most counselors, therefore, are not qualified to do projective testing. However, they still need to become familiar with projective tests since they may want to refer clients to psychologists for projective testing and often will receive client records and intake reports that contain an analysis of projective material.

Projective personality tests are intended to provide a global picture of people's emotional makeup. These tests seek to bypass many of a person's defense mechanisms and reflect unconscious feelings and motives as well as pathology that may thus far have been controlled on the conscious level. The most widely used projective personality tests are:

1. *Rorschach Psychodiagnostic*—Developed by Hermann Rorschach in 1921, this test consists of 10 ink blots. People are asked to report what they see and where it is located on the blot. An analysis of the content, form, determinants, and quantity of people's responses yields information on their wishes, attitudes, and perceptions of the world.

2. *Thematic Apperception Test* (TAT)—The TAT, developed by H. A. Murray, consists of 20 pictures. Generally, people will be shown 10 of them, selected by the examiner for relevance to a particular person. The person is asked to make up a story to explain each picture. Responses can be analyzed to provide information on the person's needs, conflicts, relationships, experiences, and overall personality dynamics.

3. *Sentence Completion*—Several varieties of this inventory have been developed. The best known is that of J.B. Rotter. Rotter's format consists of 40 sentence stems (e.g., I like...). The person completes each stem with the first words that come to mind. In this way, information is provided on concerns, feelings, and attitudes.

4. *Projective Drawings*—Typically, people providing projective drawings are instructed to draw a house, a tree, and a whole person. The drawings offer insights into people's self-images and perceptions of their families as well as their overall emotional development and intelligence.

5. *Bender Visual–Motor Gestalt Test*—This is primarily a measure of visual-motor development and learning disability. However, it also has been widely used and studied as a projective personality test. The Bender Gestalt consists of nine designs (each on a separate card) that the person is asked to copy. Analysis of the designs for accuracy, size, placement on the page, and other variables offers data on people's

interpersonal relationships, areas of concern, and emotional development.

A complete psychological assessment is likely to include most or all of the above inventories as well as an individual intelligence test. It also might include the Minnesota Multiphasic Personality Inventory, discussed in the previous section. The ambiguity inherent in the interpretation of projective tests is reduced by giving a person several of these tests. The examiner can then base interpretations on recurring patterns and themes rather than on isolated responses and can produce a more detailed and reliable report.

This section has focused primarily on tools of assessment designed to provide information on an individual. However, many other inventories also are available. They include those designed to assess environment, marital or family dynamics, or the structure of a group. Reference books cited earlier, as well as catalogs from test publishers, can help counselors select the most appropriate inventories.

PLANNING THE ASSESSMENT

The interview is the core of the process of diagnosis and treatment planning. Through an interview, counselors have an opportunity to observe and become acquainted with clients, to explore their concerns and histories, and to formulate diagnoses and treatment plans. Sometimes, however, the intake interview is not enough. There are many situations in which this might be the case: clients who have difficulty with self-expression and insight, who are hostile or resistant, who are confused or severely disturbed, or who are presenting ill-defined or unusual symptoms are likely candidates for structured assessment. Even when none of these qualities are present, testing can enhance the counseling relationship; it can provide insight, offer new ideas and perspectives, and promote discussion and exploration. However, testing also can be threatening or arduous for the client and can damage the client–counselor relationship. Consequently, counselors should try to ensure that the assessment process is both effective and expeditious; testing should not be routine or gratuitous, but should only be used to answer questions or fill in important gaps that cannot be resolved in less obtrusive ways.

Some of the most important areas that can be clarified by testing are:

1. self-image and self-esteem
2. degree and nature of motivation
3. intellectual and academic strengths and weaknesses
4. learning style and presence and extent of cognitive or learning disorders

5. needs and values
6. interpersonal skills and relationships
7. view of the world
8. moods
9. habits and behaviors
10. nature and degree of pathology
11. leisure and career interests
12. family and other environmental factors
13. likelihood of responding positively to particular modes of treatment
14. overall pattern of personal strengths and deficits

Formulating Assessment Questions

Before making the decision to use tests or inventories, counselors should ask themselves the following questions (Seligman, 1994):

1. What are the goals of the counseling process?
2. What information is needed to accomplish those goals?
3. Have available sources of information such as the client's own experiences and self-knowledge and previous records and tests been used effectively and fully?
4. Does it seem likely that testing and other forms of assessment can provide important information that is not available from other sources?
5. How should testing be planned and integrated into the counseling process to maximize its benefits?
6. What important questions can be answered by the testing?

Counselors should know the areas in which further information is needed before testing is begun. Especially if the client is to be referred to another mental health professional for testing, counselors must clarify the reasons for the assessment and communicate them as specifically as possible to the examiner. Providing the examiner with questions to answer seems particularly likely to yield the needed information. Precise questions, such as the following, are typical of those asked when people are tested:

1. Does this person have a mental disorder? If so, what is the diagnosis?
2. Does this person need hospitalization or is outpatient treatment adequate?
3. What interpersonal patterns seem to be undermining this person's social relationships?

4. Can this child perform satisfactorily in a regular classroom or is a special placement in order?
5. What is the severity of this person's depression?
6. What is this person's intellectual level?

Sometimes, such specific questions cannot be formulated and a person will be referred for or receive a general psychological assessment. In such cases, a battery of tests typically will be used, combined with an interview, to provide a comprehensive picture of the person. A group or battery of inventories might also be used even when specific questions are posed, since the answers to diagnostic questions often cannot be derived from the results of only one inventory. Rather, the answers will emerge more clearly from the nature and patterns of responses that a person gives to a number of inventories.

Selection of Inventories

Selection of specific inventories depends on a number of factors, including the purpose of the inventory, the training and credentials required to administer the inventory, the time required to administer the instrument, the reading level of the inventory, the ages for which it is appropriate, the group on which it has been normed, the inventory's validity and reliability, efforts to minimize culture and gender bias, the inventory's format (e.g., computerized, true–false), and the ways scores are obtained and presented. Test manuals can provide counselors with this information so that they can select inventories wisely.

Some examples of batteries of tests and inventories follow:

1. General assessment conducted by a counselor of a person going through a mid-life transition:
   a. California Psychological Inventory
   b. Strong Interest Inventory
   c. Lifestyle Assessment Questionnaire
   d. Profile of Mood States
   e. Values Scale
2. General assessment conducted by a psychologist:
   a. Rorschach Test
   b. Thematic Apperception Test
   c. Projective Drawings
   d. Bender Gestalt
   e. Wechsler Adult Intelligence Scale
   f. Minnesota Multiphasic Personality Inventory
3. Assessment of a high school student with career confusion:
   a. Strong Interest Inventory

      b. Otis-Lennon School Ability Test
      c. Career Maturity Inventory
      d. Differential Aptitude Test
   4. Assessment of a person with significant depression and interpersonal concerns:
      a. Millon Clinical Multiaxial Inventory
      b. Beck Depression Inventory
      c. Myers-Briggs Type Indicator

Preparing People for an Assessment

Counselors should work collaboratively with their clients in determining those questions that they hope testing will answer and in planning the assessment process to maximize motivation and reduce anxiety. Counselors should provide information on the purpose of the assessment, clarifying how it will benefit the client. They should provide details on the testing site, the length of the assessment process, the nature of the inventories to be administered, the name of the examiner, and what information the person can expect to receive from the assessment. (Of course, clients also should be informed in advance if they will not receive detailed information on their assessment, as often is the case with projective testing.) Clients should have an opportunity to ask questions and express their ideas about how to plan the testing in order to maximize motivation and cooperation as well as to ensure appropriate selection of instruments.

FRAMEWORKS FOR UNDERSTANDING PEOPLE

Once data has been gathered on a person, the counselor has the sometimes challenging task of organizing and analyzing the information. The interpretation of the assessment data generally involves comparing patterns evidenced by the client with pre-established or common patterns or frameworks. This process lends structure and confidence to the counselor's interpretations.

    Which framework to use depends on several factors—the orientation of the counselor, the nature of the person's difficulties, and the approaches to treating emotional difficulties offered by the agency where treatment is taking place. A variety of frameworks will be considered in this section. This list is by no means exhaustive and counselors should feel free to use alternate frameworks or develop frameworks that are helpful to them in assessing their clients.

Developmental

Perhaps the most basic frameworks for assessment are developmental ones. Many developmental models are available, and counselors will need to decide which is most useful and relevant to their needs. Because these models are readily available in other sources, they will only be mentioned here.

Classic and well-established developmental frameworks are exemplified by those of Sigmund Freud (Brill, 1938), Piaget (1963), and Erik Erikson (1963). Such frameworks enable counselors to assess people's psychosocial, psychosexual, and cognitive development, with particular emphasis on the early years. More recent models, such as those of Schlossberg (1992), Levinson (1986), and Fry (1992), facilitate analysis of the adult years, while others, such as those of Minuchin (1977) and Gottfredson (1981), offer perspectives on children's development.

Models are also available to help counselors assess special areas of development. For example, Super (1957) and Ginzberg (1972) developed well-supported theories of career development. Havighurst (1972) described age-related tasks. *The Family Life Cycle* (Carter & McGoldrick, 1988) extended the concept of development beyond the individual and provided a framework for examining the growth and history of a family.

Social, Economic, Cultural, and Ethnic Frameworks

Another way to view people is within the context of their social, economic, cultural, and ethnic backgrounds. This approach provides another norm or reference point against which clients' individual patterns can be compared. Literature is available to help counselors draw these comparisons, such as the work of Pedersen (1990) and Sue and his colleagues (1992). Most counselors probably also have some awareness of common views and experiences of many ethnic and socioeconomic groups and can draw on their own knowledge. Such information should be used with caution, however, and counselors should seek verification in the literature of any guidelines or patterns that they use for assessment of clients.

Psychological Aspects—General

Of particular importance to counselors and clients is the analysis of psychological variables, especially those that provide information on the short-term course of people's disorders, the urgency of their situations, and their receptivity to counseling. Chapter 5 provides detailed information on the mental status examination that yields some of this information. Generally conducted (formally or informally) during the intake or initial interview, the mental status examination provides the counselor a structure for assessing a person's current level of emotional and intellectual functioning. Signs of psychosis, such as delusions, hallucinations, incoherence, markedly peculiar behavior, or extremely inappropriate affect should be noted during the initial interview and should prompt the counselor to consult with a psychiatrist on a person's difficulties. Other psychological aspects requiring early assessment include the person's potential for suicidal or violent behavior and the person's system of defenses.

Psychological Aspects—Suicidal Behavior

Whenever people express feelings of significant depression, guilt, and hopelessness or report thoughts of suicide, counselors should assess the person's potential for self-destructive behavior. There are approximately 50,000 suicides annually in the United States. Most of these are depressed people who had given some warning of their intent and who might have been prevented from committing suicide by a combination of counseling and medication. Suicide is particularly common in men aged 45 and older, employed in professional or skilled areas, living alone, experiencing unusual stress or threat of financial loss, and abusing drugs or alcohol (Motto, Heilbron, & Juster, 1985). Men who attempt suicide usually choose a highly lethal weapon such as a gun. Factors such as confusion around sexual orientation and a family history of alcoholism, depression, or suicide (especially by one's mother) also predispose people toward suicidal ideation. Common warning behaviors of people contemplating suicide include social withdrawal, giving away important possessions, persistent insomnia, weight gain or loss, a decline in occupational or academic performance, previous suicide attempts, unsuccessful efforts to obtain help in the past, ideas of persecution, and feelings of hopelessness, failure, defeat, shame, and guilt.

Counselors suspecting that a person is having suicidal thoughts should ask directly whether the person has contemplated suicide. This line of questioning is not likely to initiate thoughts of suicide if such thoughts have not been present already. Rather, the questioning can enable clients and counselors to accept and explore the suicidal feelings and to take preventive measures.

Assessment of suicidal thoughts should explore the following areas:

1. *Duration of suicidal feelings*—Generally, a suicidal crisis is relatively brief. It may last only a few hours, is most severe at its onset, and has usually passed within six weeks (Hipple & Cimbolic, 1979).
2. *Nature of the plan and the availability of the means*—People who have a clearly formulated plan for suicide, including the use of a lethal weapon that they possess, such as a man who intends to shoot himself

with an available gun next weekend when the family is out of town, are at very high risk for suicide.

3. *History of drug or alcohol use, depression, and suicide attempts in self or family members.*

4. *Mood*—Feelings of anxiety, depression, hopelessness, and guilt have a strong association with suicide. However, people in deep despair sometimes are too discouraged and debilitated to attempt suicide. They may not have the energy to act on their suicidal thoughts until their mood begins to improve, just when the counselor thinks they are showing progress and has stopped monitoring them closely (Walker, 1981). Counselors should, therefore, pay particularly close attention to people with suicidal thoughts when their depressions begin to lift.

5. *Motivation*—People do have a reason for contemplating suicide, as irrational as that act may appear to others. They may want to end their suffering, to punish others, to find peace in an afterlife, or to escape stress or humiliation. They may hope that a suicidal gesture will bring them attention and change the behavior of others. Understanding a person's motivations is important; through knowing what people's needs are, counselors can help them find alternate routes to meeting those needs.

Although all suicidal thoughts and actions should be taken seriously because of their potential lethality, people who are contemplating suicide almost always are conflicted or ambivalent. No matter how discouraged they are, there is likely to be a part of them that wants to be helped. Counselors often can make contact with that part through a combination of empathy, hopefulness, and active intervention. A contract can be made in which the person promises not to commit suicide for a predetermined period. A list of coping mechanisms can be developed with the person for times when suicidal ideation is strong. Hot lines, hospitalization, and other emergency resources can be made available to the person. Support systems and available resources can be strengthened through the counseling process. Sometimes counselors decide to break confidentiality to notify family and friends of a person's suicidal ideation; this step must be taken with care but can be necessary if a person's life is in danger. Consultation with colleagues or supervisors can help counselors deal with decisions around suicide-prevention.

Suicidal ideation, like psychosis, can be frightening to counselors. However, the assessment of suicide risk and prevention of suicide is a critical aspect of the counselors' roles as diagnosticians and treatment planners, drawing on their helping skills and their ability to take an active stance.

Psychological Aspects—Violence

Although most clients seem more likely to harm themselves than others, counselors should be alert to the possibility that their clients might engage in physically harmful or destructive acts against others. The most important predictor of violent behavior is a past history of violence; history-taking is, therefore, of great importance whenever destructive or harmful behavior is suspected. People who are accident-prone and who drive recklessly also seem unusually likely to engage in self-destructive or violent behavior. People who commit violent acts against others are typically male, make excessive use of drugs or alcohol, have feelings of failure and low self-esteem, and have both psychological and neurological difficulties. Psychotic disorders and paranoid disorders, in particular, often are associated with violent client behavior (Walker, 1981).

Detecting neurological problems and knowing when to refer people for assessment of cognitive functioning are skills that should be possessed by all counselors, particularly those who are dealing with potentially violent clients. Although counselors generally are not trained to diagnose neurological impairment, they should watch for the following clues (Walker, 1981): visual or auditory hallucinations, difficulties in impulse control, memory disturbances, confusion, inability to learn new material, extremely concrete thinking patterns, reported visual field abnormalities, a history of head injury, prolonged alcohol or drug abuse, frequent headaches, seizures, or language disturbance. Especially when several of these symptoms are noted in a person, counselors should request a psychiatric or neurological evaluation of that client.

Psychological Aspects—Defense Mechanisms

All people use defense mechanisms. Defense mechanisms are unconscious psychological processes that help people achieve some balance between their instinctual drives and the demands of daily life. Defense mechanisms assist people in coping with reality, in deferring gratification, and in meeting their needs in socially acceptable ways.

A broad range of defense mechanisms has been identified. People can be described by the types of defense mechanisms they are most likely to use. Their preferred defense mechanisms, in turn, provide important information on the nature of their difficulties, the prognosis of their conditions, and their likely response to counseling.

The following classification and description of defense mechanisms can be useful to mental health professionals (Kaplan & Sadock, 1994; Perry & Cooper, 1989; Vaillant, Bond, & Vaillant, 1986).

- *Narcissistic or psychotic defenses*—especially evident in children and people with psychotic disorders, as well as in dreams:

  1. Delusional projection—attributing own characteristics or feelings (often persecutory) onto others and acting toward that person based on this perception
  2. Denial—refusing to acknowledge the presence of a situation or concern
  3. Distortion—extreme reshaping of external reality to meet inner needs

- *Immature defenses*—common in adolescents as well as in people with addictive, personality, and depressive disorders:

  1. Acting out—direct expression of sexual or aggressive wishes and impulses, often in a socially unacceptable way
  2. Blocking—inhibition of feelings, thoughts, or impulses
  3. Devaluation—attributing exaggerated negative characteristics to another person
  4. Fantasy—using fantasy and extreme withdrawal to avoid conflict and intimacy
  5. Hypochondriasis—transformation of negative feelings toward others, arising from loneliness, aggression or loss, into complaints of fatigue, pain or illness that are exaggerated or without physiological cause
  6. Idealization—exaggerating another's virtues in order to avoid seeing them realistically
  7. Introjection (or Identification)—internalization of characteristics of a loved or feared person in order to reduce anxiety and increase closeness with that person
  8. Passive–aggressive behavior—indirect expression of anger and hostility
  9. Projection—a milder version of delusional projection
  10. Regression—returning to an earlier situation or previous stage of development to avoid present or future anxieties or concerns
  11. Somatization—converting impulses into sensory or neuromuscular symptoms
  12. Splitting—viewing oneself or others as being all good or all bad. This may entail a shifting from idealization to devaluation

13. Turning against the self—turning inward a hostile thought about another person

- *Neurotic defenses*—common in most people:

    1. Controlling—extreme attempts to manage or direct events, people, or objects in one's environment
    2. Displacement—changing the object of an impulse, attitude, or feeling to a less threatening object without changing the impulse, attitude, or feeling itself
    3. Dissociation—seeking to avoid stress by cutting off feelings or thoughts from the rest of one's personality
    4. Externalization—perceiving aspects of one's own personality in the environment and in external objects
    5. Inhibition—limiting or renouncing specific behaviors such as sexual involvement to avoid conflict and anxiety
    6. Intellectualization—controlling feelings and impulses by thinking about them and analyzing them rather than by experiencing them
    7. Isolation—intrapsychic splitting of emotion from content and experience, leading to repression or displacement
    8. Rationalization—justification of attitudes or behaviors by selecting the most favorable motives or reasons and ignoring others
    9. Reaction formation (or Overcompensation)—managing unacceptable impulses or feelings by expressing their opposites
    10. Repression—excluding thoughts, impulses, and memories from consciousness
    11. Sexualization—attributing unwarranted sexual significance to an object, person, or activity to ward off anxiety connected with unacceptable impulses
    12. Somatization (defined above)

- *Mature defenses*—common in normal, healthy adults:

    1. Altruism—directing energies toward constructive and gratifying service to others
    2. Anticipation—goal-directed and realistic planning to deal with future difficulties, anxiety, and inner distress
    3. Compensation—overemphasizing one area to balance failure or disappointment in another or overcorrecting for a limitation
    4. Humor—using wit and humor that does not hurt oneself or others to make uncomfortable feelings more tolerable

5. Sublimation—modification of unacceptable urges into acceptable ones by changing the object or vehicle of expression (e.g., sexual tension may be discharged through sports)
6. Suppression—conscious or semiconscious postponement of gratification or exclusion from awareness of an impulse

People engaging in immature, narcissistic, or neurotic defenses are more likely to be seen in counseling than are those using predominantly mature defenses. Analysis of the nature of people's defense mechanisms can facilitate understanding and help counselors to promote increased use of mature defense mechanisms.

INDIVIDUALIZED FRAMEWORKS

Sundberg (1976) suggested three ways of thinking about a person's characteristics: types, traits, and transactions. Types can be determined through the diagnostic process, using the multiaxial assessment framework of the DSM. Traits, as defined by Sundberg, are characteristics of the person that are assessed through comparison with others. These have been considered from many perspectives in the preceding sections of this chapter. Gathering information on transactions involves looking at people in the context of their environments and examining their interactions with other people, objects, and events.

Sundberg's perspective, especially when approached in a longitudinal fashion, allows people to serve as their own frameworks for analysis. Counselors can then define typical patterns of response and behavior that characterize particular clients and can take note of changes in those patterns. Once the counselor has a sense of a person's history and repeated patterns, future patterns can be anticipated and modified. For example, a person who has consistently responded to any threat of rejection or disapproval through flight and avoidance is likely to persist in that behavior unless alternative responses are developed. Patterns and longitudinal trends typically provide more reliable and important information about people than do acute episodes or isolated pieces of information. Consideration of types, traits, and transactions, then, all are important in gaining a complete and reasonably accurate picture of a person and in minimizing the likelihood of unjustified labeling or the drawing of unsubstantiated and unwarranted conclusions.

PROCESS OF ANALYSIS

Analyzing and interpreting the information gathered on a person probably is the most challenging and the most creative part of diagnosis and treatment planning.

The process involves developing and checking hypotheses about the significance and importance of the information in order to provide insight into the person and facilitate decisions about diagnosis and treatment.

Questions to Guide the Analysis

Assume that an intake interview has been conducted and that data from that interview are available on tape, in the counselor's notes, or in the counselor's memory. In addition, previous records have been reviewed and any current assessment or testing results are available. The counselor now can begin the process of analysis by asking the following questions about the accumulated information:

1. What underlying themes or repeated issues are present in the information? These may be obvious, such as a person's repeated negative references to men (e.g., a demanding and critical father, an abusive first husband, projective testing that shows negative feelings toward men, and job losses stemming from conflict with male supervisors). Often, however, these patterns are more subtle. For example, the person may describe two recent car accidents and a series of errors at work and may have omitted many items during the testing process. Such a person may be prone to self-destructive behavior or dissociation or may be so confused and anxious he or she feels overwhelmed and out of control.

2. What items or issues were given greatest importance by the person? Counselors tend to focus on certain aspects of a person's narrative that they believe to be of particular relevance in characterizing the client. These might include the person's family situation, thought processes, or previous emotional difficulties. While this process of selective attending and exploring is sound and provides counselors a structure for information-gathering, counselors also should step into the client's shoes and determine what that person perceives as important. The client, for example, may talk at length about home repair projects. The counselor should take note of this and try to determine what the projects mean to the person. Do they represent a constant source of stress, a gratification, or the person's feeling that all aspects of his life, the house included, are falling apart?

3. What unusual pieces of information, reactions, or thoughts are presented by the person? An old newspaper adage was that if a dog bites a man, it is not news but if a man bites a dog, it is news. The same principle holds true for interpretation of client data. If a person simply

reports that he owns a dog, that piece of information might not be worth mentioning in an intake report. If, however, the person talks at length about her five dogs, fourteen cats, six gerbils, and pet hyena and states that she wishes she didn't have to work full-time so that she could be with her animals all day, this certainly is noteworthy and should be explored to determine what has motivated the person to become so absorbed in her animals.

4. What omissions or abbreviations appeared in the person's presentation? In reviewing an intake interview, the counselor may note that a person said almost nothing about her mother, although she talked extensively about her father. Another person may talk easily about his sports activities but say little about his job. Counselors should attend to these omissions and, if possible, explore them with the person.

   Sometimes the person may resist discussing these subjects or the omissions may not be noted until after the person has left. This might make analysis of the omissions difficult and the counselor should be cautious about premature interpretations. A counselor cannot be sure, for example, whether the person said little about her mother because the two have a conflicted relationship or because that relationship is comfortable and the person wanted to focus on areas in which she needed help. Significant omissions should be noted in the intake report as areas needing further exploration, or, if substantiating information is available, as highly charged or conflicted areas for the person.

5. How does a given piece of information fit in with what else is known about the person and his or her environment? Interpretations should rarely be made on the basis of a single piece of information. Rather, the counselor should seek to develop a comprehensive and coherent picture of a person that integrates and makes sense of the presented information.

6. What frameworks help make sense of this data? A previous section of this chapter discussed frameworks for analysis. Counselors may consider the frameworks described there to determine which ones are relevant to the client's major concerns. Those frameworks then could be used to enhance and structure the process of interpretation.

GUIDELINES FOR INTERPRETATION

Perhaps the greatest potential pitfall of the interpretation process is the counselor's becoming judgmental and making unjustified conclusions. While the counselor should not just report the facts, interpretations that are made should not condemn, criticize, or stigmatize the client; they should be well-substantiated; and they should generally be cautious and tentative in nature. It is preferable to talk in terms of possibilities and likelihoods rather than absolutes.

The following are four hypothetical reports by counselors, offering their analyses of the same situation, the first few minutes of a counseling session with Joan B. and her four-year-old son Kevin. The four analyses are quite different and represent distinct approaches to the process:

Example 1

Joan B. and her four-year-old son Kevin arrived for their appointment approximately 15 minutes late. They walked in and Ms. B. took the chair by the desk, pointing out some toys in the corner for Kevin to play with. While Ms. B. and I began to talk, Kevin raced around the room, waving a toy airplane, and simulating airplane noises. He then climbed on and off Ms. B's lap several times, knocking her purse to the floor. When his mother told him to be quiet while we spoke, Kevin returned to the toys and began noisily pounding blocks against each other. Ms. B. ignored this behavior.

Example 2

Joan B. and her four-year-old son Kevin arrived for their appointment approximately 15 minutes late. Ms. B. seemed oblivious to the fact that she had kept me waiting. Ms. B. took the chair by the desk and encouraged Kevin to play with some toys in the corner. Unfortunately, he chose to play with the toy plane and became quite noisy and irritating as he raced around the room, making airplane noises. Kevin then climbed on and off his mother's lap several times, knocking her purse to the floor. Ms. B. was ineffective in her efforts to quiet Kevin and seemed unaware of how to control her child's behavior. Kevin continued to make a nuisance of himself by noisily pounding blocks against each other.

Example 3

Joan B. and her four-year-old son Kevin arrived for their appointment approximately 15 minutes late, suggesting Ms. B.'s resistance to the counseling process. Ms. B. attempted to assert her control over her son by taking the chair by the desk and telling him to play with the toys in the corner. Kevin chose to play with a toy airplane, and raced around the room with the plane, simulating airplane noises. His selection of the plane seemed to represent an effort to assert his masculinity and to defy maternal control. When ignored by his mother, however, the Oedipal needs typical of his age group emerged and he approached his mother in a rather seductive way, climbing on and off her lap. Still not receiving the affection and attention he craved, Kevin knocked Ms. B.'s purse from her lap in an apparent passive-aggressive gesture. At this point, his mother tried to quiet him, but her weak ego strength and apparent fear of her son got in the way, and she was ineffective. Kevin then expressed his anger and frustration with his mother's vague and ambivalent responses to him by noisily pounding blocks against each other.

Example 4

Joan B. and her four-year-old son Kevin arrived for their appointment approximately 15 minutes late. Ms. B. did not seem aware that they were late. She took the chair by the desk and told Kevin to play with the toys in the corner. Kevin selected a toy airplane and ran around the room with the plane, simulating airplane noises. He kept glancing at his mother, as though wanting something from her, perhaps control or attention. Ms. B. did not respond to Kevin, but seemed to focus on our conversation. Apparently losing interest in the plane, Kevin put it aside and began to climb on and off his mother's lap. This seemed further indication of his wish for her attention. Only when Kevin knocked her purse from her lap did Ms. B. tell him, in a shaky voice, that he should be quiet. She seemed reluctant to exert control over him until he manifested behavior which could not be ignored. When she did attempt to modify Kevin's behavior, she seemed uncomfortable and had little success. Kevin then began noisily banging blocks against each other, apparently ignoring his mother's direction. Although Kevin is at the age when his mother's attention typically becomes very important, especially for boys, he is unusually active even for a four-year-old and does not seem to be meeting his needs well through his interactions with his mother.

Discussion

These four examples illustrate both desirable and potentially harmful approaches to analysis of client information. While none of them is perfect, some are both more useful to the counselor and more helpful to the client.

In example 1, the counselor is presenting a factual description of the scene. He is performing almost the same role as a tape recorder or video camera. While there is little in example 1 that could be viewed as damaging or inaccurate, the data is not organized in a meaningful way and is not used to provide insight into Ms. B., her son, and their relationship.

The counselor in example 2 loses too much of her objectivity and communicates a negative and judgmental picture of the clients. Words such as "oblivious," "unfortunately," "irritating," and "nuisance" are inappropriate as used here. This counselor seems more concerned with her own rights and feelings than she is with understanding the clients. Consequently, not only is this analysis inappropriately pejorative, it fails in its effort to provide useful understanding of these people.

Although the analysis presented in example 3 is thought-provoking and may even be accurate, this counselor is overinterpreting the limited amount of information available and is drawing premature conclusions. The counselor has used a psychoanalytic framework to make sense of the experience and seems to be forcing the observations to conform to that framework. Conclusions are drawn in absolute terms, based on isolated incidents rather than trends or patterns, and motivations are inferred with little justification. Descriptions such as "assert his masculinity," "defy maternal control," "passive-aggressive," and "weak ego strength" might be justifiable after lengthy data-gathering and observation of these people, but are inappropriate, based on this small sample of behavior.

Example 4 seems to be the best of the four. The counselor remains relatively objective, makes use of a developmental framework to assess Kevin's behavior, is tentative in the conclusions drawn, yet does provide some understanding of these people and their interactions. Emphasis is placed on observable behaviors rather than motivations that can only be surmised. Efforts have been made to substantiate all interpretations by describing the observations that justified them. This example is useful to both counselor and clients in that areas needing further exploration emerge clearly, working hypotheses for interpreting the dynamics of this situation are presented, and the people are described in such a way as to foster empathy and insight.

Clearly, the process of interpretation can be challenging. Some counselors are most comfortable with the noninterpretive stance assumed by the counselor in example 1, while others feel that they should try to make the sort of rapid interpretations presented in example 3. Both of these approaches do a disservice to clients and do not make good use of the special skills of counselors: their knowledge of human development and behavior, their empathy and sensitivity, their insight into people, and their understanding of human development and relationships. By drawing on these skills during the process of assessment and interpretation, counselors can facilitate diagnosis and treatment planning and can present their clients as full human beings who seem to come alive and whose lives and experiences have coherence and importance.

The next chapter focuses on information gathering through an intake interview. It includes the transcript of an interview and an accompanying analysis that further clarifies many of the points presented in this chapter.

Intake Interviews

In most mental health agencies, clients are seen for an intake interview before treatment begins. Counselors in private practice also typically conduct a comprehensive initial interview. These interviews serve the following purposes:

1. *Determining suitability of person for agency's services*: Generally, clients (or their referral sources) are knowledgeable enough about mental health services to present themselves for treatment at the sort of agency that can meet their needs. Sometimes, however, people seek or need a particular service that is not provided by the person or agency they have consulted. For example, a man with a psychotic disorder may present himself at an agency specializing in career counseling. In cases such as these, the counselor should make a referral as discussed in chapter 7.

   Sometimes people request a specific form of treatment (e.g., biofeedback, assertiveness training) not available at a particular agency. The reasoning behind the person's preference should be explored to be sure the requested treatment is well-understood by the person and seems to be a sound method of treatment for him or her. If so, a referral can be made; if not, the counselor can discuss alternative and potentially more helpful approaches with the person.

2. *Assess and respond to urgency of person's situation*: A person in a crisis, perhaps having suicidal thoughts following a marital breakup, should receive help as soon as possible. Similarly, a severely disturbed person, perhaps one who is actively hallucinating or spending money wildly during a manic episode, also needs immediate attention. One goal of the intake process is to assess the urgency of the person's situation and, if immediate intervention is warranted, to see that it is provided.

3. *Familiarize person with agency and counseling process*: Many people are apprehensive and unsophisticated about counseling. Presenting themselves for counseling may be viewed as an admission that some-

thing is wrong with them. Initial fantasies of the counseling process expressed to me by clients included having to lie on a couch and dredge up unpleasant dreams and memories, being "forced to tell the truth about themselves," and being given electroconvulsive therapy.

People's preconceptions of the counseling process should be explored and any fears or distortions alleviated by a clear, concise description of the counseling process. People also should be informed of relevant agency policies such as scheduling, fees, confidentiality, presence of a waiting list, and additional screening procedures. In addition, people should be given information on what will happen next in the treatment process, whether it is an initial appointment, further intake screening, or referral.

4. *Begin to engender positive client attitudes toward counseling*: Part of the process of helping people to feel comfortable with an agency and its procedures is the development of some positive counselor–client rapport and the communication of a sense of optimism. Even clients who will not see the intake interviewer again should leave that interview with a sense of having gained something from the interview, of having been heard, and of hopefulness that counseling will help them. The intake interviewer, as a representative of the counseling agency, plays a key role in determining whether people will return for counseling and whether they will be ready to make a commitment to that process.

5. *Gather sufficient information on presenting problem, history, and dynamics to allow formulation of a diagnosis and treatment plan*: The focal task of the intake interview is to gather enough information on the client to allow the formulation of at least a provisional diagnosis and treatment plan. Although many agencies have a recommended procedure for acquiring client information and a form on which counselors are to write a summary and analysis of the data they have received, it is the responsibility of the intake interviewer to determine what information is needed, to conduct an interview that will provide the information, and to terminate the interview when the goals of the intake process have been reached.

OVERVIEW OF THE INTAKE PROCESS

The intake process itself can vary considerably depending on several variables:

1. The personnel involved in the process

2. The ways of gathering information
3. The intake schedule and format
4. The client
5. The relationship of intake process to treatment

Intake Personnel

In some agencies, a single intake interviewer has the responsibility of gathering data on and evaluating people's mental status, the nature and dynamics of their presenting concerns, and relevant history. However, in other agencies, clients meet with several mental health professionals as part of the intake process. The mental health counselor might gather information on the presenting problems and background. A physical and mental status examination might be conducted by a psychiatrist. A referral also could be made to a psychologist for projective testing and an assessment of intelligence or to a social worker who will interview family members and make a home visit. The nature of the intake process can vary considerably, depending on who is involved in the intake process.

Information Gathering

The manner in which data is gathered is another aspect of the intake process. Some agencies rely exclusively on information provided by clients through interviews and completion of forms. Other agencies advocate a broad-based approach to collecting information and may interview family members and close friends of the client, may request academic and medical records, may administer standardized tests or other assessment instruments, and may contact teachers or employers for additional information.

Both the manner in which information is gathered and the personnel involved will be reflected in the format of the intake interview. Nearly all agencies make use of an outline or standardized procedure for intake. While some flexibility in these procedures is common, they will exert a great influence over the intake process. Samples of such formats will be provided later in this chapter.

Depth and Duration of Intake Process

Intake interviews may be as brief as twenty minutes in an emergency room, where people in crisis and those who are actively psychotic are referred for immediate treatment while others may be placed on a waiting list. On the other hand, intake procedures may take four hours or more, especially if psychological testing is involved, and may involve three or more sessions, scheduled on different days with different mental health specialists. Most mental health counselors seem to devote one to two hours to the intake process.

The depth of the interview, like its duration, is largely determined by agency policy and practice. In some agencies, intake interviewers function as selective and intelligent tape-recorders. They gather information, sort important from unimportant, and present relevant material in a concise format. They do little interpretation or analysis, viewing that as either more appropriate in treatment than in intake or as not part of the counseling process at all. Other agencies ask for a much more analytical role, viewing the interviewer as an interpreter whose goal is to understand the underlying dynamics of the client's concerns.

Nature of Client

At the outset of an intake interview, counselors need to make a rapid assessment of the client so that any urgent needs can be met quickly and the intake interview can be appropriately structured. To facilitate their efforts to understand the person quickly, counselors should consider who referred the person, the stated purpose of the referral, the person's presenting concerns, and the apparent level of the person's motivation and functioning.

The nature of and reason for the referral can provide essential information. Clients may be referred by other agencies or helping professionals who do not provide the services needed. The referral sources may be transferring responsibility for the person's treatment to the second agency, as in the case of most court referrals or referrals from employee assistance or managed care programs. On the other hand, the referral source may be seeking only a specific form of treatment for a person (e.g., career counseling, hypnotherapy for weight loss) while the referring agency continues to provide and oversee the person's treatment. Generally, the intake interviewer will have contact with the referring agency to determine why the referral was made and whether collaborative treatment is indicated.

People are also encouraged to seek counseling by family or friends. These referral sources may have a vested interest in the person's seeking counseling. Such clients may have sought counseling because of pressure from another person, perhaps a spouse who threatens marital separation unless counseling is begun. These clients may be resistant and have limited motivation toward treatment, or they may be highly motivated to maintain their relationships and lifestyle. Attitudes toward treatment usually have to be addressed early in the intake interview if productive counseling is to be undertaken.

Externally motivated clients represent only one type of client who may prove challenging to the intake interviewer. Others include the severely depressed person, the person who is psychotic, the hostile and angry person, the seductive or manipulative person, and the person expressing suicidal ideation. With such people, the interviewer's efforts to follow a standardized format and develop a comprehensive picture of the client may be frustrated. Intake interviewers must take into account the nature of people's presenting concerns and the attitudes they bring into the intake interview so that the interview can be appropriately individualized. With depressed people, for example, the interviewer might need to assume a more active and directive role, relying on clear and concrete questions and interventions that facilitate self-expression; hostile clients might require limit-setting and confrontation as a part of the interview; while the person in a crisis may require some immediate assistance and only a minimal intake process. Counselors must individualize and adapt the standardized procedures of their agencies so that, at the end of the intake process, the client is motivated and optimistic and the counselor has a useful understanding of the person's difficulties and is ready to plan the treatment.

Relationship of Intake Process to Treatment

An important determinant of the intake process is the nature and timing of what happens next. The following are some possible steps that follow the intake interview:

1. The intake interviewer will immediately begin to see the person for counseling.
2. The person will soon begin treatment with another mental health professional.
3. The results of the intake interview will be presented and discussed at a staff or case conference and a treatment plan developed at that time.
4. The person's name will be placed on a waiting list until an appropriate therapist has some available time.
5. If alternatives 3 or 4 are followed, some agencies will simultaneously assign people to an intake group to provide interim treatment. These groups can offer some continuity of treatment, bridging the time gap between the intake interview and the assignment of the person to an appropriate treatment person or group.
6. The person might be referred to a more suitable agency or source of assistance.

7. With or without the agreement of the intake interviewer, the person might discontinue contact, perhaps feeling that he or she does not have an interest in treatment at present.

Whichever of these outcomes occurs, the intake interviewer should ensure that the following procedures are followed:

1. The person leaves the intake interview with an understanding of what will happen next.
2. Urgent client needs are met quickly.
3. The process of diagnosis and treatment planning is under way.
4. Both client and intake worker have a sense of closure and comfort at the end of the intake process.
5. The intake interviewer ensures that referrals and follow-up will be accomplished. If people need time to decide whether to continue treatment or if they want to delay treatment, the intake interviewer should arrange for the person to be contacted at a later date. If the person severs contact with the agency unexpectedly, further contact usually will be made to ensure that the person has another opportunity to receive help and that the intake process was not excessively stressful or uncomfortable for the person.

CONDUCTING AN INTAKE INTERVIEW

Intake interviewers generally have little background or preparatory information on the people they will be seeing for an interview and so must be flexible, resourceful, and experienced enough to handle a broad range of clients and presenting concerns. Sometimes new counselors at an agency conduct many of the intake interviews as a way of filling their time, building up a caseload of clients, and freeing more established counselors to spend more time on treatment. This does not mean that conducting intake interviews is easier than counseling. Rather, the intake interview often is more challenging and demanding than a typical counseling session because it involves dealing with an unknown client who may not be familiar or comfortable with counseling.

At some agencies, appointments for intake interviews are scheduled. At other agencies, however, intake interviewers cover predetermined blocks of time. For example, a counselor may interview any new clients who present themselves on Mondays between 9 a.m. and 1 p.m. That enables an agency to provide immediate service to people, but can be more taxing for the counselor who may see no clients one week and five on another week. Generally, the duration of an intake interview is more flexible and variable than that of the counseling session.

Interventions

Many ways to begin an intake interview have been identified. Some mental health workers start with an ice-breaker or a series of social amenities: "How's the weather out there? ... Did you have any trouble finding a parking place? ... It's nice to see you today." Others go to the opposite extreme and begin with "Tell me what your problems are." The social approach seems to be counter-productive because it does not set the proper tone for a counseling interview, can mislead the person as to the nature of the counselor–client relationship, and can increase clients' anxiety since they have come to see an expert, not a friend. On the other hand, the problem-focused approach may clash with people's perceptions of why they are seeking counseling and may promote resistance if they are reluctant to see themselves as having problems. An approach that is professional, businesslike, and relatively nonthreatening seems ideal. The counselor might open the interview with a question such as "What brings you in today?" or "What sorts of things were you looking for help with?"

Once the counselor–client dialogue is under way and some idea of the person's presenting problem has been obtained, the counselor usually should orient the person to the purpose, nature, and duration of the intake interview. If the intake interviewer is not necessarily the counselor who will be treating the person, this should be stated at the outset, lest the client feel misled. After establishing the ground rules for the intake process, the counselor typically will then spend most of the interview further exploring the person's presenting concerns, gathering information on history and life circumstances, and gaining insight into the dynamics of the person's difficulties. Detailed information on categories of inquiry and the process of analysis are provided later in this book.

Techniques used by the interviewer will not differ radically from techniques used in counseling sessions: open and closed questions, reflection of feeling, restatement, minimal encouragers, interpretation, and summarization are likely to be the primary modes of intervention. However, the percentage of each type of intervention used in intake interviews probably will differ from its percentage of use in counseling sessions. Counselors typically take greater control of intake sessions than they do of counseling sessions; they tend to be relatively directive and intervene frequently. More questioning probably will be done than in a counseling session because information gathering is under way.

Since clients generally will not be familiar with the counseling process, interviewers should select interventions that are likely to elicit meaningful responses. Open questions seem to be the best tool for accomplishing this. (Open questions are those that call for more than a very brief response.) For example, the intake interviewer might ask, "How do you feel about your work?" rather than "Do you like your work?" Counselors might think that reflection of feeling and interpretation would have little place in an intake interview and, in fact, those modes of intervention probably are used less in intake interviews than in counseling sessions. However, those techniques still are important in giving people the sense that they are heard and understood by someone who has something to offer them, so those approaches should not be avoided by the intake interviewer. Neither should the interviewer refrain from asking questions about areas that seem very personal, such as hallucinations, suicidal ideation, sexual experiences, and financial circumstances. Most clients expect such questions and will respond openly to direct and clear questions such as "Have you thought about hurting or killing yourself?" or "Do you ever see or hear things that seem strange or that other people do not see or hear?" Questions of this nature should be phrased carefully so that they do not suggest or encourage specific responses. For example, asking "Tell me about any use you have made of drugs or alcohol in the past week" usually will elicit more information than asking "Do you have a drinking problem?" While beginning counselors, in particular, may feel they are intruding by asking such questions, they should bear in mind the difference between counseling and socializing. Most people seeking counseling are relieved to have these difficult areas discussed in an open and nonjudgmental fashion.

Recording Information

Because a great deal of information probably will be gathered in a fairly short time, most intake interviewers use either note-taking or tape-recording to assist their recall. Both approaches have advantages and disadvantages.

The client's permission must be obtained before a session is tape-recorded. Although few people object to being recorded, this can be viewed as an intrusion into the counseling process and makes some people uneasy, despite assurances of confidentiality. Counselors also may need as much time to review a tape recording as they did to conduct the intake interview. However, tape-recording has the important advantage of preserving the intake interview with minimal distortion. Moreover, once the mechanics of discussing and starting the recorder are completed, most people become oblivious to that process. During the session, then, it is less obtrusive than note-taking.

Note-taking generally is less threatening than tape-recording and requires little or no discussion in most cases. However, it has several possible disadvantages. Note-taking can prevent counselors from giving clients their full attention. Notes will almost inevitably be incomplete, possibly leading to significant omissions or distortions. In addition, clients are sometimes distracted by note-taking and may attribute significance to the instances of note-taking, perhaps even focusing more on topics that seem to precipitate note-taking. If note-taking is used, counselors should try to minimize its impact on the counseling process and to capture essential themes and interventions in the notes as well as writing down important client comments and behaviors that promote understanding.

Combining the two modes of recording information allows the counselor the option of listening to all or part of the taped session while having the notes available for quick review. Whether to tape record or take notes on sessions is an individual decision determined by counselor preference and the nature of a particular client.

Concluding the Intake Interview

Since the intake interview may not be of predetermined length, the interviewer must decide when to end the interview and inform the client that termination of the interview is imminent. The counselor should do this in a positive way and should allow at least a few minutes for client additions and questions. A typical closing interaction might be:

> Counselor: You've certainly told me a great deal about yourself. I think I have the information I need to move ahead on planning your counseling. Is there anything you'd like to add to what we've talked about?

> Client: No, I don't think so.

> Counselor: All right. Let me fill you in on just what will happen now and how long that will take. There will also be some time for you to ask any questions you might have before we wrap up for today.

The interview ends, with the counselor informing the person about the steps for scheduling another appointment and the timetable to be followed should there be a delay. The counselor also should be sure that the person is familiar with any necessary procedures before leaving the agency (e.g., paying the bill, completing forms, scheduling another appointment).

THE EXTENDED INTAKE INTERVIEW

This section of the chapter will familiarize readers with the content and process of a typical extended intake interview, including the categories of inquiry and analysis that might be part of such an interview. Also provided are a transcript of an extended intake interview and an extended intake report based on the transcript. A subsequent section of this chapter will provide categories of inquiry and examples of brief intake reports.

An extended intake may require several hours of interview time. The interviewer has a multifaceted role: establishing rapport, asking appropriate questions, making effective interventions, and analyzing the entire process in a way that facilitates treatment. Such interviews often have both overt and covert agendas. The overt agenda involves gathering useful information on the nature of people's concerns and on relevant history. Most of the questions aimed at acquiring this material will be direct; their goals, apparent. At the same time, the counselor also is gathering information on clients' mental status. This process is more subtle and often involves using observational or inferential information rather than factual material provided by the clients.

Sometimes the interviewer will make use of checklists, inventories, or questionnaires to supplement, focus, and standardize the interview process. These might be comprehensive inventories designed to help the interviewer gather a broad range of information on a person's level of functioning, presenting problems, and history. Examples of this are the Schedule for Affective Disorders and Schizophrenia (Endicott & Spitzer, 1978) and the Diagnostic Interview Schedule (Robins, Helzer, Croughan, & Ratcliffe, 1981) for adults and the Diagnostic Interview for Children and Adolescents (Welner, Reich, Herjanic, Jung, & Armado, 1987) and the Kiddie-SADS (Puig-Antich & Chambers, 1978), used to assess Affective Disorders and Schizophrenia in school-aged children. Numerous specific questionnaires on such topics as fears, level of depression and anxiety, eating problems, and use of drugs and alcohol also are available to facilitate the interviewer's exploration of a particular aspect of a person's life. Whether such instruments are used depends on agency policy, counselor preference, and client concerns.

MENTAL STATUS EXAMINATION

The purpose of a mental status examination is to obtain information on how people function and present themselves to others. When drawing conclusions about the mental status of people, formal examination generally is not involved; intake interviewers rely heavily on their observations and their knowledge of normal functioning as well as on data provided by clients. However, checklists or specific questions can help insure counselors' accuracy. A mental status examination facilitates accurate diagnosis and effective treatment planning. In addition, managed care groups are increasingly requiring a mental status assessment as part of the documentation required for authorization of treatment.

Mental status can be conceptualized in terms of the following categories (Maxmen & Ward, 1995; Shea, 1990):

1. *Appearance*

   a. General impression?
   b. Nature and appropriateness of clothing?
   c. Cleanliness?
   d. Unusual physical characteristics?

2. *Behavior*

   a. Attitude toward counselor (e.g., eye contact, willingness to respond to questions)?
   b. Habits (e.g., smoking, rocking)?
   c. Movement retardation or agitation?
   d. Tremors or tics?
   e. Other unusual mannerisms?
   f. Apparent disabilities (e.g., visual, motor, auditory)?

3. *Speech*

   a. Articulation or communication difficulties?
   b. Speech pressured or slowed?
   c. Unusual or idiosyncratic speech or word usage?

4. *Emotions*

   a. Observable emotions, including affect and immediate as well as underlying, long-standing emotional states?
   b. Range of emotions?
   c. Appropriateness of emotions?
   d. Lability of mood?
   e. Flat or blunted affect?

5. *Orientation to reality*

   a. Aware of time (hour, day, month, year)?
   b. Aware of place (where interview is being conducted)?
   c. Aware of persons (who client and counselor are)?
   d. Aware of situation (what is happening)?

6. *Concentration and attention*

   a. Able to focus on stimuli? This category is sometimes assessed by asking people to repeat at least five digits (7,3,5,2,9) or repeat three words in reverse order (shoe, tree, ask).

b. Demonstrates ability to sustain attention? A classic test of concentration is asking a person to subtract 7's from 100 (e.g., 93, 86, etc.)

c. Alert and responsive, lethargic, or distracted?

7. *Thought processes*

   a. Capacity for abstract thinking? A measure of abstraction can be obtained by asking a person to explain several proverbs (e.g., The early bird catches the worm, strike while the iron is hot) or asking for similarities (e.g., how are an apple and a banana alike? how are a car and an airplane alike?)

   b. Flight of ideas or loose associations (skipping from one topic to another)?

   c. Repetitions or perseverations?

   d. Coherence and continuity in thoughts?

   e. Responses delayed, confused, or tangential?

8. *Thought content*

   a. Suicidal ideation?

   b. Violence, aggression, rage?

   c. Delusions?

   d. Obsessions or compulsions?

   e. Fears and phobias?

   f. Ideas of suspicion or persecution?

   g. Other prominent thoughts?

9. *Perception*

   a. Hallucinations (auditory, visual, other)?

   b. Other unusual sensory experiences?

10. *Memory*

    a. Adequacy of immediate memory (5–10 seconds)? This can be assessed by the measures of attention described in item 6 above and by immediate recall of interviewer's questions.

    b. Adequacy of short-term memory? This ability can be assessed by asking about information provided earlier by the interviewer or by asking the person to repeat three unrelated words after five minutes.

    c. Adequacy of long-term memory? Recent long-term memory can be assessed by asking about events in the past few days, weeks, or months. Remote long-term memory can be assessed by asking about the person's educational or occupational history or about historical events he or she would be expected to recall.

11. *Intelligence*

    a. Educational level?
    b. Adequacy of fund of information?
    c. Level of vocabulary?
    d. Overall intelligence?

12. *Judgment and insight*

    a. Decision-making ability?
    b. Problem-solving abilities?
    c. Awareness of nature of own problems?
    d. Impulsivity?
    e. Nature of self-image, including strengths and weaknesses?

This comprehensive outline of a mental status examination is much longer than a written mental status examination usually will be. Typically, a few paragraphs is sufficient to describe mental status. An example will be provided later in this chapter.

OUTLINE OF AN EXTENDED INTAKE INTERVIEW

The following is an outline of the categories of inquiry in a typical comprehensive intake interview. Suggested questions and topics are provided to help counselors conduct such an interview. Although this outline can be useful in providing a structure for in-depth interviews and in helping to ensure that important areas of inquiry are not omitted, this outline should be viewed as a guide. Each interview will be unique and the effective interviewer will conduct intake sessions with flexibility and sensitivity to the clients' needs. Questions and topics considered will be individualized to suit the concerns, age, functioning, and level of motivation of each client.

    I. *Identifying information*

        A. Gender
        B. Age
        C. Ethnic and cultural background, religion, native language
        D. Marital and family status
        E. Educational level
        F. Occupation

    G. Place and nature of residence and cohabitants
    H. Referral source

II. *Presenting problem:* This is a brief statement of the person's chief complaints and difficulties, the person's perceptions of what has brought him or her to seek treatment at the present time, and what kind of help is sought. The presenting problem may not coincide with the interviewer's assessment of a person's difficulties. People sometimes are not fully aware of what is really bothering them, have difficulty stating their concerns clearly, or may be using a less threatening presenting problem such as career uncertainty as a comfortable way of seeking help with a more highly charged or less socially acceptable concern such as marital infidelity or child abuse.

III. *Current problems and previous difficulties:* In this section of the interview, greater exploration of clients' difficulties is undertaken. Stated and implied concerns are explored, and the interviewer begins to formulate hypotheses about the nature and dynamics of those concerns. For all problem areas explored, interviewers should obtain information about:

    A. Nature of concern
    B. Circumstances and time of onset
    C. Accompanying symptoms
    D. History of concern (initial or recurrent, frequency, duration)
    E. Dynamics of concern (what seems to cause it to develop, change, or abate? What does the person do to modify it? How do close friends and family deal with the concern?)
    F. Previous treatment for concerns and effect of treatment
    G. Impact of concern on person's lifestyle, activities, relationships, eating, sleeping, mood

IV. *Present life situation*

    A. Family relationships, conflicts, and changes
    B. Other important interpersonal relationships
    C. Occupational/educational activities
    D. Social and leisure activities
    E. Living situation
    F. Sources of satisfaction
    G. Sources of stress
    H. Typical day in person's life

V. *Family:* Although this section might involve considerable history-taking, information should be gathered not for its own sake but rather to shed light on the dynamics of the person's current situation.

A. Background information

1. Social, economic, ethnic/cultural, and religious origins and influences
2. Genetic/historical patterns
3. Significant crises or episodes
4. Patterns of physical or emotional illness in family (of particular interest is a history of drug or alcohol abuse, depression, suicide, abuse, or violence)

B. Nature of family constellation

1. Composition of family
2. Power structure of family
3. Patterns of closeness and distance
4. Family values
5. Parenting and communication styles
6. Birth order and impact on client

C. Relationships with father, mother, siblings, partner, children, and other significant family members.

In discussing each of the above relationships, the following topics might be explored:

- How is that person perceived by the client?
- What is the nature of the current relationship with that person?
- What is the history of the relationship?
- What impact or influence has that person had on the client? What sort of role model has the person provided?

VI. *Developmental history:* In obtaining a developmental history, interviewers should be selective and focus on times of greatest relevance to the person's current situation. For example, little attention typically would be paid to infancy and early childhood in an interview with a 35-year-old person experiencing career dissatisfaction. However, understanding those early years might be very important in gaining insight into the dynamics of a fire-setting 8-year-old. The following outline of developmental history is, then, a comprehensive one, provided to give direction but intended to be used selectively. For each age group discussed, counselors should ask about important events, difficulties, and successes. Information can be obtained from parents or caretakers as well as from clients themselves.

A. Infancy

   1. Birth history

      a. What were the circumstances, ages, and health of the parents at the time of the birth?
      b. Were there medical complications or problems?
      c. Was the child wanted at that time?
      d. How did the parents seem to feel about the gender of the child?

   2. Early development

      a. What was the nature of early family relationships?
      b. Who cared for the child?
      c. How did feeding progress?
      d. How did toilet training progress?
      e. How did overall development progress (e.g., crawling, walking, speech, physical growth)?
      f. Were any significant health problems present?
      g. Was there any history of habit disorders, strong fears, problem behavior, abuse or neglect, family conflict?
      h. How was discipline provided?

B. Early childhood (preschool years)

   1. What were the child's living conditions like?
   2. What was the composition of the family?
   3. What were the child's roles and relationships in the family?
   4. What was the nature of the child's early social relationships outside the family?
   5. What was the child's personality like?

C. Middle and late childhood

   1. Describe the child's early educational history. When was school begun and how was it handled?
   2. How did the child relate to other children?
   3. How did the child get along with teachers?
   4. What subjects and activities did the child particularly enjoy or do well at?

5. What subjects and activities did the child particularly dislike or have difficulty with?
6. What changes, patterns, or problems were observed in the child's family relationships?
7. What behavioral problems, if any, were present?
8. Describe the child's sense of initiative, level of self-confidence, and capacity for accomplishment.
9. What were the child's personality and emotional development like during these years?

D. Adolescence

1. What was the timetable of physical maturation (e.g., growth, menstruation, appearance of facial and body hair)?
2. How did the person react to these changes?
3. Describe the person's peer relationships, especially close friendships. Was the person isolated or involved?
4. What patterns of sexual activity and interest were manifested?
5. How did the person deal with authority figures?
6. Describe the person's academic performance.
7. What social and leisure activities were preferred?
8. What were family relationships like?
9. What were the person's career aspirations?
10. What emotional or physical problems were presented?

E. Adulthood

1. Describe the person's strengths, accomplishments, and areas of difficulty.
2. What has the person's career history been like? (Consider sequence of jobs, successes and failures, special skills, work attitudes, level of responsibility, satisfaction, relationships with supervisors and coworkers.)
3. What are the person's current educational and occupational goals?
4. What are the person's leisure and cultural activities? How much time is spent on these?
5. Describe the client's social relationships. (Consider nature, number, duration, and intensity. What role does the person seem to assume in relationships?)
6. Describe the person's adult sexual development. How are sexual and interpersonal relationships intertwined? Is the person satisfied with his or her sexual involvements and activities?

7. Describe the nature and history of the person's close relationships. (Focus especially on quality of and disappointments in relationships).

8. Is the person married or in a committed relationship? If so, what is the relationship like? What are its rewards and difficulties? What is the chronology and developmental history of the relationship? If the person is not in a committed relationship, is this anticipated or hoped for? Why or why not?

9. If the person has children, what are their genders and ages? Are more children planned? How was the partner relationship affected by the children? What have the person's relationships been like with the children? What approach is taken to parenting?

10. Are there in-laws? What are the person's relationships with them?

11. How have the person's relationships with members of the family of origin developed in adulthood?

12. What is the person's current financial situation?

13. What are the person's religious and spiritual beliefs and values?

14. Does the person have a record of arrests, incarcerations, or lawsuits? What is their nature?

15. What use does the person currently make of drugs and alcohol? Any change in this pattern over the years?

16. Has the person ever felt abused or mistreated?

17. What are the person's primary sources of satisfaction?

18. What image does the person have of him or herself?

19. What goals or future dreams are important to the person? What does he or she think life will be like in 5 or 10 years?

VII. *Medical history*

A. What past and current illnesses and accidents of significance has the person experienced?

B. Is the person currently receiving medical treatment or medication? If so, what is its nature and purpose? Does it seem to have any side effects?

C. What past medical treatments has the person received?

D. Describe the nature of any hospitalizations.

E. Has the person received previous treatment for emotional difficulties? If so, for what difficulties, when, for what duration, and of what type? What impact did the treatment have on the person's complaints? What seemed to be most helpful? Why was treatment ended?

In the following pages, readers will be provided with a verbatim transcript of an extended interview, a report written on that interview, and two additional brief intake reports. The interview format roughly follows that presented in the preceding pages and illustrates how such an interview might be conducted and subsequently analyzed.

───────── TRANSCRIPT OF AN EXTENDED INTAKE INTERVIEW

The client is Vicki Ryan, a 21-year-old Caucasian female who sought counseling at a community mental health center.

Interviewer: What brings you in for counseling today, Vicki?

Vicki: Well, I flunked out of college, my parents kicked me out of the house, my life really is a mess. My mother said she would pay for counseling and I should get some help, so I called.

Interviewer: You sound very worried about what's happened. Tell me what led up to all this.

Vicki: My freshman year at college wasn't too bad. I passed everything with C's and D's. But things really seemed to go downhill the next year.

Interviewer: How do you explain the change?

Vicki: I got involved with this guy, Matt. First I thought things were really good. I'd never had a boyfriend before and he was good-looking and smart and he seemed to like me. But then he wanted me to do things I wasn't sure about.

Interviewer: Tell me about that.

Vicki: He and his friends would drink a lot and smoke pot. They were always partying, never studying. They all had an apartment off campus. All the guys had girlfriends and they would spend the night there and so I started staying over too. We'd stay up most of the night partying and be too wasted to get to class. I could just see my grades slipping away, but Matt would get real mad if I said I had to study or go back to the dorms.

Interviewer: How did you handle that?

Vicki: I tried to explain to him that I had to study some or I wouldn't pass my courses but...he would get real mad...a couple of times he hit me.

Interviewer: What kept you in that relationship?

Vicki: Most of time he was pretty nice to me. He would tell me how good I looked and how much he liked to be with me. Nobody else seemed interested in me. I guess he didn't really care about me, but I just didn't know what to do.

Interviewer: Sounds like you've been having a difficult time for a while now. What is your situation like right now?

Vicki: After I flunked out of college, I moved back in with my mother and stepfather, but my stepfather said I had wasted all his money and couldn't live in his house until I paid him back what he had spent on my college expenses. Mom didn't say much so I figured I'd better leave. I moved in with two of my girlfriends; they're letting me sleep in their living room, and I got a job at a fast food restaurant.

Interviewer: So you seem to be alright for the moment, but you need some help in sorting out what you've been through and getting yourself back on track. Are there other areas you think counseling might help you with?

Vicki: My relationship with my parents isn't too good. I guess I could use some help with that. And especially after what happened at college, I feel pretty bad about myself. Real discouraged. I don't seem to have the energy to do much.

Interviewer: So there are several areas we need to talk about besides the immediate problem. The way we usually work here is to start with a long interview, what's called an intake interview. In doing that, I'll be gathering a lot of information about your background, about what led up to this point, so we can understand as well as possible what is going on with you now and try to figure out how we can help you at this time. Then, if you and I agree that counseling might help you, I will arrange for you to start seeing one of our counselors. How does that sound to you?

Vicki: Sounds okay.

Interviewer: We'll certainly talk further about the difficulties you're having now, but I'd like to get some information about your background and what led up to this situation. That will give me a better understanding of what's going on. Let's start with your family, since that's another area of concern for you. Who are the important people in your family?

Vicki: Well, there's my mom and my dad. My parents were divorced about 15 years ago and I've been living with my mom since then. I don't see much of my dad. He works for an airline and is based in New York. He's always traveling. I get postcards every once in a while and he usually remembers to call on my birthday.

Interviewer: How often do you see him?

Vicki: Maybe once or twice a year.

Interviewer: Tell me some more about what your father is like and how you two have gotten along.

Vicki: You know, I feel like I don't really know him. I can't remember much from before the divorce, just a lot of yelling. Since then, it's mainly just postcards. He got remarried right after the divorce and has another family now. He just seems real busy and doesn't have much time for me.

Interviewer: How do you feel about that?

Vicki: I'd like it to be different. When I was younger, I had thoughts about going to New York and getting a job with the airline so I could be with him more, but that's silly. He's always nice to me when I see him, brings me presents and so on, but he doesn't know me either and doesn't know what to give me. Last year he sent me pearls for my birthday. Look at me. Can you just see me with my torn jeans, my Grateful Dead tee shirt, my nose ring, and my pearls?

Interviewer: I hear a wish to be closer to your father, but also a real distance between you.

Vicki: Yes. Now, my mom and I really used to be close. She would call me her little princess and we were just like best friends after she got divorced. We'd go shopping together and to the movies and really have fun. But I knew she wanted to get married again, and then she did.

Interviewer: Tell me about that.

Vicki: She married my stepfather when I was 8. She changed a lot then. She was pretty sad after the divorce, but she went out and got a job and started to have a career. She learned computers and got a good job, but she quit when she got married again. Now she just stays home. She plays bridge and paints and stuff like that. My stepfather doesn't want her to work and she does whatever he wants her to.

Interviewer: What is your stepfather like?

Vicki: He's always telling people what to do. We've had some problems.

Interviewer: Problems?

Vicki: I don't really want to talk about that right now.

Interviewer: Alright, maybe we'll get back to that later. Who else is in your family?

Vicki: I have two brothers. They're both a lot older than me. They're 30 and 34. They're both married, and Rick, the younger one, has two kids. We get along okay. Rick always tries to give me advice about guys. He's the one I'm closest to. They both went away to college and hardly ever came back home again. They're real successful; Jeff is a stockbroker and Rick is a lawyer. My dad tells me he's real proud of them. I guess my mom is too. You know, sometimes I think they didn't really want me, I think I was just an accident.

Interviewer: Sounds like you wish they'd tell you they were proud of you too.

Vicki: Yeah, but what is there to be proud of?

Interviewer: You're feeling pretty bad about yourself. Let's take a look back and see how long you've had those feelings. How about during your early childhood, when your parents were still married, what memories do you have of that period?

Vicki: Not too many. I remember my parents yelling at each other. First my dad would leave. Then my mom would ask my brothers to watch me and she would go after him. If my brothers weren't there, sometimes she would take me with her, driving around looking for my father, I think in bars or nightclubs. He would drink a lot...I think he still does. We had a nice house then, real big with a pool. After the divorce, we moved to an apartment, but my mom has her big house again.

Interviewer: Do you remember anything particular about your development or experiences during those early years that your parents might have told you?

Vicki: Mom said I was a difficult baby, much harder than my brothers. I think I had colic or something. Then, when I started to walk, she said I would follow her around everywhere, would hardly let her go to the bathroom alone. That's about all I know.

Interviewer: Sounds like those were difficult years for you and your family. How about when you were older, elementary school?

Vicki: I remember that real well. My dad left for good right before I started first grade and I remember crying for at least a week or so when I'd go to school. Things settled down after a while. I made some good girlfriends, got involved in sports. I was pretty good at soccer and swimming. I was sort of an average student, I did ok, didn't like it much. I never studied much; I could remember things real well and so I never had to study to get by. Mom was always trying to get me to take classes, dancing, piano, singing. I never liked any of it and eventually she stopped trying. I guess the hardest part was when my mom remarried.

Interviewer: What made that hard?

Vicki: My stepfather...he did some things to me.

Interviewer: I can see this is difficult for you to talk about, but it would help us know how to help you if you could talk about what happened.

Vicki: I don't want my mom to find out. I never told her. Is everything I say about this confidential?[1]

Interviewer: Yes, it is, unless you or anyone else is in any danger now.

---

[1] Some states require that child abuse be reported even if the survivor is no longer a minor, although that was not the case when and where this interview took place. Vicki was given complete written information on guidelines for confidentiality before the intake interview began.

Vicki: No, not anymore. He would come into my room at night and touch me. In places he shouldn't touch me. If I'd cry or tell him to go away, he'd say he was just showing his love for me. But then he'd tell me not to tell anyone or he would hurt me. Once I decided to tell my mom. I told her I wanted some time alone with her. I guess he figured out what I was going to do and he closed the car door on my hand. I broke a finger. He said it was just an accident and Mom believed him but I knew and figured I just better keep my mouth shut.

Interviewer: What a painful time that must have been for you!

Vicki: You better believe it. He stopped when I was about 12, but it went on for three years. I read a lot about kids who are sexually abused but my stepfather never made me have sex with him. Is what he did still sexual abuse?

Interviewer: Yes, it certainly is. How do you think that has affected you?

Vicki: Well, probably it has something to do with the problems I've had with guys. In high school, all my friends were starting to date and sometimes I even got asked out, but I just wasn't interested. All I wanted to do was sports. But then in college, living away from home, I felt real lonely. I didn't know anybody at first and so I started dating. Nobody special until I met Matt, but it's like I went from one extreme to another. I told you I had sex with him...he was the first. I hated it, but I knew I had to or he'd leave me. Now, I'm not interested again. If guys are like Matt or my stepfather, why bother?

Interviewer: You're pretty angry at the way these men have treated you.

Vicki: I sure am, but then I wonder why I couldn't make them stop. With Matt, I could just walk away and never come back, but I didn't.

Interviewer: Sounds like you're blaming yourself. Have you discussed this with anyone else or gotten any counseling before to help you?

Vicki: No. Except for my high school counselor helping me plan my program and find a college that would accept me, I never talked to a counselor before. I did talk with some of my girlfriends about Matt. Some of them said it was terrible and I should get rid of him, but then a couple of them told me that their boyfriends hit them too, so I thought, maybe that's just the way it is. I'd just drink a lot so I wouldn't think about it.

Interviewer: Tell me about your use of drugs and alcohol.

Vicki: It started in high school. Just pot and alcohol then and just on weekends at parties. Just a couple of beers or a couple of drags. Then my freshman year of college, not much at all. I dated some, but just these nerds. Most of the time I stayed by myself, I watched television, stared at my books. Then it started again when I met Matt. We would drink almost every day, lots, and drugs too. Usually just pot unless somebody had something else. Sometimes I didn't even know what I was taking.

Interviewer: How about now?

Vicki: Well, I don't have any money for drugs and I wouldn't want to do them anyhow. I still drink some.

Interviewer: Tell me about your drinking over the past week.

Vicki: Not all that much. I had three or four beers on Friday and Saturday. My roommates and I opened a big bottle of wine on Sunday and finished it off by Tuesday.

Interviewer: Let me shift gears for a while and ask you about some areas we haven't touched on much. I'd like to try to fill in some gaps. How about your health?

Vicki: I'm in pretty good health. Just the usual, strep throat, the flu, and so on over the years.

Interviewer: What medications have you taken?

Vicki: Just stuff for colds, aspirin. Oh, and I used to have asthma when I was real young but I'm ok now. I do worry about weighing too much but that's my only physical problem.

Interviewer: What is your height and weight?

Vicki: I'm 5'3" and weigh 122.

Interviewer: Any changes in your weight or eating lately?

Vicki: I've lost about 10 pounds in the past few months, without even trying. I don't seem to have much of an appetite.

Interviewer: How about your sleeping?

Vicki: Some changes there too. I have trouble falling asleep; it seems I just keep thinking and thinking about what a mess I'm in and what I should do.

Interviewer: Have you ever felt so bad you've thought about hurting yourself or killing yourself?

Vicki: Yeah, I guess so. When I was 9 or 10 and my stepfather started messing with me. And then when my stepfather said I had to move out. I felt pretty hopeless. But I would never really kill myself...I just thought about it...but not now.

Interviewer: So you're not in any danger now?

Vicki: No, definitely not.

Interviewer: Have you ever seen or heard things that other people didn't or that seemed strange?

Vicki: You mean like hearing voices or something? No, I never did.

Interviewer: Any legal problems or concerns?

Vicki: A couple of speeding tickets, but that's it.

Interviewer: What part has religion played in your life?

Vicki: Not much anymore. I was brought up Catholic, but my parents weren't very observant. My stepfather is Protestant, but he and my mom never go to church anymore. For a couple of months in college, I started going to church again. I thought it might help me. But it really didn't have anything to do with what I was going through and so I stopped. I guess I believe in God but I wouldn't really say I'm religious. One of my roommates calls herself a humanist; maybe that's what I am.

Interviewer: Religion seems to be an area that you're still trying to sort out. Tell me about your ethnic background.

Vicki: My great-grandparents came to the United States from Europe. I think most of them were Irish. They settled around Boston and we've been living in New England ever since. I really don't know much more about them. All my grandparents are still alive and I see my mother's parents often. My grandma Nancy was real good to me when I was little, and we're still pretty close. She likes to take me shopping and out to lunch.

Interviewer: So she's a special person in your life. How about jobs that you've had?

Vicki: Not much. My parents never wanted me to work while I was in high school. They said it would hurt my grades, and they gave me all the money I needed. The summer after high school I got a job in a fast food restaurant, mainly just to be with my friends who were working there. That's where I'm working now.

Interviewer: How do you feel about your job?

Vicki: It's a job. What can I say? I feel sort of like a robot when I'm there. Put the burgers on the grill, turn them over, put them on the buns, wrap them up, start all over. Doesn't take much brain power.

Interviewer: Not very rewarding for you. Have you thought about how you might change that?

Vicki: Not really. I just feel stuck. I flunked out of college. I have no money. What can I do?

Interviewer: You sound pretty hopeless. I hope counseling can help you find some ways to make your situation better. Just a few more questions. How about interests or activities you're involved in now?

Vicki: Not much. I work afternoons and evenings, come home, go to sleep, wake up, watch the talk shows in the morning, play with my cat, and go to work. What a life!

Interviewer: How would you like your life to be?

Vicki: Well, I'd like to have a decent place to live, maybe out in the country. I could imagine myself being a forest ranger or working on a farm, but that doesn't pay very well. I'd like to earn enough to buy a car, but I don't care about luxuries. I'd like to have a dog or two and lots of cats. Some good friends. A better relationship with my mother and father. Feel better about myself. Maybe a boyfriend, but he'd have to be very different from anyone I've ever dated.

Interviewer: You do have some ideas about what you would like your life to be like. The challenge now is to figure out how to get there.

Vicki: That's it, alright.

Interviewer: Well, you've told me a great deal about yourself today. Is there anything else you would like to add that you think I ought to know about you?

Vicki: No, I think you covered most of the important stuff.

The session now concludes by discussing the next step in counseling with Vicki, setting up an appointment for her to continue counseling with the interviewer or another counselor.

NATURE OF AN INTAKE REPORT

The report of an extended intake interview typically consists of the following information, illustrated in the report of the interview with Vicki later in this chapter:

1. Information on mental status
2. Summary and analysis of person's history and dynamics of current concerns
3. Conclusions and recommendations of the interviewer

The first two sections have been outlined in the previous pages. They may be organized and presented according to the format offered in this chapter, or the format may be varied to meet the needs of a particular client, interviewer, or agency. The third section contains the conclusions drawn by the intake interviewer and sets forth the treatment plan. That section might consist of the following categories:

A. Summary of data from consultants, records, referral sources
   1. Medical and psychiatric evaluations
   2. Psychological assessment
   3. Other available data
B. Diagnostic impression
   1. Person's strengths and weaknesses
   2. Concerns that call for therapeutic intervention
   3. DSM diagnosis
C. Treatment plan (See chapter 6 for additional details on this section.)
D. Prognosis

REPORT OF EXTENDED INTAKE INTERVIEW

Client: Vicki Ryan   *Interviewer:* Helen Goldberg, LPC
Birthdate: 2/3/74   *Date of interview:* 8/9/95

Identifying Information

Vicki Ryan, a 21-year-old single white female, sought counseling at the New England Community Mental Health Center at the suggestion of her mother. Ms. Ryan currently lives with two roommates and is employed at a fast-food restaurant.

Presenting Problem

During the past year, Ms. Ryan had been a sophomore at a state university located approximately 200 miles from her home. She reported that she had failed most of her courses during that year, apparently as a result of little studying, extensive involvement in social activities, and drug and alcohol use. Her boyfriend during that time had hit her on several occasions. Ms. Ryan stated that when she returned to live with her mother and stepfather, her stepfather told her she could not live with them until she repaid the money she had "wasted" through her poor academic performance. Reported symptoms included feelings of self-blame and discouragement, problems in eating and sleeping, and a lack of direction. Drug and alcohol use also seemed excessive. In addition, long-term family and relationship problems were presented, including sexual and physical abuse by her stepfather, little contact with her biological father, and a disappointing relationship with her mother.

Mental Status Examination

Ms. Ryan presented for the interview wearing clothes that were clean and suitable for the weather but that gave a strong message. She wore a Grateful Dead tee shirt, torn jeans, multiple earrings, and a gold stud in her nose. She had no unusual physical characteristics and seemed to be an appropriate weight for her height. She related well to this interviewer, made consistent eye contact except when discussing the abuse she had experienced, and manifested no unusual behaviors. Her speech sometimes seemed slowed, but Ms. Ryan generally was articulate and expressed herself clearly. She appeared depressed and reported some prior suicidal ideation as well as physiological signs of depression. Her affect varied little and was consistent with the serious topics she was discussing.

Ms. Ryan seemed in good contact with reality and manifested no difficulties in concentration, attention, or memory. Her thinking was clear and coherent and she was capable of some insight, though her judgment was sometimes flawed. She appeared to be of at least average intelligence, although her academic history raises questions about her learning abilities. She is experiencing low self-esteem and self-blame and does not have good problem-solving abilities. At the same time, she has many strengths; she is open and expressive, she is motivated to make changes, she has had some rewarding relationships over the years, and, at the moment, is in a safe situation.

Present Problems and Previous Difficulties

Ms. Ryan presented long-standing difficulties in mood, goals and direction, self-esteem, and family as well as other relationships. Particularly important are several years of sexual and physical abuse by her stepfather (e.g., fondling, threats, closing a car door on her hand) and depression around the time of her parents' divorce when she was about 5 years old. Her presenting concerns (depression, goals and direction, substance use, and relationships) seem related to her long-standing difficulties with males, her apparent sense of powerlessness and discouragement, and her lack of consistent support and caring relationships.

Present Life Situation

Ms. Ryan's depression as well as her stressful financial and family circumstances at present have led her to adopt a very restricted life style. Although she is employed and does not report work-related problems, her primary leisure activity seems to be watching television. She maintains some contact with her mother, a grandmother, and several women friends, but has few if any sources of pleasure at present.

Family

Ms. Ryan comes from an upper-middle class family, most of whom are Irish Catholic. Her biological father is an executive, employed by the airlines. Ms. Ryan expressed a wish for a closer relationship with him, but the two now seem all but estranged. Her relationship with her mother has been an inconsistent one, possibly enmeshed following the parents' divorce, but more distant since the mother's remarriage. Ms. Ryan does not view her mother as a good role model and spoke disparagingly of her mother's current marriage. Ms. Ryan reported good relationships with her two brothers, 9 and 13 years older than she, although those relationships, too, seem to be distant. The most troubling relationship is with her stepfather, who reportedly sexually and physically abused the client. She presented information that suggested alcohol abuse in her biological father and depression in her mother. Ms. Ryan speculated that she had been an "accident" and seems to see herself as an unwanted and unappreciated addition to her family.

Developmental History

With the important exceptions of her parents' divorce and remarriage and the reported abuse by her stepfather, Ms. Ryan reports a fairly uneventful developmental history. She was actively involved in sports, perhaps the only subject in the interview that sparked much enthusiasm. She described herself as an average student who studied little but performed satisfactorily because of a good memory. She apparently had girlfriends but did not begin to date until college. She became sexually active during her sophomore year but derived little enjoyment from that experience. Her sexual activities seemed to grow out of her wish to please her boyfriend and her difficulty in asserting her own needs. Her involvement in an emotionally and physically abusive relationship during college seems to echo her earlier abuse by her stepfather and her perception of her mother as doing almost anything to please her current husband.

Medical and Treatment History

Ms. Ryan reports a childhood history of asthma. Otherwise, she apparently is in good physical health. She has not had any significant medical treatments nor has she had previous counseling.

Risk Factors

Ms. Ryan presented several risk factors. She reported some suicidal ideation, although she maintained that she was not in danger of hurting herself. She seems to have made considerable use of drugs and alcohol during her last year of college and continues to consume alcohol in substantial amounts (e.g., several glasses of wine or beer per day over the weekend). In addition, her history of abuse raises concern that she will involve herself in another abusive relationship.

Diagnostic Impression

Although Ms. Ryan presently seems to be taking adequate care of herself and has housing and employment, her social and occupational functioning clearly seems impaired. She is struggling with depression, feelings of failure and self-blame, and a history of abuse and difficult family relationships. At the same time, she has many strengths: motivation to change, intelligence, communication skills, physical health, and a vision of a more positive future. She seems to be an appropriate candidate for counseling at present. A multiaxial assessment of Ms. Ryan follows:

Axis I.   296.32 Major Depressive Disorder, recurrent moderate
            304.80 Polysubstance Dependence, in partial remission
            300.4 Dysthymic Disorder, early onset (provisional)
Axis II.   V71.89 No diagnosis on Axis II
Axis III.   None
Axis IV.   Academic failure at college, family conflict, financial
            difficulty
Axis V.   52

The treatment plan for this case, which usually would be the last section of the intake report, is discussed later in this chapter as well as in chapter 7.

THE BRIEF INTAKE INTERVIEW

Many mental health agencies use a briefer approach to intake interviews. Such interviews typically last 30 to 50 minutes and culminate in a relatively short written report. This approach is particularly prevalent in agencies that are understaffed or advocate one of the brief, solution-focused, or strategic approaches to treatment, discussed in subsequent chapters.

The primary goals of the brief intake process are similar to those of the extended process. They commonly include the following:

1. Assessing and dealing with the urgency of the person's concerns
2. Gathering demographic data
3. Orienting the person to the policies and procedures of the agency as well as to the counseling process
4. Understanding the person's presenting problem and reasons for seeking help at the present time
5. Evaluating mental status
6. Obtaining information on the person's current situation
7. Gathering salient information on relevant history, especially previous treatment
8. Developing a diagnosis and treatment plan

In a brief intake interview, particular emphasis is placed on presenting concerns. The brief model assumes a less analytical approach, generally accepting the person's statement of his or her goals with only limited exploration. Far less attention is paid to history-taking and only minimal examination of underlying dynamics is undertaken.

Information Sheet

An intake interview, whether brief, extended, or in-between, often begins with the gathering of some factual information from the interviewee. Sometimes this information is obtained by a receptionist, clerical worker, or mental health aide rather than by the mental health professional who will be conducting the interview.

A sample of such an information sheet is provided here. It has been completed with data obtained from a person whose brief interview report will be presented in the following section.

Models of Brief Intake Interview Reports

Although the content areas of brief intake reports are fairly consistent, the formats used tend to vary from one agency to another. What follows are two brief intake reports, completed according to two different models. The first of these is based on an interview with Chanta Sok, the client whose data is provided on the information sheet. The second report is based on Vicki Ryan, the client whose extended interview and report were presented in the previous section.

INFORMATION SHEET FOR CHANTA SOK

NAME: Chanta Sok
ADDRESS: 452 Wayne Street, Arlington, Virginia
HOME PHONE: (703) 555-3854 WORK PHONE: (703) 555-8345
DATE OF BIRTH: 2/21/57
PLACE OF BIRTH: Cambodia
SEX (underline one) Male   Female AGE: 39
RACE: Asian
MARITAL STATUS: Widow
EDUCATION: Completed equivalent of eighth grade
OCCUPATION: Restaurant manager

SALARY: Varies—approximately $45,000 per year
REFERRAL SOURCE: Dr. Sareoum Kry, physician
Have you ever been seen at this Mental Health Center before? No
Have you ever received previous counseling? No
If YES, please give date last seen:
Have you ever been treated in a psychiatric hospital? No
Place of hospitalization
Date of hospitalization: from   to
Are you taking any medication? If YES, what?

INTAKE REPORT ON CHANTA SOK

Intake Interviewer: L. Dunn, Ph.D.
Date: 1/11/97

1. *Presenting symptoms*: About two weeks ago, Ms. Sok was in an automobile accident while riding in a taxi. The driver of the taxi was killed. Later that day, Ms. Sok became unable to see. No medical explanation could be found for her loss of vision.

2. *Mental status examination*: Ms. Sok was brought to the interview by her adult son. She was appropriately dressed and was oriented to time, place, person, and situation. No unusual behaviors were noted, and she seemed in good contact with reality. Ms. Sok manifested an extremely flat affect, with considerable depression in evidence. Although she had lived in Cambodia until 17 years ago, she spoke English well. However, her replies to the interviewer's questions were minimal and eliciting information was difficult. Gaps in memory were evident and, at her request, her son responded to many questions for her.

3. *Relevant history*: Ms. Sok was born in Cambodia. She was married at age 16 and has two children, a son, now 22, and a daughter, now 18. Early history is unremarkable until 17 years ago when, during a period of civil unrest, her father and husband, both government officials, were murdered. Ms. Sok had hidden herself and her children and was not physically harmed but saw the murder of her husband and father. A few months later, she left Cambodia and with the help of relatives moved to Arlington, Virginia, with her mother and children. Although she has established an apparently successful life for herself and her children, Ms. Sok stated that she has never gotten over the loss of her

husband and father and has frequent vivid images as well as night-mares of their murders.

4. *Present situation*: Ms. Sok owns a four-bedroom townhouse where she lives with her mother and two children. She has been employed in a restaurant for five years and now is manager of that restaurant. Her social contacts seem to be limited to family and friends from church; she stated that her long work hours prevent her from having any leisure time.

5. *Prior treatment*: Ms. Sok reported no previous psychotherapy and no significant medical complaints or treatments prior to her present loss of vision.

6. *Multiaxial assessment*:

Axis I.   300.11 Conversion Disorder, severe, with sensory deficit
          309.81 Posttraumatic Stress Disorder (provisional)
          Rule out 300.4 Dysthymic Disorder
Axis II. V71.09 No diagnosis on Axis II
Axis III. Blindness reported; no medical cause determined
Axis IV. Observed murder of husband and father, serious automobile accident in which driver was killed
Axis V.   Current: 50
          Highest: 75

Ms. Sok apparently is experiencing Posttraumatic Stress Disorder with underlying depression in response to witnessing the murder of her husband and father. The recent automobile accident seems to have exacerbated her symptoms and, because of its similarity to the trauma she experienced, pre-cipitated the blindness, perhaps a symbolic statement that she had seen too much to bear.

7. *Overview of treatment*: Individual counseling is recommended for Ms. Sok. She seems likely to benefit from a supportive counseling rela-tionship that gradually helps her to express the reactions she had to the accident and to recognize the connection between the present event and her earlier trauma. She will need help in dealing with the murders of her family members in order to develop her coping skills and help her deal with the present situation. In addition, she probably would benefit from some cognitive-behavioral interventions to alleviate her depression and increase her leisure and social activities. The support systems of her family and church may be used to accelerate achieve-ment of treatment goals.

BRIEF INTAKE REPORT FOR VICKI RYAN

Client: Vicki Ryan
Counselor: Helen Goldberg, L.P.C.
Date: 2/17/97

1. *Presenting symptoms and concerns*: Ms. Ryan, a 21-year-old white female, sought counseling after she had failed most of her courses during her sophomore year of college and was told she could not return to live with her mother and stepfather until she repaid the college tuition money she had "wasted." During her last year of college, she reportedly made excessive use of drugs and alcohol and was in a dysfunctional and abusive relationship with a boyfriend. Ms. Ryan reported feelings of depression and discouragement, self-blame, and low self-esteem. Some prior suicidal ideation was expressed, although the client did not seem to be in danger. Changes in eating and sleeping patterns also were reported.

2. *Mental status examination*: Ms. Ryan related well to this examiner. She seemed well-oriented to reality and manifested no unusual behaviors. Her communication skills were good, and she expressed herself clearly. Memory seemed intact, and intelligence appeared to be at least average. Affect seemed flat and depressed. Insight showed some impairment.

3. *Relevant history*: Ms. Ryan reported a history of troubled family relationships, including her parents' divorce about 15 years ago, overinvolvement with her mother after the divorce, and loss of closeness with her mother after her remarriage several years later. Particularly noteworthy is reported sexual and physical abuse of Ms. Ryan by her stepfather. She also is troubled by a distant relationship with her biological father.

4. *Present situation*: Ms. Ryan presently is living with two women friends and is employed at a fast food restaurant. She reported financial difficulty and seems to have few leisure activities.

5. *Prior treatment*: No significant medical or psychological treatment was reported.

6. *Multiaxial assessment*:

   Axis I.   296.32 Major Depressive Disorder, recurrent, moderate
              304.80 Polysubstance Dependence, in partial remission
              300.4 Dysthymic Disorder, early onset (provisional)
   Axis II.   V71.89 No diagnosis on Axis II

Axis III. None

Axis IV. Academic failure at college, family conflict, financial
difficulty

Axis V. 52

7. *Overview of treatment*: Ms. Ryan seems likely to benefit from weekly cognitive-behavioral counseling, emphasizing interventions designed to alleviate depression, reduce drug and alcohol use, and promote coping skills. Attention also will need to be paid to her experiences of abuse; she needs to understand the impact this has had on her and make better relationship choices in the future. Family dynamics and inter-actions with mother and biological and stepfathers also should be a focus of treatment. Individual counseling is recommended initially; however, once some progress has been made, this client seems likely to benefit from family counseling, involvement in a 12-step program, and participation in a support group for women who have been abused. She also needs career and leisure counseling. A psychiatric evaluation to determine her need for medication has been requested.

MAKING THE TRANSITION FROM INTAKE TO TREATMENT

An intake interview generally will culminate in the formulation of a diagnosis and a treatment plan as it has in this report. Detailed information on diagnosis is provided in chapter 3 and on treatment planning, in chapters 6 through 9. In some agencies, the intake interviewer has the responsibility for determining the diag-nosis and treatment plan, while in others this is accomplished through a case conference.

Case conferences are used by many agencies to make diagnosis and treatment planning a group process, presumably increasing accuracy because input from a number of people is obtained. The case conference also often serves as the vehicle for assigning clients to mental health therapists.

A typical case conference will be a regularly scheduled weekly meeting, perhaps 1–2 hours in duration, of all mental health workers in a particular agency or division of an agency. Each person who interviewed new clients that week will present the group with a brief summary of the history and concerns of that client and the interviewer's impressions of the client. Other staff will have an opportunity to ask questions of the interviewer, and then the group will collabo-rate to determine a diagnosis and treatment plan for the client. Typically, once those have been agreed upon, the case will be assigned to an appropriate mental health professional, taking account of the expertise of the staff members, their interest in particular types of clients and approaches to treatment, the treatment needs of the client, and the schedule constraints of both clients and staff members. Case conferences also can be used to help counselors with ongoing clients. More information on case conferences is presented in chapter 10.

The transition from intake interview to treatment may be affected by the presence of a waiting list or by the client's financial circumstances. If the agency maintains a waiting list, a determination must be made as to how long a particular person can comfortably delay treatment and what sorts of interim services or referral sources might be provided. This process can be facilitated by designating someone as the case manager or person responsible for ensuring the expeditious provision of services to a particular client. The delay of treatment can be a frustrating and disappointing experience for people, who often bring with them feelings of ambivalence and apprehension about seeking mental health services. People should be informed of the nature and expected duration of any delay and encouraged to maintain their commitment to treatment. Clients can easily fall by the wayside or be lost in the procedural intricacies of an agency; steps should be taken to prevent those outcomes.

Finances can present another potential roadblock to treatment. Some agencies have sliding fee schedules, based on clients' incomes, while others do not. Some mental health therapists are eligible to receive third-party payments while others are not. Some people have medical insurance that will pay all or part of the cost of treatment of emotional disorders while others do not have such coverage. Treatment planning must take account of costs and financial resources as well as other potential barriers to effective treatment and identify ways to provide people with the help they need as soon as possible.

The Nature and Importance of Treatment Planning

According to the *Diagnostic and Statistical Manual of Mental Disorders*, the initial or intake interview and the multiaxial assessment are the first two steps in effective counseling. Those steps provide counselors with the information they need for the third step, the development of a treatment plan.

"Treatment planning in counseling is the process of plotting out the counseling process so that both counselor and client have a road map that delineates how they will proceed from their point of origin (the client's presenting concerns and underlying difficulties) to their destination, alleviation of troubling and dysfunctional symptoms and patterns, and establishment of improved coping mechanisms and self-esteem" (Seligman, 1993, p. 288). Treatment planning plays many important roles in the counseling process:

1. A carefully developed treatment plan, well grounded in research on treatment effectiveness, provides assurance that counseling with a high likelihood of success is being provided.
2. Written treatment plans allow counselors to demonstrate accountability and effectiveness. Treatment plans, in combination with post-treatment evaluations, can substantiate the value of the work being done by a counselor or by an agency. They can assist counselors in obtaining funding for programs and in receiving third party payments and can provide a sound defense in the event of a malpractice suit.
3. Use of a treatment plan that specifies goals and procedures can help counselors and clients to track their progress. They can determine whether goals are being met as planned and, if not, can make appropriate revisions in the treatment plan.
4. Treatment plans also provide a sense of structure and direction to the counseling process. They can help counselors and clients to develop

shared and realistic expectations for that process and promote optimism that progress will be made.

This chapter will present a systematic and comprehensive model for treatment planning.

SUITABILITY FOR COUNSELING

Before counselors begin to develop a treatment plan to guide their work with a particular person, they must determine whether that person is likely to benefit from counseling. In order to assess this, counselors should look at three areas:

1. Level of person's motivation
2. Characteristics of the person
3. Nature of the problem

Motivation

People come to counseling from various referral sources and with varying degrees of motivation. Asking people, "What led you to seek counseling at the present time?" is a good place to begin to assess motivation. A reasonable estimate of the person's motivation generally can be made by examining the following:

1. Nature of referral
2. Urgency/magnitude of difficulty
3. Nature of precipitating event

Nature of Referral

People may seek counseling on their own initiative, at the suggestion of another person, or via a professional referral. Self-referred clients usually have taken a look at their lives and feel that some change is warranted; they have selected counseling as a way to achieve that change. Generally, people who are self-referred are motivated to participate in counseling, although they still may have unrealistic expectations for that process.

People sometimes are referred to counseling by their family or friends. This type of referral can take many forms. A positive example is the person who is motivated by another's success with counseling. Such a person might say to the counselor, "You seem to have helped my friend Ann when she was going through some rough times at work, and now she's a supervisor. I'm having trouble at work now and Ann said maybe you could help me, too." This person has some incentive to seek counseling but may not fully understand that process.

People who seek counseling largely because of pressure from another person may not be motivated to engage in counseling. An example of this is a client who wore his wife's clothes for sexual arousal. She was troubled by this behavior and insisted that he seek counseling. This man's motivation for counseling was questionable. He did not express an interest in change to please himself but, rather, because it had been demanded by his wife. Sometimes, however, people have difficulty taking responsibility for seeking counseling even though they want help; they may view counseling as an indication that something is wrong with them. Such people may really be self-motivated but may need the smoke screen of a referral as a temporary self-protection. On the other hand, these clients may resent the source of referral (e.g., the demanding spouse) and may transfer that resentment to the counselor. While other-referred clients may be excellent candidates for counseling, the counselor should take time to explore their expectations and strengthen their intrinsic motivation for counseling.

Motivation also may vary considerably among people who have been referred to counseling by another professional, such as a physician, minister, lawyer, or other therapist. Some of these clients may be highly motivated and may have been referred so they can obtain less expensive or more appropriate services. However, others may have been referred for compulsory counseling, perhaps as a condition of parole, and may be more resistant. Involuntary clients typically have more extrinsic than intrinsic motivation toward counseling and may manifest considerable resistance to the counseling process. Treatment planning with them must take account of the nature of their motivation. Short-term contracts and concrete, readily attainable goals generally should be established. Their progress should be assessed at regular intervals.

Urgency and Magnitude of Difficulties

The urgency and magnitude of a person's difficulties often provides valuable information on the nature and level of motivation, as does the nature of the event that led the person to seek counseling. However, urgency does not necessarily suggest high motivation. For example, Bettina, diagnosed with alcohol dependence, presented for counseling upon learning that she was pregnant. She had been told that her alcohol use could harm the fetus, so she viewed her concern as an urgent one. However, Bettina had little genuine interest in changing her lifestyle or examining her attitudes and behaviors; she refused to attend AA meetings and discontinued counseling after a few sessions.

A crisis does seem to make people more receptive to the counseling process but, of course, is not a guarantee they will be sufficiently motivated to persevere with counseling. All the crisis does is open the door to the counselor. Whether the counselor is allowed through that door depends on the skills of the counselor and the levels of motivation and discomfort of the client.

Counselors occasionally encounter people whose motivation is so low that they cannot be engaged in the counseling process. Such people may refuse to disclose more than identifying information, may be verbally abusive toward the counselor, or may misunderstand the nature of counseling. If efforts to clarify the nature of counseling, develop rapport, and help the person to identify some goals do not succeed, the counselor probably should suggest that counseling may not be appropriate at present. A referral for other services can be made or, if warranted, an appointment for a follow-up visit in a few weeks or months can be scheduled. These actions do not necessarily represent failure for either client or counselor but, simply, an acknowledgement that counseling is not the cure for all ills.

Characteristics of the Client

Most counseling modalities are aimed toward people who are not severely impaired in terms of their verbal and cognitive skills and who have a reasonable degree of organization in their lives. Such people are likely to keep scheduled appointments, to follow through on suggested tasks, and to engage in a dialogue about their concerns.

People without those characteristics tend to pose more of a challenge to the counselor and call for particularly careful treatment planning. Support systems may have to be enlisted to enable clients to keep scheduled appointments. Counseling sessions may have to be held in the client's home or in inpatient or day treatment facilities. Verbal tactics may have to be deemphasized while behavioral and teaching models are used extensively. The field of counseling today is sufficiently broad to accommodate the needs of people who are not the affluent, articulate, and self-disciplined clients so often depicted in early case studies. However, the person who has little intrinsic motivation toward counseling, who has difficulty keeping appointments, and whose verbal skills are well below average may benefit more from treatment modalities other than traditional counseling.

Nature of the Problem

In order for people to benefit from counseling, they must have concerns that are amenable to treatment by counseling. Categories of common concerns are:

1. Relationship and communication difficulties
2. Confusion about goals and direction
3. Poor or unclear self-image
4. Indecision
5. Troubling behaviors or habits
6. Depression or anxiety
7. Difficulty coping with a crisis or loss

Clearly, counseling is appropriate for a wide range of concerns. However, people sometimes present with goals or concerns that are outside the scope of the counseling process. Examples of these are:

1. People who really want to make someone else change
2. People seeking the counselor to be their friend or defender
3. People asking for information beyond the counselor's range of expertise (e.g., on financial affairs or divorce law)
4. People who want the counselor to force them to do something (e.g., lose weight)
5. People who are focused on persuading the counselor to take a particular point of view (e.g., to recommend that they be awarded disability payments after an accident)

Goals like these are not too far afield from the counseling process. For example, people who are seeking friendship through counseling can be encouraged to reflect on their social relationships and develop ways to form better friendships outside counseling. However, if the presenting concerns cannot be redefined through the counseling process, such people should be referred to other sources of help. Counselors should bear in mind, though, that people's presenting problems often are not what is really troubling them, and considerable effort should be channeled toward clarifying their underlying concerns before it is determined that counseling is not warranted.

Counseling as the primary treatment intervention also has a low probability of success with some manifestations of mental disorders. People with severe personality disorders and a history of treatment failures, people who unwaveringly externalize the source of their difficulties, people with oppositional and other problems who seem to derive gratification from showing the counselor to be ineffective, and people who are out of contact with reality typically make challenging clients. Although some of these people certainly would benefit from treatment, their motivation must be addressed before an effective treatment plan can be developed, and counseling should be combined with medication or other approaches to treatment.

Frances, Clarkin, and Perry (1984) concluded, "The findings of outcome research demonstrate psychotherapy to be, on the average, significantly more effective than no treatment" (p. 214). Sixty to 70% of people improve in response to counseling, and some of those who do not improve would probably have deteriorated further without help. Occasionally, however, no treatment or another treatment is the best recommendation.

MODEL FOR TREATMENT PLANNING

Few generally accepted models for treatment planning are available. However, the DO A CLIENT MAP, developed by this author (Seligman, 1990), has been adopted by many agencies and clinicians. The first letters of the 12 steps in this format for treatment planning form its name, serving as a mnemonic device. The purpose of the plan is, of course, to map out the counseling process for a given client. This format of treatment planning includes:

1. *D*iagnosis, according to the DSM
2. *O*bjectives of treatment
3. *A*ssessments
4. *C*linician
5. *L*ocation of treatment
6. *I*nterventions
7. *E*mphasis
8. *N*umber of people ("Nature" in the original version of the MAP)
9. *T*iming
10. *M*edication
11. *A*djunct services
12. *P*rognosis

Whatever format for treatment planning is followed, counselors will find that they must make decisions regarding the 12 elements in the MAP. The rest of this chapter will describe these elements in greater detail.

DIAGNOSIS

A multiaxial assessment or diagnosis, according to the DSM, is the first step in a treatment plan. The details of the plan stem from the information provided in the diagnosis of a person's mental disorders and conditions, physical conditions, stressors, and level of coping. Chapter 3 of this book provides guidelines for making a multiaxial assessment according to the DSM.

Early in the counseling process, either while determining the suitability of clients for treatment or shortly thereafter, counselors and clients should work on the formulation of objectives. Objectives or goals may change and evolve as counseling progresses, and new goals may replace old ones as gains are made. Nonetheless, objectives are necessary in order to develop a treatment plan, to assess progress, and to give direction to the counseling process.

Having a model of what it means to be psychologically healthy can help counselors gather information and establish objectives. Witmer and Sweeney (1992) identified five areas of optimal health and functioning:

1. *Spirituality*—a sense of inner peace, clear values, optimism, enjoyment of life, and direction.
2. *Self-regulation*—having self-worth and self-esteem, being physically fit and healthy, feeling resilient and in control of one's life, having creativity and problem-solving skills as well as a sense of humor, and being realistic, spontaneous, and intellectually stimulated.
3. *Work*—paid employment, volunteer activities, education, or home and family activities that afford people psychological, social, and economic benefits.
4. *Friendship*—having support systems and positive interpersonal relationships.
5. *Love*—having a long-term relationship that is mutually intimate, cooperative, trusting, and sharing.

Considering people's strengths and difficulties in these five areas can facilitate the determination of objectives that will promote healthy development. When formulating objectives, counselors should think not only in terms of ameliorating problems and pathology, but also should view people from preventive and developmental perspectives, seeking to help people establish more rewarding lives and master the skills they need to cope successfully with future difficulties.

Establishing objectives should be a mutual process, involving both clients and counselors. Sometimes counselors believe they know what would be best for clients and what their goals should be. However, shared goals are more likely to facilitate the counseling process and motivate the client. Counselors should begin the goal-setting process, then, by eliciting objectives from the client, rephrasing them if necessary, and writing them down. Some people have difficulty articulating goals. Counselors can facilitate that process by asking questions such as the following:

- What exactly are you like when you are experiencing this difficulty?
- Before you developed this problem, how did you feel and what was your life like?
- Suppose a miracle happened overnight, and when you woke up in the morning all these difficulties had been resolved. How would you know? What would be different? (deShazer, 1991).
- If you resolved this problem, what differences would other people notice? What would you be doing that you are not doing now?

Once the client's goals have been thoroughly explored, attention can shift to the counselor's objectives if they have not been brought up by the client. Counselors have the right to suggest goals to clients and even to make them a condition of treatment. For example, a counselor might say, "I know that your primary concern is the conflict you have had with your last three supervisors. However, that conflict seems related to the use you are making of alcohol. I don't think I can help you with your work problems unless we also try to change your use of alcohol. How would you feel about adding an objective related to reducing or eliminating your use of that substance?"

The identified objectives should be clear and measurable. Clients often express goals such as "feeling better about myself" and "getting along better with others." While such changes may well be made through the counseling process, they are vague objectives and are difficult to measure. Such objectives make developing a treatment plan and assessing progress very difficult. Consequently, counselors should work with people to determine, for example, exactly how they will know they are getting along better with others. Will they have fewer fights with colleagues, have lunch with friends more often, or have a longer list of people they would want to invite to a party? Regardless of the treatment modality used, goals should be defined as concretely as possible. Subjective self-report data (e.g., "I really do have more self-confidence these days.") are indicators of counseling progress. However, such feelings can be ephemeral and may not be solid building blocks in the counseling process. People seem to develop the soundest self-help skills and the greatest sense of their own competence and independence if they understand what they have done to effect positive changes in their lives and what the specific indications of those changes are.

Gintner (1995) delineated a five-step process to establishing objectives:

1. Describe the problem as specifically as possible.
   Example: Gets to work late most mornings.
2. Transform the problem into an objective by stating it as something that needs to be increased, decreased, or done differently.
   Example: Arrive at work by 9 a.m.

3. Make the objective measurable by stating it in terms of at least one of the following:

a. Frequency (e.g., changing the number of times a behavior is performed).

b. Intensity (e.g., reducing score on the Beck Depression Inventory to 20 or less).

c. Duration (e.g., spend at least 30 minutes in uninterrupted conversation with my husband).

d. Amount (e.g., write 10 pages per day).

4. Establish the criteria for achieving the objective.
Example: Increase time spent exercising to at least 30 minutes a day, four days a week.

5. Identify a time frame for achieving the objective.
Example: By the end of the month....

Phrasing objectives in quantifiable terms is optimal. However, sometimes the limited insight or experience of the client or the nature of the objective makes that difficult. In such circumstances, counselors can establish an informal rating scale for their client's use. For example, the counselor might say, "On a 1 to 10 scale, where would you say your self-esteem is now?...Where would you say it was before you became depressed?...Where would you realistically like it to be in three months?...In a year?" Most people have no difficulty using these rating scales, despite their unscientific nature, and they provide a useful vehicle for measuring change.

Counselors often think of objectives in terms of short-term, medium-term, and long-term. "Short-term" usually refers to objectives that can be accomplished in days or weeks; "medium-term," in weeks or months; and "long-term," in months or even years. Short-term objectives always should be developed, regardless of the anticipated duration of the counseling process. Short-term objectives, easily accomplished and evaluated, provide both counselors and clients with a sense of progress, optimism, and reinforcement. Examples of short-term goals are calling to obtain information on the high school equivalency test, initiating communication with a family member, or reducing consumption of ice cream to twice a week.

Medium- and long-term objectives guide the overall direction of the counseling process. Examples of medium-term goals are remaining alcohol-free for three months, identifying and applying to four colleges that are consistent with a person's academic and career interests, and beginning a home business. Long-term objectives would only be developed if long-term counseling is anticipated or if client and counselor understand that those are goals that will be pursued after the completion of counseling. Long-term goals might include completing a college degree, confronting a parent who abused the client many years earlier, and obtaining a more rewarding job.

ASSESSMENT

In order for counselors to establish objectives that are clear and realistic, they must have a good understanding of the nature and possible causes of their clients' difficulties. If the intake interview does not provide that understanding, counselors probably will want to add an assessment component to their treatment plan. Assessment may be done by the counselor, by another mental health professional, or by a specialist in another field.

Counselors can use inventories of abilities, personality, interests, and values to assess their clients. Other mental health professionals can use tools that may not be available to counselors. For example, the psychologist can administer a battery of projective tests, the school psychologist can determine intellectual and learning abilities, and the psychiatrist can assess whether neurological impairment is present. Detailed information on assessment tools used by counselors and other mental health professionals is presented in chapter 4 of this book. Assessment also may be provided by other professionals, with physicians being an especially important source of information. For example, they can help counselors determine whether a sexual dysfunction or an anxiety symptom has a medical basis, whether someone diagnosed with Anorexia Nervosa is in danger, or whether a child is growing at an appropriate rate. Assessment can provide information not otherwise available to counselors and can serve as a double-check on the counselor's own interpretation of a problem. Adding an assessment component to a treatment plan can increase the likelihood of determining interventions that are likely to be successful.

CLINICIAN

According to Sexton and Whiston (1991, p. 343), "...the ability of the individual counselor can have a major impact on the process and outcome that exceeds the impact made by any technique or approach." Herman (1993) agreed, stating, "...nonspecific factors such as therapist personal characteristics may be the primary determinants of successful outcome" (p. 29) and "...the quality of the therapeutic bond has a significant impact on therapy outcome" (p. 30). Evidence is accumulating that counselors' personal and professional qualities can have a profound impact on the nature and effectiveness of the counseling process, regardless of the counselor's theoretical orientation.

Counselor qualities associated with a positive outcome include communication of empathy and concern, involvement in the counseling relationship, credibility as perceived by the client, and communication of positive regard and warmth (Sexton & Whiston, 1991). Effective counselors typically assume a collaborative rather than an authoritarian stance in relation to their clients, prepare clients for the part they will play in the counseling process, and encourage active client involvement, a problem-solving attitude, and a sense of appropriate responsibility for their difficulties. Effective counselors communicate genuineness, respect, and immediacy. They are interested in and committed to their profession and view their clients as being capable, trustworthy, dependable, adequate, and friendly (Terry, Burden, & Pedersen, 1991). These counselors pay attention to the development of a working alliance and take the time to establish mutually agreed upon objectives with their clients. Clients who anticipate positive and realistic outcomes from counseling and whose expectations are congruent with those of their counselors are more likely to achieve those outcomes (Beutler, Crago, & Arizmendi, 1986).

Corey, Corey, and Callanan (1988) identified 10 personal characteristics that all counselors should strive for. These include goodwill, the ability to be present for others, recognition and acceptance of personal power, an individual counseling style, willingness to be open and vulnerable, self-respect, willingness to serve as role-models for others, ability to take risks and admit mistakes, an orientation toward personal and professional growth, and a sense of humor.

Part of treatment planning is identifying a suitable counselor for a client. Many variables should be considered when matching counselor and client, in addition to the characteristics mentioned above. Experience, of course, is an important counselor variable. Once the diagnosis or the mode of treatment has been determined, whether potential counselors have the necessary skills and experience must be ascertained. If, for example, a person seeks marital counseling from a counselor who is not skilled in that process, the counselor should refer the person to another counselor, if indeed marital counseling seems warranted.

A related but perhaps more difficult issue is that of the counselor's comfort. Although it is important for counselors to maintain a strong measure of objectivity and generally to refrain from imposing their own values on their clients, counselors will inevitably have feelings toward their clients and their behaviors. These reactions often are strongly colored by the counselors' own backgrounds and experiences. When these reactions bear little relation to the reality of the clients' behaviors but are more a reflection of the counselors' inner experiences, the reactions are termed "countertransference." An example is the counselor who was severely punished for lateness as a child and who becomes extremely angry with a client who is 10 minutes late. Other counselor reactions may be more grounded in objective reality. For example, many counselors would feel angry and upset when a client describes an incident in which he sexually abused his 6-year-old daughter.

Neither countertransference reactions nor other emotional reactions to clients are, in themselves, problems or grounds for referral. However, counselors should attend to and seek to understand their own feelings. Strong emotional reactions to clients, especially of a countertransference nature, perhaps should prompt counselors to seek further supervision or some counseling for themselves. Especially if more than a few counseling sessions have taken place, efforts should be made to avoid referring a client due to the counselor's emotional reactions, since that action might be perceived by the client as a rejection and could be countertherapeutic. Only in extreme circumstances should a referral be made because the counselor's affective reactions to a person prevent the development of a positive counseling relationship.

Counselors occasionally are aware in advance that they are likely to be emotionally uncomfortable working with a particular person. An example might be the counselor who does not want to counsel people considering abortions because he is morally opposed to abortion or the counselor who has been raped who fears that her anger will interfere with her work with a person who has been convicted of rape. In such cases, the counselors' supervisors can be made aware of those constraints, and the clients can be channelled unobtrusively to other counselors. However, counselors in mental health agencies may have little opportunity to choose their clients. In general, counselors should try to deal with their biases and work through negative reactions so that they can counsel a broad range of clients.

Research suggests that personal qualities of the counselor, discussed earlier, are likely to be more important than demographic variables. Nevertheless, the impact of demographic counselor variables also should be considered during treatment planning. Age, gender, and ethnic and cultural background of the counselor are probably the most important of these, although others, such as the counselor's marital status, whether he or she is a parent, or religious preference also can affect the counseling process. Few clear answers are available as to how clients and counselors should be matched with respect to demographic variables (Pietrofesa, Hoffman, & Splete, 1984). In assessing these variables, particular notice should be taken of:

1. Great disparities between counselor and client—a 65-year-old client, adjusting to retirement, may have some difficulty accepting help from a 25-year-old counselor.

2. Great similarities between counselor and client—a client who is having difficulty coping with the pressures of becoming a single parent may overidentify with or become envious of a counselor who also has recently become a single parent.
3. Strong feelings on the part of the client toward particular groups—a client who has always assumed a passive role in relation to women may have difficulty engaging in a productive counseling relationship with a female counselor.

Of course, these are only hypothetical examples; very different reactions may ensue. The 65-year-old retiree may find that the youthful counselor sharpens his awareness of the breadth of his life experiences, leading to increased self-confidence. The single parent may benefit from the empathy and support he receives from the counselor in similar circumstances. The client who has had difficulty relating to women may learn a new way to interact with women through a female counselor. There is no precise way to predict the impact of demographic variables on the nature of the counselor–client relationship. However, counselors should still attend to such variables and draw on their insight and clinical skills as well as client preferences to effect productive counselor–client matches and to handle the impact of such variables on the counselor–client relationship.

LOCATION

Determining the type of counseling agency or practice best able to help a particular person is another important step in treatment planning. Whether treatment should be provided in an outpatient setting, at a day treatment center, or in an inpatient (residential or hospital) facility can be determined by examining the following variables:

1. Nature, severity, progression, and duration of symptoms
2. Threat to self or others
3. Nature and effectiveness of previous treatment
4. Cost effectiveness
5. Support systems and living situation
6. Preferences of client and significant others
7. Likelihood of client keeping outpatient appointments
8. Overall objective of treatment (e.g., symptom removal, rehabilitation, maintenance)
9. Person's catchment area or geographic location
10. Insurance coverage and financial resources

Counselors should pay particular attention to the level of supervision and the frequency of treatment needed by the person.

People should be seen for counseling in the least restrictive environment that can provide them the safety and services they need. This means that a person with Paranoid Schizophrenia and homicidal ideation clearly should not be treated in most private practices, while the person with an Adjustment Disorder with mild depressive features probably is ideally suited for treatment in a private practice. Determining location of treatment may be unnecessary if the client already has sought out an appropriate counseling facility. However, if this has not happened, a referral may be indicated.

INTERVENTIONS

Intervention is really the heart of the treatment plan. Here clinicians specify exactly what they will do to accomplish the objectives that have been determined. The interventions section of a treatment plan has two parts. First, clinicians indicate the theoretical framework that will guide their work with a particular person. Ten theoretical models of counseling (cognitive, behavioral, reality, person-centered, psychodynamic, rational emotive behavior therapy, Adlerian, integrated, and eclectic) are discussed in detail in the next chapter, while others are briefly reviewed. Although some situations call for a relatively pure theoretical approach, counseling is more likely to involve an eclectic or integrated approach. If so, the treatment plan should specify the nature of that approach. For example, the counselor might plan to begin with a person-centered approach to build rapport and strengthen self-esteem, then shift to a cognitive-behavioral approach to mobilize the person and reduce dysfunctional thinking, and finally shift to a psychodynamic approach to promote understanding of underlying concerns and patterns in order to build coping mechanisms and reduce the likelihood of a recurrence.

In the second part of the Interventions section of the treatment plan, counselors list the specific techniques they will use, such as *in vivo* desensitization, imagery, discussion of earliest memories, or assertiveness training, to accomplish their objectives. Each specific technique usually is linked to the objective each is designed to accomplish. Techniques associated with the major theoretical approaches to counseling are reviewed in the next chapter.

Considerable research through the 1980s and 1990s has focused on the area of differential therapeutics, seeking to determine which models of counseling are most effective and under what circumstances they are most likely to be effective. Overall, research has found little difference between approaches in terms of outcome (Altekruse & Sexton, 1995). Counseling effectiveness can best be explained by factors common to many approaches and by the skill and personal style of the counselor (Sexton & Whiston, 1991). Research also has indicated that treatment focused on insight and exploration of client's emotions, traditionally viewed as essential ingredients of counseling, does not bear a significant relationship to outcome and therefore is not always a required part of counseling.

Although research on counseling effectiveness does not support the validity of a prescriptive approach, in which certain interventions always are indicated for treating a particular mental disorder, research does provide some guidelines as to what is likely to be effective and what is not. The following section organizes most of the mental disorders and conditions described in the DSM into seven broad categories, listed roughly in order of prognosis, along with treatment recommendations for each category.

1. *Problems of Adjustment and Life Circumstance*—This section includes the Adjustment Disorders and the conditions that are not mental disorders, such as Bereavement, Occupational Problem, or Phase of Life Problem, listed in the DSM. These difficulties are very common; approximately 10% of adults and 32% of adolescents will experience an Adjustment Disorder (Maxmen & Ward, 1995). People with these difficulties typically are reacting to a particular situation, a specific stressor (e.g., divorce, relocation, loss) or a circumstance (e.g., retirement, career dissatisfaction). They need help in gaining a clear and realistic perspective on their situation, perhaps via reading and information gathering; emotional support to give them the strength to address their difficulties; and identification, development, and mobilization of coping mechanisms they can bring to bear in dealing with the present concerns. Problems in this category typically respond very well to short-term counseling following a crisis intervention model. Treatment may even promote personal growth.

2. *Behavioral Disorders*—Included in this category are those disorders that are characterized by problems in habits, behaviors, or impulses, such as Substance Use Disorders, Sexual Dysfunctions, Paraphilias, Conduct and Oppositional Defiant Disorders, Attention Deficit Disorders, Eating Disorders, Sleep Disorders, and Impulse Control Disorders (e.g., Pyromania, Kleptomania, Pathological Gambling, and Trichotillomania). People with these disorders typically manifest a cycle of dysfunction in which they have a build-up of tension and a craving for some harmful activity. The tension is eventually released through the activity, and then a quiescent or regretful period may follow until the tension starts to build again.

Treatment of these disorders will be primarily behavioral in nature, using such techniques as goal setting, contracting, stress management, and response prevention. Peer support groups such as Rational Recovery or Overeaters Anonymous as well as group counseling are important additions to treatment; the role models offered by the group members can promote development of coping mechanisms and provide reinforcement. Family counseling and education are other important ingredients in treatment of these disorders. Some of these disorders, such as the Eating and Sleep Disorders, often benefit from medication as well as counseling. Although most people with these disorders respond positively to treatment, relapse is common and must be addressed in treatment.

3. *Mood Disorders*—Included in this group are Major Depressive Disorder, Dysthymic Disorder, Bipolar Disorder I and II, Cyclothymic Disorder, and Depressive Disorder NOS. Major Depressive Disorder may be the disorder most often treated in both inpatient and outpatient mental health settings. Depression, a feature of most of the disorders in this section, has been shown to respond well to both cognitive-behavioral therapy and interpersonal psychotherapy, a form of psychodynamic psychotherapy. Psychotropic medication is nearly always combined with counseling in the treatment of Bipolar I and II Disorders and Major Depressive Disorder and also may be used for the other Mood Disorders. Interventions that encourage physical activity, experiences that provide pleasure and promote feelings of competence, and self-help opportunities are especially useful in ameliorating depression. Suicidal ideation often accompanies depression and must be addressed in treatment. People with these disorders, like people with the disorders in the previous group, typically respond well to treatment but have a high likelihood of relapse.

4. *Anxiety Disorders*—Anxiety Disorders are characterized by a combination of worry, fear, and apprehension along with physical manifestations of the anxiety, such as avoidance, withdrawal, fatigue, and muscle tension. In a one-year period, approximately 12.6% of the population will experience an Anxiety Disorder (Maxmen & Ward, 1995). This category includes such disorders as the Phobias (Specific, Social, and Agoraphobia), Panic Disorder, Obsessive-Compulsive Disorder, Acute Stress Disorder, Posttraumatic Stress Disorder, Generalized Anxiety Disorder, and Separation Anxiety Disorder. These disorders usually respond well to cognitive-behavioral interventions, particularly relaxation and desensitization. Supportive interventions can enhance the impact of the cognitive-behavioral interventions by

encouraging people to deal with their fears. Disorders triggered by a traumatic experience typically benefit from group counseling with people who have undergone similar experiences, while Obsessive-Compulsive Disorder almost always requires medication in addition to counseling.

5. *Disorders That Combine Physical and Psychological Complaints*—Included in this category are the Somatoform Disorders, the Factitious Disorders, and a broad range of Mental Disorders Due to a General Medical Condition. Counselors should work collaboratively with physicians in the treatment of these disorders. The physicians must determine whether a medical condition is present and what treatment it requires. Typically, people with these mental disorders focus on their physical complaints and neglect other areas of their lives. The body often becomes their vehicle for self-expression. Counseling can help by increasing socialization and activity levels in these people and by facilitating their awareness and verbalization of their feelings. Secondary gains of the physical complaints need to be identified and possibly reduced. Techniques such as relaxation and pain management also can be useful. A combination of person-centered/supportive counseling and cognitive-behavioral counseling, then, usually is indicated for these disorders. Disorders in this group, particularly Factitious Disorder, often are treatment-resistant and may require lengthy and intensive treatment.

6. *Personality Disorders*—These deeply ingrained and long-standing disorders may cause less impairment than some of the Mood, Anxiety, Somatoform, and Impulse Control Disorders but typically are more treatment-resistant. Personality Disorders are very common and are present in approximately 15% of the general population and 30–50% of clinical populations (Gunderson, 1988). Treatment of Personality Disorders can be very lengthy, often three to five years (Millon, 1981). At the same time, people with Personality Disorders tend to want rapid assistance with their difficulties and usually do not have a great deal of insight or intrinsic motivation to make changes. In light of this conflict, treatment of these disorders tends to be most successful when it has two phases. In phase one, active, directive, and structured approaches such as cognitive and behavioral counseling predominate, focused on ameliorating the person's presenting concerns. Once some progress has been made, and if the person is willing to engage in long term treatment (often not the case for these clients), psychodynamic interventions can be combined with the cognitive-behavioral ones to help the person address long-standing concerns and patterns as well

as underlying problems. Specific interventions will vary, depending on which Personality Disorder is diagnosed; for example, people with Schizoid Personality Disorders usually need help with assertiveness, communication, and socialization while people with Histrionic Personality Disorders need help in developing insight, making sound decisions, and managing their emotions.

7. *Cognitive, Psychotic, and Dissociative Disorders*—People with these disorders typically have difficulty maintaining a clear sense of reality. They may have memory loss, confusion and disorientation, or delusions and hallucinations. The primary treatment for people with Cognitive or Psychotic Disorders usually is medication. However, supportive counseling that promotes adjustment and maximizes functioning can be very helpful as well. Dissociative Disorders vary considerably as do their treatment; people with Depersonalization Disorders may need only some help in reducing anxiety while people with Dissociative Identity Disorders typically need long-term psychodynamic psychotherapy.

EMPHASIS

Once counselors have determined the theoretical model and perhaps also the interventions they will use in treating a particular person, they will need to determine how that approach will be adapted to the needs and personality of that client. Counselors can consider the following dimensions in deciding how they will individualize their counseling or what aspects of a given approach they will emphasize:

1. *Level of directiveness and structure*—People who respond best to a counseling approach that is active, structured, and directive usually are those who are not very comfortable with verbal interaction or self-disclosure, who may have limited motivation and insight, and who have concerns that are urgent and behavioral in nature. On the other hand, people who are self-motivated, insightful, and functioning fairly well but who are prone to self-doubts and low self-esteem seem to respond better to approaches that rely more on the client to give direction to the session.

2. *Level of support and confrontation*—Confrontation may sound like a threatening process, but it simply entails calling people's attention to discrepancies. An example of a gentle confrontation is, "I'm confused by what you are saying. Earlier in the session, you talked about how

tight finances were and how you were trying to save money to buy a house; now you are telling me that you are planning a costly wedding in an elegant hotel. Help me understand how all this information fits together." In general, people who are both resistant to counseling and fairly resilient are good candidates for confrontation, while people who are fragile or in poor contact with reality might benefit more from a supportive approach.

3. *Level of exploration*—Exploratory counseling encourages people to look beyond their presenting concerns and may focus on the antecedents of those concerns, earlier difficulties, dysfunctional and recurrent patterns, and family dynamics. While presenting concerns certainly will not be ignored, efforts will be made to understand them from a holistic or lifelong perspective. This process may entail loosening some defenses, raising clients' anxiety levels, and opening up some concerns that previously had been suppressed, denied, or avoided. People who are suitable for an exploratory emphasis in counseling should have the emotional resources necessary to take a close look at their developmental concerns and life patterns. Ideally, they should have the time and motivation to engage in counseling that goes beyond their presenting concerns and should have an interest in personal growth. People who do not fit these profiles may benefit more from counseling that strengthens their existing defenses and maintains a present-oriented focus.

All of these dimensions are on a continuum; counselors should think not in terms of whether they should be confrontational or supportive but, rather, where on the continuum ranging from very confrontational to very supportive they should focus their counseling with a particular person. Counselors also should keep in mind that all these variables are likely to shift during the counseling process. A person in crisis may require a strong dose of supportive counseling, but, once the crisis has been resolved, that same person may benefit from exploring the impact that early family dynamics have had on his/her development and so may move into a more exploratory counseling relationship.

NUMBER OF PEOPLE

Another aspect of treatment planning is determining how many people and which people will be involved in the counseling process. Three broad categories are reviewed in answering this question: individual counseling, group counseling, and family counseling.

Individual counseling is the most common form of treatment. Almost any concern that is amenable to counseling can be treated through individual counseling. Sometimes it is used because it seems more likely to help the person than would group or family counseling. For example, the person may be extremely shy and anxious, very angry and hostile, in poor contact with reality, or coping with an urgent crisis. People such as these are more likely to benefit from individual counseling, at least initially. Individual counseling may also be the method of choice for pragmatic reasons. An appropriate group may not be available or the client's family may refuse to attend counseling sessions. In cases such as these, counselors can use techniques that bring some of the advantages of group or family counseling into the one-to-one counseling session. Role playing or use of the empty-chair technique can help people to deal with family or other interpersonal issues in individual counseling. Counselors can view clients through a family dynamics perspective even though family members may not be present. Homework assignments, focusing on client interaction with others, can further broaden the scope of individual counseling.

Group counseling, like individual counseling, can be employed for both therapeutic and pragmatic reasons. Some counseling agencies rely heavily on group counseling because it allows them to provide services to more clients than they could help through individual counseling. While group counseling probably is better than no counseling at all for most clients, group counseling should not be thought of as simply a more efficient approach to counseling than individual treatment. Group counseling is particularly suited for some concerns and is contraindicated for others.

On a superficial level, people with interpersonal difficulties seem likely to benefit from group counseling. However, participation in a counseling group does require at least a minimal level of confidence and communication skills. It also can be a more stressful and anxiety-producing situation than individual counseling, at least until the group has developed a supportive and cohesive environment. Consequently, people who have severe depression or anxiety, have very weak interpersonal skills, or are in crisis probably should not be placed in group counseling until their symptoms have been somewhat reduced. However, for the reasonably well-functioning person who could benefit from practice in communication skills and who is confident enough to benefit from peer feedback, group counseling can be very effective in improving socialization skills and helping clients become more aware of how others react to them.

Counseling groups also can help people feel less alone and can help them learn from the insights and efforts of others in similar situations. Such groups also can be very supportive to fragile or emotionally damaged clients. Homogeneous counseling and support groups have been formed for people in marital or career transitions, for people who have been abused, and for people with life-threatening illnesses, to cite just a few. Disorders involving problem behaviors such as Substance Use Disorders, Eating Disorders, and Intermittent Explosive Disorder, as well as disorders that develop in response to a trauma (Acute Stress Disorder and Posttraumatic Stress Disorder) also are likely to benefit from group counseling. Additional information on group counseling is presented in chapter 9.

Even if group counseling is not the primary mode of treatment, it can be a valuable source of additional help for some people. Such people might be in individual and group counseling concurrently or might be referred to a counseling or support group after some progress has been made through individual counseling. Alternatively, group counseling might be recommended to deal with one aspect of a person's concerns while individual or family counseling is used for other aspects. However, the realities of the counseling situation should be considered. Many people cannot afford the money or time required to participate in several modes of treatment simultaneously. Similarly, many agencies, especially those of a nonprofit nature, do not have the resources to supply people with both group and individual counseling. Again, treatment planning will need to be pragmatic as well as therapeutic.

Family counseling has been growing in importance as a mode of treatment. Approaches to family counseling are considered further in chapter 8. Some counselors believe that nearly all difficulties stem from family dynamics and prefer to see an entire family together for counseling whenever possible. Other counselors use family counseling more selectively. When planning the treatment, counselors should consider the relevance of the person's family background and circumstances to the presenting problems, the willingness of the person to involve family members in counseling, and the proximity and reported motivation of those family members. Family counseling probably should be included in the treatment plan of most disorders involving children and adolescents, Substance Use Disorders, and severe Psychotic and Cognitive Disorders to help families cope more effectively with those disorders. The cost-effectiveness of family treatment should also be considered as well as the severity of disturbance in the family and the interrelationship of members' symptoms. Interrelated symptoms typically indicate that family treatment would be useful. If all of these considerations suggest that family counseling is warranted, counselors then should consider who should be present (e.g., spouse, children, siblings, parents, grandparents). Type of family counseling also must be determined.

Family counseling, like group counseling, can be combined with other modes of treatment. A common pattern is for a person to be seen for a few sessions of individual counseling followed by some joint sessions with a spouse or parent and then by the resumption of individual treatment once the counselor has gathered information on family dynamics and helped to improve family interaction and communication. Although family counseling may be the most effective mode of treatment in some cases, it is possible to effect changes in a family by working with an individual, especially if a counselor is adept at assuming a family dynamics perspective regardless of who is present at the counseling session.

TIMING

Many decisions enter into planning the timing of the counseling process. Counselors must decide the length of the counseling sessions, their spacing and frequency, their approximate number, and whether counseling will be time-limited. Pacing and sequencing of the counseling process also may be considered as part of timing. Timing is determined by the interaction of several factors: the motivation of the client, the diagnosis, the objectives, and constraints such as the person's financial circumstances or the limits imposed by managed care on the number of sessions.

Length of Sessions

Traditionally, counseling sessions are 45 or 50 minutes in length. However, sometimes reasons exist for deviating from that time frame. Children and people with significant cognitive or intellectual deficits may feel more comfortable with shorter sessions, while families sometimes need longer sessions in order to give everyone an opportunity to air their concerns.

Frequency of Counseling

People usually are seen for counseling once a week. However, here, too, reasons exist for change. People who are in crisis, who present a danger to themselves or others, or who are experiencing severe symptoms often need to be seen more frequently. On the other hand, people who have made significant progress and are moving toward completing counseling may shift to bi-monthly or monthly sessions as a comfortable way to leave counseling. Intermittent treatment sometimes is used for people with chronic concerns to help them maintain their stability and monitor their functioning.

Duration of Counseling

Although usually counselors cannot determine exactly how many sessions people will require to meet their objectives, counselors should have an idea of the anticipated duration of the counseling process. Crisis intervention, the briefest form of counseling, is designed for people with immediate concerns, often accompanied by a high level of disruption. A man whose wife was killed in an accident, leaving him with three young children and feeling suicidal and overwhelmed, or an adolescent who was raped and has been unwilling to return to school are examples. Short-term counseling generally has been regarded as involving 8–20 sessions (Maxmen & Ward, 1995). However, an increasing emphasis on brief counseling from managed care, understaffed agencies, and clinicians themselves has led to a decline in the number of sessions usually considered short-term counseling. Short-term counseling is commonly indicated when an otherwise well-functioning person presents a relatively circumscribed concern. The widowed father described above, for example, might become a candidate for short-term counseling once he has dealt with his crisis; short-term counseling might help him to grieve the death of his wife, improve his parenting skills, resume a social life as a single person, and redefine his future goals.

Short-term counseling also may be indicated for a person with limited motivation who has multiple long-standing problems. An example is a 52-year-old woman who presented concerns about her mother. The daughter sought counseling for help in deciding whether to place her mother in a nursing home and in coping with her guilt and anger toward her family who was insisting that the aged mother had become too great a burden for them. During counseling, the counselor learned that the woman was experiencing considerable marital strain and had been feeling some depression and lack of direction since her youngest child entered college. However, she was not motivated to look at these issues at present, but only wanted help with her concerns about her mother. (She returned for career and marital counseling a year later.)

Medium-term counseling, defined roughly as longer than 20 sessions but shorter than 50 sessions, often is needed for people with two or more coexisting mental disorders, with long-standing or severe symptoms, or with the more serious Axis I disorders. However, counselors should bear in mind that most of the progress, during counseling, seems to occur by the 8th session, and after six months of treatment, almost 75% of the ultimate change has occurred (Altekruse & Sexton, 1995). Justification needs to be provided for mediium or long-term counseling.

Long-term counseling is becoming increasingly unusual, although extended treatment of some disorders, such as Personality Disorders or Dissociative Identity Disorders, still is indicated. Counselors should be cautious about recommending long-term counseling. It can tax a person's finances and schedule and may lead to undesirable dependency on the counselor. Counselors should be sure that long-term counseling really is the best treatment for the person. According to Frances and his colleagues (1984, p. 170), "Most studies fail to demonstrate a significant advantage of longer treatment."

Clients sometimes ask how long counseling will take. The experienced counselor probably can offer the person a general idea of how long it usually takes to deal effectively with the sorts of concerns the person presents. Questions about duration typically reflect some apprehensions about counseling, and these should be explored. If the question reflects a reluctance to make a significant commitment of time and energy to counseling, the counselor might suggest that the person agree to a predetermined number of sessions, after which the counseling would be reevaluated. Time-limited counseling can focus and intensify the process and can contribute to treatment effectiveness.

Flexibility and change are in order in determining duration, and counselors may find that crisis intervention can turn into medium-term counseling while motivational changes may halt plans for long-term counseling. Frequency of contact also is difficult to predict and should be determined by client needs and progress throughout the course of counseling.

Pacing and Sequencing

Treatment plans should take account of people's readiness for change and be paced accordingly. A gentle, gradual approach to counseling might be used with a fearful, fragile person with few support systems, while a more rapid approach to change might be adopted with a usually well-functioning person in a situational crisis. The sequence of treatment elements is another aspect of counseling, closely linked to pacing of treatment. A fragile client may first be seen in individual counseling and then, when confidence has grown, be placed in a counseling group to improve social skills. A more stable client might be able to tolerate concurrent career and family counseling. Pacing and sequencing, then, also should be considered in treatment planning.

MEDICATION

Medication sometimes is prescribed to people in counseling to help them overcome debilitating anxiety, depression, mood swings, panic attacks, psychosis or other severe symptoms. Although counselors are not qualified to prescribe medication, the following reasons indicate why it is important for counselors to be knowledgeable about the types and effects of drugs that are commonly used to treat emotional disorders:

1. Clients may already be taking prescribed medication. Knowledge of that medication, its purpose and side effects, can provide counselors with important information about the person's condition. It also can

give the counselor an idea of how the person functioned before taking medication and what the person might be like without it.

2. By knowing what medication can and cannot do for people, counselors can judge when to refer a person to a psychiatrist for medication.

3. Counselors typically see clients more frequently than a collaborating psychiatrist who prescribes medication for those clients. Consequently, the counselors are in a better position to monitor treatment compliance and the effectiveness of the medication and to suggest another visit to the psychiatrist if the medication does not seem to be helping.

4. Similarly, counselors are likely to learn before a consulting psychiatrist of a change in a client's medical condition, such as a pregnancy or the diagnosis of a physical illness. Such information should prompt a strong recommendation from the counselor that the client taking medication contact the psychiatrist immediately.

5. In addition, clients may not be as open with a psychiatrist, seen for brief monthly medication sessions, as they are with a counselor whom they see weekly. For example, a person who is abusing alcohol may not disclose that to a psychiatrist, but may share this information with the counselor. Some drugs, such as the benzodiazepines, can be fatal if combined with alcohol. The well-informed counselor can remind the client of any dangers associated with the medication being taken and can ensure that the psychiatrist has full information on the person's condition.

6. Medication brings many benefits but also can cause a wide range of sometimes serious and occasionally lethal side effects. Common side effects include anxiety, appetite changes, bowel changes, breast enlargement, breathing difficulty, cardiovascular changes (heart rate, blood pressure), confusion, depression, dizziness, drowsiness, facial grimaces, faintness, gastrointestinal upset, hair loss, headaches, impaired coordination, jaundice, light sensitivity, memory impairment, menstrual irregularities, mouth dryness, muscle spasms and tremors, nausea, nightmares, pains, panic, perspiration, rashes, restlessness, ringing in ears, sexual difficulties, sleep disturbance, slurred speech, tingling sensations, tongue changes, urinary changes, visual abnormalities, weakness, and weight change.

When clients take medication, counselors may have difficulty determining whether symptoms are caused by emotional factors or are side effects of the medication. Side effects also can be confusing and upsetting to clients. Some side effects, such as hair loss, sexual dysfunction, and weight changes, can have an adverse impact on people's self-images and their interpersonal relationships, while others, such as confusion, heartbeat irregularities, and pain, can be frightening and dangerous. Counselors should be aware of the potential side effects of commonly prescribed medications and should consult with physicians, with the client's permission, when possible side effects are reported.

A brief overview of the major categories of psychotropic medication is presented here. Additional information can be obtained from the annual compendium of pharmaceuticals and biologicals, the *Physicians' Desk Reference,* available at nearly every medical facility in the United States. Briefer references, such as *The Pill Book, The Complete Guide to Drugs* and *The Essential Guide to Prescription Drugs* are updated regularly and also can be useful and convenient references.

The following are the major categories of medication commonly used to treat mental disorders and their symptoms:

1. *Benzodiazepine/Anti-anxiety medication*—These include Librium, Valium, Xanax (Alprazolam), Ativan, Klonopin, BuSpar, Serax, and others. They are prescribed to reduce anxiety, panic attacks, and insomnia; can facilitate withdrawal from drugs or alcohol; enhance the effect of antipsychotic medication; and serve as muscle relaxants (Bender, 1990). However, these drugs have addictive properties and can be lethal when combined, in excess, with alcohol. More judicious use is being made of these medications, but they are still frequently prescribed.

2. *Lithium*—Lithium is highly effective in the treatment of Bipolar Disorders. It seems to act by controlling the acute manic episodes and reducing the severity of the depression. Lithium also can be effective in ameliorating the symptoms of Cyclothymic Disorder, recurrent Major Depressive Disorder, and Schizoaffective Disorder. Although 80–90% of people with Bipolar Disorders show significant improvement in response to Lithium, they may need to be maintained on the drug for many years and require regular blood tests because the medication can upset the electrolyte balance.

3. *Heterocyclic Antidepressants*—Examples of this category of medication include Elavil (Amitriptyline), Tofranil (Imipramine), Norpramin (Desipramine), Pamelor (Nortriptyline), and Anafranil (Clomipramine). They are particularly useful for people experiencing Major Depressive Disorders (especially those accompanied by Melancholia) and Panic Disorders but also are used to treat Enuresis, Posttraumatic Stress Disorder and a variety of other disorders. Clomipramine has been found effective in treating Obsessive-Compulsive Disorder and Trichotillomania. The onset of the effect of these drugs typically

requires 10 to 14 days. Four to six weeks may be needed for the full impact of the drug to be felt, so rapid improvement should not be anticipated. Weight gain and several other side effects frequently are associated with this category of medication. An overdose of tricyclic antidepressants can be fatal, so they should be prescribed cautiously for people experiencing confusion or suicidal ideation.

4. *Monoamine Oxidase Inhibitors* (MAOIs)—A second category of antidepressant medication, MAOIs, includes Marplan, Nardil, and Parnate. They, too, require several weeks to take effect and are used in the treatment of such symptoms as depression, panic attacks, anxiety, phobias, obsessional thinking, hypochondriasis, and depersonalization. MAOIs seem to be particularly effective in the treatment of depression accompanied by one or more of the above symptoms. The ingestion of certain foods (e.g., ripened cheese, beer, wine, and yeast) or use of nasal decongestants in combination with these drugs can cause an adverse reaction.

5. *Serotonin Selective Reuptake Inhibitors* (SSRIs)—This group of medications is newer than the above groups and seems to be growing in use despite some controversy surrounding their impact. Examples of this category of medication include Prozac (Fluoxetine), Paxil, and Zoloft. These seem to have fewer side effects than earlier medications and are effective in treatment of depression and associated difficulties such as Eating Disorders and Somatoform Disorders (Maxmen & Ward, 1995).

6. *Antipsychotic Medication*—This category includes the phenothiazines, such as Thorazine, Prolixin, Mellaril, and Stelazine, and the non-phenothiazines, such as Clozaril (Clozapine) and Haldol (Haloperidol). These medications are used primarily to reduce psychotic symptoms and to prevent relapse of Schizophrenia and other Psychotic Disorders. Some have other important uses; Haldol, for example, is used to treat Tourette's Disorder, and several of these drugs can ameliorate the symptoms of Pervasive Developmental Disorders or severe Cognitive Disorders. These medications can cause anticholinergic side effects such as dry mouth and constipation. Medications such as Artane and Cogentin may be combined with antipsychotic medication to address these side effects. Long-term use of some of these medications can lead to Tardive Dyskinesia, characterized by such symptoms as facial grimacing and tongue protrusion. One of the newest antipsychotic medications, Risperdal (Risperidone), is drawing considerable attention because it seems to have fewer side effects than other antipsychotic drugs.

7. *Barbiturates*—These drugs, including Amytal, Nembutal, and Seconal, produce prompt and sustained sedation. They often are given to people to relax them prior to surgery and are effective in reducing insomnia and anxiety. However, the use of these drugs is limited because they are readily addictive, have many side effects, and can be lethal if an overdose is taken. They also can cause drowsiness and may interfere with driving. Nonbarbiturate sedatives also are available such as Placidyl and Quaalude. Both their effects and their dangers are similar to those of barbiturates.

8. *Other medical treatments*—Wellbutrin and Effexor are other antidepressant medications that show promise because of their relatively minimal side effects and strong impact on depression. Carbamazepine (Tegretol) is used to treat mood instability and explosiveness, especially if Lithium has been ineffective and if the mood changes are related to temporal lobe epilepsy or a manic episode. Methadone and Naltrexone are used to help people who have been dependent on narcotics. Naltrexone may also be helpful to people who are diagnosed with alcohol dependence. Disulfiram or Antabuse is another medication that has been used in treatment of alcohol abuse or dependence. Ritalin (Methylphenidate) and Cylert are often used to treat Attention-Deficit/Hyperactivity Disorders.

Although not a form of medication, electroconvulsive therapy (ECT) is sometimes recommended by psychiatrists and may be helpful when medication and counseling have not been successful. ECT has received a great deal of negative publicity, and some counselors are surprised to learn that it is still being used. ECT works quickly and is at least as effective as antidepressant medication in relieving acute depressions, especially those characterized by melancholia. However, ECT can cause temporary or permanent memory impairment, is more costly and less convenient than medication, and often results in only short-lived improvement (Frances et al., 1984). Consequently, ECT should almost always be accompanied by other forms of treatment and generally is used only after other treatment approaches have failed.

Research has found that a blend of counseling and medication is often superior to either alone (Frances et al., 1984). Counselors and their clients should not construe a need for medication as an indication that counseling has failed. Rather, a referral for medication is one more tool that counselors can include in their treatment plans to enhance their effectiveness.

Counselors should not specify particular medications in their plans but should leave that decision up to the psychiatrists. The treatment plans should indicate only whether or not a referral for a medication evaluation is needed.

That decision will be based primarily on the nature and severity of a person's symptoms. If a medication evaluation is indicated, counselors should obtain written permission from the client to confer with a psychiatrist and should refer the person to a psychiatrist with whom they have a collaborative relationship. The following indicates the probable need for a medication referral and can guide counselors in deciding whether to include such a referral in a treatment plan:

- *Always*—Psychotic Disorders, Tourette's Disorder, Cognitive Disorders, Bipolar I and II Disorders, Obsessive-Compulsive Disorder, Substance-Related Disorders, Pervasive Developmental Disorders, Mental Disorders Due to a Medical Condition.
- *Almost always*—Major Depressive Disorder.
- *Usually*—Attention-Deficit/Hyperactivity Disorder, Eating Disorders, Cyclothymic Disorder, Sleep Disorders, Panic Disorders.
- *Sometimes*—Substance Use Disorders, Mental Retardation, Conduct Disorder, Anxiety Disorders, Somatoform Disorders, Dissociative Disorders, Factitious Disorders, Sexual and Gender Identity Disorders, Impulse Control Disorders, Personality Disorders.
- *Rarely*—Adjustment Disorders, Learning Disorders, Oppositional Defiant Disorder, Other Conditions that are not mental disorders.

Of course, people with some of these disorders such as Factitious and Somatoform Disorders probably will already have on-going contact with physicians. Even if psychotropic medication is not indicated, counselors should confer with these physicians with the client's permission.

ADJUNCT SERVICES

Most clients benefit from adjunct services, sources of help, support, and information that are outside of the counseling relationship. These can enhance and contribute to the effectiveness of counseling and help people make progress toward their goals between counseling sessions.

The nature and provision of adjunct services should be determined in the course of treatment planning. The counselor's plan to use adjunct services should address the following questions:

1. *When* should the adjunct services be provided? For example, should they begin immediately or not until some improvement has been made in a person's mood?
2. *What adjunct services* should be recommended? Typically, the counselor will suggest not only the type of adjunct services that are needed but also sources for these services.

3. *What connection* will be maintained between the counselor and the provider of the adjunct services? Will the counselor simply give the person the name of an agency or service provider without follow-up? Will the counselor follow up at a distance by occasionally inquiring about the person's involvement with and reactions to the adjunct services? Or will the counselor contact directly the providers of adjunct services so that they can work as partners in implementing the person's treatment plan? Clients who are fearful, fragile, confused, resistant, or in poor control of their impulses typically will require considerable support in their efforts to obtain adjunct services. A close connection between a counselor and the provider of adjunct services also is indicated if the services are closely related to the counseling process (e.g., career counseling, assertiveness training) rather than representing other disciplines (e.g., tutoring, speech therapy).

4. *Who* will oversee the treatment plan? One of the pitfalls of a multifaceted treatment plan is the lack of clarity surrounding the question of who will oversee, coordinate, and take responsibility for the implementation of that treatment plan. Designation of a primary counselor or case manager should be done soon after an intake interview is completed.

5. What will be the *sequence* of the adjunct services? Sometimes several adjunct services are recommended as part of a treatment plan. To be most effective, the plan should specify whether the services should be sequential (e.g., communication skills training should precede a person's involvement in a social organization), concurrent (e.g., exercise class and a weight control program), or determined by client preference and availability of services.

The needs of the client, the philosophy of counseling and preferred style of the counselor, and the parameters of the setting where treatment is being provided all determine the choice of adjunct services that are most likely to be helpful to the person and how they are used. The following is a list of frequently used adjunct services that can be incorporated into a treatment plan.

1. *Skill development*—tutoring, study skills, assertiveness training, parenting, job-seeking skills, academic courses.

2. *Focused counseling*—career counseling, art therapy, biofeedback, sex therapy.

3. *Personal growth*—values clarification, relationship enhancement, image-building.

4. *Peer support groups*—twelve-step programs such as Alcoholics Anonymous and Overeaters Anonymous, Rational Recovery, support

groups for people with severe illnesses or disabilities, men's or women's support groups, Tough Love.

5. *Alternate care or living arrangements*—halfway houses, group homes, low-income housing, day treatment centers, foster homes, shelters for the homeless, homemaking services, facilities providing nursing care or rehabilitation.

6. *Professional services*—physical examinations, gynecologists and urologists, other specialized physicians, legal assistance, financial planning, accounting, divorce mediation, acupuncture, employment agencies.

7. *Other health-related services*—weight-control programs, exercise classes, physical rehabilitation, meditation.

8. *Organizations for socialization and leisure activities*—social clubs, organized sports activities, special interest groups (e.g., bridge clubs, gardening clubs), cultural societies or groups, religious or spiritual organizations, nature-oriented activities (e.g., Sierra Club, hiking or biking groups), Parents Without Partners, professional associations.

9. *Governmental services*—aid to dependent children, food stamps, Social Security, unemployment compensation, subsidized housing.

The nature of most of the preceding services is self-evident. Counselors will encounter additional services through experience. Knowledge of the communities in which they work and the typical needs and resources of people in those communities should enable counselors to seek out and select appropriate adjunct services for their clients.

PROGNOSIS

Prognosis is the last piece of the treatment plan. It indicates what the likelihood is of accomplishing the objectives that have been listed in the treatment plan according to the methods listed in the plan. Prognosis is determined by many factors including the natural course of a particular mental disorder, the presence of coexisting disorders, the highest level of functioning of the client, the duration and severity of the disorder, the pattern of onset of the disorder (acute disorders typically have a better prognosis), the client's age at onset (later usually is better), the availability of social supports and adjunct services, the nature of the treatment plan, the skill and experience of the counselor, and the client's expectations and compliance with treatment. Approximately 65% of clients make positive changes as a result of counseling (Altekruse & Sexton, 1995). Usually these changes are enduring. However, 6–7% of clients deteriorate during counseling

(Sexton & Whiston, 1991). Adjustment Disorders, Depressive Disorders, and Anxiety Disorders typically have a positive prognosis while the outlook for helping people with Personality Disorders, Schizophrenia, Eating Disorders, Substance Dependence, Factitious, and Gender Identity Disorders is not as positive.

Terminology used to describe prognosis includes excellent, very good, good, fair, poor, and guarded. For people with multiple diagnoses, the prognosis may differ for each of the disorders. Counselors should strive to develop a treatment plan that is likely to have an optimistic prognosis. This involves identifying realistic objectives as well as interventions that have proven their value.

Chapters 7, 8, and 9 provide additional information on theories and techniques of individual, family, and group counseling to facilitate the treatment planning process. Sample treatment plans can be found in each of those chapters for counselors to use as models to guide their treatment planning.

Theories and Techniques of Individual Counseling

Counseling is effective! Study after study has arrived at conclusions similar to that of Sexton and Whiston (1991, p. 345): "…while some clients do improve on their own, in comparison, those in counseling improved more and at a faster rate…." By 1980, clinicians had clearly established that their work was effective. They then turned their attention to determining why it worked, when it worked, and what they could do to make it work better.

This area of inquiry was launched by the 1980 study of Smith, Glass, and Miller. They used meta-analysis to summarize the results of all controlled studies they could locate on psychotherapy outcome, a total of 475 studies. The results indicated that psychotherapy was effective and that the two year relapse rate was small. However, when Smith, Glass, and Miller tried to draw more specific conclusions about effectiveness, their findings were limited. They did discover clear evidence that cognitive, cognitive-behavioral, and behavioral interventions were highly effective with a broad range of disorders. The psychodynamic approaches were nearly as effective in treating social, career, and academic concerns; fear and anxiety; Somatoform Disorders; and antisocial and addictive disorders. The humanistic and developmental approaches did not receive the same support; however, far less research was available to assess those approaches.

Research since the Smith, Glass, and Miller study has sought to provide more definitive information on treatment effectiveness. However, that endeavor has been a challenging one for several reasons. The outcome of counseling depends not only on the treatment that is provided but on existing factors in the client, the counselor, and the setting, and on their interaction during the therapeutic process. In addition, over 400 separate schools of psychotherapy have been identified (Lazarus & Beutler, 1993).

This complex situation makes it unlikely that one theoretical model will emerge as superior. Nevertheless, counseling should not be a haphazard process. Prochaska and Norcross (1994) observed that the following processes of change permeated most approaches to counseling: feedback, education, corrective emotional experiences, stimulus control, self- and social-liberation, counterconditioning, reevaluation, and contingency management. Nearly all counseling approaches also provide information on human functioning, on how problems arise, on interventions, and on desired outcome (Hershenson, 1993). Gilliland, James, and Bowman (1989) found that most counseling approaches followed a common pattern of treatment: problem exploration; problem definition, including exploration of affective, cognitive, physical, and behavioral aspects; identification of alternatives; planning; action and commitment to change; assessment and feedback. Most theoretical models of counseling, then, have an underlying similarity.

The challenge for counselors is not to find the one perfect approach to counseling, but to develop a sound treatment plan that matches treatment to disorder and client. As Sexton (1995, p. 56) put it, "...a counselor's overall approach is not important, but the match of the specific technique with the presenting concern of the client may be important." In other words, clinical protocol is more important than general theoretical approach. "It is...the skillfulness of the counselor that is the most significant factor...A skilled counselor who skillfully applies techniques that focus clients on their presenting concerns, and who uses various techniques matched with clients' presenting concerns, will be effective regardless of [his or her] theoretical perspective" (Sexton, 1995, p. 57).

Reflecting this conclusion, increasing numbers of counselors are gravitating toward eclectic and integrated models. McWhirter and McWhirter (1991, p. 74) provided a useful definition of eclecticism: "Eclecticism means to select methods or doctrines from various sources or systems." It is not "...an indiscriminate and arbitrary collection of scraps and pieces" but rather draws specific concepts and techniques from identified sources, implements them in unified ways, and integrates them via the style and personality of the counselor.

Altekruse (1995) reported that 40.2% of mental health counselors surveyed described their theoretical orientation as eclectic. Specific orientations reported by the counselors who were surveyed included cognitive-behavioral and rational emotive therapy, 17.4%; humanistic/existential/person-centered, 11.7%; Adlerian, 6%; psychoanalytic, 5.7%; developmental, 4.3%; reality therapy, 3.2%; transactional analysis, 2.5%; gestalt, 1.4%; and other, 7.5%.

Whether counselors identify themselves as eclectic or affiliate with one of the specific approaches to counseling, effective counselors now need to have knowledge of and facility with a broad range of approaches and interventions.

Although research has not yet provided recipes for the treatment of each disorder and client (and probably never will), most counseling approaches seem to work better with certain types of people or concerns than they do with others. This chapter will consider the major approaches to individual counseling in relation to diagnosis and treatment planning. (The major approaches to group and family counseling are considered in later chapters.) This book assumes that readers possess some familiarity with the salient theories of counseling. Consequently, although a review of the essential ingredients of these approaches will be provided, the intent of this book is not to teach theories of counseling. Neither is it the intent to encourage counselors to become chameleonlike and adopt a different approach to counseling for every person they see. Most counselors develop their own counseling styles that they are understandably unwilling or unable to modify radically. However, counselors can shift their styles within broad parameters, can borrow from a variety of counseling approaches, and can develop ways of relating to and helping each person that is uniquely suited to that person's needs. The purpose of the next three chapters is to provide counselors some guidelines for accomplishing that. In this chapter, models of individual counseling will be described and their application to Vicki Ryan, presented in chapter 5, will be discussed.

PERSON-CENTERED COUNSELING

Person-centered counseling, formerly known as self-theory, client-centered counseling, non-directive counseling, or relationship theory, is an approach to counseling originated by Carl Rogers in the 1940s. It has continued to evolve, becoming more eclectic and advocating a more active role for counselors (Gilliland et al., 1989). Although the general acceptance of this model seems to have declined in recent years, it has had a profound impact on the field of counseling, providing the basis for many, more recent counseling approaches.

Description of Approach

The overriding principle of this approach is the idea that if the counselor can provide clients with a genuine relationship in which they feel understood and accepted, receiving what Rogers called unconditional positive regard, their self-esteem will blossom and they will increasingly be able to draw on their own resources to help themselves. This humanistic, experiential-existential approach espouses the belief that each person is unique and has the ability to strive toward self-actualization and reach his or her full potential. The person-centered model is characterized by the following qualities:

1. Present-oriented
2. Holistic
3. Emphasis on person's experience, perceptions, agenda, and goals (phenomenological)
4. Focus primarily on lifelong development and self-actualization, although specific problems are considered
5. Empathic, accepting, genuine, and congruent counselor
6. Focus on feelings, emotions
7. Concreteness and specificity encouraged
8. Little use made of tests, exercises, information-giving
9. Client–counselor relationship of great importance
10. Encouragement of person's self-awareness, exploration, self-esteem, and competence

Techniques associated with this approach to counseling include:

• Acceptance, unconditional positive regard
• Empathy, reflection of feeling
• Support, encouragement
• Clarification, open questions
• Goal setting
• Genuineness, modeling, rapport-building

Application to Clients

Some elements of the person-centered model, such as empathy, concreteness, and a focus on the present, pervade many approaches to counseling. Others, such as the emphases on emotions, self-actualization, and the counselor–client relationship, characterize some approaches but not others. Clearly, aspects of the person-centered model can be integrated into other approaches to counseling without making full use of this model. However, the person-centered model is particularly well-suited for some clients.

The concerns typically presented by these people are encompassed by the following DSM categories:

1. Adjustment Disorders
2. Other Conditions That May Be a Focus of Clinical Attention, particularly Phase of Life Problems, Relational Problems, Occupational Problems, Bereavement, Identity Problems, Religious or Spiritual Problems, and Acculturation Problems

People in these groups generally have some effective coping skills, are in good contact with reality, are capable of forming a collaborative relationship with the counselor, are motivated, and are not severely impaired. Their GAF scores on Axis V of the multiaxial assessment probably are relatively high. Such people usually can accept the responsibility placed on them by the person-centered model, have resources that they can draw on, and are interested in engaging with the counselor in the treatment process. They can tolerate the sometimes leisurely pace of the Person-centered model and can make changes in emotions, perceptions, and self-concept leading to changes in behavior, thinking, and relationships. People who experience person-centered counseling seem to develop a greater sense of well-being and the ability and courage to take greater responsibility for their lives.

A relatively structured and active version of the person-centered model also may be useful with people with low GAF scores. Because this model is a supportive and positive one, it can be useful with people who are feeling fragile and unsure of themselves. It also can be helpful to people with Psychotic or Cognitive Disorders. Although medical treatment usually will be the primary approach to helping these people, many can benefit from a supportive, affirming, and non-demanding counseling relationship that helps them maximize their functioning, promotes their self-esteem, and enhances their adjustment.

Vicki Ryan, presented in chapter 5, certainly would benefit from elements of the person-centered approach, particularly the emphasis on development of self-esteem, self-awareness, and communication skills. She probably would respond well to an accepting, supportive counselor. However, her difficulties seem too urgent and serious for this to be the primary mode of intervention.

BEHAVIORAL COUNSELING

Behavioral counseling is a very different model from person-centered counseling. Originating with the work of B. F. Skinner in the late 1930s and 1940s, the behavioral model of counseling has become an essential tool for most counselors.

Description of Approach

Behavioral counselors generally believe that personality is shaped by environmental reinforcers. If undesirable traits and behaviors have been learned, then behavioral counseling can be used to teach and reinforce positive behaviors while eliminating maladaptive ones. Behavioral counseling is characterized by the following dimensions:

1. Generally present-oriented, though some attention is paid to understanding how problems developed

   2. Problem/symptom focused
   3. Emphasis on behavior
   4. Counselor primarily responsible for agenda of sessions
   5. Concreteness and specificity encouraged
   6. Unlearning and learning, leading to behavioral change, are the goals
   7. Considerable use made of information-giving, inventories, homework assignments, and a wide variety of other techniques
   8. Client self-awareness, overall growth, and emotional responses deemphasized
   9. Interface between person and environment explored
  10. Goal directed, including regular evaluation of progress and revision of treatment plans if indicated

The behavioral model has been criticized for neglecting people's inner needs. Most modern behaviorists do, however, view the counselor–client relationship as quite important. Empathy and acceptance of the person are communicated and time is taken for accurate listening, the development of rapport and a collaborative counselor–client relationship, and understanding of the place of people's symptoms in their overall life patterns. Nevertheless, the ultimate goal of behavioral counseling is symptom removal and behavioral change; the counseling relationship is viewed as an important condition for change rather than the cause of change.

Behavioral counseling follows a fairly predictable pattern: establish goals, monitor the identified behaviors, change conditions, establish rewards and/or consequences, solidify and extend gains, evaluate, and maintain progress. The following techniques are associated with behavioral counseling:

- Establishment of baseline or current severity of problem
- Goal setting, contracting, record keeping (e.g., charts, diaries)
- Use of rewards and penalties
- Aversion therapy (e.g., time out, imagery, Antabuse)
- Natural consequences
- Incompatible alternatives
- Reinforcement schedules
- Cueing, anchoring
- Satiation, flooding
- *In vivo* or imaginal desensitization
- Biofeedback and other forms of relaxation
- Role-playing
- Modeling by self or other
- Acting as if one is someone who is admired
- Activity schedules

- Token economies
- Assertiveness and other skill training

Application to Clients

People for whom behavioral counseling is likely to be effective are those who present disorders of behavior or habit control. Behavioral counseling can be particularly helpful to children or adults who lack the motivation or verbal facility for extensive self-exploration. Behavioral counseling typically is short-term and time-limited in nature and so may appeal to people who do not have the interest, patience, or resources to engage in a prolonged counseling experience and who are seeking circumscribed and measurable changes. Such people are most likely to have disorders such as the following:

1. Attention-Deficit/Hyperactivity Disorders
2. Conduct Disorder
3. Oppositional Defiant Disorder
4. Pica
5. Elimination Disorders (Encopresis, Enuresis)
6. Substance Use Disorders
7. Phobias (Specific Phobia, Social Phobia, Agoraphobia)
8. Sexual Dysfunctions
9. Paraphilias
10. Some Sleep Disorders, especially Insomnia and Circadian Rhythm Sleep Disorder
11. Trichotillomania

Behavioral counseling also can be helpful in modifying the behaviors of people with Personality Disorders, Cognitive Disorders, Psychotic Disorders, Eating Disorders, Obsessive-Compulsive Disorders, and Adjustment Disorders, although behavioral counseling will need to be combined with other approaches in treatment of those disorders. Behavioral techniques often accelerate client growth and change even though another model of treatment is primary. For example, a person with low self-esteem and strong feelings of interpersonal insecurity may require the pace and support of a person-centered counselor but also may benefit considerably from assertiveness training and techniques for developing communication skills.

Because behavioral counseling usually is the treatment of choice for Substance Use Disorders, it is likely to be an important element in Vicki Ryan's treatment plan. In addition, increasing her activity level and improving her communication and assertiveness skills can reduce Vicki's depression and contribute to her self-esteem. However, behavioral counseling alone may not be enough to address her depression.

REALITY THERAPY

William Glasser first described reality therapy in the 1960s, and that approach to counseling has evolved and gained in popularity since. It has been adopted by many substance use treatment programs and correctional facilities and is used in many schools because of its emphasis on prevention and responsibility.

Description of Approach

Reality therapists generally believe that people who behave responsibly and in a socially acceptable manner, seeking to fulfill their needs without depriving others of the same ability, in a way that attends to the framework of the real world, will be most likely to meet their needs and develop what Glasser called a success identity based on feelings of love and self-worth. This philosophy is embodied in the three R's of reality therapy: right, responsibility, and reality. Control theory, an aspect of reality therapy, seeks to help people meet their basic psychological needs for survival, belonging, power, fun, and freedom.

Reality therapy can be characterized by the following dimensions:

1. Present and future oriented, remedial as well as preventive
2. Emphasis on importance of counselor–client rapport and involvement
3. Focus on behavior, not emotion
4. Client self-evaluation, goal-setting, planning, and contracting
5. Elimination of punishment and excuses; people learn through the natural consequences of their behavior
6. Emphasis on what and how, not why
7. Perserverance; if one approach doesn't work, try another

Reality therapy uses many of the same techniques as behavioral counseling as well as some techniques borrowed from cognitive therapy. Additional techniques associated with reality therapy include:

- Caring confrontation
- Planning and making written commitments to responsible behavior
- Use of natural consequences
- Limit-setting, within the session
- Encouragement of positive addictions such as exercise or meditation

Many similarities exist between behavioral counseling and reality therapy. However, reality therapists place greater emphasis on the establishment of a warm, understanding counseling relationship. In addition, although reality therapists focus on present behavior, they also are concerned with self-esteem and the person's environment. Reality therapy is designed to help people reach the point where they can give and receive love and perceive themselves as valuable members of society.

Application to Clients

Glasser developed his approach while working with adolescent girls who had been placed in a residential program because of their delinquent behavior. These girls generally were mistrustful of counseling, had little initial motivation to change, and were not experienced or interested in exploring their thoughts and emotions. Glasser developed a model that would be effective with people like these who have difficulty meeting their own needs without violating the rights of others, who often behave irresponsibly, and who tend to disregard or defy social norms. Such people might suffer from the following DSM disorders and conditions:

1. Conduct Disorder
2. Oppositional Defiant Disorder
3. Substance Use Disorders
4. Factitious Disorders
5. Disorders of Impulse Control including Pathological Gambling, Pyromania, Intermittent Explosive Disorder, and Kleptomania
6. Personality Disorders, especially Antisocial Personality Disorder
7. Adult, Adolescent, or Childhood Antisocial Behavior

People with difficulties such as these tend to be resistant to treatment and have problems that manifest themselves behaviorally. Reality therapy often is effective in helping people with this combination of characteristics. This approach also can be a useful part of a treatment program for people in crisis, people with Psychotic or Paranoid Disorders, people who are depressed, and people with Somatoform Disorders (Gilliland et al., 1989).

RATIONAL EMOTIVE BEHAVIOR THERAPY

Rational emotive behavior therapy (REBT), previously known as rational-emotive therapy, was first developed by Albert Ellis in the 1950s. Ellis, like Glasser, became disillusioned with the psychoanalytic model and sought an approach to counseling that was more effective at ameliorating the problems that his clients were presenting. The seeds of Ellis' psychoanalytic training are evident, however; he viewed emotional difficulties as stemming from a pattern of childhood development that leads people to care too much about what others think of them and encourages behaving in ways that will win favor. People with these attitudes tend to be other-directed, have little confidence in their own skills and attributes, and have beliefs that Ellis termed irrational. These beliefs, such as the thought that people must be fully competent, adequate, and achieving in all areas in order to be viewed as worthwhile, are characteristic of people who awful-ize, as Ellis put it. They overgeneralize, focus on should's and must's, think in extremes, feel disaster is lurking around every bend, and believe they have little control over their lives. Behavioral and affective difficulties grow out of these dysfunctional thoughts.

Description of Approach

Ellis' model views the onset of difficulties and their resolution according to a five-step sequence:

A—An *activating* event occurs.
B—The individual's *belief* system comes into play; rational or irrational thoughts emerge.
C—These thoughts lead to adverse *consequences*.
D—The counselor's role is to *dispute* the irrational ideas.
E—New *emotional consequences* can then take place.

Ellis and his associates have modified his approach over the years, now advocating an approach that seeks a deeper philosophical change and improved self-esteem, promoting long-range fulfillment. REBT has become more humanistic, preventive, growth-promoting, and eclectic, drawing on behavioral and affective approaches as well as on cognitive interventions.

REBT is characterized by:

- Emphasis on the present, though past and future both receive attention
- Thoughts viewed as the key to changing both emotions and behavior
- Counselor assuming a directive and instructional role; rapport is necessary but not sufficient for change
- Confrontation of dysfunctional thoughts via disputing, debating, defining, discriminating
- Reduction of ideas to absurdity, other uses of humor
- Using frequent homework assignments, especially involvement in rewarding activities, bibliotherapy

- Skill training
- Practicing and reinforcing positive cognitions

Reality therapy and REBT have in common an emphasis on encouraging people to value and take responsibility for themselves. Both stress the importance of action through contracts and homework assignments, but for Ellis cognitive change is primary, while for Glasser behavioral change leads to change in other areas. Ellis looks more at the person's internal dynamics, while Glasser is more aware of the person's environment.

Application to Clients

Although both REBT and reality therapy place the counselor in a directive role and stress behavioral change, Ellis' approach seems to call for a higher degree of motivation and commitment on the client's part. Furthermore, REBT's emphasis on cognitive analysis and restructuring seems best-suited for people who have a fair amount of verbal fluency, intellectual ability, and self-discipline. REBT is particularly appropriate for people who are confused by dysfunctional emotions and are having difficulty bringing their thinking skills to bear on an issue, but who are not psychotic. Such people might be experiencing the following disorders:

1. Mood Disorders, especially Major Depressive Disorder and Dysthymic Disorder
2. Anxiety Disorders, especially Generalized Anxiety Disorder
3. Adjustment Disorders

For the more severe of these disorders, such as Bipolar Disorders, medication or other treatment modalities often are combined with REBT to accelerate progress.

REBT and reality therapy might well become part of the treatment for Vicki Ryan. She feels like a failure, has feelings of discouragement and hopelessness, and tends to think in extremes. She does not know how to meet her needs. The action-oriented, cognitive focus of REBT as well as the behavioral emphasis of reality therapy are likely to alleviate her depression and increase her activity level. However, these approaches probably would have to be adapted and combined with other approaches to address her history of abuse, her substance use problems, and her family and relationship difficulties.

Both REBT and reality therapy are characterized by their developers as serving a broad spectrum of the population. Both have been modified for use by teachers as well as by counselors and are ways of helping troubled people as well as those who function satisfactorily to think, feel, and act in healthier and happier ways. Although these modes of treatment certainly are not ideal for all people, they do have broad application and can supplement many other approaches.

COGNITIVE THERAPY

Cognitive therapy, a newer approach to counseling than those discussed above, was developed by Aaron Beck and his colleagues who, like Glasser and Ellis, became disillusioned with the effectiveness of psychoanalysis. Related to and yet different from REBT, cognitive therapy assumes that affect and behavior are influenced by underlying assumptions or cognitions derived from previous experiences. This is a directive, structured approach that seeks to identify and correct distorted cognitions. Although behavior and emotion receive attention in this model, more attention is paid to cognition.

Description of Approach

Cognitive therapy differs from REBT in the approach used to effect change in thinking. Cognitive therapy consists of specific learning experiences designed to teach people to:

1. Monitor and record negative automatic thoughts
2. Recognize links between cognition, affect, and behavior
3. Reality-test dysfunctional automatic thoughts
4. Substitute correct cognitions for ones based on misinterpretation (cognitive restructuring)
5. Identify and change dysfunctional beliefs that lead to biased and distorted cognitions (Beck, Rush, Shaw, & Emery, 1979)

Additional techniques associated with cognitive therapy include:

- Hypothesis testing
- Mental and emotional imagery
- Cognitive and covert modeling
- Thought stopping
- Self-talk
- Keeping diaries of events, thoughts, reactions, arguments
- Letter writing
- Rating activities for mastery and pleasure
- Beck Depression Inventory and other inventories
- Hourly mood graph
- Affirmations

- Systematic assessment of alternatives
- Stress inoculation
- Cognitive rehearsal
- Hypnotic suggestion
- Reframing

Application to Clients

Cognitive interventions nearly always are combined with behavioral interventions for a particularly powerful treatment plan. Either alone or in combination with behavioral techniques, Cognitive therapy is likely to be effective with people experiencing:

1. Mood Disorders, especially Major Depressive Disorder
2. Anxiety Disorders, especially Phobias, Generalized Anxiety Disorder, Panic Disorder
3. Adjustment Disorders accompanied by depression or anxiety

Cognitive interventions also might be helpful, along with other interventions, for people with Somatoform Disorders, Personality Disorders, and a broad range of other disorders.

Cognitive therapy is a sophisticated and complex approach that has received considerable attention and support in recent years. The apparent usefulness of the model, especially with people who are depressed and suicidal, makes it an approach with which all counselors should be familiar. It seems to be the forerunner of a group of time-limited, directive, cognitive, strategic approaches that have attracted considerable attention and that seem to be establishing new direction for the field of counseling.

Vicki Ryan's depression certainly was connected to some dysfunctional thoughts. She perceived herself as a failure and was pessimistic about her ability to form positive relationships with men. Cognitive therapy would be a valuable approach for addressing those cognitive distortions and alleviating her depression.

INDIVIDUAL PSYCHOLOGY/ADLERIAN COUNSELING

Alfred Adler, a student of Freud's, developed an approach now known as individual or Adlerian psychology. In the past 15 years, a resurgence of interest in this approach has developed, especially among those who counsel children.

Description of Approach

Adler's approach has a strong philosophical base. The model is a pheno-menological, holistic, and humanistic one. It postulates that people are motivated by needs for both pleasure and social acceptance. Adler believed that children have strong feelings of inferiority that they strive to overcome throughout their lives by seeking achievement and mastery and that people's lifestyles and goals form early in their development. Adlerian counseling, then, tends to focus on the child and on the parent–child interaction. More recent theorists, such as Rudolph Dreikurs, Raymond Corsini, Donald Dinkmeyer and others, have elaborated and updated Adler's theory so that the approach now is widely used not only with children and their families, but also in adult personal counseling, career counseling, and marital counseling.

The Adlerian model of counseling is characterized by:

1. Emphasis on early childhood development and its impact on present attitudes and behavior
2. Increasing self-awareness and behavioral change
3. Holistic examination of person and environment
4. Stress on counselor–client relationship
5. Use of interpretation (sharing hunches or intuitive guesses)
6. Development of personally rewarding and socially responsible goals and modes of achieving them

Adlerian counseling encourages use of the following techniques:

- Examination of life script and style of life
- Interpretation
- Empowerment and encouragement
- Analysis of birth order and family constellations
- Exploration of early recollections
- Analysis of dreams
- Immediacy and confrontation
- Avoiding the tar baby (avoiding pitfalls)
- Spitting in client's soup (dispelling illusions)
- Natural and logical consequences
- Development of social interest

The Adlerian model differs from many of the newer approaches to counseling in that it emphasizes the importance of early childhood development and seeks to foster insight and understanding. It usually is less symptom-focused and more oriented toward improving one's overall ability to deal with life in a rewarding and socially responsible way. Like REBT and reality therapy, however, it is a broad-based approach that can be used by teachers and parents as well as by counselors.

Application to Clients

Conceptually, the Adlerian model seems to have something to contribute to almost all counseling situations. Although it is an analytical approach, the Adlerian counselor assumes a fairly directive role and offers hunches or interpretations. Consequently, this model does not require the client to be either motivated or communicative. However, the approach does seem best suited to people who are neither severely disturbed nor confronting an urgent problem or issue (e.g., abuse, alcohol dependence). Individual psychology seems most appropriate for people who are experiencing emotional upset of long duration and who are having difficulty developing self-confidence, mobilizing themselves, and finding a rewarding direction. This approach also is very effective in counseling children who are able to comprehend and communicate reasonably well. People for whom this model seems likely to be helpful might be described as experiencing:

1. Conduct Disorder of Childhood or Adolescence (especially if mild)
2. Oppositional Defiant Disorder
3. Separation Anxiety Disorder
4. Mild depression or anxiety, not stemming from a crisis
5. Identity Problem
6. Childhood or Adolescent Antisocial Behavior
7. Parent–child Problem
8. Other Relational Problems
9. Occupational Problem

Vicki Ryan certainly could profit from Adlerian counseling. She is very much affected by childhood experiences, has little sense of self and of direction, and probably would benefit from developing her social interest. Initially, however, her situation seems too urgent for reliance on this approach. Beginning her counseling with a cognitive-behavioral approach to help her reduce her alcohol use and stabilize her life probably would benefit her most. Then, when she is ready to address less urgent concerns, Adlerian counseling can be integrated into her treatment.

PSYCHODYNAMIC PSYCHOTHERAPY

Psychodynamic psychotherapy, like Adlerian counseling, is derived from Freud's psychoanalytic system of psychology. However, while psychoanalysis has waned in popularity, psychodynamic psychotherapy has received increasing attention and support. Sifneos, Klerman, Malan, and others have adapted the psychoanalytic model to modern counseling, leading to the development of brief psychodynamic psychotherapy and interpersonal psychotherapy.

Description of Approach

Psychodynamic psychotherapy typically seeks to ameliorate a recurrent focal concern or dysfunctional pattern, often problems in relationships, and helps people handle similar concerns more effectively in the future. Dysfunctional patterns in the person's past are explored in order to understand their impact on present functioning. Underlying emotions are uncovered and processed. Some attention is paid to transference, dreams and fantasies, defense mechanisms, and the unconscious, but far less than would be done in conventional psychoanalysis.

Techniques associated with psychodynamic psychotherapy include:

- Analysis of transference
- Exploration of dysfunctional patterns
- Relationship of history to present concerns
- Discussion of dreams and fantasies
- Processing of early memories
- Hypnotherapy
- Making the unconscious conscious
- Interpretation
- Working through

Application to Clients

Brief psychodynamic approaches can be effective in treating depression, anxiety, and situational disorders reflecting repeated patterns, while long-term psychodynamic approaches are useful with more deeply ingrained disorders, once any initial crisis has passed. The following disorders and conditions are likely to respond well to treatment via a psychodynamic approach:

1. Major Depressive Disorder
2. Dysthymic Disorder
3. Generalized Anxiety Disorder
4. Dissociative Identity Disorder
5. Most Personality Disorders (e.g., Borderline, Dependent, Avoidant)
6. Relational problems reflecting repeated dysfunctional patterns

Vicki Ryan certainly manifests repeated dysfunctional patterns, especially in her relationships with men. Psychodynamic psychotherapy could help her gain insight into those patterns and effect changes in her relationships. However, this approach to treatment, like Adlerian counseling, seems best used as a secondary or later approach in Ms. Ryan's treatment, with more cognitive and behaviorally-oriented interventions used first to help with her immediate situation.

GESTALT COUNSELING

Gestalt counseling, developed by Fritz and Laura Perls, had a powerful impact on the field of counseling in the 1960s. Although its use seems to have declined since then, it is an established approach in the field.

Description of Approach

Gestalt therapists, as their name suggests, emphasize wholeness of experience. They seek to help people gain access to neglected aspects of themselves, bring closure to unfinished experiences, develop a greater sense of responsibility, and become more aware of their potential. Counselors using this approach typically assume a directive role, in which they may frustrate, interpret, lead, and interact with clients. Counselors' attention to the whole picture leads them to attend to mind and body; affect, behavior, and cognition; and person and environment. Their focus is primarily on present experiences. Gestalt therapists believe that most people in modern Western society neglect bodily reactions and emotions. The Gestalt approach to counseling, then, emphasizes reintegration of the self by increasing people's awareness of nonverbal reactions and of their emotions.

The Gestalt approach to counseling uses a broad range of techniques such as the following:

1. Awareness emphasized, especially of affect and non-verbal responses
2. Focus on what and how, not why
3. Exploration of dreams and fantasies
4. Giving voice and action to physical sensations, nonverbal cues, emotions
5. Empty chair
6. Top dog/under dog (reflecting parts of the personality)
7. Exaggerating feelings and actions
8. Confrontation
9. Homework

Application to Clients

Because of its confrontational nature and its emphasis on making the unconscious conscious, the Gestalt model generally is not appropriate for people who
are severely disturbed, are in a crisis, or are poorly motivated. The model appears
most useful for people who tend to intellectualize, have trouble clarifying their
feelings, and cut themselves off from aspects of themselves (e.g., the person who
neglects relationships and overemphasizes work). Gestalt counseling also might
be useful with people presenting psychosomatic or other physical symptoms that
are linked to emotional difficulties. Such people may benefit from attending to
and making better use of the bodily messages that they send and receive. People
for whom Gestalt therapy seem useful might present with the following:

1. Cyclothymic Disorder
2. Dysthymic Disorder
3. Generalized Anxiety Disorder
4. Somatoform Disorders
5. Factitious Disorders
6. Adjustment Disorders
7. Psychological Factor Affecting General Medical Condition
8. Some Other Conditions (e.g., Occupational Problem, Phase of Life
   Problem, Relational Problem)

For the more severe of these disorders, the Gestalt approach generally
should be used only if client motivation and emotional strength are adequate and
if the approach is combined with or tempered by other approaches. The Gestalt
approach seems well suited to many of the problems resulting from the pressures
of modern life. It is a rich model with a broad repertoire of techniques that can
be used to enhance or expand on other models of counseling even if the primary
mode of treatment is not Gestalt.

Techniques such as exploration of dreams and fantasies and the empty
chair technique (for conversations with her parents, stepfather, and Matt) might
be very helpful to Vicki Ryan. However, she seems too fragile and in too much
of a crisis for Gestalt therapy to be the initial counseling approach.

ECLECTIC AND INTEGRATED MODELS OF COUNSELING

A trend toward eclecticism in counseling has been gaining ground since the
1940s. Existing approaches, such as those described in this chapter, are becoming
broader and more flexible, and effective counselors usually exhibit an extensive
repertoire of interventions (Gilliland et al., 1989). The 1990s witnessed a

particular effort to develop integrated models of counseling, although most counselors who do not adhere to a specific theoretical model are probably better described as technical or systematic eclectics, borrowing from several theoretical models, than true theoretical integrationists (Prochaska & Norcross, 1994).

Multimodal Behavior Therapy

The first well-known integrated model of psychotherapy was multimodal behavior therapy. Arnold Lazarus developed this approach to counseling which integrates and expands on many of the approaches discussed in this chapter. Lazarus' model enables counselors to take a systematic and comprehensive look at a person, determine areas of strength and weakness, and develop a treatment plan designed to have a multifaceted impact. Multimodal therapists view counseling as a holistic learning process and believe that change in one aspect of a person will affect and be encouraged by change in other aspects of that person.

A sevenfold model for assessing the person and planning the treatment is used in this approach. The acronym, BASIC I.D., represents the model:

B   Behavior (observable habits and activities)
A   Affect (feelings and emotions)
S   Sensation (physical concerns, sensory responses)
I   Imagery (images and fantasies)
C   Cognition (beliefs, thoughts, plans, philosophies)
I   Interpersonal relations (relationships with others)
D   Drugs, biology (broadly defined as biological functioning)

Assessment of these seven areas leads to the development of a modality profile to guide the counseling process.

Multimodal counseling is characterized by:

1. Counselor assuming a directive, responsible role
2. Limited attention to antecedent and precipitating factors; focus largely on the present
3. Holistic attitude
4. Objective evaluation of progress

In addition, techniques such as the following are associated with each of the seven areas of focus (Prochaska & Norcross, 1994):

- Behavior—reinforcement, consequences, extinction, conditioning
- Affect—recognizing and expressing feelings, abreaction
- Sensation—relaxation, pleasuring

- Imagery—visual imagery, changing self-image
- Cognition—cognitive restructuring, education
- Interpersonal—modeling, social skills training
- Drugs/biology—improving nutrition and exercise, changing drug and alcohol use

The behavioral origins of the multimodal approach are evident. However, this approach has gone beyond behaviorism and has attempted to establish a broad and flexible comprehensive model. Even if a person presents difficulties in only one or two of the seven areas, the BASIC I.D. framework enables counselors to perform a psychological assessment of people to ensure not only that presenting or obvious problems receive attention, but that all important areas of functioning are explored. This model also helps counselors define and build on people's strengths as a way of reducing problem areas.

Multimodal counseling has a contribution to make to almost every sort of client concern. However, some types of people, difficulties, and circumstances lend themselves particularly well to this sort of approach. Although the counselor takes primary responsibility for assessing people according to the BASIC I.D. and suggesting the details of the treatment plan, this model seems most likely to work with a client who is reasonably well-motivated, in satisfactory contact with reality, and capable of at least a moderate level of planning, organizing, and self-monitoring. People who present a range of diverse concerns (e.g., depression, eating problems, and poor social skills) might be particularly responsive to the multimodal model because it can help them develop a systematic approach to their concerns and can help relieve feelings of being overwhelmed and discouraged, common in multiproblem clients.

Developmental Counseling and Therapy (DCT)

A newer integrative therapeutic approach is developmental counseling and therapy (DCT), for individual counseling, and the related systemic cognitive-developmental therapy (SCDT) (Ivey & Rigazio-DiGilio, 1991; Rigazio-DiGilio, 1994). DCT/SCDT is consistent with a developmental approach to counseling; it redefines pathology as developmental blocks or delays that need to be alleviated in order to free the person for further growth. This holistic model considers mind, body, and context and seeks to match treatment approach to a person's developmental orientation.

The DCT/SCDT model postulates the existence of the following four cognitive-developmental orientations, based on the work of Piaget:

1. *Sensorimotor*—People in this stage are present-oriented. They typically rely on their senses and are not introspective. They tend to be

reactive and easily overwhelmed. Counseling focuses on eliciting their experiences and understanding.

2. *Concrete-Operational*—People in this stage can describe and plan, following a linear model of causality. They have difficulty with empathy, generalization, and change. Counselors can work with these people most effectively if they focus on facts, sequential descriptions, and perceptions of events.

3. *Formal Operational*—These people are analytical, can see their place in their environment, and can see patterns and multiple perspectives. However, they often emphasize reflection at the cost of action and have trouble changing basic assumptions. They need to focus on roles, relationships, and patterns of thoughts, feelings, and behaviors.

4. *Dialectic/Systemic Operational*—Although people in this group also may focus too much on analytic thinking, they have a capacity for integration, for challenging their own assumptions, and for understanding context and complexity. They need help in reviewing their assumptions and alternatives, changing patterns, and integrating aspects of their lives.

Although research is needed to demonstrate the effectiveness of this theoretical model, it seems to mesh well with the viewpoints of most mental health counselors, may apply to a broad range of people and disorders, and provides useful guidelines for treatment planning and selection of interventions.

Thinking-Feeling-Acting (TFA) Model

The thinking-feeling-acting (TFA) model, developed by Mueller, Dupuy, and Hutchins (1994), is another holistic model that seeks to match interventions to clients. Using the Hutchins Behavior Inventory, counselors adopting this model identify a person's strengths and limitations in three areas: thinking, feeling, and acting. Strategies are then adapted both to the person's primary orientation and to areas that need development.

Adaptive Counseling and Therapy/Readiness Model (ACT)

The adaptive counseling and therapy/readiness model (ACT) also seeks to match therapist approach to client needs (Nance & Myers, 1991). Therapeutic approaches are described in terms of two dimensions, support behavior and directive behavior. The model defines four counseling orientations in terms of these dimensions. Approaches that are low in directiveness and high in support are basically supportive approaches; those that are high in directiveness as well as support emphasize teaching; those that are low in support and high in directiveness stress telling; while those that are low in both dimensions emphasize delegating. This approach, like TFA and DCT/SCDT, shows promise but needs further study.

OTHER MODELS OF TREATMENT

Several other specific theoretical models, not as widely accepted as those discussed earlier in this chapter, have also contributed to the counseling profession and are worthy of mention.

Existential Therapy

Developed by Rollo May, Yalom, Frankl, Binswanger, Bugental, and others, the existential model is a phenomenological and humanistic approach that seeks to help people know and express themselves fully. Using such techniques as life review and paradoxical intervention, this model helps people to discover meaning in their lives, make rewarding choices, and develop responsibility and self-confidence. Existential therapy seems best suited for fairly healthy people experiencing mild depression, anxiety, or situational difficulties and who need a sense of meaning and direction in their lives.

Constructivism

A series of approaches have been developed, primarily during the 1990s, that emphasize an epistemological viewpoint. Their advocates believe that knowledge is not an objective representation but, rather, a creation of thought and language that grows out of social interactions (Guterman, 1994; Steenbarger, 1991). These approaches are known by a variety of names, including ecosystemic counseling, constructivism, social constructivism, interactional counseling, subjectivism, and narrative therapy. They emphasize change and process rather than content and take the position that people have a logic and wisdom in their lives that counselors need to understand. Advocates of these models typically believe that clients and counselors should co-create definitions of problems and directions for change, with the therapeutic relationship being an integral element in the change process. Language, metaphors, stories, and dialogue are viewed as other important ingredients in the process of change.

Transpersonal Approaches to Counseling

Derived primarily from eastern traditions and beliefs, these approaches strive to help people to develop their spiritual side and transcend the limits of body and matter (Tart, 1992). Like the constructivist approaches, they have not yet been well researched but seem to be growing in use, perhaps because they offer an alternative to the overcommitted and busy lives of so many people.

Additional Models

Several hundred other approaches to counseling are available, including social learning theory, Jungian therapy, and a broad range of expressive therapies (e.g., art therapy, mythopoetic therapy, play therapy, poetry therapy). Approaches to counseling are constantly being developed and modified. This chapter was not intended to provide a comprehensive discussion of all existing models of counseling. Rather, its purpose was to help readers appreciate the broad range of available counseling approaches and develop an ability to evaluate the suitability of these approaches for a variety of client concerns.

Many counselors align themselves with one or two approaches to counseling. They may characterize themselves, for example, as reality therapists or cognitive-behavioral counselors. Their preferred approach to counseling probably has been selected for several reasons: the counselors' exposure to that model through training and experience, the suitability of that model for their work setting or client population, the compatibility of that model with the counselors' personal style and philosophy, and their confidence in the effectiveness of that model.

Even though most counselors have preferred modes of counseling, counselors tend to be eclectic. That is, even when they make greater use of one approach than of others, they may borrow from other modes of counseling to adapt the process to the unique needs and concerns of each client. Describing a counselor as eclectic, then, does not provide much information about the counseling style and attitudes of that counselor. The best treatment often is provided by a counselor knowledgeable and flexible enough to use appropriate ingredients of several theories. Counselors should be able to justify their approach, selecting interventions that have proven their effectiveness in addressing particular problems or disorders and systematically tailoring them to individual client needs.

SAMPLE TREATMENT PLANS

This section presents three abbreviated counseling cases and shows how treatment plans have been developed to suit the particular needs of these clients.

These examples are designed to illustrate the application of principles discussed in this chapter as well as chapters 3–6.

Case 1—Jill Stone

"My husband says if I don't get back to myself by the end of the month, he's getting a divorce, and probably he should. I'm no good to anybody anymore." These were Jill Stone's opening words when she sought counseling. Jill, a 44-year-old white woman, was married to John, 47. They had three children: Arthur, 17; Benjamin, 15; and Carol, 12. Jill reported that, until three years ago, their lives had been good. John made a good salary as an engineer; Jill had chosen to stay at home with her children as her mother had done and found that very rewarding.

Then everything changed. Jill was diagnosed with cancer in her left breast. She struggled through surgery and radiation, feeling hopeless and discouraged. Those feelings of depression did not leave her, even though she managed to go on with her former lifestyle within a month of her first diagnosis. She had a persistent fear that she had not seen the end of cancer, and she was right. Two and a half years later, cancer was found in her right breast. Because this time Jill had some cancerous lymph nodes, her treatment required a mastectomy, chemotherapy, and radiation. Her hopelessness deepened, and this lively and independent woman became needy, dependent, and demanding, clinging to her husband and daughter, and blaming her family for not helping her feel better. She no longer took pleasure in her life, felt guilty because of her disease, was exhausted, and had gained over 35 pounds in the past three years.

Jill was the youngest child in her family of origin with two older brothers. Her mother had died of metastatic breast cancer at 48, when Jill was 24. Jill's family had been a close-knit, expressive one that was devastated by the death of their mother. Jill married John shortly after her mother's death.

John was the oldest of five children. His family, unlike Jill's, had serious financial and emotional difficulties. John had little contact with the family after he finished college.

Diagnosis

Axis I.	296.22 Major Depressive Disorder, single episode, moderate, with melancholic features
	300.4 Dysthymic Disorder, late onset, moderate
Axis II.	V71.09 No diagnosis on Axis II

Axis III. History of neoplasm, malignant, right and left breasts
Axis IV. Cancer and its treatment, conflict with family
Axis V.   55

Objectives

Short term:

1. Talk with husband about postponing decision on ending marriage
2. Initiate self-help program for coping with cancer.
3. Reduce depression (reduction of at least 3 points on the Beck Depression Inventory).

Medium term:

1. Reduce depression further (reduction of at least 10 points on the Beck Depression Inventory).
2. Restore quality of marriage to former level as measured on a self-report inventory.
3. Initiate weight loss and exercise program.
4. Promote awareness of the impact of family patterns on the current family situation (e.g., the legacy of cancer, family communication patterns) demonstrated by having Jill write about these patterns and discuss them with her husband and children.

Assessment

1. Beck Depression Inventory.
2. Informal rating scales of quality of marriage (e.g., communication, intimacy, mutual support, understanding).
3. Millon Clinical Multiaxial Inventory, to provide additional information on diagnosis and treatment.

Clinician

Jill probably would work best with a female counselor about her own age who has experience in counseling cancer survivors.

Location

Counseling should take place in an outpatient setting, perhaps a private practice or community mental health center that offers a broad range of services.

Interventions

The overriding theoretical model for counseling this client will be cognitive-behavioral counseling; this approach is effective in reducing depression and promotes coping skills that will help Jill deal with the impact of cancer. Once initial goals have been achieved, psychodynamic interventions will be integrated with the cognitive-behavioral ones to help Jill understand the impact family patterns and dynamics have had on her and her family.

Specific interventions will include:

1. Teaching communication skills and using role-playing to facilitate communication with husband.
2. Teaching relaxation and visual imagery focused on coping with cancer and its treatments.
3. Identifying, disputing, and replacing dysfunctional cognitions in order to reduce depression.
4. Planning a program of activities that seem likely to provide feelings of pleasure and mastery; these should include activities with family, friends, and alone as well as both sedentary and strenuous activities. This program will help reduce depression, promote involvement with others, improve self-esteem, and contribute to improved health and weight.
5. Developing a genogram and family history of Jill and John's families of origin and their present family to promote awareness of family dynamics.

Emphasis

Particular attention will be paid to providing support to Jill and building a strong therapeutic alliance with her. Her counseling will be structured and directive at first, but will gradually allow her to play an increasing role in her treatment.

Number of People

Counseling should initially be individual, with couples and family counseling combined with individual counseling as soon as Jill's depression begins to lift or if Jill is not successful in persuading her husband to defer his decision on the future of their marriage.

Timing

Jill will initially be seen twice a week, for 50-minute sessions. As soon as her depression begins to lift and she is productively engaged in counseling, sessions will be reduced to once a week. Counseling of approximately 3–6 months duration is anticipated.

Medication

Jill will be referred to a psychiatrist to determine the need for medication to help relieve her depression. In addition, contact will be initiated with her oncologist to help both Jill and her counselor gain greater understanding of the impact of Jill's disease and its treatments on her mood and physical condition.

Adjunct Services

Jill will be referred to a peer support group for women who have had breast cancer. A support group for families affected by cancer will also be recommended. In addition, Jill will be encouraged to join the National Coalition for Cancer Survivorship or a similar organization that can inspire hope in cancer survivors. Participation in a regular exercise program and a lecture series on healthy eating also will be encouraged.

Prognosis

The prognosis for alleviating Jill's Major Depressive Disorder is excellent, but because that disorder tends to recur, relapse prevention should be addressed in the treatment. The prognosis for alleviating the Dysthymic Disorder is very good, in light of its late onset and its apparently reactive nature.

Case 2—Manuel Ortiz

Manuel Ortiz is an 8-year-old Latino boy who was referred to a community mental health center by his school counselor. About a year ago, Manuel was sexually abused by his teacher, a middle-aged man with red hair. The teacher threatened to harm Manuel's family if Manuel refused to cooperate with the abuse or told anyone and so Manuel kept silent about the experience. After several months, another child reported the teacher, who was subsequently prosecuted and imprisoned. Manuel continued to keep the abuse to himself until a middle-aged man with red hair came to give a talk to his class. Manuel began crying uncontrollably, was taken to the counselor's office, and finally told her of the abuse.

Manuel's teachers and family had noticed behavioral changes in him over the previous year. He frequently had bad dreams from which he awakened confused, frightened, and disoriented. He often seemed anxious and distressed when away from home or his parents, and spoke frequently of fears that his parents would be killed. Manuel had some medically unverified physical complaints and had missed many days of school. As a result, his academic performance had declined and his teacher thought he might need to repeat third grade.

Manuel lived with his parents and older brother. Both parents worked outside of the home; his mother was a teacher and his father was an anesthesiologist. Manuel's brother was doing well in the seventh grade. Although his family was a stable and caring one, Manuel reported he felt his parents had little time for him and always seemed busy.

Diagnosis

Axis I.   309.81 Posttraumatic Stress Disorder, chronic, severe
Axis II.   V71.09 No diagnosis on Axis II
Axis III. Deferred
Axis IV.   Abuse by teacher, academic difficulties
Axis V.   60

Objectives

Short-medium term:

1. Help Manuel process and cope with his abuse, as evidenced by his ability to talk about it appropriately with his counselor and his parents and by a reduction in associated symptoms.
2. Attend school daily, except in the case of a verified medical illness.
3. Reduce number of bad dreams from approximately one per week to no more than one per month.

Medium-long term:

1. Improve academic performance, as evidenced by Manuel's completing third grade with an average of C or better.
2. Improve Manuel's communication with his parents as evidenced by self-report on a rating scale and amount of time spent in positive interaction with his parents.
3. Increase amount of time spent outside school with friends and in rewarding leisure activities to an average of two hours per day.

Assessment

1. Assessment of intelligence and academic abilities, using the Wechsler Intelligence Scale for Children and the Wide Range Achievement

Test, as well as information on standardized tests Manuel took at school.

2. Children's Personality Questionnaire to provide better understanding of Manuel.
3. Inventory of fears and phobias.

Clinician

Counselor should have experience in dealing with sexually abused children and should not resemble the abusive teacher. Manuel should be asked whether he prefers a man or a woman for his counselor to maximize his comfort with the counseling process.

Location

Outpatient counseling agency, focused on counseling children and families.

Interventions

Manuel presents difficulties on many fronts. Consequently, a multimodal approach will be used to guide his treatment. Specific interventions will include the following:

- *Behavior*—Manuel will identify rewarding and largely noncompetitive activities that interest him and that will afford him more contact with family and peers. A schedule will be developed to gradually increase time he spends in those activities. In addition, his parents will be encouraged to become more involved in his homework and to reinforce his regular attendance at school.
- *Affect*—Manuel will be encouraged to talk about the abuse he experienced and to express his feelings connected to that event, the threats he received, and his subsequent silence. Play therapy sessions also will be used to facilitate expression of feelings.
- *Sensation*—Relaxation techniques will be taught to counteract Manuel's anxiety and bad dreams.
- *Imagery*—Drawing, as well as conversation, will be used to help Manuel process some of his negative mental images connected to the abuse. In addition, visual imagery will be used to help him replace those images with more positive ones.

- *Cognitions*—Manuel remains fearful, even though his abuser is in jail. Manuel also blames himself for not fighting the abuser and believes that his family is ashamed of him. These dysfunctional cognitions will be clarified, disputed, and replaced with more functional cognitions.
- *Interpersonal relations*—Training in communication skills, as well as involvement in a counseling group for abused children, should help Manuel regain self-confidence and build peer relationships.
- *Drugs, biology*—A healthy diet and a program of regular exercise will contribute to the accomplishment of the identified objectives.

Emphasis

Manuel will need a very supportive counselor who can set a gradual pace to the counseling, emphasizing successes and reinforcement of gains.

Number of People

Counseling, initially, will be a combination of individual and family counseling. Later, Manuel's involvement in a counseling group for children who have been abused will be encouraged.

Timing

Ideally, Manuel should be seen once a week for individual counseling and once a week for family counseling. Individual sessions will initially be 30 minutes in length, in light of Manuel's anxiety, and will be increased to 45 minutes when he can tolerate longer sessions. At least four to eight months of treatment is anticipated.

Medication

A referral for a medical examination will be made to provide information on Manuel's many physical complaints. A referral for a medication evaluation does not seem indicated at present.

Adjunct Services

Tutoring probably would benefit Manuel as well as involvement in a reading club or similar activity that promotes both learning and peer involvement.

Prognosis

In light of his youth and his supportive family, Manuel's prognosis seems to be very good.

Case 3—Flame

Flame is a 27-year old white female who has been incarcerated for the third time, following her arrest for robbery and assult. (Flame was previously convicted of prostitution and possession of cocaine. She also has been arrested many other times for a wide range of crimes including shoplifting, selling cocaine and heroin, and assault.)

Both of Flame's parents used drugs and alcohol extensively. When Flame was 10, her father killed her mother during a fight. Flame witnessed the murder and shortly thereafter ran away from home. She has been living on the streets ever since, supporting herself through prostitution and selling illegal drugs. When she was incarcerated, she needed to be detoxified because of her heavy use of cocaine, heroin, and alcohol. Flame has been married and divorced twice. She had one child who was taken away from her and another who was given up for adoption. She was pregnant at the time she was seen for counseling and stated that she wanted help so she would not lose this child too.

Flame reported that she had not been feeling well for several months and had experienced persistent gastric distress. However, she had not sought medical attention for her physical problems.

Diagnosis

Axis I.   304.80 Polysubstance Dependence, in partial remission
Axis II.   301.7 Antisocial Personality Disorder
Axis III. Deferred; reports gastric distress
Axis IV.   Incarceration, pregnancy
Axis V.   30

Objectives

Short term:

1. Eliminate use of alcohol and illegal drugs.
2. Initiate plan for self-care, including medical evaluation and prenatal care.

Medium term:

1. Improve coping mechanisms (e.g., stress management, verbal self-expression) as evidenced by a daily diary of stressful incidents and coping responses.
2. Develop realistic plans for her discharge from prison, including finding employment, housing, and making non-drug related friends.

Long term:

1. Establish a stable, self-sufficient, and non-criminal lifestyle for herself and her child.
2. Learn to talk about, work through, and accept her very difficult early history.

Assessment

Substance Abuse Subtle Screening Inventory and Minnesota Multiphasic Personality Inventory to provide additional diagnostic information; inventories of interests, aptitudes, and achievement levels to facilitate career counseling.

Clinician

Flame may benefit from a counselor who could serve as a role model for her. She will need a clinician who is experienced in treating people with a history of criminal behavior and drug and alcohol use and in addressing resistance.

Location

Flame is incarcerated at present and will be counseled while in prison. She will then be referred to her parole officer and a community mental health center for continued treatment. The facility should be able to provide regular drug and alcohol screenings.

Interventions

Reality therapy will initially be the theoretical framework for counseling Flame. However, she probably will benefit later from psychodynamic psychotherapy to help her understand how she has been affected by past experiences and patterns. Initial interventions will include:

1. Education on the impact of drugs and alcohol.
2. Behavioral contracting to facilitate abstinence from drugs and alcohol.

3. Development of coping mechanisms to help Flame remain free of drugs and alcohol; this would include relaxation, thought-stopping, distraction, visual imagery, and other stress-management techniques.
4. Involvement in life skills classes at the prison to facilitate future planning.
5. Bibliotherapy, focused on reading biographies of people who have overcome difficult backgrounds.
6. Keeping a diary of stressors and coping responses.

Further interventions will be planned, based on Flame's response to treatment.

Emphasis

Counseling will need to be structured and directive, yet facilitate the development of a good counselor–client rapport.

Number of People

Concurrent group and individual counseling is recommended for maximum impact.

Timing

Counseling while Flame is incarcerated will take place on a daily basis. Individual sessions will be 45 minutes in length; group sessions, 90 minutes. Once she is released from prison, she should have at least two contacts per week with helping professionals for at least three months. Long-term counseling is anticipated for this client.

Medication

Flame will be referred for a thorough medical evaluation. Antabuse and/or Methadone may help her to stop her use of illegal drugs and alcohol.

Adjunct Services

Participation in Alcoholics Anonymous and Narcotics Anonymous is essential. In addition, Flame should continue to take life skills classes to help her learn such skills as parenting, budgeting, job seeking, and meal preparation. She will be referred to the Department of Social Services for help in locating subsidized housing and financial assistance and to the Department of Vocational Rehabilitation for job training and help in finding employment.

Prognosis

Flame reports strong motivation at the present time. However, the rate of recidivism is high for people with her diagnoses and the prognosis probably can be viewed as no better than fair.

SAMPLE CASES

Readers are encouraged to develop their skills by completing treatment plans, following the DO A CLIENT MAP, for the following cases:

1. Dee, aged 10, has always been very shy and has not enjoyed parties and group gatherings. About six months ago, while she was at a party, a bunch of balloons burst right behind her. Since then, she had refused to attend any parties and cries when her parents insist that she attend school on days when parties are scheduled. On several occasions, when balloons were brought into the classroom, she developed extremely high anxiety and had to leave the room. She even became anxious when watching parades that featured balloons on television. Other than these difficulties, Dee does well at school, seems to have good relationships with family and teachers, and is well-behaved.

2. Evan, a 25-year-old man, sought counseling at the suggestion of his father. He reported that his father thought there was something wrong with him because he didn't have a girlfriend. In fact, Evan had never had a date and had never had an interest in close relationships. He had graduated from college and was successfully employed as a computer programmer; he had a computer at home and rarely went to the office, preferring to work by himself. He raised purebred dogs, devoting a great deal of time and energy to his pets. Although he did not enjoy showing them, he did sell them and enjoyed photographing them. He stated that although he did not feel very close to his family, he was in contact with them and had dinner with them once a month. He described his life as stable and satisfactory and reported no particular difficulties other than his current conflict with his father.

3. Nancy, a 29-year-old woman, sought help in deciding how to handle an unplanned pregnancy. She had become pregnant on her first date with a man she had met at a bar. She subsequently informed him of her pregnancy, but he expressed no interest in continuing their relationship and advised her to have an abortion as soon as possible. Nancy

seemed upset, confused, sad, and angry. She also reported mild depression since the death of her mother three years ago.

History-taking indicated that Nancy was living with her widowed father. She had completed high school and had worked as a secretary for the same firm for the last 10 years. She was bored and dissatisfied with her work but had not taken steps toward change. Her social life was extremely limited. However, she did occasionally drink enough alcohol to bolster her courage. She occasionally dated men she met in bars. She had had only a few sexual experiences and assumed that her partners would take responsibility for birth control.

4. Rachel, age 34, sought counseling after her husband requested a divorce. Rachel was a plump woman, dressed in exotic, flowing robes. She wore a great deal of jewelry that clanged when she waved her hands, something she did frequently. Rachel had recently learned that her husband was having an affair with a co-worker. When she confronted him with this, he stated that he had been very unhappy in their marriage and wanted a divorce. Rachel responded by breaking a set of dishes and threatened to kill herself if her husband left her. She acknowledged that she, too, had affairs but said they didn't matter because she didn't care for the men and was only trying to relieve her boredom. Rachel's history revealed a long-standing pattern of impulsive behavior in which she was easily influenced by others. Toward the end of the session, she invited her male therapist to join her for a cocktail at a nearby restaurant.

5. The client, a 47-year-old man who insisted on being called Gauguin, was brought to counseling by his wife. She reported that throughout most of their 10-year marriage, her husband had been very stable except for two periods when he seemed quite depressed for three or four months. Now she was seeing a new side of him. The client reported that he had recently realized that he was destined to be a famous painter like the original Gauguin. He was making plans to sell the family home so that they could move to the South Seas, where he was sure he would be inspired to paint his masterpieces. He had painted as a hobby for many years but had never spoken of aspirations like these. The client's wife reported that he seemed to be sleeping little, had become much more talkative, and was neglecting his responsibilities in their home mail-order business in order to spend time painting furiously or attending private art exhibitions to which he had not been invited.

Diagnosis and Treatment Planning for Families

Family counseling has been growing in use and influence for more than 50 years. Research indicates that couples and family counseling is more effective than individual counseling in the treatment of family concerns (Frances et al., 1984). Most counselors today include family counseling in their repertoire of skills and, even if engaged in individual counseling, obtain information on their client's family of origin and current family. Family counseling theory not only offers a variety of approaches for helping families, but also provides a framework for understanding individuals in a family context. In a way, then, family counseling is a point of view, useful in the diagnosis and treatment of individuals as well as couples and families.

This chapter provides counselors with a framework for analyzing and diagnosing family difficulties as well as a review of the major approaches to family counseling. The chapter assumes that readers have some prior knowledge of family counseling or that they will acquire further learning in this area if they intend to practice family counseling.

As early as the 1920s, Alfred Adler, Rudolph Dreikurs, and others recognized the impact of the family on children's development, and mothers usually were interviewed when their children were brought in for treatment. Some attention was paid, during those years, to prevention of family difficulties, usually through family-life education programs. The 1930s saw the beginning of marriage counseling, initiating a pattern of seeing family members together. Stress and conflict in families escalated during the 1940s as a result of World War II, leading to increased attention to family difficulties. During that same decade, the

American Association of Marriage Counselors, the precursor of the American Association for Marriage and Family Therapy, was founded, providing a professional organization for therapists who specialized in counseling families.

Several researchers gave great impetus to the development of family counseling in the 1950s. Murray Bowen, on the East Coast, and the Palo Alto group (Jay Haley, Gregory Bateson, John Weakland, Don Jackson, and others), at the Mental Research Institute on the West Coast, explored the interaction between Schizophrenia in one family member and the behavior of the rest of the family. Bowen drew attention to the process of intergenerational transmission while Bateson and his colleagues emphasized the importance of the double-bind, a form of communication in which incompatible messages are transmitted simultaneously. For example, a parent might verbally encourage affection but then act cold and unresponsive when the child becomes affectionate. During the 1950s and even later, both the double-bind and the "schizophrenogenic" mother, defined as a "domineering, aggressive, rejecting, and insecure woman" who gave mixed messages, were believed to contribute to the development of Schizophrenia in families (Nichols, 1984, p. 19). The first book on family therapy was published during the 1950s (Thomas, 1992).

In the next decade, Virginia Satir's *Conjoint Family Therapy* (1967) focused attention on less disturbed families and on the importance of family communication and the family unit. Satir also initiated training of family therapists. Nathan Ackerman founded the first family therapy journal, *Family Process*. Salvador Minuchin made an important contribution to the family counseling movement during the 1970s by focusing attention on family structure and ways in which it could be modified to improve family functioning. Outcome studies on the effectiveness of family therapy were initiated, with the growth in theoretical approaches to family counseling. Certification and licensure of family therapists began during the 1970s.

Innovative approaches to family counseling in the 1980s generally advocated a brief, directive, and problem-focused approach to treatment, exemplified by strategic family therapy developed by Haley and Madanes (Madanes, 1981). Attention to assessment tools in family therapy, models of self-help for families such as marital enrichment and parent effectiveness programs, and integrated models of treatment increased along with a growing awareness of the importance of family differences and special needs.

During the 1990s, family therapy became well established. The American Counseling Association added a division for family counseling, the International Association of Marriage and Family Counselors (IAMFC), which published the first issue of its journal in 1993. The 1990s saw continued emphasis placed on diverse techniques and eclectic models encompassing aspects of brief, structural, strategic and systemic family therapy. Innovators in family therapy during this decade focused on epistemology, the process of knowing and describing social construction of reality. New models of family counseling emerged that emphasized understanding a family's view of their lives and of the impact of the therapist–family interaction on those perceptions.

This overview of the development of the field of family counseling is necessarily cursory. However, it does offer readers a context in which to consider current approaches and methods of treatment. More information on the major approaches cited in this section will be provided later in this chapter.

ASSESSMENT OF FAMILY FUNCTIONING

No taxonomy comparable to the DSM exists for use in the diagnosis or assessment of family functioning. However, the list of categories or dimensions for understanding families that appears in this chapter been drawn from the relevant literature and provides a comprehensive framework for analyzing families.

These assessment categories, as well as selected theories of family counseling, will be illustrated with reference to the Wood family. This African American family consisted of John Wood, age 49; his son, John, Jr., age 19, from John's first marriage; John's present wife, Olivia, age, 35; her son, Nathan, age 8, from her first marriage; and Keesha, age 2, the daughter of John and Olivia.

John was a successful businessman who owned a printing company. His first wife was killed in an automobile accident approximately six years ago.

Olivia had been married briefly to Nathan's father, Neil, but was divorced before the birth of their child. Olivia attributed the divorce to her first husband's abuse of alcohol and his infidelity. She and Nathan have had no contact with Nathan's father since the divorce. Olivia reported that Neil was incarcerated. Prior to her marriage to John four years ago, Olivia supported herself and Nathan by working as a waitress while trying to establish a career as an artist. She has had some success as a fabric painter and has sold quite a few of her designs.

John, Jr. was a freshman in college, living with John and Olivia. He was majoring in business and worked in his father's printing company during summer vacations.

Nathan was in the third grade. He had been diagnosed as having Attention-Deficit/Hyperactivity Disorder, Predominantly Hyperactive-Impulsive Type, and a Learning Disorder in reading. A Developmental Coordination Disorder also was suspected. Nathan had been a difficult child since birth. Although he was affectionate and reasonably well-behaved in light of his hyperactivity, he was boisterous and awkward and had little academic success. Attention from his mother as well as special help at school enabled him to pass each grade, but he seemed to be falling further behind his class each year.

Keesha thus far was a delight to the family, a healthy and happy child. Her father doted on her and Nathan seemed especially attached to Keesha.

Presenting Problem

Family counseling, like individual counseling, usually begins with an exploration of the presenting problem that led the family to seek help and of the kinds of changes the family would like. With families, as with individuals, presenting concerns may not represent the fundamental issues troubling the family. Satir (1967) observed that often families seek help for a child with a behavioral problem. Satir dubbed this child the Identified Patient (IP) and found that the IP often was the healthiest family member, acting out in order to obtain help for the family. The attribution of a family concern to an individual member can make determination of the family's difficulties a challenging task. This task can be further complicated if family members have divergent views of family problems. Nevertheless, the family's presenting concerns must be understood and evaluated as part of the assessment of the family.

When Olivia and John Wood presented for counseling, they did, indeed, have rather different conceptions of the family's problems, with each one attributing those problems to a different person. Both agreed that they had been arguing more and more and that the comfortable and loving family environment they had envisioned when they married had not materialized. John blamed these problems on Nathan; he stated that Nathan's noisy, acting-out behavior destroyed the peace and quiet he had valued in his home and that Olivia spent so much time with Nathan and Keesha as well as with her art work that she had little time left for him. Olivia, on the other hand, attributed their difficulties to John, Jr. She believed that he was abusing alcohol and spending too much time with friends rather than his studies. She also complained that John denied the existence of these problems and continued to give John, Jr. money for car payments and social activities that would be better spent on a private school for Nathan.

Transgenerational Family History

Bowen (1974) believed that families could best be helped if they were viewed from a longitudinal perspective. This promotes understanding of what is called the intergenerational or transgenerational transmission process, in which patterns and traits are passed on from one generation to the next. Bowen used a genogram (diagram of generations) to facilitate this process. A partial genogram of the Wood family is provided (Figure 8.1). In a genogram, females are

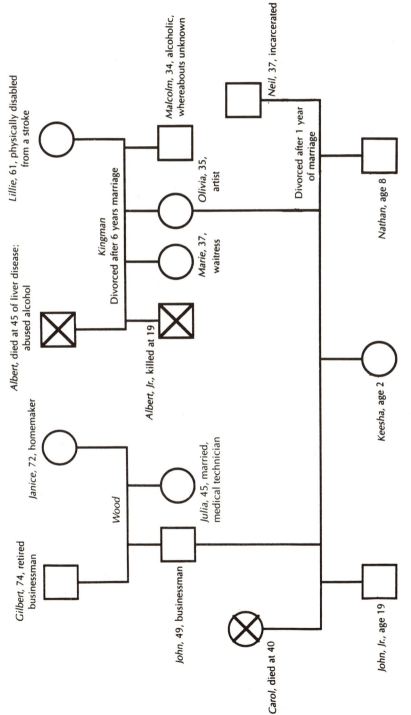

Figure 8.1. Genogram of the Wood family.

represented by circles; males, by squares. An X indicates a deceased family member. Siblings are listed in order of birth, from left to right. The husband's family is placed on the left, the wife's on the right.

John and Olivia came from very different family backgrounds. John's family had been a traditional, middle-class one. His father established the business that John now owned. His mother was a homemaker who had been very involved with church and family activities. Values of stability, family unity, and financial success were important in the family.

Olivia, on the other hand, came from a more chaotic family. Her mother had been the mainstay of the family, even during the years when her parents were married. Her father, Albert, abused alcohol, was employed sporadically as a construction worker, and often stayed away from home for several days at a time. Olivia had little contact with her father from the time of her parents' divorce when she was five years old until his death.

Detailed information on John's and Olivia's siblings is not included in this abbreviated genogram but would be included in a full genogram. Olivia's older brother was accidently shot and killed at age 19 during a conflict between neighborhood gangs. Her sister Marie has been divorced twice and supports herself and her three children by working as a waitress while her brother Malcolm, who had a problem with alcohol since about age 10, has not had contact with the family in nearly 15 years. John's only sibling, Julia, is married, has two children, and works as a medical technician.

Although more exploration would be needed to determine the nature of the transgenerational transmission process in these families, the following patterns can be noted:

1. Substance abuse (Albert, Malcolm, Neil).
2. Gender roles that were consistent within families but diverge between families; men were in charge in the Wood family while Olivia's family was characterized by strong, nurturing women and unreliable men.
3. Children and the role of parenting were valued in both families.

Other patterns of importance that might have an impact on the present family:

1. Both John and Olivia reportedly were the favorite children in their families, with both having strong ties to their mothers.
2. Both John and Olivia have had to cope with the loss of loved ones. John continued to grieve over the death of Carol, his first wife, and sometimes compared Olivia unfavorably to Carol.

Other patterns are likely to emerge with further exploration and could shed light on the dynamics of the present family.

Carter and McGoldrick (1988) found that, like individuals, families go through relatively predictable developmental stages and concluded that these are important in understanding families. They stated, "The family life cycle perspective views symptoms and dysfunctions in relation to normal functioning over time and views therapy as helping to reestablish the family's developmental momentum." (p. 4) Carter and McGoldrick identified six stages in the family life cycle, listed below, along with some of the challenges typically associated with each stage.

I. Leaving home: single young adults.

   A. Separating from family of origin and achieving independence and responsibility for self.
   B. Establishing and acting on career, financial, and personal goals.
   C. Developing intimate peer relationships.

II. Marriage: The new couple and family.

   A. Forming and making a commitment to a new family system.
   B. Maintaining both separateness and intimacy.
   C. Redefining relationships with parents and friends to accommodate the partner; defining relationships with in-laws.

III. The family with young children.

   A. Making space for children.
   B. Establishing comfortable and compatible styles of parenting.
   C. Maintaining the spouse relationship.
   D. Coping with role changes, new demands on time and finances, responsibilities.
   E. Realigning relationships with family and friends to include parenting and grandparenting roles.

IV. The family with adolescents.

   A. Increasing boundary flexibility to accommodate adolescents' need for separation as well as the needs of aging grandparents.
   B. Coping with midlife changes in marriage, career, values.

V. Launching children and moving on.

   A. Handling financial and emotional changes often associated with children in college and grandparents needing help.
   B. Reinvesting in and redefining the marriage.

C. Changing roles—establishing adult relationships with grown children, dealing with disabilities and death of older generation, becoming grandparents.

VI. The family in later life.

A. Maintaining functioning of self and couple in light of sexual, physical, and role changes.
B. Coping with aging, illness, and death.
C. Establishing grandparenting (sometimes great-grandparenting) roles.

In general, families have the most difficulty dealing with events the first time they happen (e.g., birth of the first child), events that are unanticipated and unwanted (e.g., miscarriage, the sudden loss of a job), and events that occur at ages that differ from the norm (e.g., the birth of a child to a couple in midlife). The process of children's leaving home seems to be a particularly difficult stage or transition. Of course, each family has its individual patterns of development and its unique reactions to important events.

The family life cycle can best be understood in its temporal context. Social patterns such as the usual marriage age, the typical number of children, the acceptability of divorce, and gender roles are in constant flux and have an impact on how people negotiate the family life cycle.

The family life cycle of the Wood family is complicated. Before John and Olivia married, both were single parents, John with an adolescent and Olivia with a young child. When they married, they entered the second stage, the new couple, while having to cope with other stages. John became the parent of two young children at an age when most of his peers were launching their children and Olivia became the mother of an almost-launched adolescent with whom she had had little opportunity to establish a relationship. Parenting responsibilities made it difficult for the couple to carry into their marriage the romance and closeness of their year of courtship, and both felt disappointed.

The age difference between John and Olivia and the patterns of their age groups also were important. John grew up viewing women in traditional roles, and that had been the pattern of his first marriage. He was unprepared for Olivia's independence and commitment to her career; he had implicitly assumed that her career involvement would decline when she married and gave birth to Keesha. Olivia, on the other hand, had looked forward to the increased time she would have to develop her artistic skills because of the financial stability of her second marriage.

Family Structure

Many factors determine the structure of a family. In addition to the composition of the family, these include:

 a. Birth order, gender, and ages of children
 b. Patterns of alliance and avoidance, similarity and difference
 c. Formal and informal hierarchy and power structure
 d. Structure of family of origin

In a healthy family structure, the parents have a strong bond and are close to each other. Siblings also have a strong subsystem, with strong alliances also developed between same-gender, parent–child and sibling dyads. Patterns often reflecting family difficulties include each parent's being closest to a child of the opposite gender, rather than to each other, and the children having the most power in the family.

The structure of the Wood family is diagrammed in Figure 8.2. Although John and Olivia still have some connection to each other, both feel closest to

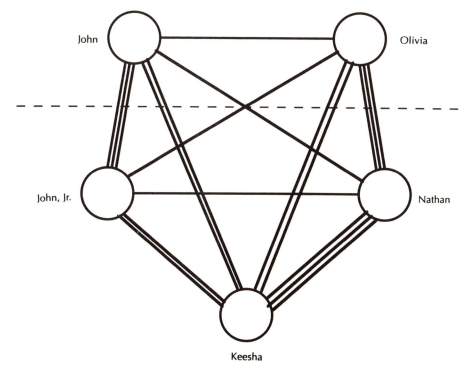

Figure 8.2. Diagram of the structure of the Wood family.

their first child and most distant from their step-child. Nathan has not been able to bond well with either John or John, Jr. and remains closest to the females in the family. Keesha is the only recipient of the entire family's affection.

Birth order provides additional information on family structure. The configuration of John, Jr. and Keesha replicates John's family of origin (older brother, younger sister) and is familiar and comfortable to him. High expectations were held for him as the oldest child and only boy and he has transmitted those expectations to John, Jr. Olivia recalled her older brother Albert, Jr. as a problem and viewed him as one reason for her parents' divorce. Older brothers, then, have a bad image for her, although she does relate well to Nathan and Keesha. As often happens with middle children, Olivia followed an unconventional and artistic path, one that was accepted in her family where personal qualities were emphasized over conventional achievement. This experience seems to have enabled her to be tolerant of Nathan's special needs.

Communication and Interaction Styles

Many frameworks are available for categorizing styles of communication in family members. One of the most useful was developed by Satir (1983). She postulated the existence of five modes of communication:

a. Placator—the self is viewed negatively and the person almost always agrees with others.
b. Blamer—the self dominates, and other people and the context of the situation are ignored.
c. Computer or Super-reasonable—the context matters most to this intellectualizing person; people and their feelings are ignored.
d. Distractor or Irrelevant—communications generally ignore both people and context.
e. Congruent communicator—this person takes account of the self, of others, and of the context.

While nearly everyone tends to shift styles depending on the situation, most people do have a preferred style of communicating.

John typically uses Blamer and Super-reasonable styles of communication. Olivia, too, often assumes the Blamer style, although she sometimes is a Placator, especially in relation to issues around Nathan. Nathan, himself, is a Distractor, while John, Jr. leans toward the Super-reasonable style of communication but can use Placator, Blamer, and Distractor modes to avoid incurring his father's anger.

Communication styles may also be described as visual, auditory, or kinesthetic. For Olivia, the visual mode is an important one, and she seeks to present an attractive appearance as a way of showing her feeling for John. However, John emphasizes a kinesthetic mode and sometimes finds Olivia to be distant.

Triangulation is a frequent pattern of communication in dysfunctional families. Typically, that involves both parents communicating to each other through a child. Although that pattern was not present in the Wood family, Keesha could evolve into the conduit for communication between her parents.

Family Rules, Roles, and Values

All families have rules that are stated or expressed as well as norms, values, or expectations that may or may not be clearly stated. Rules typically are specific, such as curfews and assignment of chores. Norms and values tend to be less clear than rules and might include such messages as, "The children are expected to do well in school and to go to college," or "Don't talk about a family member's alcohol use." John placed great emphasis on education and, consequently, viewed John, Jr. as successful and Nathan as a disappointment because of their very different academic experiences. Olivia was brought up in a family that was damaged by uncontrolled and unacknowledged alcohol use and saw the harm that could do; she is now trying to limit John, Jr.'s alcohol use but is encountering resistance from John.

All family members have roles determined by a combination of their official status in the family (e.g., father, youngest child) and by the needs of the family and the functioning of each individual. John viewed his father as the head of his family of origin and himself as head of the family in his own marriages. However, Olivia's mother had been in charge of her family and, as a single parent, Olivia had to take charge of her household. She was not used to yielding power to a man and envisioned her marriage as a partnership. Before Olivia's second marriage, one of Nathan's roles was to give a focus and purpose to his mother's life. Now that role was less important to Olivia, but Nathan still struggled to maintain his position as center of his mother's life. As in the Wood family, rules and roles are important sources of information about family functioning.

Ethnic, Cultural, and Socioeconomic Background

Ethnic, cultural, and socioeconomic patterns play a significant role in determining family functioning. Although interpretation of background information presents risks of stereotyping and overgeneralizing, a cautious exploration of these areas can provide valuable understanding of the dynamics of a family.

Although both John and Olivia were African American, their socioeconomic backgrounds were different. John's father came from a poor family of origin but used his business and financial abilities to create a comfortable life for his family. His emphasis on financial success has been transmitted to John. John disapproved of Olivia's family of origin and believed that Olivia should be grateful that he had rescued her and Nathan from financial instability. Olivia's background was reflective of patterns sometimes associated with African Americans, including strong women, artistic accomplishment, and a nontraditional family structure. Olivia found herself sometimes disapproving of John's traditional attitudes, wanting him to take on some of her energy and flexibility. Similar ethnic backgrounds but different cultural ones have led to discrepant values between John and Olivia.

Differentiation of Self

Bowen (1974) postulated a differentiation of self scale, with scores ranging from a low of zero to a high of 100. He used this scale as a measure of how individualized and separated people were from their families. Those at the low end (0–25) of the scale tend to have enmeshed and symbiotic relationships with their families and are self-centered and dominated by emotion. People who fall above the midpoint on the scale typically are more inner-directed, rational, and secure, respect others, and have fairly well-defined opinions, beliefs, and values. Although people within a family can differ considerably in their degree of differentiation, some families promote differentiation while others inhibit it. People tend to choose spouses and to raise children with levels of differentiation comparable to their own. Bowen saw differentiation of self as a key ingredient in family health; one of the primary goals of his approach to family therapy is to increase client self-differentiation.

Levels of differentiation in the Wood family fell in the middle range (25–75) with Olivia perhaps the most differentiated. This family was not what Bowen called an undifferentiated family ego mass; however, family members did feel pressure to conform to family and societal values rather than to develop their own value systems.

Significant Physical and Mental Conditions

When a person in a family has a significant illness, disorder, or disability, it inevitably has an impact on that person's family. The impact can take many forms. In some families, the affected family member becomes the focus of the family's energy, either uniting the family or detracting from other family relationships. The affected family member may be viewed as a source of shame and embarrassment or as a source of pride. A severe or long-standing disability in a family also shapes the way that family interacts with the outside world. In some families, the disability causes the family to withdraw and exclude outsiders who may intrude on the family grief or exacerbate their shame. In other families, the disability becomes a conduit for communication as family members expand their outside contacts in an effort to find medical treatment, information, and support to help them handle the condition. The ways in which families handle illness and disability provide information on the nature and level of their coping abilities and their attitudes toward family cohesiveness and community involvement.

Nathan's Learning Disorder and his Attention-Deficit Disorder propelled Olivia into active involvement with his school system in an effort to obtain the help Nathan needed. Her younger brother had presented similar symptoms (although the disorders had never been diagnosed) and so Olivia was familiar with young boys who demand a great deal of attention. John, however, was unfamiliar with symptoms like Nathan's and was embarrassed by Nathan's constant talking and inability to sit still. John found himself avoiding family activities and preferred time alone with Olivia. Their differing attitudes toward Nathan's difficulties was another source of conflict in the family.

External Sources of Stress and Support

External sources of stress and support can have a considerable impact on a family's homeostasis. Some families have a strong and extensive support system, perhaps including extended family, work colleagues, neighbors, and fellow members of religious or leisure organizations. Such families typically are more able to handle stress and change than isolated nuclear families. Helping families to build support systems can be an important counseling strategy.

Families also have to cope with stress coming from outside sources. The company where a family member is employed may suddenly close, a child may be mistreated by schoolmates, or a fire may destroy family possessions and impose an unanticipated financial burden.

Families of origin as well as friends provided some stress and considerable support to the Wood family. John's parents lived in a retirement community nearby and were involved with John, Jr. and Keesha, although they, too, had difficulty accepting Nathan. Olivia's mother was disabled, and Olivia provided her both financial and practical help. Olivia belonged to a group of independent artists and had formed some friendships in that group, while John was well-respected in his church and community. Involvement in shared baby-sitting in their neighborhood enabled Olivia to get acquainted with nearby families. John, Jr.

had many friends at college and in the neighborhood. Although Nathan had few peer supports, he did have good relationships with his teachers.

Dynamics of Symptom Maintenance

Symptoms of dysfunction often serve a purpose in a family and are almost always intertwined with the overall dynamics of the family. Counselors usually seek to understand the role of the symptom in order to effect its change or elimination. Behavioral sequences, leading to the emergence or manifestation of a symptom, provide one clue to comprehending the nature of the symptom. Other clues are provided by an examination of the family structure and the needs of individual members.

Neither John, Jr. nor Nathan were happy with their parents' marriage. Both had enjoyed being the center of attention and were having difficulty yielding that position. The current intensity of Nathan's symptoms, in particular, seemed to reflect his dismay with his present family situation. For John and Olivia, too, previous difficulties also brought benefits. Both were understandably proud of their roles as single parents; compromising the values and attitudes they held before the marriage conflicted with their self-images and so has been resisted.

Strengths

Although the focus of analysis thus far has been on problems, the Wood family also had many strengths, as do most families. Olivia and John were dedicated parents and responsible, intelligent adults with their own interests. Their marriage resulted from a courtship of over a year, during which they became good friends as well as lovers. They enjoyed each other's company and wanted to build a life together. These, and other strengths, will help them to resolve the concerns they presented in counseling.

Special Circumstances

In addition to exploring the 12 preceding aspects of families, counselors also should take account of any special concerns or circumstances that might be present in the family. These include the impact of divorce, death, or blending of families; adoption; occupational stressors; and the presence in the home of people outside the nuclear family. Remarried families, like the Wood family, typically must cope with complex, conflicting, and ambiguous new roles and relationships; divided loyalties; and feelings of mistrust, guilt, and anxiety (McGoldrick & Carter, 1988). All these factors should be considered in the process of family assessment.

STRUCTURED ASSESSMENT OF COUPLES AND FAMILIES

Although interviews are the primary vehicle for gathering information on families, many inventories as well as nonstandardized approaches to assessment have been developed or adapted for use with families. These can help counselors to gain insight into families and also can be useful in promoting increased self-awareness and mutual understanding within families. A sampling of these tools is presented here to give readers some idea of what is available.

Many inventories have been developed since the 1970s to assess marital satisfaction and adjustment. Among the best known and researched are the Family Adaptability and Cohesion Evaluation Scales (FACES) (Olson, 1986). This brief inventory is designed to measure cohesion and adaptability to change in families. Also useful in the assessment of family functioning are the Parent–Adolescent Communication Scale, the Family Satisfaction Scale, the Family Environment Scale, and Children's Report of Parent Behavior Inventory (Amerikaner, Monks, Wolfe, & Thomas, 1994).

Other inventories have been designed to describe the nature of an intimate relationship, highlighting its strengths and weaknesses. Particularly useful for this purpose is the Myers-Briggs Type Inventory (MBTI), published by Consulting Psychologists Press. A computerized scoring of a couple's MBTI scores yields information on probable strengths and issues created by the combination of their personalities. For example, a couple in which both partners are characterized by introversion is likely to be very comfortable sharing quiet time but may have difficulty maintaining relationships with family and friends.

In addition, a wide range of specific inventories are available for use with families; they provide assessment of such dimensions as dual-career relationships, conflict resolution skills, parenting styles, problems and attitudes of children and adolescents, sibling relationships, family beliefs, and co-dependency (Fischer & Corcoran, 1994; Fredman & Sherman, 1987).

Many nonstandardized approaches to assessment also are available for use with families (Holman, 1983). These not only provide information but can be used as vehicles for discussion to promote family awareness. The genogram, discussed earlier in this chapter, is one of these, described particularly well by McGoldrick and Gerson (1988). Another is the ecomap, designed to provide a picture of the organizational patterns and relationships in a family. Completed in conjunction with a family, large circles represent systems in a family environment (e.g., friends, extended family, recreation, work, culture), small circles represent females, and small squares represent males. Arrows signify flow of energy or resources while lines and spacial relationship of figures indicate nature and extent of involvement. *Incomplete sentences* also yield family information and promote discussion. Family members are asked to complete a series of sentences individually and in writing (e.g., What I value about my family is…, The biggest problem we face is…). Responses then are shared and discussed. Another useful tool is the *family sculpture*; family members arrange themselves to create a physical representation of the family. This can be adapted to family needs by asking a particular person to create the sculpture, by asking for a sculpture of the ideal family, or by sculpting the family at a specific time. Discussion of the sculpture while people are still in position can be particularly powerful.

TREATMENT PLANNING FOR FAMILIES

Once an assessment has been made of the family, the counselor is ready to formulate a treatment plan. Chapter 6 provided an overview of the DO A CLIENT MAP, including aspects that must be considered in formulating treatment plans for individual clients. With minor variations (indicated below), these dimensions are also considered when planning the treatment of a family. Because these dimensions were explored in depth in chapter 6, they are presented only briefly here, with emphasis given to their application to family counseling in general and to the Wood family in particular.

Diagnosis—Use of the DSM in assessment of individuals within a family is strongly recommended. That process can shed light on family problems and patterns of interaction. For example, in the Wood family, Nathan has been diagnosed with a Learning Disorder and an Attention-Deficit Disorder; these disorders have an impact not only on his functioning at school but on his role in the family, his closeness with his mother, and his difficulties with his stepfather. John, Jr. may be diagnosed with Alcohol Abuse, once further information is obtained. Although neither Olivia nor John seem to have mental disorders, John may have Obsessive-Compulsive Personality Traits while Olivia may have Histrionic Personality Traits, reflecting very different personal styles.

Objectives—Family members and counselors should collaborate to determine appropriate objectives. For the Wood family, specific objectives include the couple's having positive time together, behavioral changes in Nathan and John, Jr., and improved shared decision-making regarding such areas as finances and Nathan's education.

Assessment—The primary approach to assessment with families, in addition to interviews, is the inventories and nonstandardized procedures discussed above. Outside referrals can also provide useful information. For example, people presenting with Sexual Dysfunction usually would be referred for a medical evaluation.

An important purpose for assessment of families is determining their suitability for treatment. Counselors need to determine whether the family can make a commitment to and benefit from counseling or whether the process is likely to be sabotaged by the destructive participation or absence of one or more family members. The Wood family certainly seemed suitable for counseling; both Olivia and John were motivated to improve their family relationships and neither was severely impaired. Nathan and John, Jr. also had a profound impact on family dynamics and should participate in at least some family counseling sessions. Keesha probably should not be included in family sessions because of her age, but observing family interaction with her for one session might be informative.

Clinician—In determining who will provide counseling to a family, consideration should be given to whether one or two counselors (usually a male and a female) should be involved as well as to the possible importance of such counselor variables as age, gender, background, and experience. No particular guidelines seem essential in selecting a counselor for the Wood family. However, they might respond best to a counselor in midlife who has experience in helping people with problems related to remarried families, parenting, and communication.

Location—Family counseling usually takes place in outpatient settings, although it can be combined with individual and group counseling for people in hospitals or day treatment programs.

Interventions—Determining interventions for families, as for individuals, involves identifying a theoretical orientation as well as appropriate specific interventions. These choices are guided by many factors, including the motivation of the family, the nature of their difficulties, and the composition of the family. Further information on theories of family counseling and their application to the Wood family is provided in the next section of this chapter.

Emphasis—Theories of family counseling, like those of individual counseling, should be adapted to particular clients. Counselors should determine whether a family is fragile and has few strengths and insights, requiring a great deal of support, or whether the family is cohesive and motivated to examine past influences and underlying dynamics. The Woods are a relatively healthy, verbal, and expressive family. At the same time, they tend to blame their children for their difficulties and, as a whole family, are unlikely to be receptive to long-term, exploratory counseling. They would probably benefit most from counseling that is somewhat structured and problem-focused but that also builds communication and other family skills.

Numbers—Counselors need to determine whether to see an entire nuclear family, a couple, a subsystem (e.g., parent–child, siblings), or a nuclear family plus extended family such as grandparents. In addition, individual sessions with one or more of the family members might be indicated. Families also may be seen alone or with other families or couples in group therapy. Sessions with the Wood family probably will include Olivia, John, Nathan, and John, Jr. in most sessions but couples sessions, sibling sessions, and parent–child sessions also might be held.

Timing—Family counseling sessions, like those of individuals, usually are scheduled on a weekly basis, although each session may be longer than 50 minutes to allow time for all family members to speak and interact. Contracting for a specified number of sessions is often used with families as a way to address varying motivation within a family. Most models of family therapy are relatively brief, but some, like Bowen's intergenerational family therapy, tend to be lengthy. The Woods probably would respond best to counseling that is short or medium in duration, with weekly sessions of at least 60 minutes.

Medication—If any family members have severe symptoms that may be alleviated by medication, a medical referral can facilitate the process of family counseling. Nathan already is receiving medication. for his Attention-Deficit Disorder. No other need for medication was presented by the Wood family.

Adjunct services—Families, like individuals, benefit from activities that give them support and information, increase their socialization and activity levels, and provide them rewarding and pleasurable experiences. Al-Anon groups might provide John and Olivia with information on alcohol abuse. Participation in Alcoholics Anonymous might help John, Jr. More shared family activities, such as outings to the beach and family hikes, that provide time together in rewarding ways can increase the cohesiveness in this family.

Prognosis—This predicts the likelihood of the family's achieving its objectives according to the treatment plan that has been developed. In light of their motivation and emotional health, the prognosis for ameliorating the difficulties of the Wood family is very good.

THEORIES OF FAMILY COUNSELING

Many diverse approaches to family counseling are available. Some of the most important approaches are reviewed here. Guidelines are provided to help readers understand the kinds of families or situations for which each approach is particularly useful. This section is not designed to teach theories of family counseling but rather to enable counselors to integrate these approaches into their treatment plans in an effective way.

TRANSGENERATIONAL FAMILY THERAPY

The roots of transgenerational family therapy are in Freudian psychoanalytic thought. Developed by such theorists as Murray Bowen, James Framo, and Ivan Boszormenyi-Nagy, this long-term model of family counseling seeks to understand the present family by looking at the families of the past, from whom some of the patterns, role, behaviors, and attitudes of the present family have been acquired. Murray Bowen probably is the best-known proponent of this approach. Bowen, who died in 1990, initially focused his work on families with a person with Schizophrenia. He continued his work at the Georgetown Family Center, in Washington, D. C., which he founded and which continues to teach his approach.

Bowen viewed the family as a system. He believed that people within that system did not function independently but that change in one person would affect the system just as change in the system would have an impact on all family members.

The following concepts are integral to Bowen's theory of family therapy:

1. *Differentiation of self*—This describes the extent to which people can think, feel, and act for themselves, assessed on a 1–100 scale.
2. *Intergenerational* (or transgenerational or multigenerational) transmission process.
3. *Birth order* and *sibling position*.
4. *Family triangles*.
5. *Nuclear family emotional system*—This includes the focus and intensity of emotion in the family, the nature of the marital relationship, and the functioning of individual family members.
6. *Family projection process*—One member of the family projects uncomfortable or unacceptable feelings onto other family members.
7. *Emotional cutoff*—A family member, often a young adult, establishes physical and emotional distance from the family in order to achieve some independence. This often characterizes the efforts of people who are poorly differentiated to separate themselves from enmeshed families.
8. *Nodal events*—These are particular crises or happenings that shape a family.
9. *Family secrets*—Secrets such as infidelity, abortions, and substance use are common in families and can be at the heart of family dysfunction.

In working with families, Bowen assumed the role of coach or consultant. His style, and that of most of his followers, was cognitive and unemotional, leading people on a slowly paced journey toward gathering information, understanding their nuclear and families of origin, and increasing differentiation. Bowen sought to increase intimacy, objectivity, and understanding and to decrease emotional reactivity, anxiety, and increasing fusion in families. He often spent three years or more working with a family, using genograms, family interviews, and other tools.

Because he believed that an individual could have an impact on a system and vice versa, Bowen would work with an individual, a couple, or a family. His approach, then, can be useful regardless of whether an entire family is present for counseling. In its purest form, transgenerational family therapy seems suitable for only a select group of people, those who are not in an immediate crisis and who have the time, energy, finances, and inclination to undertake a lengthy and often analytical exploration of their families. A modified version of this approach, however, provides both a way of conceptualizing family functioning and many useful techniques that have broad application. A genogram, for example, can promote understanding in families where the intergenerational transmission process has had a major influence on current functioning.

The Wood family might not be willing to engage in an extended examination of their family background and so they might not be good candidates for Bowen's approach. However, the genogram and several other concepts associated with this approach, including the importance of birth order and differentiation do have relevance to that family, so might well be incorporated into their counseling.

EXPERIENTIAL/HUMANISTIC/COMMUNICATIONS APPROACHES

Virginia Satir, who developed conjoint family therapy, is the best known proponent of an approach that focuses on family communication. (Other proponents include Carl Whitaker and the Duhls.) Satir believed that although requests for counseling often are prompted by the apparent dysfunction of one family member, the identified patient or IP frequently is the healthiest member of the family and is simply reacting to the overall dysfunction in the family (Satir, 1983; Satir, Banmen, Gerber, & Gomori, 1991). Satir's goal, then, was to shift the focus of the counseling from the IP to the family, especially to the couple, and to help the family reestablish intimacy, caring, cohesiveness, and communication.

The following concepts are important in this model:

1. The partner relationship is integral to the health and functioning of the whole family.

2. Obtaining a family life chronology, beginning with the partners' families of origin and focusing on the development of the partner relationship, is important in reestablishing positive family feelings.

3. Low self-esteem in family members is a frequent cause of difficulties; counseling should promote individual self-esteem along with maturation and responsibility.

4. Clear and congruent communication is essential to healthy family functioning.

5. Differing styles of communication or perception (e.g., visual versus kinesthetic) can lead to conflict and need to be addressed.

6. Separateness and individuation of family members is essential to healthy family functioning.

7. Process usually is more important than content; counseling should emphasize the process of family communication rather than specific symptoms which probably are messages of hurt or blocks.

8. Family rules, norms, and secrets exert a powerful influence on family dynamics.

Satir's holistic approach, with its echoes of Carl Rogers, probably seems familiar to most counselors. Satir viewed herself as a role model and resource person, teaching families new ways to interact and supporting their efforts to change and grow. Her focus was largely on the present, and she emphasized strength rather than pathology. Exercises and techniques such as analysis of communication stance (Placator, Blamer, Super-reasonable/ Computer, Distractor/Irrelevant, Congruent communicator), family sculptures, family reconstruction, Parts Parties (helping people value multiple aspects of themselves), awareness enhancement, meditation, touch, and reframing are important ingredients in this model.

Satir's model encourages involvement of the entire nuclear family in the counseling process, even though counselors may not meet with all family members in all sessions. Her model is particularly suitable for families in which the partner relationship has weakened and where family communication is confusing, incongruent, and limited. Satir's communications approach seems best suited for people who are not in crisis and who have at least a moderate degree of motivation and verbal ability. Of course, nearly all families seeking counseling have some difficulty with communication. Consequently, aspects of Satir's approach, like Bowen's, have a great deal to offer almost all families seeking counseling.

In many ways, the communications model is well suited to treatment of the Wood family. Nathan and probably also John, Jr. were viewed as the IPs; however, the primary family difficulties stemmed from the interaction of John and Olivia, who no longer had the sense of unity and closeness that led them to marry. They were drifting away from each other and becoming overinvolved with their biological children. Family members communicated in limited and ambiguous ways and little open dialogue was present. Nathan, as well as Olivia and John, seemed to have issues of self-esteem. The members of this family were motivated to seek help and seemed capable of learning to communicate clearly and directly. Satir's model also provides a mix of supportiveness and directiveness, likely to be appreciated by this family.

STRUCTURAL FAMILY THERAPY

Salvador Minuchin is viewed as the primary developer of structural family therapy. (Maurizio Andolfi, who studied with Minuchin, is also associated with this approach.) Minuchin has had a long association with the Philadelphia Child Guidance Center, which provides training and counseling in this model. Minuchin advocated taking an active and involved approach to family counseling, becoming a part of the family system himself, if necessary, in order to challenge and change the family structure and views of the world (Minuchin & Fishman, 1981).

The following concepts are important in structural family therapy:

1. *Family structure*—This includes patterns of transaction, styles of communication, coalitions, and boundaries. In healthy families, boundaries are clear yet flexible. They provide well-defined lines of responsibility and authority and facilitate independence while protecting the family. Parents are allies and are in charge of the system yet are free to be childlike at times. Children have secure and clear roles, yet can occasionally and appropriately assume parental functions.
2. *Subsystems*—Subsystems are essential to family functioning. These include the partner subsystem, sibling subsystems, and various combinations of parent–child subsystems (e.g., the female family members' subsystem). In well-functioning families, subsystems are flexible and respond to the situation at hand.
3. *Adaptation to stress*—The manner in which families handle and adapt to stress provides information on the family structure and sources of both strength and weakness. Culturally or environmentally related stressors have received particular attention from Minuchin.

Minuchin used a broad range of techniques such as enactment, reframing, unbalancing, diagrams, and metaphors to join the family, to evaluate their functioning, and then to solve the problems and restructure the family, perhaps by escalating stress or using a family member as a sort of co-counselor. Structural family therapy is an active and creative approach that often is effective in overcoming resistance and engaging even difficult families in the therapeutic process. It also is a valuable approach to helping families with boundary issues, weak parental subsystems, excluded or enmeshed family members, and related concerns. This approach often is combined with strategic interventions, discussed later in this chapter.

Important structural issues were present in the Wood family. Olivia and John were reasonably effective parents, but did not have a strong spouse subsystem. Boundaries between parents and children were not always clear, and the mother–son (Nathan) and father–son (John, Jr.) subsystems seemed enmeshed. However, although a structural approach to working with this family might well be effective, the family structure was not severely dysfunctional. Attention to structural issues might, therefore, best be accomplished in the context of another approach, such as the communications model.

BEHAVIORAL FAMILY COUNSELING

Behavioral family counseling, an active, directive, and symptom-focused approach, is similar to behavioral counseling with individual clients. It is based on social learning theory and is particularly useful for dealing with couples or parent–child issues where a behavioral change is desired (Stuart, 1980). Proponents of this model include Richard Stuart and Aaron Beck.

Behavioral family counseling typically begins with an assessment of the current family situation, the nature and level of the undesirable behavior, and its secondary gains. Inventories and checklists are used to facilitate assessment. A contract might be developed, with both partners or the parents and children agreeing to make specific behavioral changes. Any rewards or consequences are then specified. A range of behavioral techniques (e.g., role playing, modeling, shaping, rehearsal, reinforcement, time out, token economies, contingency contracting, negotiation and conflict management, anger management, sex therapy) might be used to facilitate the change. Important skills such as problem solving, parenting, communication, and decision making might be taught. Structured efforts to improve relationships also play an essential role in this model. Couples might be encouraged to set aside a certain amount of time each day to be alone and talk, or they might set up Caring Days when they engage in behaviors their partner has identified as reflecting love and caring such as a massage, sending flowers or a card, preparing a special meal, or arranging a special evening. Family meetings provide a forum for sharing concerns. Follow-up sessions evaluate progress and, if necessary, modify the contract or the treatment plan.

Counselors using a behavioral model usually view themselves as educators, coaches, and expert consultants, although they do not ignore the importance of rapport. They design behavioral change programs, write up contracts, and regularly assess progress.

The behavioral model is most likely to be effective when family concerns are fairly specific and circumscribed and when the underlying relationships are basically sound. For example, this approach can help parents develop techniques for managing their children's behavior and can help couples find a comfortable way to share household chores. Often, however, counseling that begins in a behavioral mode will unearth structural or communication difficulties, necessitating an alternate or combined mode of counseling.

Nathan's behavior might be improved through behavioral counseling. John and Olivia could be helped to establish clear behavioral guidelines for Nathan, with rewards given if they are followed and, possibly, consequences dispensed if they are violated. Basically a child who is eager to please, Nathan might well accept the guidelines and learn to moderate his behavior. This approach might also help Olivia and John negotiate financial and household responsibilities, but other interventions seem indicated to address structural and communications problems.

ADLERIAN FAMILY COUNSELING

Alfred Adler, Rudolph Dreikurs, Don Dinkmeyer, and Jon Carlson are the names most strongly associated with Adlerian counseling or individual psychology. This approach originally focused primarily on the parent–child interaction and sought to help parents to facilitate the healthy development of their children.

The following ideas are important to this theory (Christensen, 1991):

1. Feelings of inferiority, stemming from childhood, often are related to family difficulties as people try to overcome those feelings and become their ideal selves.
2. Birth order is important in determining family roles and relationships.
3. Pampered or neglected children and children with physical or intellectual deficits are particularly likely to present problems.
4. Natural consequences, encouragement, respect, and realistic expectations help children and families to develop in positive ways.
5. Family conferences and democratic family structures contribute to the development of strong and healthy family constellations.
6. Families should be considered in their social context.

Adlerian counselors typically work with parents and children, both together and individually. Teachers also might be included in family counseling sessions. Counselors following this approach tend to be directive, interpretive, and present-oriented. They are concrete and combine supportive and educational approaches.

The focus of the Adlerian approach on encouragement and health rather than on pathology makes it useful with a broad range of families, but it is particularly well-suited to families where a conflict between parents and children is present. Dinkmeyer and Carlson (1984) adapted this model for use with couples. They have defined marital happiness as a combination of self-esteem, social interest, and a sense of humor. Using an analysis of the partners' life styles, they promote marital happiness and enrichment by emphasizing strengths, facilitating understanding, and building responsibility and social interest.

Aspects of the Adlerian approach seem useful in helping to conceptualize and treat the difficulties of the Wood family. The family council could be a helpful stimulus to family communication and might promote cohesiveness in the family. Viewing Nathan as a child who has feelings of inferiority and who is striving for power in self-destructive and socially unacceptable ways can lead to the development of effective approaches to helping him. Techniques of marital enrichment might be very helpful to John and Olivia. In addition, discussion of the impact of birth order might promote understanding of family roles. However, the Adlerian model does not address directly the communication concerns of the Wood family and so probably would not be the best method for helping them.

STRATEGIC FAMILY THERAPY

Strategic family therapy, developed by Jay Haley and Cloé Madanes, draws heavily on the work of Milton Erickson. This theory views symptoms as a metaphor for the family difficulties and advocates an active approach to removing the symptom and simultaneously improving the overall family functioning (Haley, 1987).

Principles important in this theory include:

1. Family structure and hierarchy are both important; the parents must be clearly in charge of the family.
2. Transitions often precipitate family dysfunction. The departure of the children from the home is a particularly stressful transition.
3. The counselor is responsible for finding a way to alleviate symptoms and help the family. If one approach doesn't work quickly, another approach should be tried until the goal is accomplished.

   4. The counseling focuses on actions; thoughts, feelings, and insights are
      secondary.

Strategic family therapy is a directive, carefully planned, action-oriented
approach, with the counselor in charge. A wide range of techniques is used.
Paradoxical interventions are a particularly important ingredient of this approach. These involve a reversal of the person's perceptions or expectations. For
example, a setback may be predicted for a family that is making good progress,
and a couple that seeks help because of constant fighting might be told to
schedule arguments. These interventions serve to jostle the family's dysfunctional patterns and reduce the power of the symptom. This often leads to a
modification in family dynamics and the elimination of the symptom. The family
then is likely to be receptive to learning new skills and behavioral patterns. Other
important techniques in this approach include directives, prescribed ordeals
paired with symptoms, relabeling, redistributing symptoms, rituals, and enactment.

Haley and Madanes believed that this approach could be helpful to all
families, regardless of the nature of their concerns (Madanes, 1981). This
approach is particularly effective with resistant or passive families, families with
limited verbal or analytical abilities, families experiencing stressful transitions,
families in crisis, and families with dysfunctional hierarchies.

A strategic approach might be effective in reducing Nathan's symptoms
and improving family functioning. In order to do this, the counselor might tell
the family that Nathan is acting out because he does not know how a young man
is supposed to act; John and John, Jr. would then be encouraged to engage in
rewarding activities with Nathan to model appropriate behavior. Their attention
and acceptance might help Nathan feel more comfortable in the family and
reduce his enmeshment with his mother. Other interventions can be developed
to strengthen the partner relationship and promote shared parenting. However,
moderating this directive approach with some attention to the development of
communication skills and promoting understanding of the challenges of blended
families could make counseling even more effective with this family.

BRIEF/SOLUTION-FOCUSED FAMILY THERAPY

Developed by Steve deShazer, Michele Weiner-Davis, William O'Hanlon, and
others, and drawing on the work of the Mental Research Institute, solution-
focused family therapy is a brief, problem focused model (Becvar & Becvar,
1993). It emphasizes strengths and resources as well as past successes and helps
people use those to make small but rapid changes. This approach is structured

and goal-oriented, using a broad repertoire of strategic interventions, as well as understanding of the reciprocal relationships in a family, to promote change. Strongly associated with this model is deShazer's (1991, p. 113) Miracle Question: "Suppose that one night there is a miracle and while you were sleeping the problem that brought you to therapy is solved: How would you know? What would be different? What will you notice different the next morning that will tell you that there has been a miracle? What will your spouse notice?" Another special feature of this model is the use it sometimes makes of an observing team who give feedback, messages, and clues to the counselor and the family (Thomas, 1992).

Solution-focused family therapy advocates short-term counseling, typically 6–12 sessions. Because of its emphasis on health and rapid resolution of problems, it has considerable appeal for counselors, clients, and managed care organizations and is growing in use.

This model also has some ideas to offer the Wood family. The Miracle Question, in particular, can help the family to identify times both before and after Olivia and John's marriage when family members felt happier and interacted more successfully. Both Olivia and John have coped with serious difficulties in their lives; John dealt with the death of his first wife and being a single parent while Olivia, too, experienced loss and the challenges of being a single parent to a demanding child. Coping strategies that helped them through those times can be mobilized now.

CONSTRUCTIVIST/NARRATIVE APPROACHES TO FAMILY COUNSELING

Several of the pioneers in family counseling, including Adler and Satir, took a phenomenological approach in which they tried to understand the family's conception of reality. Solution-focused and other modern approaches to family therapy have built on this concept and assume a constructivist position that views reality as "multiperspectival" (Becvar & Becvar, 1993, p. 297). Each family member has his or her own understanding of the family and its difficulties based on that person's views and the language used to describe the family. Constructivist therapists emphasize epistemology, the process of knowing and describing the social construction of reality (Amatea & Sherrard, 1994). They begin by speaking the clients' language and accepting their perspectives, seeking the logic and wisdom in their lives. Change is promoted by shifting those perspectives and modifying language so that resources and solutions are evoked.

New approaches to family therapy have built on these concepts and advance an approach to counseling that emphasizes a process of dialogue

(Becvar & Becvar, 1994). Counselors listen to clients' unique stories and then use words, metaphors, and circular questions as well as their own story about a family or client to effect change. Although focus usually is on presenting problems, these models are less structured than solution focused models and emphasize a more collaborative client–counselor relationship. Variations on this model include constructivism, which views people as self-organizing systems whose perceptions of reality shape experience; interactional counseling, which also emphasizes the constructions of the perceiver but places particular emphasis on the importance of social interaction and communication (Steenbarger, 1991); and narrative therapy, which uses written communications between clients and counselors to shape perceptions and effect change.

OTHER MODELS OF FAMILY COUNSELING

The most important models of family counseling have been reviewed in this chapter. However, several other models, including the Milan approach to counseling with families and psychodynamic family psychotherapy are used by many family counselors and will be mentioned here briefly.

Milan Systemic Family Therapy

This approach was developed by Mara Selvini Palazzoli and her colleagues in Milan, Italy, and by Penn and Hoffman in the United States. It is an epistemological approach that integrates strategic and behavioral techniques (Selvini Palazzoli, 1985; Thomas, 1992). Repetitive sequences, feedback loops, and coevolution in families in which each family member affects others receive particular attention in this model. Using techniques such as circular questioning, rituals, and prescriptions (often that the parents take a vacation together away from their children), this model involves extended sessions and observers who provide feedback to the therapists.

Psychodynamic Family Counseling

Freudian theory is the basis for this approach to counseling families, developed by Nathan Ackerman, Kirchner and Kirchner, Scharff and Scharff, Harville Hendrix, and others. The goals of this approach are to increase ego strength and reduce interactions based on past figures and experiences by improving insight (Thomas, 1992). Techniques include a detailed history taking with emphasis on family of origin, free association, use of transference and countertransference, exposing family secrets, questioning, observing defenses, interpretation, and working through. This approach continues to have appeal and usefulness for some counselors and families.

EXAMPLE OF A TREATMENT PLAN FOR A FAMILY

This chapter has reviewed the most important approaches to working with families and couples. All of the major approaches discussed here had something to offer the Wood family, although some seemed more useful than others. Treatment planning for families, then, even more than for individuals, is a flexible process that involves assessing family dynamics, determining the most appropriate mode of treatment, and integrating that information with the skills and preferences of the counselor to determine an effective way to counsel a family.

The last section of this chapter provides a sample treatment plan for another family. It also gives readers descriptions of three additional families for use in practicing treatment planning for families.

TREATMENT PLAN FOR THE SCHWARTZ FAMILY

The Schwartz family includes Denise, age 35, Peter, age 37, and Jeffrey, age 4. This is the first marriage for Denise and Peter. Their first child, a boy they named Jeffrey, was born one year after the marriage. Jeffrey died of a genetic disorder when he was 18 months old. Their second child, who Denise insisted be named after their first child, was born about three years later. Denise had a miscarriage between the two births.

Denise and Peter met in college and married, following a courtship of nearly five years, during which Peter completed law school. Denise works part-time doing telemarketing from home, but spends most of her time caring for Jeffrey. She is overprotective, seems sad, and is very concerned about her marriage. She suspects Peter of having an affair. Peter works full-time as a lawyer, seems tense and preoccupied, and minimizes Denise's concerns. Denise was the oldest child in a large, enmeshed family. Peter was the youngest of three, with two older sisters. His mother abused alcohol and his father was in the military and was away from home for long periods of time.

Jeffrey presents with unpredictable behavior; he vacillates between aggressive acting out and clinging overdependency. The family sought counseling at the suggestion of Jeffrey's preschool teacher. Denise hopes that counseling also will improve her relationship with Peter.

Diagnosis of Family Members

Denise:

   Axis I.   300.4 Dysthymic Disorder, moderate
   Axis II.   Dependent personality traits
   Axis III. None
   Axis IV.   Marital conflict
   Axis V.   65

Peter:

   Axis I.   300.02 Generalized Anxiety Disorder, mild
   Axis II.   Obsessive-compulsive personality traits
   Axis III. None
   Axis IV.   Marital conflict, pressure at work
   Axis V.   70

Jeffrey:

   Axis I.   312.9 Disruptive Behavior Disorder NOS
   Axis II.   V71.09 No diagnosis on Axis II
   Axis III. None
   Axis IV.   Conflict in parents' marriage
   Axis V.   55

Assessment of Family Functioning

This family presents with problems of loss, disruptive behavior, and poor communication. They seem to be repeating some transgenerational patterns; Denise overfunctions as the caretaker while Peter has withdrawn, both physically and emotionally. He had been the center of attention as a child and when he and Denise first married and is having difficulty with Denise's absorption in Jeffrey. This family is in stage III, the family with young children. Role changes and maintaining the spouse relationship, common challenges in this stage, are particularly difficult for this couple. Denise and Jeffrey seem enmeshed, not surprising in light of the family history. However, Peter has been all but cut off from the family system and may have formed intimate relationships outside of the home. Family members have divergent communication styles; Peter tends to be Super-reasonable; Denise, both Blamer and Placator; and Jeffrey is a Distractor. Congruent communication is limited. Family values also are in conflict; Peter's values tend to be material while Denise emphasizes parenting. Both Denise and Peter come from European Jewish backgrounds; this is a source of commonality. Extended family are a resource and assist with babysitting and finances. Neither Denise nor Peter have clear and positive self-images; both have an external locus of control. This, as well as other factors, made it difficult for them to establish a strong marriage and cope with their losses together. As a result, they have become distanced and disapproving of each other. However, they have many strengths; they have stayed together despite great loss, they are verbal and intelligent, they once had a loving and rewarding relationship, and both are motivated to make a good home for Jeffrey.

Objectives

1. Improve ratings of marital happiness and security.
2. Increase time Denise and Peter spend together as a couple.
3. Reduce the frequency of Jeffrey's aggressive behavior and increase his independence.
4. Reduce Denise's depression and Peter's anxiety.
5. Enable couple to grieve and discuss their losses openly.

Assessment

1. Scale to measure marital happiness.
2. Beck Depression and Anxiety Inventories.
3. Baseline measure of Jeffrey's behavior.
4. Medical evaluation of Jeffrey.

Clinician

Beyond experience in helping families deal with loss and grief, no special clinician characteristics seem indicated.

Location

Outpatient counseling in a private practice, community mental health center, or family counseling agency.

Interventions

An eclectic approach will be used that initially emphasizes a communications approach, then shifts to a combination of behavioral and structural interventions. The humanistic or communications model will be used to help the couple express and understand their feelings, develop congruence in their communications, and increase their self-esteem. This model can help them regain the closeness they had when they married and can facilitate their efforts to grieve their losses. Once they feel more secure in the marriage and with themselves, behavioral techniques such as Caring Days and scheduled talks and dates will be used to promote closeness in the couple while clear rules and appropriate use of reinforcement and time out can help modify Jeffrey's behavior. Structural interventions, such as joining and unbalancing, will help to restore the parental hierarchy.

Emphasis

Although support will be an important ingredient in treatment with this family, they can handle a moderately paced approach that focuses them on their concerns.

Numbers

Family and couples counseling will be the primary modes of treatment.

Timing

Weekly 50-minute sessions will be scheduled, for approximately 3–6 months.

Medication

If rapid improvement is not evident in both Jeffrey's behavior and Denise's depression, they will be referred to a psychiatrist for assessment.

Adjunct Services

Family and couple activities that are pleasurable and rewarding are essential to this family. Peter and Denise will be encouraged to resume ballroom dancing lessons that they had begun and enjoyed shortly after their marriage. Peter might benefit from involvement in an ACOA group while Denise might join a support group for mothers of young children. An outside activity for Jeffrey such as pre-kindergarten or gymnastics can promote independence, self-esteem, self-control, and peer involvement.

Prognosis

Prognosis is good to very good for accomplishment of objectives via this treatment plan.

Cases for Treatment Planning

Case 1. The Stuart family consists of George, 52, a school principal; his wife Jody, 52, a librarian; and their children, Susan, 20, Mark, 17, and Lucy, 12. All three children were adopted. Susan and Mark have both been high achievers and are athletically inclined. Lucy is mildly mentally retarded. Her self-care is poor and she is in a special program at school. She is very attached to her father and to Susan and is hostile toward her mother. Jody wants to become more involved in her career and resents Lucy's caretaking demands. She has been encouraging George to send her to a boarding school which he is reluctant to do.

Case 2. Steve Stern, age 46, and Roberto Alvarado, 35, have been living together for five years and view each other as life partners. Steve was married for 15 years before he met Roberto and has two children, Mari, age 12, and Howard, age 10. Roberto would like the children to view him as a stepparent but Steve has kept contact between Roberto and the children to a minimum. His explanation is that his ex-wife would deny him visitation rights if she knew the truth about his relationship with Roberto. The two also have cultural differences; Steve's background is Jewish and Roberto's is Latino. Steve is the oldest of two; Roberto is a middle child in a family of five children. Roberto works as an accountant and Steve is employed in sales.

Case 3. The Young family includes Arlene, 33, Fred, 35, Fred, Jr., 14, and Bobby, 10. Arlene is very talkative and attractive. She expresses long-standing dissatisfaction with her marriage. She has had a number of poorly-concealed affairs which have generally gone unnoticed by her husband. She recently prompted the family's decision to seek counseling by charging expensive furs and jewelry to her husband and then concealing the bills. Fred is a highly intelligent and successful business executive. He reported no awareness of marital difficulties until his wife's recent spending spree. He views that as the main issue and wants help in controlling his wife's money management. Fred, Jr. is quiet and intense. He is a good student, well behaved and scholarly, but with little peer group involvement. He was conceived on his parents' third date and was the reason for the marriage, although he is unaware of this. Bobby is cute, talkative, and manipulative. He is intelligent but does not do well at school. He is a leader among his peers and clearly is the favorite of both parents.

Assessment and Treatment Planning for Groups and Organizations

Linda Seligman and Bonita Marcus Moore

Since the 1960's, therapy and counseling groups have come into increasing use to meet a wide diversity of educational and therapeutic needs (Corey, 1995). Increasingly, counselors see the use of groups as a vital adjunct to their individual counseling. Counseling groups are being used extensively in specialized settings ranging from treatment programs for eating disorders to pain centers to business and industry settings (Morran, 1992). Many factors have driven the rising popularity of group treatment. The group offers an opportunity for the person to move beyond the dyadic client–counselor relationship and to draw upon the insights, perspectives, and feedback of other members of the group (Corey, 1995; Ratican, 1992). The group participant can practice new skills of self-expression, communication, and socialization in the group setting (MacLennan & Dies, 1992). A counseling group can provide a safe environment for the rapid reduction of the feelings of isolation which many clients present. As they interact with other people who have similar problems, their own difficulties can seem more understandable and less frightening; clients can internalize these perceptions and become more accepting of themselves (Ratican, 1992). The group experience can create a sense of belongingness which probably could not be achieved in individual counseling.

Yalom (1995, p. 1) identified 11 therapeutic factors in group counseling which he believed set in motion the complex process of therapeutic change:

1. Instillation of hope
2. Universality
3. Imparting information
4. Altruism
5. Corrective recapitulation of the primary family group
6. Development of socializing techniques
7. Imitative behavior
8. Interpersonal learning
9. Group cohesiveness
10. Catharsis
11. Existential factors

These factors have been associated with positive change in a variety of treatment modalities, but have a particularly strong association with successful group counseling.

Beyond the therapeutic benefits of group work, economics also contributes to the popularity of group work. Counselors in many settings are expected to address a broad range of complex issues and to serve a large number of clients with limited resources (staff, time, and money) (Brown, 1994; Ehly, 1993). The group format offers a means for meeting this challenge.

This chapter will suggest a framework for assessing the dynamics of counseling groups and for providing group treatment. It will also review the various aspects of the counselor's role in providing group treatment in a variety of settings. Although no standard format exists for the diagnosis of group concerns, assessment procedures and treatment modalities are available for counseling groups and will be discussed in this chapter.

The group counselor's primary task is to clarify the nature and concerns of the group (diagnosis) and to develop strategies for dealing with those concerns (treatment planning). To do so, the counselor considers the group's composition, motivation, environment and dynamics.

COMPOSITION

The counselor may be leading a preexisting or preformed group, or may be in the position of forming new groups to meet identified needs. The preformed group is likely to occur in an organizational setting, where the counselor is called in to provide consultation services, perhaps promoting cohesiveness and productivity in a group of employees. A predetermined group may also be found in a community setting, where the counselor is asked to provide services to an identified clientele such as ex-offenders or negligent parents. Although the people composing these groups may not have met as a group before, the counselor may have little or no flexibility in determining the composition of the group.

More often, however, the counselor has the flexibility to construct a counseling group based on certain criteria. These criteria include the following:

1. *Number of members*—The ideal number of participants in a counseling group is approximately seven or eight, according to Yalom (1995), and certainly no fewer than six or more than fourteen (Gladding, 1995). Sensitivity training groups may be somewhat larger, with 12–16 members considered a comfortable size (Yalom, 1995). When groups are very small (four or fewer), members tend to feel pressured to perform or contribute, and the opportunities for interaction are diminished. On the other hand, when groups are too large, some members may feel discouraged from participating, while a subgroup of members may dominate the group (Gladding, 1995). The optimal number of members ultimately should be determined not by formula but primarily on the basis of several factors: the number of group leaders, the ages of participants, and the goals of the group. For example, a bereavement group for young children probably should be relatively small (Healy-Romanello, 1993), while a personal growth group for college students might provide more opportunity for interaction if composed of approximately twelve group members and two co-leaders.

2. *Nature and history of concerns*—A counseling group typically has one or more important concerns, such as coping with abuse or developing assertiveness, that need to be understood and addressed. The counselor should assess the group's homogeneity with respect to the focal concerns. Greater homogeneity in background and concerns usually leads to greater group cohesiveness and a more intense group experience (Corey, 1992). A homogeneous group may be especially useful when members primarily need support or help dealing with specific common problems (Gladding, 1995). On the other hand, a heterogeneous group may more accurately recreate a social microcosm, which may be of significant therapeutic value to some participants (Yalom, 1995). Heterogeneous groups may be particularly appropriate for personality change and other issues requiring intensive and long-term group counseling (Gladding, 1995).

3. *Relevant demographic characteristics*—Often, demographics are important factors in group membership. For example, many counseling

groups are limited to one gender or age group. Survivors of childhood incest may be most effectively treated in a same-gender group. Lifespan development issues such as retirement might be best addressed in a group of people in mid-life or older. Career and job issues may be quite different for affluent clients than for those from a low socioeconomic level. There also has been some indication that ethnic homogeneity in counseling groups might be most effective in addressing issues related to racial identity development (Bowman, 1993). Potential members may be screened with a view to characteristics such as age, gender, and background.

4. *Relevant personal characteristics*—Not all people are appropriate for group counseling, so screening for suitability is essential. People who would be particularly inappropriate for group membership generally are those who are extremely hostile or aggressive, out of touch with reality, suicidal, highly suspicious, antisocial, or in a crisis (Corey, 1995). Appropriateness for the group also needs to be assessed with reference to the composition and goals of the group. For example, people who abuse substances may be excluded from membership in certain personal growth groups, where their presence may detract from the group's goals; however, group counseling focused on dealing with addiction issues may be a highly effective format for working with these same people (Corey, 1995). The goals of the individual participants should be compatible with those of the group as a whole (ASGW, 1989).

5. *Financial circumstances*—Potential members' financial circumstances must be reviewed if there is to be a fee or if eligibility for membership in the group is contingent on meeting low-income guidelines.

6. *Open vs. closed group membership*—A group which allows for a flow of members entering and leaving the group can provide stimulation and vitality, as well as programming flexibility. However, group cohesion and trust is often more difficult to achieve in an open group than it is in a group whose membership is stable and whose duration is specified. A closed group also is more likely to maintain continuity of issues and relationships, since its membership is more stable. However, it may be difficult to maintain a closed group over an extended period of time. As months pass, some members may leave the group, and the diminished size of the group may inhibit its effectiveness (Yalom, 1995). Group counselors need to decide whether open or closed groups are most likely to accomplish their goals.

The use of an example can clarify the process of initiating and leading a counseling group as well as the nature and importance of some of these relevant variables. The adult division of a county school system took on the task of providing basic skills education and vocational training for low-income single parents and displaced homemakers. As part of this effort, counselor Jane Clemes was hired to coordinate the program as well as to provide personal, educational, and career counseling to the group.

The counselor established the following criteria for participation:

1. Participants had to be residents of the jurisdiction providing funding.
2. All participants had to be single mothers; widowed, divorced, or separated homemakers; or single pregnant women.
3. Participants had to meet established income guidelines.
4. Participants had to be over the age of 21; or, if under 21, had to be high school graduates. (This criterion was established because non-high school graduates under 21 were eligible for other services in the area.)
5. Participants had to be competent in reading, writing, speaking, and understanding English.
6. Participants had to appear to be able to function successfully in a group setting, manifesting no severe personality disorders, or hostile, violent, or suicidal behavior.
7. Participants were required to be free of substance use disorders.
8. Participants were self-referred and voluntary.
9. Participants had to express motivation to become employed upon the completion of the program.

Jane determined that, given the resources she had, she could provide training and counseling services to 16–18 program participants. To accommodate such a large number, she planned on having two counseling groups.

Jane then planned an outreach program. She distributed press releases and fliers throughout the community. In response to inquiries these generated, she met with area human services providers and explained the planned program in greater detail. Her publicity effort generated telephone inquiries from 60 people. Jane conducted her initial interviews during those telephone contacts, obtaining rudimentary information regarding each caller's educational and employment background, current life situation, and expressed interests. She then sent a printed questionnaire to 55 of the callers, referring the remaining five to other programs or resources more closely matching their expressed situations or needs.

The 40 questionnaires which she received back gave Jane information about the applicants' demographic and personal characteristics. Those who appeared eligible for the program were contacted for an intake interview in person. Following the interviews, 24 people signed up for the program. They ranged in age from 25 to 54, reflected a range of racial and ethnic backgrounds, and all had children. There was considerable variability in their education and work backgrounds.

Jane decided that a closed membership format would be most appropriate for the groups. Because applications continued to filter in after her initial screening, she requested funding to begin another group at a later date. She felt that it was important to keep the first groups closed and time-limited, to maintain continuity and to assure a smooth flow from counseling to vocational training.

MOTIVATION

The members of a group, especially a preformed group, may have widely varying levels of interest in treatment. Some members may be motivated to seek treatment, but unwilling or hesitant to express themselves in a group setting. Some may focus exclusively or primarily on the group leader and disregard or resist input from other group members. Those who are in the group involuntarily, such as people assigned to the group by the courts or managers in a corporation engaged in an organizational development effort, may be resistant to the entire experience. Counselors need to obtain an accurate reading of people's interest in counseling before it is begun so treatment planning can take account of likely sources of resistance.

During the intake interviews, Jane tried to determine the level of applicants' motivation. Several of the applicants were there at the urging of their mothers, siblings, boyfriends, or social workers. One reported that her divorce attorney thought it would look good if she were involved in a career counseling and training program. Although Jane did not feel that this information should lead her to reject people from the program, it did influence her decision to accept 24 applicants into the program, in anticipation that several might not actually begin the program. In fact, only 16 people did participate. This was a good size, Jane felt, for the goals and format of the support groups she planned to conduct.

ENVIRONMENT

Consideration of the group's environment includes an exploration of the members' home base, be it a community, work setting, or school, and the environment in which treatment will be provided. Of particular importance is an examination of those factors that might promote or inhibit the success of the group. For example, the sociopolitical factors influencing the community might have a bearing on the effectiveness of the counseling group. If treatment is delivered in a high-crime area where personal safety is at risk, this factor must be considered in planning the location and timing of meetings, as well as possible transportation arrangements for group members. If the group is conducted in a school or corporate setting, the institutional climate, including the level of trust in the organization, may have an impact on the likelihood of success of the group.

In preparation for her counseling, Jane made a concerted effort to understand the participants' environments. The community mental health center at that time was hosting a series of lunches to bring together community leaders and human services workers. Jane attended those in order to get to know and be known by the professionals who were likely to serve her clients. These luncheon meetings had the additional purpose of exposing Jane to a multitude of resources and referral sources which she knew would be of use to her clients.

GROUP DEVELOPMENT AND DYNAMICS

Groups, like people, go through a series of developmental stages. These stages have been described with slight differences, but with remarkable consistency, by group stage theorists (Corey, 1995; Kormanski, 1988; Yalom, 1995):

Stage 1:   *Orientation and exploration*—The primary task of the initial stage is to establish structure and goals.

Stage 2:   *Conflict and interpersonal dominance*—This stage is characterized by increased anxiety, defensiveness, and jockeying for control.

Stage 3:   *Working stage*—This is a period of great cohesiveness, high productivity, and intermember harmony.

Stage 4:   *Consolidation and termination*—This stage is characterized by summarizing, integrating, and interpreting the experience of the group.

Group dynamics can be assessed through understanding and examining the following aspects of a group:

1. Cohesiveness of group—How close-knit, committed, and involved are the group members?

2. Level of trust—Are the members able to take risks and to self-disclose appropriately? To what extent are they able to move beyond surface

conversation, to deeper levels of interaction? Do they focus their trust solely on the group leader, or do they trust other members as well?

3. Nature and degree of communication—How openly do members communicate? Who communicates with whom? What styles of communication characterize individual members and the group as a whole? For example, do the group members communicate well in cognitive areas but have difficulty sharing their emotions?

4. Group decision-making style—Is it democratic or authoritarian? Are decisions made efficiently or laboriously?

5. Formal and informal roles assumed by members—What styles of participation are typical of the group members? Do some members seem to dominate group interactions? What is the structure or hierarchy of the group? Do some members seem to have more power or influence than others? Do some appear to play supporting roles? Are there identifiable rescuers or scapegoats? What patterns of influence are exerted by group members? Who has assumed leadership roles and functions?

6. Rules and norms accepted by the group—What expressed and implicit policies and procedures guide the operation of the group? Most groups have norms that influence when members arrive for meetings, the regularity of attendance, the amount of self-disclosure and confrontation that occurs, the power given to the designated leader, and the topics considered in group meetings.

7. History of treatment—What counseling interventions have been made previously with this group? What impact have they had on the group? These variables are of particular significance to the counselor who is beginning counseling with a group that is already formed or functioning, such as a counseling group that has received some treatment but that is now being reevaluated or assigned to a new counselor, a peer support group being assessed for professional intervention, or a group that had been formed in another setting (e.g., a work group or a classroom group), now referred for counseling. However, these same variables are also of importance to counselors assessing the progress of their own ongoing groups.

PLANNING THE TREATMENT

Once the needs and dimensions of the group have been assessed through interviews, questionnaires, research, observation, or other means, the counselor is ready to plan the treatment. This plan may follow the format of the DO A

CLIENT MAP, presented in chapter 6, including the following elements: *D*iagnosis, *O*bjectives, *A*ssessments, *C*linician, *L*ocation, *I*nterventions, *E*mphasis, *N*umbers, *T*iming, *M*edication, *A*djunct Services, and *P*rognosis (Seligman, 1990).

Diagnosis

The first step is to understand the needs, concerns, strengths, and weaknesses of those people who will be the focus of treatment. Initially, the counselor may have had a broad description of the group membership. However, assessment, conducted during an intake interview, will provide specific diagnostic and descriptive information about the participants. Determining whether any of the participants has a mental disorder and its nature is especially important.

Jane felt that the 16 people who arrived for the first group counseling session comprised an appropriate group. Although they showed some diversity in ethnic, educational, and employment backgrounds, their commonalities seemed more significant than their differences. All appeared to be in periods of major transition in their lives, and all seemed to have arrived at that point involuntarily. For the most part, the women seemed apprehensive about what lay ahead of them and unsure of their own capabilities to cope. Most expressed a strong desire to take care of their children, to provide a good and stable home for them despite tumultuous circumstances, and to give their children a better life than the women had had. Several of the participants expressed a desire to improve themselves so that they could be a role model and an inspiration to their children. None of the women had incapacitating mental disorders or medical conditions and none presented a danger to themselves or others. However, some were experiencing Adjustment Disorders or Dysthymic Disorders.

Objectives

As with individual counseling, objectives should ideally be established before the treatment is planned. However, counselors and clients in a group may have more difficulty reaching a consensus on goals and objectives. Counselors working with groups may need to assume a more active role in goal setting, inferring appropriate and shared goals and objectives from information provided during the assessment process.

Jane derived her groups' goals not only from information gleaned in contacts with the participants, but also on the basis of predetermined goals built into the overall program. Those goals were to empower the women so that they could formulate career-life goals, develop marketable skills, and eventually become economically self-sufficient.

In addition, the participants had expressed the following goals, which Jane integrated into the design of her program:

1. to improve self-image and feelings of self-worth
2. to develop a sense of optimism and a vision of a brighter future
3. to build strategies for coping with stress
4. to learn assertiveness skills in order to be unafraid to speak up for themselves.

Assessment

Assessment in counseling groups refers to assessment of both the individual members or potential members and the group as a whole. Qualitative as well as quantitative approaches may be helpful to the counselor in designing a treatment plan and course of action for a counseling group.

Qualitative Approaches to Assessment

Many techniques are available for assessing the needs of a group. The intake interviews can generate a wealth of information on individual needs, goals, and expectations. The interviewer can gather information about the participant's personal history, motivation for treatment, environmental stressors, and ego strength (Yalom, 1995). Observation of the participants or potential participants can yield important data for diagnosis and treatment planning. Observation may be most feasible in a school or residential setting, where the person's behaviors and interactions may be accessible to trained observers. However, even in the context of the intake interview, the interviewer can make observations that can facilitate understanding of the person's interpersonal interaction patterns. Questionnaires administered prior to the establishment of a group also may help the counselor to establish common concerns or needs relevant to the theme or focal issue of the group.

As the group progresses, journals, shared with the counselor (and sometimes with other members), can provide a means for generating qualitative information on the progress of the group. That information may be a valuable aid to the development of personal insight as well as in shaping treatment and establishing a record of progress.

In organizations, qualitative assessment of the organization, prior to the inception of group counseling, may be used to generate information that will promote effective treatment planning for the group. A framework used for diagnosing organizational effectiveness has been described as the seven-S's of the organizational system: strategy, structure, systems, staff, style, skills, and shared values

(Waterman, Peters, & Phillips, 1980). Information in these areas can be garnered through individual and focused group discussions, as well as review of documents including regulations, organization charts, and workflow diagrams.

In the case discussed in this chapter, Jane had limited access to information about her group participants. However, the inquiry call, application questionnaire, and intake interview together yielded enough information for her to have some sense of participant needs and goals. Particularly useful were questions included on the intake questionnaire related to the participant's personal history and goals, as well as information regarding other treatments and disabilities. During the intake interview itself, Jane explored the participant's expressed goals and underlying experiences and influences leading to those goals. These issues were again discussed during the initial phase of the group.

Quantitative Approaches to Assessment

Quantitative measures also have been used to add information on the diagnosis and evaluation of a counseling group. However, some question exists as to whether quantitative measures can adequately distinguish subtle (but significant) changes in the group members (Corey, 1995). The *How Encounter Groups Work* questionnaire developed by Lieberman, Yalom, and Miles (1973) has been demonstrated to yield useful data for evaluation of a group experience (Kivlighan, Johnsen, & Fretz, 1987). The Fundamental Interpersonal Relations Orientation questionnaire (FIRO) also has been used to measure interpersonal behavior of group members. This instrument profiles the individual on the basis of three interpersonal needs: control, inclusion, and affection (Yalom, 1995).

Practitioners make use of a wide variety of quantitative assessment instruments to measure relevant constructs in group members as a means of identifying needs and of assessing nature and impact of the group experience. Pre-group and post-group administration of such instruments may indicate changes. For example, the A-COPE measure of coping factors in adolescents (Patterson & McCubbin, 1987) has been used to measure impact of group counseling on twelve coping factors (ventilating feelings, seeking diversions, developing self-reliance, developing social support, solving family problems, avoiding problems, seeking spiritual support, seeking out close friends, seeking professional support, engaging in demanding activity, turning to humor, and relaxing) (Carty, 1993). The Social Support Inventory (McCubbin, Patterson, Rossman, & Cooke, 1982) has been used to assess new parents' support systems, and has been adapted to measure social support in other groups and populations as well (Carty, 1993). The categories of social support measured by this instrument include emotional, esteem, network, appraisal, and altruistic support. Other instruments available for measuring such factors as locus of control, depression, and dependence/independence also may be useful in assessing individual changes stemming from group counseling.

Little evidence exists that standard psychological tests are useful as predictors of group behavior. Studies of the MMPI, Rorschach, Thematic Apperception Test (TAT), Sentence Completion, and Draw-a-Person have yielded little useful information for prediction of group behavior (Yalom, 1995).

Clinician

Group counselors must attend to three dimensions of their groups: the group as a whole, the individual members of the group, and the interactions among the group members. Corey (1995) identified traits in the group leader who is most likely to succeed in this challenging role:

1. *Sense of presence*—Counselors should be emotionally available to all of the group members.
2. *Personal power*—This attribute comes from a feeling of self-confidence.
3. *Courage*—Effective leaders are able to take risks, admit mistakes, and act on hunches and intuitions.
4. *Willingness to confront oneself*—Leaders must be able and willing to do whatever they expect of the other group members.
5. *Sincerity and authenticity*—Effective group leaders are able to engage clients in working with them by being direct, caring, and challenging.
6. *Sense of identity*—Group counselors should be centered, self-aware, and committed to positive personal change.
7. *Belief in the group process*—Group leaders must be advocates for the potential of group counseling and therapy, and should convey that enthusiasm to the group members.
8. *Creativity*—Effective group leadership requires spontaneity and inventiveness.

Co-leadership can bring a positive dimension to the group experience (Corey & Corey, 1992). In the group environment, effective communication and relationship skills manifested by co-leaders can provide a unique form of modeling. By sharing the task of group management, co-leaders can more effectively balance the complex demands of attending to the people in the group, their interactions, and the group as a whole.

Jane decided to use a co-leader in her group because of the richness of experience she felt the arrangement would afford. She also believed that she and her co-leader could provide a model of effective communication and collaboration from which the participants could learn.

Location

Counselors charged with leading groups do not always have a great deal of flexibility regarding location. When there is flexibility, the counselor should attend to environmental factors which might influence the quality of the therapeutic or growth experience. The location selected for the counseling group should be one that is likely to maximize attendance and promote a sense of comfort and belonging. It also should have facilities that are appropriate to the group including a room that is large enough to accommodate the members. If counselors think that a particular client group will feel uncomfortable, stigmatized, or inconvenienced by meeting at a mental health facility, group meetings might be scheduled at area churches, libraries, or community centers or at the homes, schools, or work places of group members. In addition, the location should be easy to get to, with ample parking for those who drive, and access to public transportation if participants are unable to drive. If child care is likely to be a concern of group members, appropriate facilities and child care providers may be essential to the success of the group as well.

Physical comfort should certainly be taken into consideration, because such annoyances as uncomfortable chairs, extreme temperatures, and poor acoustics may inhibit the therapeutic experience. Counselors should be sure that the setting conveys a relaxed and comfortable climate and communicates a sense of security and privacy.

In some situations, a location that is less convenient might be more appropriate. For example, groups in organizations may find the worksite to be too distracting or too threatening for them to achieve real productivity; therefore, an off-site location might be best. If children feel that they might be teased by other children because of their involvement in a counseling group, they may enter the group experience with heightened fear or resistance. Therefore, the school counselor might want to choose an inconspicuous location for the group sessions.

Jane decided to conduct the group sessions in a community center that was familiar to many of her group members. The community center was housed in a building which at one time had been the neighborhood's middle school. Now it was a hub of activity for a variety of age groups. Jane felt that this environment would be familiar to many of the women who had grown up in the neighborhood, and would provide a nice bridge to their planned future training programs.

Interventions

There are several different ways of conceptualizing the work of a counseling group. Is it to be primarily educational or therapeutic? *Educational groups* typically provide didactic information and skills training, while *therapeutic groups* focus more on exploring and developing understanding of feelings and modifying cognitions and behaviors. Some group theorists characterize therapeutic groups as either therapy groups (focusing on remediation, treatment, and/or personality change) or counseling groups (focusing on growth, development, prevention, self-awareness, and releasing blocks to growth) (Corey, 1995). In an organizational context, groups have been described as transactional or transformational. In the *transactional* group, tasks may involve communication, problem solving, and decision-making as their key elements. In the *transformational* group, the emphasis is on increasing awareness, acceptance, and divergent thinking (Kormanski, 1988).

MacLennan and Dies (1992) described four types of counseling groups:

1. *Prevention groups*—set up primarily for outreach and mental health education. For example, a community mental health center might develop communication groups for adolescents to teach them interpersonal skills that generate positive coping skills.

2. *Problem-oriented or remedial groups*—instituted to provide help with specific problems. A group for caretakers of people with Alzheimer's disease is an example of such a group, providing both support and resolution of a variety of specific problems. Similarly, counseling groups might focus on a specific diagnostic group such as people with Eating or Dissociative Disorders.

3. *Life adjustment groups*—set up to respond to situations that demand changes in a person's self-concept, self-management, and/or lifestyle. Separation and divorce adjustment groups are an example of this type of group.

4. *Indirect counseling groups*—arising out of activities such as recreational or religious involvements. Many churches have groups for single parents, for example.

Regardless of the conceptual framework selected, group counseling is most likely to be effective if accomplished within the context of a defined framework.

Many methods are available to facilitate learning and personal change in groups, such as didactic presentations, sharing of experiences, role playing, or brainstorming sessions. Many theories and techniques of group counseling also have been developed to promote personal change. (These will be further discussed later in this chapter.) Often, a combination of interventions seems best suited to accomplishing a group's goals. Counselors should have a rationale for the approaches to treatment that are used and the sequence of their interventions.

Jane saw her task as providing both education and counseling toward personal growth, development, and self-awareness. Therefore, she planned a format that included some didactic presentations, brainstorming to generate ideas and information, and role playing exercises. In addition, she used cognitive and behavioral techniques to promote personal change. Her overriding theoretical framework, reality therapy, helped group members meet their needs in responsible ways.

Emphasis

The goals of the group will help to determine the emphasis. The amount of structure and degree of directiveness depend on the nature and needs of the participants and the goals of treatment, as well as the counselor's theoretical orientation (Corey & Corey, 1992). In the initial stage of a group, a greater degree of structure can help members to understand expectations and to develop a sense of confidence and safety. However, an overly structured or directive style may result in nonparticipation or overdependence upon the leader. Consequently, groups often become less structured by the leader and more member-driven as they develop.

Numbers

Often participants in group counseling and therapy groups are involved concurrently in individual or family counseling. With the clients' permission, the group leader should maintain contact with any other professionals involved in providing treatment to group members to ensure the compatibility of treatments.

Four of Jane's group members indicated that they were receiving individual counseling. Their counselors agreed in advance to their clients' participation in group counseling. Jane contacted each of the counselors to make sure that the treatment she was planning would not interfere with any other aspects of their treatment plans.

Three of the participants who were not receiving counseling services elsewhere showed symptoms of depression. Because she did not have the time or resources to offer these participants intensive treatment, Jane referred them to other mental health professionals for further assistance.

Timing

The timing of group counseling, including the length and frequency of sessions and the duration of treatment, are important aspects of the treatment plan. Most groups meet for one and a half to two hours at a time. Generally, a session of less than an hour is too short to accomplish much work. However, the group's productivity usually diminishes after two hours, and the discussion may become tedious and exhausting (Yalom, 1995). Most groups meet once a week (Corey,

1995). Those which meet less often generally have difficulty maintaining an interactional focus. It may in fact be therapeutically desirable for a group to meet twice a week or more, but this is often impractical, due to scheduling conflicts as well as financial constraints (Yalom, 1995).

The length of a closed-membership group generally depends on the nature of the particular concerns involved. Groups formed to assist participants in coping with a life crisis such as loss of a job or relationship might be of short or medium duration, meeting for less than six months. Groups formed to deal with a long-term concern, such as childhood abuse, might meet for a much longer period. The duration of the group may be specified at the outset, or it may be left open.

Brief group therapy is a format that is gaining in use and popularity, driven by demonstrated effectiveness in many situations, as well as by its economic advantages. In this format, the group leader must keep the group focused on its particular goals, in order to reach closure in a short period of time (generally 20 sessions or less).

Jane planned to have her groups meet once a week, in the morning, from 10 A.M. to 12 noon, for ten weeks. She believed that this amount of time would allow the participants to develop a basic level of trust, to establish some new communication skills and patterns of interaction, and to develop some new strategies for coping with life transitions and decisions. Although Jane felt that a longer period could also be beneficial, her funding constraints, as well as the scheduling complexities of the group members, argued for the most efficient use of group time. Jane also thought that having a definite, foreseeable end point to the group experience would motivate participants to use their time productively.

Medication

Medications and dietary supplements are often indicated as an important addition to counseling. Although group counselors are generally not able to prescribe medication, they are often in a position to note clients' emotional, behavioral, or other difficulties that might benefit from medication and can observe side effects of medications as the group members interact with others. Atypical speech or cognitive or affective difficulties may be more easily identified in a group situation than in brief one-to-one interactions in a psychiatrist's office. Group members' complaints about such side effects as sleeping difficulties, appetite changes, or visual, sexual, or digestive difficulties may provide important information about the impact of medication (Kottler, 1994). Thus, it is important that group counselors have an awareness of members' medication profiles, as well as a knowledge of possible side effects of medications. Observation of symptoms may prove quite important in participants' treatment. Counselors should refer group participants to a psychiatrist when a need for medication or the adverse impact of a medication is noted.

Adjunct Services

The counseling group provides a safe environment for trying out new behaviors, interacting with others, and developing heightened awareness of oneself and of others. However, the time spent in group represents a small percentage of the person's week. Thus, counselors often develop resources that will reinforce progress made in the group and will continue the development of skills or insights achieved during group time.

Homework assignments or suggested tasks are a useful means of extending the therapeutic experience. These may be assigned individually to specific members of the group, or to all members of the group. Assignments may be made by the group leader in a structured group or may emerge from the group members' interactions with one another. For example, a member might agree to a group suggestion to speak with a particular person or to try out a new behavior learned during the group session, and to report back on this action at the next group meeting.

Bibliotherapy is a widely used adjunct to both individual and group therapy. Themes or issues which emerge during a group session may be explored further through outside reading of short stories, novels, plays, or self-help books. Often counselors develop their own printed materials for psychoeducation (Kottler, 1994).

Journal keeping can also be an extremely effective means of extending the therapeutic group experience. Writing in a journal following group sessions can help a person reflect on what was happening in the session, analyze and develop meanings from the experience, and create closure which may have been missing from that particular person's experience in the group. Kottler (1994) judged journaling to be the "single most useful therapeutic adjunct available to group members" (p. 282).

Some group counselors develop questionnaires or logs in which members record their reactions to the group session. This provides a structured format, helping them to remember, reflect, and evaluate, as well as to record feelings or thoughts which they were unable or unwilling to share during the group session. This activity provides information that is not only useful to the participant but is also helpful to the counselor.

Videotapes may provide useful feedback to group members (Cooker & Nero, 1987), and may be used either during or following group sessions. Participants watching their own interaction patterns in the group may find that videotapes yield useful and unique insights (Kottler, 1994). Videotaped movies may provide some of the same benefits as bibliotherapy in providing a means for viewers to see other people in situations or with concerns similar to their own.

Self-help or support groups (also referred to as mutual aid groups) may be a useful adjunct to counseling. Generally leaderless and low-cost or no-cost, these groups can provide an opportunity for people to continue the work they started in counseling, or to obtain practice and reinforcement of skills learned. Overeaters Anonymous (OA), Parents Anonymous, job clubs, and Rational Recovery are examples of self-help groups that are available in many communities.

Prognosis

The prognosis for success in a group is dependent in large part on the positive attitude of the counselor and how that attitude is conveyed to the members. Counselors can "plant a favorable prognosis" (Kottler, 1994, p. 62) by preparing the members to expect a positive experience. From the first telephone contact, through the intake interview and the initial group meeting, the counselor has rich opportunities to plant the expectation of success in the member's mind. This reinforces the first of Yalom's therapeutic factors discussed earlier in this chapter, the instillation of hope, which is a major factor in determining the group's success. During the life of the group, the counselor can further facilitate a positive prognosis by drawing the group's attention to any progress made and encouraging the group members to support and reinforce each other's gains (Kottler, 1994).

OTHER ASPECTS OF TREATMENT PLANNING FOR COUNSELING GROUPS

The DO A CLIENT MAP clearly can be used in treatment planning for groups as well as for individuals and families. However, the group counselor also should incorporate budgeting and evaluation into the treatment planning process.

Budgeting

Budgeting is an essential item to be considered by many counselors who are planning group treatments or programs. Budget exerts a powerful influence over all aspects of program development and must be taken into account throughout the planning process. Frequently, the counselor has the responsibility to determine potential sources of program funds. Typical sources might include participant fees; resources, often in the form of space and staff time, from a mental health agency; grants from federal, state, or local government, the United Way, or other funding agencies; donations of money, facilities, or services by community-based organizations, local charitable groups, or business foundations; or third-party payments from insurance companies.

Budget planning is essential for counselors who are trying to secure grants to fund their programs or for those who are working on a contractual or consultant basis. In these situations, the costs of the program often will have to be projected well in advance of the actual experience. A budget that is unrealistic or excessive can cause the loss of grants or the awarding of contracts to other service providers. Grant or contract budgets are likely to have little flexibility, so counselors must be sure that they can implement their program within the boundaries of the budgets that they have requested. Generally, the budget for a group program or experience will encompass the following items, as indicated in Jane's program budget which follows:

BUDGET FOR GROUP COUNSELING

Personnel
    Counselor: 120 hours @ $28 per hour (includes 40 hours of actual group sessions, plus 30 hours for intake interviews, 16 hours in pre-intake preparation, 6 hours in forms preparation and review, 10 hours meeting with participants before and after group sessions, and 18 hours in evaluation-related activities) $3360

    Co-leader: 50 hours @ $17 per hour $ 850
    Secretary: 43 hours @ $10 per hour $ 430
    Benefits (FICA): 7.65% of salaries $ 355
Facilities (meeting room, offices, telephones, utilities, furniture, computers, software, office equipment, custodial and repair services)   (donated)
Printing (photocopying services donated) $ 40
Office supplies (most supplies donated) $ 25
Postage (use of postage franking machine donated) $ 25
Client travel reimbursement (for 3 participants @ 23 cents per mile) $ 138
Client child care @ $12 per hour $ 600
Materials and supplies $ 72

In her grant proposal, Jane reflected the in-kind (donated) expenses according to a standard formula provided by her employer.

Counselors whose training has focused primarily on mastering the theories and techniques of counseling may be surprised and dismayed to discover the diverse pragmatic skills that are required of the counselor involved in program development. However, for counselors to deal effectively with the broad range of client needs, the growing demand for accountability, and the limited funds available for mental health services, they must have a mastery of a wide range of therapeutic, educational, and administrative skills.

Evaluation

Accountability is of paramount importance for counselors. Because available funds for mental health services are declining in most settings, those who disburse such funds want to make sure the money is well spent. Mental health service delivery agencies as well as charitable and governmental funding agencies consequently are requiring evaluation of programs to determine whether they have met their goals and whether continued funding is indicated. To receive grants and other funds for services, counselors must demonstrate that they are accomplishing something worthwhile.

Beyond the need for accountability is the need for feedback to inform practice. Program evaluation can serve counselors and their employers both by providing data to guide improvement and enhancement of current programs and techniques and by providing information for use by others offering similar services. Evaluation is particularly important if comparable group experiences are planned in the future or if similar client groups need services. Evaluation then can be used not only to assess the effectiveness of a particular program of intervention but also to guide the development of future programs.

Several approaches are available for evaluating the impact of group counseling and programs. An overview of some of these will be provided here. However, counselors will need some knowledge of research methodology or the help of a research consultant when planning their evaluation procedures, to be sure the procedures they select are valid.

Evaluation is facilitated if goals are stated in such a way as to be specific and measurable. Assessment of goal attainment usually can best be accomplished by the use of a control group that can be compared with the treatment group. This might occur if treatment could not be provided to all of the potential members of a group experience. Pre- and posttreatment evaluation could then be done of both groups to determine whether the group that received help made more positive changes than the group that was kept on the waiting list. However, the investigator would need to be cautious in drawing conclusions and would need to determine whether the two groups were really otherwise comparable and what other factors may have influenced the treatment and control groups.

Generally, the effectiveness of any program is evaluated in light of the objectives originally set for the group. With or without a control group, the most common method of evaluating program or counseling effectiveness involves the administration of inventories or questionnaires before and shortly after the group experience. A third administration of the instruments might occur in a follow-up, some months later, to provide information on the development or persistence of any changes over time.

Standardized tests and inventories determined to be reliable and valid, with norms based on groups similar to the one receiving treatment, typically provide the most trustworthy information. Sources discussed in chapter 4 can help counselors select appropriate instruments. Often, however, the counselor will find it useful to gather subjective reactions to the specific interventions employed in a particular group. In such cases, a specifically designed questionnaire may be the best instrument. For groups with poor reading or writing skills, oral interviews, group discussion, or follow-up telephone interviews might provide useful data (Mawson & Kahn, 1993).

Evaluation data also can be gathered by looking at the perceptions significant others have of the impact of the group experience on the participants. In a school setting, for example, the counselor might ask teachers for their observations of any changes in behavior of students involved in counseling groups. Another approach to evaluation involves obtaining data on demonstrated behavioral changes. The counselor or collaborating evaluator may engage in unobtrusive observation to gather this data. While the direct cause-and-effect relationships between the treatment and these changes may be difficult to determine conclusively, such data can be strongly suggestive of the value of the group.

Jane's evaluation strategy consisted of the collection of qualitative data by three instruments: posttreatment questionnaires, which included both quantifiable information on a Likert scale (mostly agree/mostly disagree) and open-ended questions; interviews conducted with participants informally at the conclusion of the group; and a follow-up questionnaire mailed about six months after the conclusion of the treatment.

GROUP COUNSELING IN CONTEXT

The counselor may apply the skills of group leadership to a variety of contexts. The group counselor usually is situated in mental health settings, schools, or organizations.

The Mental Health Counselor

Typically, the mental health counselor is employed in a private or group practice, in a specialized or community mental health agency, or in a hospital. In hospitals, counselors may conduct groups for people with similar mental health or physical problems, for those about to leave the hospital and re-enter the community, or for families and caregivers. In private or group practice, or in agency settings, the counselor may be called upon to lead special population groups, such as groups for women, for men, for adult children of alcoholics, for people with eating disorders, for people in crisis, for people over age 65, for people who are HIV-positive, for people with cancer, or for people abusing drugs or alcohol (Corey, 1995). In a study of employment of mental health counselors in community agencies, West et al. (1987) indicated that 68% of agencies responding involved their counselors in conducting group therapy.

In the community, counselors are sometimes called upon to lead support groups. These groups may be largely self-directed, but are in need of a professional to foster communication and to facilitate the group process. Shulman and Gitterman (1986) presented the role of the counselor in such groups as assisting the individuals in engaging with the groups, rather than in actually directing the groups.

The School Counselor

Group treatment can be especially effective in the school setting because young people, as they develop, often look to their peers, rather than to adults, for acceptance, validation, and support (Ehly & Dustin, 1989; MacLennan & Dies, 1992). Counseling groups offer a particular advantage over individual counseling to many adolescents in that they can actually help the youth in their struggle to separate and achieve independence from adults. This format can appear far less threatening to many young people than the prospect of having to develop a close relationship in one-to-one counseling with an adult (MacLennan & Dies, 1992). As community problems become increasingly complex, the schools are called upon more and more to provide services that address the emotional and social needs of the students (Ehly, 1993). The school counselor is often the person to whom this task falls.

School counselors typically lead groups for education, prevention, and remediation. The goals of group counseling in the school are to help children to:

1. deal more effectively with specific problems or issues
2. obtain support
3. access relevant information

4. develop new skills
5. increase understanding of themselves and others (Brown, 1994).

Even at the elementary school level, counselors find themselves in the position of leading therapeutic as well as educational groups. At the middle and secondary school levels, counseling groups can serve as change agents, helping adolescents through the confusing process of transition and improving their self concepts, self-management skills, and interactions with others. A growing body of literature has addressed special groups for children, such as groups for children of divorce (Kalter & Schreier, 1993), for children dealing with bereavement (Healy-Romanello, 1993), and for children with behavior disorders (Braswell, 1993), as well as leadership training groups for teens (Powell, 1993) and social skills training (Gresham & Elliott, 1993).

In addition, school counselors increasingly are offering counseling groups to parents. These groups may address specific needs of parents, or may be designed to help them deal with their students' educational, vocational, personal, and social needs.

Counselors in Organizational Settings

Counselors are involved in group work through a variety of roles in business, government, and industry settings. Among these are:

- human resource administrators
- career counselors
- vocational rehabilitation specialists
- consultants (internal and external)
- trainers/educators
- EAP (Employee Assistance Program) treatment providers (Counselors in the World of Work, 1988).

Counselors in any of these roles may be called upon to provide psychoeducational groups, aimed at problem prevention or remediation. Often, counselors in these positions conduct workshops or group sessions as a way of becoming acquainted with employees, gaining more knowledge of the workplace culture and issues, and making themselves and their services more accessible and more visible to employees.

Workplace groups can be especially effective in treating people's work-related problems. Group stress reduction approaches involving relaxation training have been shown to be both economical and effective in treating employees in particularly stressful work situations. Workplace groups are also suitable treatments for people manifesting behaviors which have been popularly characterized as the Type A personality, Fear of Failure (FOF), and the impostor phenomenon. The Type A personality is one which is typified by overly ambitious striving, frequently coupled with a low level of personal satisfaction. Groups have been successful in helping people put the work role in perspective and define more realistic goals for themselves (Lowman, 1993). Studies have shown that FOF has been lowered through participation in workplace counseling groups (Rajendran & Kaliappan, 1990). The impostor phenomenon characterizes people who incorrectly believe that they have succeeded inappropriately and will soon be discovered to be a fraud. Group treatment has been found to be effective in resolving this syndrome as well (Clance & O'Toole, 1987; Steinberg, 1986).

A growing field of opportunity for counselors interested in group work is service as internal or external consultants. Rapid changes in the modern work environment, brought about by technological advancements, global competition, and an escalating diversity of personnel, have caused major and fundamental shifts in the structures and patterns of behavior in organizations. Counselors can apply their understanding of group dynamics to the organizational environment and thus help an organization to:

1. Assess and modify the culture of the organization, to meet changing demands and environments and to improve morale and productivity;
2. Acquire new insights into the dysfunctional aspects of employees' patterns of behavior as a basis for developing a more effective organization;
3. Ensure that the organization remains engaged in a process of continuous improvement and revitalization (Beer & Spector, 1993).

Organizational consultation addresses not only individual concerns, but also the issues involved in complex human systems. Thus, clinical skills in diagnosis and treatment planning must be combined with an understanding of organizational interactive systems in general, as well as the culture of the particular organization being served. The consulting relationship is inherently more complex than the traditional dyadic or group counseling relationship because of its triadic nature: the counselor, the consultee (employing organization), and the client system (group). Such consulting relationships are normally issue-focused, concentrating on the systemic aspects of the situation rather than on the individual members. Kurpius and Fuqua (1993) identified four modes of consultation:

1. *Provision*—The consultee identifies a specific need and contracts with the counselor for the direct provision of services to meet that need. For example, if the consultant is employed to resolve systemic prob-

lems in communication, she or he might design and implement an intervention to enhance employee communications.

2. *Prescription*—The consultant collects information about the organization, makes an expert diagnosis, and prescribes a treatment plan. This is also termed *expert* consultation. The consultant might review the organization, for example, and diagnose areas of conflict. The treatment plan might consist of conflict management training sessions, which could be conducted in-house.

3. *Collaboration*—The consultant and consultees work collaboratively in defining, designing, and implementing a process for planned change. This is also termed *process* consultation. Using this model, the counselor might interview members of an organization in order to ascertain their perspectives on problem areas, and then report the findings back to them. Acting in a facilitative role, the counselor would then help the members to examine and analyze the data and develop a strategy for problem-solving. The counselor could promote agreement on goals and objectives, and work to ensure continuing commitment to change throughout all levels of the organization. In addition, the counselor might develop an evaluation strategy in collaboration with the members.

4. *Mediation*—This model often involves a process-collaboration model. Mediators are often used in unionized organizations to provide an unbiased yet knowledgeable perspective. The consultants assist the two parties in coming to agreement on certain issues, but do not become involved in developing or implementing a treatment plan.

Just as counseling people (individually and in groups) provides a mechanism for realizing the developmental potential of the individual, organizational consultation provides a mechanism for realizing the developmental potential of the organization (Kurpius & Fuqua, 1993). In addition, it offers a broad range of challenging opportunities for counselors.

APPROACHES TO GROUP COUNSELING

Approaches to group counseling include models that have been developed for individual counseling and then adapted to group settings, those that have been developed for both individual and group counseling, and those that have been developed primarily or exclusively for group settings. This chapter reviews all of these but focuses most on those approaches that are particularly well suited to group counseling settings.

Chapter 7 reviewed many theories of individual counseling. All of them, especially person-centered counseling, behavioral counseling, reality therapy, rational emotive behavior therapy, Gestalt therapy, Adlerian counseling, and psychodynamic psychotherapy also have been discussed in the literature as approaches to group treatment. Although some adaptation of those models occurs when they are used with groups, the approaches remain basically the same. Consequently, the application of those approaches to group settings will be discussed only briefly here. Readers are referred to chapter 7 for additional information on the nature and application of those models. As stated elsewhere, this book assumes that the reader already has some familiarity with models of group counseling. This section will not seek to teach these approaches to the reader but, rather, will review the salient characteristics of the models and discuss their use in the process of diagnosis and treatment planning.

Models Commonly Used in Both Individual and Group Counseling

An impressive array of theoretical approaches to group counseling are available. Counselors are increasingly discovering that they can draw from a diverse range of orientations without subscribing exclusively to any one (Gilliland et al., 1989). The eclectic or integrative model of counseling provides a means of planning a group experience not just according to one theoretical model, but rather in such a fashion that interventions may be adapted to the situation (including goals of treatment, needs of the members, and beliefs of the leader or co-leaders) (Corey & Corey, 1992). When asked about their theoretical orientations, many professionals now respond not in terms of a single, rigid orientation, but, rather, a blending or integration of several conceptual frameworks (Kottler, 1994). Thus, it is more important than ever that the group counselor come to the table with an understanding of not just one theoretical perspective, but of the broad range of approaches to group counseling.

Cognitive Group Counseling

Cognitive counseling is an approach initially developed for individual counseling, but is ideally suited for group work. Focusing on beliefs and thinking patterns, this approach is based on the assumption that people have the potential to be both rational and irrational, and have the capacity to understand their own thinking. If they change their dysfunctional thinking, it will change how they feel and what they do.

This approach is especially useful when working with people who have good verbal skills, who have at least average intelligence, and who have the ability to identify feelings and behaviors. It often is used in combination with behavioral techniques to treat depression and anxiety or mild/situational disorders. Cognitive group therapy has been found to be effective in treating such diverse concerns as child sexual abuse (Watson & Stermac, 1994), weight control (Lewis, Blair, & Booth, 1992), Anxiety Disorders (Cadbury, Childs-Clark, & Sandhu, 1990; White, Keenan, & Brooks, 1992), anger and violence (Deffenbacher, McNamara, Stark, & Sabadell, 1990; Towl, 1993), and marital discord (Montag & Wilson, 1992). It generally is not appropriate for people who are psychotic or in a state of crisis. The group setting provides the opportunity for people to explore their thoughts and beliefs with other group members and to receive their feedback. Additionally, the group provides the members with a safe setting in which to internalize observations of faulty thinking on the part of other members of the group, facilitating their ability to identify and modify dysfunctional thinking patterns in themselves.

Rational Emotive Behavior Therapy (REBT)

One of the most important applications of cognitive therapy (Gilliland et al., 1989), REBT emphasizes and clarifies the relationships among thinking, feeling, and behavior in an effort to address peoples' views and beliefs about external events or situations (Corey, 1995). It is direct, active, and didactic (Donigian & Malnati, 1987). It seeks to minimize self-defeating thoughts and help the person to acquire a more realistic, tolerant outlook. The central task of REBT is to foster self-understanding and change behavior.

REBT, formerly known as RET (Corey, 1995), has been one of the most widely used therapies (Gilliland et al, 1989). Albert Ellis, its originator, also has espoused REBT as a method of fostering personal growth and a positive atmosphere in a classroom setting. In a group counseling context, REBT tends to be a leader-centered technique with the group generally focusing on the concerns of one member at a time. Because of the prominent role of the leader, however, the counselor develops a position of power which may be counterproductive or dangerous (Corey, 1995). At its best, REBT is a complicated technique which requires a great deal of sophistication and skill on the part of the counselor.

Behavioral Group Counseling

Behavioral counseling focuses on current manifestations of behavior rather than on historical antecedents, and establishes treatment goals which are specific, concrete, objective, and measurable (Corey, 1995). This approach is based on learning theory (Gilliland et al, 1989). Behavioral goals, rather than insight and introspection or exploration of feelings, form the framework and direction for counseling (Corey, 1995).

Behavioral counseling frequently is used in group settings. The presence of other members provides additional sources of feedback and reinforcement while the microcosm of the group environment gives people a safe arena for trying out new behaviors (Gladding, 1995). Typically, behavioral counseling groups are composed of people with similar behavioral concerns (such as Eating Disorders, Phobias, or Sexual Disorders) (Corey, 1995), so that opportunities for behavioral rehearsal, modeling, group support, and social rewards and punishment are maximized.

The effectiveness of behavioral counseling is measurable, and this approach provides both a firm basis for research (Corey, 1995) and the accountability which has particular importance in the current managed care environment. However, with its focus on specific problems, rigid adherence to this approach may not address underlying concerns and past influences (Gilliland et al., 1989).

Reality Therapy

Behavioral in nature, reality therapy is based upon the assumption that people are fundamentally self-determining (Corey, 1995; Gilliland et al, 1989). This approach focuses on clients' strengths and sense of responsibility as they relate to present behavior. Active and directive, reality therapy is effective in ameliorating behavioral problems, and is generally of short-term duration. Reality therapy has been applied by its developer, William Glasser, to a school setting and has been viewed as a way to promote self-esteem (a success identity) in young people and to help them learn realistic and responsible ways of meeting their needs.

Reality therapy has great versatility in application to group work. With its emphasis on accountability, action, and thinking, this approach is useful in fostering immediate change (Gladding, 1995). Reality therapy is especially useful in effecting behavioral changes in at-risk or troubled youth (Clagett, 1992; Cominskey, 1993; Williamson, 1992), in people who abuse substances (Honeyman, 1990), and people who have been raped (McArthur, 1990). However, the appropriateness of applying reality group therapy to a multicultural population has been questioned (Corey, 1995). People from some cultures have been socialized to avoid speaking assertively or directly, or to focus little on their own personal needs (Wubbolding, 1990); thus, the approach might need to be modified when used with culturally diverse groups. Reality therapy provided the theoretical basis for Jane's counseling group. Reality therapy's strategies for helping people clarify their needs, establish goals, and responsibly seek to achieve them seemed ideal for Jane's clients.

Person-Centered Group Counseling

Person-centered counseling emphasizes communication of genuineness, empathy, and unconditional positive regard. The underlying assumption of this model is that people have the potential for growth and self-determination (Corey, 1995). This can be facilitated through counseling that enhances self-esteem and promotes self-acceptance.

Carl Rogers, the founder of this approach, popularized the use of encounter groups and personal growth groups. These groups proliferated in the 1960s and continue to be used today. They usually are designed for relatively healthy people whose primary goals are to heighten self-awareness, achieve contact with others, and attain a new level of intimacy. The focus of these groups is on the present (Yalom, 1995). More recently, person-centered counseling has led to the growth of community groups (Gladding, 1995) designed to build a sense of community as well as to enhance the members' self-exploration and facilitate cross-cultural communication (Corey, 1995).

The person-centered approach lends itself well to a group setting, as participants in groups following this model can receive acceptance and develop genuine and congruent relationships not only with their counselors, but also with the other members of the group. These groups provide a safe climate and models of open and honest communication (Corey, 1995). The person-centered approach is not problem-centered or goal-oriented, but, rather, focuses on relationships, feelings, attitudes, and perceptions (Gilliland et al., 1989).

This approach is appropriate for mild adjustment and situational difficulties, especially those involving problems of self-esteem and self-confidence, stage-of-life issues, and establishment of goals and direction. Well-functioning, motivated clients who are not in crisis are most likely to benefit from this approach. Its strength is in its underlying sense of optimism, but the approach is usually not effective alone for resistant or dysfunctional clients (Gladding, 1995). Jane integrated elements of person-centered group counseling into her treatment plan in order to promote a sense of safety and enhance self-esteem. However, person-centered group counseling by itself did not offer the structure needed by Jane's clients.

Gestalt Therapy

Gestalt therapy is an active, here-and-now, holistic approach which integrates all aspects of the person's life and emphasizes accountability and responsibility. It assumes that the solutions to problems are within the self, and the goal of counseling is to remove obstacles to finding those solutions. The Gestalt model offers a variety of techniques to facilitate this process, and the role of the

Gestalt counselor is to make creative application of these techniques to problem-solving (Zinker, 1991).

The Gestalt model is used in both group and individual counseling. Even in groups, however, the focus of Gestalt counseling tends to be on individual members (Shaffer & Galinsky, 1989). Little attention is paid to facilitating member interaction. The presence of other group members can, however, promote self-awareness and vicarious learning. Often, the significance of a member's statement or behavior will be emphasized by having that member make the rounds, go up to all of the group members and announce or demonstrate an important insight or piece of behavior. The presence of others sometimes can increase the threat posed by Gestalt counseling, an approach that often involves pressure and confrontation. However, the threat also can be diminished by the support of the group and the freedom it affords members to chose their levels of participation in the group experience. Resistant members and those who engage in excessive intellectualization and rationalization are particularly likely to benefit from feedback provided in Gestalt counseling as well as from seeing aspects of themselves in other members.

The Gestalt approach is most appropriate for use with relatively healthy, high-functioning people displaying medically unverified physical symptoms, difficulty accessing feelings, or mild to moderate anxiety and depression. This approach can help people to take control of their lives and their feelings. However, it requires skillful use; Gestalt counselors run the risk of threatening and pressuring clients (Gladding, 1995; Corey, 1995). Additionally, this approach may not cross cultures very well, due to its confrontational nature (Sue & Sue, 1990). In addition, Gladding (1995) expressed concern that this approach lacked empirical evidence for its effectiveness.

Adlerian Group Therapy

The Adlerian approach, also known as individual psychology, focuses on the social determinants of behavior (Corey, 1995). Adlerian group therapy is insight-oriented, rational, and non-deterministic. It is predicated on the notion that a life script is developed during a child's early years but is open to change during the course of development. Counseling is goal-directed and focuses on developing and strengthening the person's ego and sense of empowerment and modifying dysfunctional life scripts (Gladding, 1995).

According to this theory, people are primarily social beings, motivated by social forces and striving to achieve certain goals (Corey, 1995; Corsini, 1988; Gladding, 1995). Thus, the group context is the logical setting for Adlerian therapy, providing a social context for goal attainment.

The Adlerian group counselor is active, confrontive, self-disclosing, and interpretive (Gilliland et al., 1989). This approach may be useful for addressing parent–child problems, acting-out behaviors, marital difficulties, career concerns, self-confidence issues, and relationship problems. It is an optimistic, positive, empowering and nonjudgmental approach. However, Adlerian groups require fairly high-functioning, insightful clients. Because of its emphasis on the person-in-the-environment, the Adlerian approach is particularly well suited to working with such cultural groups as Native Americans, Latinos, African Americans, and Asian Americans (Corey, 1995).

Psychodynamic Group Psychotherapy

An extension of Freudian psychoanalysis, psychodynamic group psychotherapy tends to be an interpretive, insight-oriented, directive, long-term treatment model. Its theoretical foundation is the assumption that dysfunctional behavior is rooted in an adaptive response to some inner pain which originated in the past and which, over time, has become counterproductive (Rutan & Stone, 1993).

The group setting provides excellent opportunities for fostering therapeutic insights and understandings. The anxiety and discomfort created by being in a group of strangers can stimulate regression, transference, and defense mechanisms. By observing these phenomena, the counselor can assist the participants in recognizing and interpreting their own responses, thereby gaining understanding of their reactions not only within the group environment but also outside of that microcosmic situation. The group offers a safe environment for emotionally charged interchanges and therefore can help participants to understand and consciously change their characteristic responses to interpersonal interactions (Kauff, 1993).

Psychodynamic group counselors tend to take the position of both expert and emotional participant in the group. Within the group, they alternate between the role of detached observer of the group process and its members and the role of emotionally engaged participant whose affect is available for observation by the other members. The counselor uses this role duality to reflect back to the members responses which might not otherwise be obvious or apparent to them. The counselor also uses the safety of the group environment to become the object of transference for members, as a way of allowing them to observe, interpret, and discuss emotions and reactions which, in other environments, might be too frightening, embarrassing, or threatening to acknowledge (Rutan & Stone, 1993).

The psychodynamic model of group counseling has been found to be effective in a variety of situations. Persons working through issues relating to severe trauma such as violence and abuse seem particularly to benefit from the psychodynamic treatment model (Friedman, 1994; Kanas, Schoenfeld, Marmar, & Weiss, 1994). This model also has been effective in treating Eating Disorders (Riess & Rutan, 1992) and in substance abuse relapse prevention (Khantzian, Halliday, & Golden, 1992).

Models Used Primarily in Group Settings

While the models discussed above all are direct outgrowths of theories developed initially for individual counseling, several models have been developed primarily or exclusively for use in group work. These models are based on the assumption that the group format provides the ideal environment for helping people.

Transactional Analysis (TA)

Transactional analysis (TA) was developed by Eric Berne in the 1950's and nearly always is conducted as a group experience (Corey, 1995). The approach focuses on helping people first to change their feelings and then to change their behaviors. According to TA, each person identifies with one of the following positions: I'm ok, you're ok; I'm not ok, you are ok; I'm ok, you're not ok; or I'm not ok, you're not ok. The second position is thought to be the most common. However, TA's underlying philosophy begins with the premise that we are all ok, and that we all are basically lovable and capable of growth and self-actualization. An important goal of the counseling experience is to help the participants to arrive at the belief that I'm ok, you're ok.

TA theorists also believe that there are three primary ego states: parent, adult, and child (Gladding, 1995). The child embodies creativity, joy, and spontaneity; the parent includes the conscience as well as long-standing traditions, beliefs, and values needed to guide daily functioning; and the adult is the assimilator, the rational evaluator and decision maker. All people have and need all three ego states. However, difficulties can develop when an imbalance exists among the three or when one or more of the ego states tends to come into play at inappropriate or self-destructive moments. Another goal of TA is to raise people's awareness of their ego states (Corey, 1995).

TA also pays particular attention to transactions between people (especially between group members and group leaders), to structural analysis (analysis of ego states), to group members' games (repetitive, self-destructive, often dishonest patterns of behavior), and to scripts or blueprints for life (Garvin, 1987). TA groups are designed to help people to develop productive life scripts as well as to make desired changes (Gilliland et al., 1989).

TA groups tend to be leader-centered, to make considerable use of instruction and exercises, to emphasize long-term treatment, and to focus on one person at a time (Gladding, 1995). Although TA has been used with a broad and heterogeneous client group, its use does not seem well-suited to people with Personality Disorders characterized by limited motivation for treatment, since the approach requires intensive work on the part of the individual. This model would also be inappropriate for use with people with Psychotic Disorders who may be too confused to participate effectively in such groups. In addition, people in crisis or with specific, circumscribed concerns might not be best served by the lengthy process of TA. In practice, TA seems best suited to people who are very verbal and highly motivated and who seem likely to benefit from a structured, leader-centered experience. Such people might be experiencing long-standing depression or anxiety.

This approach normalizes concerns, and frames them in language which is easily accessible (Gilliland et al., 1989). However, TA runs the dual risk of being either over-simplified or overly complex (Gladding, 1995). Counselors must be aware of their own ego states, as well as those of the group members. Transactional analysis, to be used effectively, requires considerable work on the part of the counselor as well as the group members.

Psychodrama

Psychodrama was introduced in the United States in the 1920's by Jacob L. Moreno and has been developed by Zerka Moreno, his wife, as well as other followers (Corey, 1995). This model has been adopted by a wide diversity of counselors, including those emphasizing behavioral, Gestalt, cognitive, psychodynamic, and Adlerian approaches (Kottler, 1994). Psychodrama emphasizes action and interaction, present behavior and emotion, spontaneity, creativity, and reality-testing (Corey, 1995). It encourages participants to act out difficult areas or episodes in their lives and to try out new methods of behavior (Battegay, 1990). In addition, psychodrama provides a format for participants to receive feedback from others, to release inhibiting and dysfunctional feelings, and to assume greater responsibility for their lives.

Psychodrama may be used as the predominant mode of treatment in a small group, as an occasional alternate mode of treatment, or as a technique for short-term counseling or demonstrations with a large group. Because the nature of the drama can be geared to the needs of a particular person, it is suitable for use with a wide range of people and would only be contraindicated for people who are so confused, depressed, or anxious that they could not function as participants in the drama. This approach has been demonstrated to be particularly useful for:

1. The elderly and people with Alzheimer's disease (Huddleston, 1989; Martin & Stepath, 1993; Remer, Morse, Popma, & Jones, 1993)
2. Adult survivors of childhood abuse, including those diagnosed with Dissociative Identity Disorder (Altman, 1992)
3. Children and adolescents, for whom the action orientation of this approach may be especially suitable (Brady, 1991; Dushman & Bressler, 1991; Guldner & O'Connor, 1991; Kottler, 1994; Lee, 1991; Sasson, 1990)
4. People with Substance Use Disorders (Duffy, 1990)
5. Adult survivors of assault (MacKay, 1989)
6. Work groups involved in problem solving (Gillis & Bonney, 1989).

However, this approach can have negative consequences if the counselor is inadequately trained or skilled, or does not have a clear understanding of its process and purpose (Kane, 1992).

T-Groups

Also termed training groups, T-groups were developed by Kurt Lewin and colleagues at the National Training Laboratories (NTL) in Bethel, Maine in the 1940s. Like encounter groups, T-groups were an outgrowth of person-centered counseling. However, T-groups are process-oriented, rather than personal growth-oriented (Gladding, 1995). They are fairly unstructured, but are task oriented, with a here-and-now orientation. Often used as laboratory training in connection with organizational development efforts, this format can be intensive, involving confrontation of members regarding their behaviors. This model is predicated on the assumption that participants learn best by being objectively and directly confronted by observations of their own behavior and how it affects others (Yalom, 1995). T-groups have been widely used to address specific organizational problems or issues, such as leadership effectiveness, communication skills, or problem-solving in organizations (Corey & Corey, 1992). The group provides an environment in which participants can experiment with new behaviors and try out new ideas, and has been referred to as "therapy for normals" (Yalom, 1995, pp. 490-491).

Skillful group leadership is essential. A poorly led group runs the risk of harming the individuals within the group or the macro system within which the group functions. When the T-group model is applied to organizational settings, there is particular opportunity for abuse, and caution must be exercised. The counselor or leader must have a strong indication from the outset that management is committed to both the group process and the transference of new skills and strategies from the group to the real work of the organization. Otherwise, those members who have risked self-disclosure may find themselves later penalized, rather than rewarded, for their efforts.

Tavistock Groups

The Tavistock group approach was initiated in England by Wilfred Bion and developed by A.K. Rice and Margaret Rioch. The Tavistock approach typically is implemented at a weekend or week-long institute or conference. Tavistock groups are similar to T-groups in that they are designed to promote the personal and professional growth of people who are not suffering from significant emotional disorders. However, the structure of Tavistock groups and the leadership model they follow are quite different from those of T-groups.

The primary emphasis of the Tavistock group is on developing the members' abilities to function effectively in work groups. The focus of the Tavistock group is on members' relationships to the group culture (Yalom, 1995). In this leader-centered model, the counselor plays the role of observer and interpreter, with analyses often grounded in a psychoanalytic framework. The leader's interpretations frequently result in the group members becoming initially demanding and dissatisfied with the leader. However, as the group becomes more able to use its own resources and develops insight into the group process, members' frustrations tend to lessen and they develop appreciation of the open and accepting qualities of the group environment.

Bion characterized the emotional pattern of a group according to the dichotomy of work group (W) or anti-work (basic assumption) activity (BA) (Gladding, 1995). He further described three recurring emotional states which are a part of all group interactions: aggressiveness, optimism, and helplessness. Bion stated that group functioning is complicated by conflict, and that it is the task of the counselor and work group to expose, clarify, and work through those conflicts. The group leader's role is impersonal and interpretive; observations and interventions are limited to the group as a whole, rather than to individual members. This approach has inspired controversy due to the impersonal role of the therapist as well as negative indications from outcome research (Yalom, 1995).

Theme-Centered Interactional Method (Theme Groups)

Theme-centered counseling was developed primarily by Ruth C. Cohn. Typically conducted as time-limited, relatively short-term group experiences (1 to 15 sessions), theme-centered counseling groups have a predetermined theme that is announced and briefly described by the group leader at the start of each session. Issues of autonomy and interdependence are particularly important to this approach as members explore their own thoughts and feelings and react to the theme and the input of the other members.

Theme-centered groups are generally well-structured by the leader (and by the existence of a theme) and take a positive and personal approach. Leaders tend to be genuine and empathic and draw heavily on person-centered techniques. Although the leader keeps the group working productively and appropriately focused on the theme, members are encouraged to take responsibility for their own participation and learning during the sessions. Deflections from the theme are accepted if they are important to members and relevant to group goals; rigid adherence to the theme is not necessary.

Although the theme-centered approach to group counseling never gained the widespread use and attention enjoyed by other models discussed in this section, it is included because it seems to be an extremely flexible technique that offers a balance of structure and support. These qualities make this approach appropriate for use with a broad range of people, including severely disturbed clients who are not appropriate for treatment in most group settings. Theme groups that emphasize present-oriented and pragmatic concerns have been used in conjunction with other modes of treatment in day-treatment centers and psychiatric facilities to promote interaction, symptom abatement, and development of clients' coping mechanisms.

Brief Therapy Groups

Brief therapy groups can encompass a broad range of goals, including support, social skills training, cognitive-behavioral change, or psychoeducation. This model is not new, but has come into widespread use in the 1990s, as economic factors play an increasing role in delivery of mental health services. However, brief therapy groups are not merely shortened versions of traditional therapy groups, but rather follow the model of brief solution focused therapy in determining specific and measurable goals, maintaining a present time orientation, and attending to planning and efficiency (Yalom, 1995).

Brief therapy groups can be appropriately used to deal with an acute life crisis, such as job loss or bereavement; with a developmental crisis such as adjustment to college or retirement; or with a particular symptom such as binge eating (Yalom, 1995). Brief therapy groups focus primarily on interpersonal, rather than intrapersonal, concerns (Klein, 1993).

ROLES OF THE GROUP COUNSELOR

Counselors interested and skilled in group counseling have a wide variety of interesting opportunities and settings open to them. These include the following.

The Counselor as Fund-Raiser

Today's counselors must be skilled not only in clinical methods and administrative functions but also in generating the funds needed to conduct their groups. These funds may be generated through grant-writing, through lobbying government officials, through marketing programs to potential clientele, or through providing fund-raising programs and services. For many counselors, this is the most unexpected, and yet the most critically important role to learn. In an era of increasing budgetary constraints, counselors in all contexts must be aware of fiscal needs and resources and be creative in generating funds in order to sustain their group work.

The Counselor as Mediator

Group counselors may take on the role of mediator between individuals in a group, or between groups within an organization. In a diversity of settings, including marriages, schools, and corporations, group counselors are being called on increasingly to mediate disputes and to facilitate conflict management.

The Counselor as Teacher/Trainer

Group counselors can teach interpersonal as well as self-management skills within a group context. Many school counselors take on the role of trainer of peer counselors. They also work with school faculty and staff, teaching interpersonal skills, conducting diversity training, or working with other special issues in a primarily didactic role. Counselors in corporate settings or human services agencies also are called upon to train their clients as well as their colleagues in special skills such as assertiveness, time management, and conflict resolution.

The Counselor as Human Resource Specialist

Counselors serving human resource management functions have an increasing role in organizations. These counselors may facilitate employee development or design human resource development systems, including training, coaching, or mentoring programs.

The Counselor and Organizational Development

Counselors who understand organizational systems may find they have a role in organizational development. Operating either as consultants or as employees of an organization, organizational development specialists design and modify management systems to meet the changing needs of that organization and of society.

The Counselor as Supervisor

Counselors may supervise clerical and administrative staff, students, and other counselors and mental health professionals. The role of supervisor usually entails some of the routine clinical skills which all counselors should possess, including listening skills, problem-solving, communication, and planning abilities. The role of supervisor also is quite different in nature from that of counselor, and this role-shift may cause great difficulty if unanticipated. Training in counselor supervision can alleviate some of the strain and uncertainty which often accompany a role change from counselor to supervisor.

APPLICATION OF GROUP COUNSELING

With some exceptions, group counseling, especially as the primary or sole method of treatment, is most suitable for people who are in reasonably good contact with reality; who have cognitive, behavioral, or emotional concerns rather than specific situational problems; who are not severely anxious, depressed, or deficient in interpersonal skills; and who seem capable of benefiting from overall personal development. Group counseling can help people develop trust, increase self-awareness, become more sensitive to the needs and feelings of others, experiment with new behaviors, increase self-confidence and a sense of identity, develop responsibility and the ability to engage in effective reality testing, have a sense of belonging and acceptance, improve social and communication skills, modify troubling thoughts and feelings, and work on individual issues. Although group counseling is not a viable form of treatment for all people and should not be viewed as simply a more efficient and economical variation on individual counseling, it plays an important role in the treatment of many people and can be particularly useful as an adjunct or supplementary approach to individual or family counseling.

CASES FOR DIAGNOSIS AND TREATMENT PLANNING

The following brief cases are presented to give readers an opportunity to diagnose the needs of groups and develop a treatment plan designed to meet those needs. Readers should feel free to fill in the gaps in these cases by adding information that seems necessary to the process of diagnosis and treatment planning.

Case 1. You are a counselor at an urban university in which there have been a number of incidents of reported rapes and dating-related sexual violations. You have decided to conduct a counseling group for people who have experienced these incidents, and also would like to attempt outreach to other people who may not have reported their incidents. Describe how you would go about setting up the group and the plan you would follow in conducting the group.

Case 2. As a counselor in a community-based organization, you have observed recently that many middle-aged, middle-income professionals have been seeking emergency services due to the sudden loss of their jobs. You have decided to apply for a grant from a local charitable organization in order to provide group counseling services to this population. Write a plan for the counseling services you would provide. Include in your plan the specific information you would need to include in your grant proposal, following the DO A CLIENT MAP format.

1. *D*iagnosis and statement of need
2. *O*bjectives
3. *A*ssessments and evaluation plan
4. *C*linician and other staff required
5. *L*ocation
6. *I*nterventions and services offered
7. *E*mphasis
8. *N*umbers
9. *T*iming
10. *M*oney required (budget)
11. *A*djunct services
12. *P*rognosis

Case 3. Directors of a small training firm have contracted with your counseling practice to help them improve morale within the firm. Their business volume has decreased markedly in the past 18 months, and upper management has broadcast a strong warning throughout the firm to cut expenses. However, since the company went through a downsizing several months ago, communications seem to have become stymied, several key employees resigned abruptly, internal conflicts have escalated, and the company's productivity has plummeted. Design a plan of action for the organization, including a description of the qualifications of staff you would assign to this project; the type of personnel from the training firm whom you would involve; and the nature of any interventions you would recommend.

Case 4. In the middle school where you are a counselor, several teachers have indicated that they have been having difficulties with students who come from divorced or divorcing families. These difficulties have been quite diverse, ranging from acting-out behaviors to frequent absenteeism to withdrawal and, in one case, a suspected Eating Disorder. Indicate how you might provide group counseling to these students, including the selection of members, objectives, theoretical approach, interventions, and description of how counseling will be provided within the context of the school.

Writing and Record Keeping in Counseling

The growth and professionalism of the counseling field as well as the increasing emphasis on accountability has led to an expanding need for counselors to document and substantiate the value of their work. A survey of administrators of mental health agencies indicated that "ability to write clearly, concisely, and in a professional style" was one of the three most important skills they sought in masters level counselors (Cook, Berman, Genco, Repka, & Shrider, 1986, p. 150).

Written records of the counseling process can accomplish several goals:

- Provide direction to the counseling process, thereby increasing client motivation
- Facilitate authorization for treatment and third-party payments
- Ease transfer of a client from one counselor to another
- Transmit information on a client from a consultant or previous therapist
- Track the progress of the counseling process and facilitate movement from one session to the next
- Facilitate revisions in treatment plans if clients are not making good progress or have achieved most of their goals
- Protect the counselor in the event of a lawsuit or other challenge to competence by demonstrating that appropriate treatment has been provided
- Facilitate supervision and case conferences
- Provide a written record at the termination of counseling that can be helpful if the client returns for counseling at a later date

Two types of written reports that counselors prepare, a write-up of an intake interview and a treatment plan, already have been discussed in this book. This chapter will present information on other reports prepared by and for counselors, including referrals for assessment, assessment reports, requests for treatment authorization, professional disclosure statements, requests for information, progress notes, mid-treatment evaluations and requests for authorization of additional counseling sessions, safe-keeping contracts, transfer summaries, written reports for case conferences, and closing reports.

ASSESSMENT REFERRALS AND REPORTS

Counselors frequently write and receive reports on the testing, assessment, or psychometric evaluation of clients. Sometimes a psychometric evaluation involves the writing of two reports. One will be written to the psychometrician (usually a psychologist) by the client's counselor or caseworker, requesting the assessment. The other, written by the psychometrician, will provide an analysis of the test results and respond to the counselor's questions. Wolber and Carne (1993, p. 1) wrote of psychological reports, "Probably no other form of evaluative reporting provides the mental health practitioner with a comparable in-depth view of the subject. A well-written psychological report can clarify personality dynamics and explain overt behavior. It is capable of providing answers to differential diagnostic issues and pointing a finger at possible etiology. A good psychological report can explain to the reader the effects of the interaction of cognitive and intellectual factors upon personality. The psychological report can provide an 'x-ray' of the personality, depicting dynamic factors at a level below the manifest personality or overt behavior of the subject. A well-constructed psychological report provides for a normative comparison concerning the functioning of an individual and an integrated and coherent presentation of relatively objective data. Hypotheses and recommendations can be formulated from the information provided from a psychological report. Often major decisions are based on the findings and recommendations of the psychological report."

Assessment reports are based not only on test data but also on observations and inferences drawn from an interview with the client, usually before the testing is begun, and from observation of behavior during the assessment process. Psychological reports tend to be more analytical and interpretive than reports based solely on intake interviews. This is appropriate because the tests and inventories have been studied extensively and their interpretation has been validated by empirical research. As much as possible, however, psychometricians should make their reports clear, free of jargon, and useful to practitioners. The reports should respond to the referral questions and enable the mental health professional to help the client more effectively.

Wolber and Carne (1993) described their typical assessment reports as three or four single-spaced pages in length. Psychological reports generally are written in the third person and should be person-focused rather than test- or theory-focused (Groth-Marnat, 1990). Usual components of a psychological report include information on who the client is, the reason for referral, presenting problems, the assessment instruments, background information on the client, behavioral observations during the assessment, the client's intellectual and cognitive functioning, personality (emotional, intrapsychic, and interpersonal), diagnostic impressions, recommendations, and a summary (Drummond, 1988; Wolber & Carne, 1993).

Referral for Assessment

Sometimes counselors feel stymied by clients' lack of progress, confused about the nature of their difficulties, uncertain as to the degree of pathology present, or simply in need of more information than the clients are providing. At such times, counselors might refer clients to a psychologist or psychometrician for testing and evaluation. (See chapter 4 for additional information on the testing process.)

Counselors often prepare a brief written referral report to provide the psychometrician some background information on the person to be assessed and the reason for the referral. This helps the psychometrician develop some rapport with the client and select those tests and inventories that are most likely to yield the needed information and provide answers to the counselor's questions. The following items typically are discussed in a referral report:

1. Identifying information on client (e.g., age, ethnic and cultural background, marital status)
2. Presenting problems
3. Reason for referral (referral questions)
4. Brief overview of client's background (development, health, family situation, educational/occupational history)
5. Treatment history
6. Summary of previous psychological and psychiatric tests
7. Client's attitude toward the assessment process

The following report exemplifies the information typically provided prior to a psychometric evaluation. The next section includes the test report that was prepared in response to this referral.

THE CENTER FOR COUNSELING AND CONSULTATION
PSYCHOLOGICAL REFERRAL

Client: Edwin (Ed) Ables   *Counselor:* Joyce Waters, M. Ed., LPC

Presenting Problems

Edwin Ables, a nine-year-old white male in the fourth grade at Watkins Mill Elementary School, was brought to counseling by his mother. She reported that since his parents' divorce two years ago, Edwin's behavior at school, as well as his academic performance, has been declining. In addition, he has become hostile and disobedient at home.

Reasons for Referral

1. To assess Ed's level of intelligence and academic abilities and provide clarification on the nature of his academic difficulties.
2. To provide insight into the dynamics of Ed's behavioral changes.
3. To determine the degree of pathology that is present.
4. To clarify the diagnosis and facilitate treatment planning.

Background

Until two years ago, Ed resided with his biological parents and sister who is three years older than he. Although Ed's interest in school varied, depending on the subject, he received above-average grades and did not present behavioral problems either at home or at school. When his parents divorced two years ago, Ed's mother gained custody of the children. Ed's father travels extensively on business and, although he has maintained contact with the children, sees them infrequently and irregularly.

Ed's physical development reportedly was normal and he has had no serious illnesses. He does have several male friends in his neighborhood, but lately they seem to have been withdrawing from him.

Treatment History

Ed has been seen for one counseling session with his mother and two sessions of individual play therapy. During all three sessions, he spoke little and avoided interaction with this counselor as much as possible. He evidenced little interest in the play materials except for a model airplane which he took apart and put together again for most of one session. His apparent reluctance to engage in counseling led me to make this referral for psychological testing.

Previous Test Results

No previous psychological assessment of Ed has been conducted.

Attitude toward Assessment

Ed may manifest some resistance to the assessment process, but with some encouragement can probably be persuaded to cooperate.

The Assessment Process

The person conducting the assessment is usually a doctoral-level psychologist. However, counselors are increasingly conducting assessments, especially in cases in which information is needed on a person's career development, disabilities, or potential for rehabilitation. Although most counselors are not qualified to administer projective tests and many are not trained in the use of individual intelligence tests, a battery of tests still can be compiled, consisting entirely of tests that can be used by counselors, which provides a comprehensive picture of a person's overall functioning and can answer most referral questions. This section will provide an evaluation of Ed, completed by a psychologist, as well as an evaluation of another client, completed by a counselor, to illustrate both forms of assessment reports.

Although people may be assessed without a referral report or any guidance from the client's counselor, that is unusual. In such cases a comprehensive test battery, assessing the following areas, might be administered.

1. Intellectual and academic abilities—The Stanford-Binet Intelligence Scale or one of the Wechsler Intelligence Scales most often are used to measure intelligence, while such tools as the Wide Range Achievement Test provide information on academic skills.
2. Personality—Psychologists typically use a battery of projective tests including the Rorschach Test, the Thematic Apperception Test, the House-Tree-Person, and perhaps a sentence completion inventory. Both psychologists and counselors also assess personality through objective inventories such as the Minnesota Multiphasic Personality Inventory, the Millon Clinical Multiaxial Inventory, the California Psychological Inventory, the Beck Depression and Beck Anxiety Inventories, as well as other inventories discussed further in chapter 4.

3. Perception and organicity—The Bender Visual Motor Gestalt Test (Bender Gestalt) is frequently used to provide information on these areas as well as supplementary data on personality dynamics and intellectual functioning.

Measurement of career-related interests, aptitudes, and values typically is not done as part of a comprehensive assessment unless such information was requested beforehand by the client's counselor or therapist or unless the psychometrician believes that such information would be particularly important to the referring person or agency (e.g., a rehabilitation counseling agency).

The referral report for Ed indicated that information was needed in the following areas of functioning: personality, behavior, interpersonal relationships, intelligence, and abilities. Information also was sought to provide understanding and treatment guidelines for his current behavioral, academic, and attitudinal changes. A report of the psychological evaluation of Edwin Ables follows. It is organized according to a typical framework.

Assessment by a Psychologist

ASSESSMENT REPORT

Client: Edwin (Ed) Ables   *Psychologist:* Clayton Chang, Ph.D.

Tests administered: Wechsler Intelligence Scale for Children-III
                      Wide Range Achievement Test
                      House-Tree-Person
                      Bender Visual Motor Gestalt Test
                      Thematic Apperception Test
                      Rorschach Test

Reason for Assessment

At the time of the evaluation, Edwin (Ed) Ables, a nine-year old white male, was being seen for outpatient counseling by Joyce Waters, LPC, who referred Ed for an evaluation. Information was requested on Ed's intellectual functioning and academic abilities as well as on the dynamics and recommended treatment of Ed's current behavioral, interpersonal, and academic difficulties, apparently related to his parents' divorce two years ago.

Background

The client was brought to the evaluation by his mother, who reported that Ed had been fighting and arguing at school as well as presenting academic difficulties. She stated that Ed was in the fourth grade in a regular classroom. He resided with his mother and sister, age 12. Ed's parents were divorced approximately two years ago and Ed presently has infrequent contact with his father. Mrs. Ables reported that her own relationship with Ed is inconsistent and vacillated between conflicting and getting along well. She perceived Ed as feeling torn between his parents and stated that he seemed to be having difficulty coping with their divorce. She also reported that Ed manifested some social problems and tended to play with the younger children in the neighborhood rather than socializing with his peers, who lately have avoided contact with Ed.

Impression of Client

Ed was well-groomed and casually though appropriately dressed. He is of average height and weight, looked approximately his stated age, and presented a positive appearance. Ed initially appeared resistant to the testing process. He refused to remove his hat and coat and spoke little to the examiner at the outset. As the evaluation progressed, Ed became more involved in the testing process. He gradually established a satisfactory degree of rapport with this examiner and generally showed little significant resistance after the first twenty minutes of the assessment.

Assessment of Abilities

On the Wechsler Intelligence Scale for Children, Ed achieved a verbal IQ score of 101, a performance IQ score of 118, and a full-scale IQ score of 109, placing him in the average range of intelligence. However, the disparity between Ed's verbal and performance scores is significant and probably reflects a mild learning disability that affects his reading abilities. This should be investigated further. The test protocol reflected considerable subtest scatter, suggesting that Ed's intellectual abilities have not developed smoothly and probably have been adversely affected by both emotional and learning difficulties.

Ed's intellectual strengths include his grasp of spatial organization and his capacity for visual motor coordination. He has a good grasp of planning and cause and effect relationships. He has sound judgment and clearly is aware of the socially appropriate way to behave. In fact, some indications suggest that he may sometimes be excessively conventional or conforming.

Ed's grasp of verbal concepts and his verbal skills are relatively weak. Arithmetic problems, presented verbally, also presented difficulty for him. Ed was easily distracted and sometimes gave up prematurely on tasks. On the other hand, he enjoyed the challenge presented by some of the timed tests and became highly motivated and competitive when he was working against the clock. He generally worked quickly and was not careless in his performance.

The Wide Range Achievement Test was used to assess Ed's intellectual abilities. He did best on the arithmetic section, emphasizing computation rather than problems. His arithmetic score was at the fifth grade level and in the high average range while his reading and spelling scores were at the third grade level and in the low average range.

Although Ed's intelligence level suggests that he could perform satisfactorily in a regular classroom, the imbalance in his intellectual faculties probably makes it difficult for him to complete tasks that emphasize verbal skills and that do not involve clear and relatively brief time limits. His ability to handle some tasks very easily while having considerable difficulty with others may well be frustrating and confusing to Ed. I suggest that his mother request an educational evaluation to determine whether special help or modifications in Ed's assignments might better accommodate the imbalance in his intellectual abilities.

Assessment of Personality

Ed is experiencing considerable anxiety and depression. However, he seems to have gained some control over these feelings through his high activity level. Although Ed is capable of a satisfactory level of impulse control, his acting out behavior seems to be a way for him to alleviate depression and anxiety and so becomes a rewarding behavior despite its adverse consequences. Ed is a rather unreflective boy who has little capacity for insight or empathy. He tends to be action-oriented and prefers to deal with problems and upset through activity rather than through discussion.

Ed seems to have low self-esteem. He is very concerned about his weak performance at school and perceives himself as incompetent and helpless. He wants to improve his academic performance but does not know how to make the change and feels hopeless and pessimistic. Ed also seems to feel different from his peers, viewing himself as strange and even menacing. His parents' recent divorce seems to have contributed to these feelings of differentness as does Ed's strong underlying anger. In relationships, Ed prefers a dependent stance; however, when that is prevented, he distances himself and becomes angry and disappointed. This pattern is especially characteristic of Ed's relationship with his father who bears the brunt of his anger. His mother, his sister, and his peers also are viewed as having let him down. Ed feels that his mother is pushing him away, possibly through her efforts to have Ed spend more time with his father. Ed is uncomfortable with this yet does not want to disappoint his mother.

At present, Ed is having some difficulty figuring out who he is and establishing satisfactory ego boundaries. Although he has some inner strengths, he feels as if he is on a road toward destruction and is aware that he needs some help.

Diagnosis

Axis I.	313.81 Oppositional Defiant Disorder, moderate
	300.4 Dysthymic Disorder, early onset, moderate
	315.00 Reading Disorder (provisional)
Axis II.	V71.89 No diagnosis on Axis II
Axis III.	None
Axis IV.	Separation from father, conflict with mother and teacher, declining academic performance
Axis V.	60

Recommendations

Both counseling and academic help seem indicated. Ed may well show some initial resistance to those interventions, but that resistance is likely to diminish with time and patience. Although Ed does not manifest severe pathology, the nature of his difficulties can have a strong adverse impact on his future development if not ameliorated soon. Because Ed is not very verbal or insightful, he may have difficulty involving himself in a conventional counseling relationship. Play therapy, providing both choices and clear limits, is likely to be especially helpful as is behavioral counseling, giving him acceptable ways to express and manage his feelings of anger and frustration. Family counseling, with Ed, his mother, his sister, and, if possible, his father also is indicated to help Ed cope with the impact of the divorce, to help him express himself to his family, and to establish more consistent contact between Ed and his father. An academic evaluation is recommended to clarify the nature of Ed's apparent Learning Disability, focused on verbal and reading skills. Subsequent tutoring and educational changes should not only improve his academic performance but also his self-esteem and optimism.

Psychological Assessment by a Counselor

The following assessment report was written by a licensed professional counselor and illustrates the use of objective tests of ability and personality, as well as information gleaned from an interview, to provide useful recommendations.

ASSESSMENT REPORT

Client: John Marino   *Counselor:* Clare Alvarado, LPC, CCMHC

Tests Administered

Wechsler Adult Intelligence Scale
COPSystem (CAPS ability battery, COPS interest inventory, COPES work values survey)
Millon Clinical Multiaxial Inventory

Reason for Evaluation

John Marino, an 18-year-old white male, was referred for an evaluation after his conviction for car theft. John is being considered for participation in a pre-release program that will provide him with job training and employment and prepare him for his release from prison in six months. However, during his initial interview for that program, John seemed withdrawn and depressed and had considerable difficulty responding to the interviewer's questions. An assessment was requested to determine his suitability for the pre-release program and, if that was recommended, to provide suggestions as to how to help him formulate future plans.

Background

At the time of his arrest, John was in his senior year of high school in a special education class. He was living with his mother and two younger brothers; the whereabouts of his father were unknown. John reported an interest in engaging in noncompetitive sports such as in-line skating and biking and in watching football and basketball games. He stated that he had dated little and had no close friends. He acknowledged occasional use of marijuana and alcohol prior to his incarceration. He does not have clear career goals but is interested in completing high school.

Impressions of Client

John is a tall, slender man who appears his stated age. John initially gave a negative impression when seen for the assessment. He seemed disinterested in what was going on around him and was dressed in clothes that were soiled. John did not have good verbal skills, volunteered little information about himself, and was difficult to engage in discussion.

Test-Taking Behavior

However, as the assessment progressed, John became more involved and responsive. Despite his initial negative reaction to the assessment process, he was cooperative and motivated throughout the process. He was interested in and curious about the testing and often asked to have another chance or an explanation of tasks he had failed. John is a reasonably persistent worker with a satisfactory grasp of trial-and-error learning. His concentration and attention were satisfactory and he had little difficulty following directions. His short term memory was above-average. He worked at a satisfactory rate of speed on visual-motor tasks but manifested considerable slowness on tasks that called for verbalization or writing.

Abilities

On the Wechsler Adult Intelligence Scale, John achieved a verbal IQ score of 87, a performance IQ score of 86, and a full scale IQ score of 85, placing him in the low average range of intelligence and between the 11th and 25th percentiles. This instrument yielded no evidence of learning disability or severe pathology. John has poor reading skills although he can read and perform simple mathematical computations. Despite his disinterested demeanor, John is very much aware of what is going on around him, knows of what is expected of him, grasps situations fairly quickly, and can plan appropriate actions. However, John has developed little interest in academic pursuits. His fund of information and his vocabulary are particularly poor. He also tends to have a low energy level.

John's scores on the Career Ability Placement Survey (CAPS) battery were consistent with his scores on the WAIS. All eight scores were below average, but his scores in mechanical reasoning, manual speed and dexterity, and spatial relations were relatively high (4th stanine) while scores in language usage and verbal reasoning were quite low (2nd stanine).

Personality

Assessment of John's personality yielded no evidence of severe pathology but did highlight some areas of concern. John seems to be a guarded and suspicious young man who is well-defended and resistant to self-disclosure. He tends to be rigid and constricted and has difficulty dealing with anger appropriately. He is a fairly passive person who wants to be liked but who has little genuine interest in other people. His social skills are weak and he is not interested in working on these skills in order to relate better to others. Some underlying depression was noted, but John seems to be masking and denying these feelings with a bland exterior. He does not seem to be troubled by significant anxiety.

Interests and Values

The COPSystem interest inventory suggested that John's strongest interests are in outdoor and skilled technology areas. Lowest interests were in arts, communication, and science, professional. The values inventory indicated that John valued privacy and being concrete and realistic; values such as aesthetics, social concern, and leadership were not important to him. These are consistent with John's expressed and manifest interests and abilities.

Diagnosis

Axis I.	311 Depressive Disorder Not Otherwise Specified
	305.00 Alcohol Abuse (provisional)
	305.20 Cannabis Abuse (provisional)
Axis II.	V62.89 Borderline Intellectual Functioning
	Paranoid and Schizoid Personality Traits
Axis III.	None
Axis IV.	Incarceration
Axis V.	55

Recommendations

John has more potential than is initially evident. He can profit from educational experiences and should be able to learn skills that will facilitate his employment. He can be motivated and hard-working, although he needs to develop goals and direction, improve his life skills, and receive some occupational training. John probably would be most successful in a hands-on job in which he has clear direction but can work fairly independently, producing a visible product. One of the current opportunities at the pre-release center involves training and employment in bicycle repair and an option such as this one may be well-suited to John's preferences and abilities.

John seems to have the capacity and motivation to benefit from and successfully complete the pre-release program. Standards should be set for him that are realistic yet mildly challenging. Counseling is recommended to help him deal with personal issues including his underlying depression and the conflict he seems to experience between his tendency to withdraw from others and his wish to be liked. Attention also should be paid to John's impulse control and his use of drugs and alcohol, probably a greater problem than John acknowledged. John is a young man with some motivation and strengths; counseling and occupational training at this time has the potential to make an important difference in his future.

REQUESTING TREATMENT AUTHORIZATION

Another written report that counselors might prepare early in the counseling process is a request for authorization of treatment. With the spread of managed care, counselors increasingly are required to justify the need for counseling before payment for sessions is authorized. Typically, a few sessions will be authorized by telephone, affording the counselor time to prepare and submit a written request for authorization of treatment. These reports usually are relatively brief. The following is a request for treatment authorization for Sharon Miles, a 45-year-old woman, organized according to an outline typical of such requests.

Clinical condition (reasons for seeking treatment, current condition, severity, duration, impairment, previous treatment):

Presenting concerns included long-standing mood instability, significant depression, and weight gain of over 75 pounds, resulting in physical problems. Although client is managing family demands reasonably well, she has few leisure activities and marital conflict is reported. Symptoms have been present at least since suicide of mother six years ago. There is no history of psychological treatment.

Brief mental status (abnormal findings only): Moderate depression and anxiety, mood instability, some impairment in behavior and thinking.

Diagnoses:

    Axis I.   301.13 Cyclothymic Disorder, moderate
    Axis II.   V71.09 No diagnosis on Axis II
    Axis III. Obesity, asthma, arthritis reported
    Axis IV.   Marital conflict
    Axis V.   58

Treatment goals and focus of treatment:

1. Reduce depression, stabilize mood
2. Improve self-esteem, activity level
3. Reduce marital conflict, improve communication
4. Reduce weight to healthy level
5. Facilitate grieving for death of mother

Counseling will be primarily cognitive-behavioral in nature, involving clear goals and specific steps to meet them. Some psychodynamic and supportive techniques will be used to help client deal with impact of past on present.

Types, orientation, frequency, and duration of sessions: Individual counseling, once a week for 50 minutes. Occasional couples or family sessions as needed. Anticipate total of 20 sessions. Will be referred to psychiatrist for medication evaluation, weight control program.

Prognosis: Good for relief of depression and anxiety and for improvement of marriage; fair for weight reduction.

Based on requests such as these, managed care companies determine whether to authorize counseling. Often, authorization will be for a limited number of sessions, perhaps 5–10. If continued treatment is indicated, the counselor will have to submit a progress report, justifying the need for additional sessions.

PROFESSIONAL DISCLOSURE STATEMENT

A professional disclosure statement now has become a standard part of counseling (Paradise, 1990). This statement provides information on counselors' training and areas of expertise and acquaints clients with guidelines that are important in the counseling process. Typically, this statement will be read and discussed during the first counseling session, both client and counselor will sign the document to indicate their agreement with its policies, and then the client will be given a copy of the document as a reminder of the information. This statement provides protection for both clients and counselors; once it has been discussed and signed, neither can legitimately deny knowledge of the policies and procedures contained in the statement.

The following specific information usually is included in a professional disclosure statement:

1. Counselor's qualifications, including degrees, where obtained, licenses and certifications
2. Theoretical orientation
3. Areas of expertise and counseling services provided
4. Information on the counseling relationship
5. Client responsibilities
6. Fee structure, when payments are expected, use of third-party payments, use of collection agencies in the event that payments are not made
7. Policies on missed appointments, cancellations

8. Information on privileged communication and confidentiality
9. Information on recording of sessions
10. Policy in the event of an emergency

────────────────────────────── **Sample Professional Disclosure Statement**

COUNSELING AGREEMENT FOR CLIENTS OF
DR. LINDA SELIGMAN

The purpose of this agreement is to provide important information about my background and the policies of the Center for Counseling and Consultation. Counseling is more likely to be successful if we have a mutual understanding of the counseling process.

I have a Ph.D. in Counseling Psychology from Columbia University. I am licensed as a Counselor and as a Psychologist in Virginia and Maryland and am a Certified Clinical Mental Health Counselor (CCMHC) and a National Certified Counselor (NCC). I have been the Director of the Center for Counseling and Consultation since 1985.

My practice includes adolescents, adults, couples, and families. I provide individual, group, and family counseling. I have particular expertise in counseling people who are coping with cancer, people with Mood or Anxiety Disorders, people with relationship or self-esteem concerns, people with career difficulties, and people with a history of physical or sexual abuse. My primary theoretical orientation is cognitive-behavioral. However, I am trained in and draw on a wide variety of other approaches including brief psychodynamic and solution-focused psychotherapy, reality therapy, and Adlerian psychotherapy.

Within the next session or two, we will establish goals for our work together and I will then plan a treatment that seems likely to help you achieve those goals. I have found counseling to be most effective if we work collabora-tively; I expect you to come to your sessions on time, to complete any tasks we agree upon, and to do your best to talk about those concerns, behaviors, thoughts, and feelings that are bothering you. If anything about our counseling troubles or disappoints you, I strongly encourage you to talk about that in our session so that we can address your concerns.

My current fee is _____ for a 50 minute session. Payment should be made at the end of each session unless we make other arrangements. I will be glad to provide you with statements and to complete your insurance forms as needed. A charge of $15 per 15 minute segment also will be made for consultation by telephone. No charge will be made for brief telephone conversations to schedule, change, or confirm appointments.

If you need to cancel or change an appointment, please give me at least 48 hours' notice. If that is not done, you will be charged for any missed appointments. Please be aware that insurance companies do not make payment for missed appointments.

Confidentiality is maintained as part of the counseling process in accord with the ethical standards of my profession. Your written authorization is required for any release of information or records, such as to your physician. Use of insurance forms to obtain third-party payments serves as authorization of release of information to your insurance company. Exceptions are made to this policy on confidentiality only in the event of court order, imminent danger to you or another person, or abuse of children, the disabled, or the elderly. An exception also may need to be made in the event of nonpayment of fees necessitating the use of a collection agency. Please be aware that I cannot guarantee that confidentiality of information released to insurance carriers will be maintained by those agents.

With your permission, tape recordings will sometimes be made of our counseling sessions. These will be used for professional purposes only and confidentiality will be maintained.

Messages may be left on my voice mail at any time. Voice mail will be checked regularly by myself or one of my associates between 7 a.m. and 10 p.m., seven days a week, and I will return your calls as soon as possible. I also will give you the telephone numbers of emergency services that you can access at other hours or in the event you need immediate help at any time.

Please sign below to indicate that you have reviewed, understand, and are in agreement with the policies in this agreement.

Client: _____   Date: _____
Counselor: _____   Date: _____

INTAKE QUESTIONNAIRES

Along with their professional disclosure statements, many counselors give clients an intake or life history questionnaire to be completed during or after the first session, depending on its length. Counselors can easily develop these forms to meet their needs. A brief intake form might ask for name, address of home and place of employment, telephone numbers, date of birth, insurance information, presenting concerns, medical conditions, medications, treatment history, names and ages of immediate family members, and person to contact in the event of an emergency. Suggestions for information to be included in longer question-naires can be drawn from chapter 5.

SAFE-KEEPING CONTRACTS

Dealing effectively with a client's suicidal ideation is one of the most challeng-ing and important tasks of the counselor. Sometimes a written contract can facilitate that process. Although it may seem strange to ask someone to sign a contract agreeing not to commit suicide, such a process communicates the counselor's concern as well as the seriousness of the situation and provides encouragement and alternatives.

Sample Safe-Keeping Contract

I agree that between now and July 1, I will not overdose on my medication, cut myself, drive in a reckless manner, or otherwise endanger my life. If I have thoughts about harming myself, I will instead follow the steps agreed to by my counselor and myself.

Steps are listed, including sources of emergency assistance and activities that are likely to reduce suicidal ideation. Agreement would then be signed and dated by both client and counselor.

RELEASE OF INFORMATION

Counselors often want to communicate with people who are acquainted with or who have provided treatment to a client such as family members, teachers, school counselors, physicians, lawyers, or psychiatrists. Unless the client is in imminent danger or is a minor, the client's written permission must be obtained before the counselor can talk with anyone about the client or even acknowledge that the person is in treatment with the counselor. The following is an example of a release of information.

Example of Release of Information

I authorize *(name of sending person or agency)* to release to *(name of receiving person or agency)* at *(address)* the following information: *(specify information to be released)* pertaining to myself or my child *(name of child)* for the following purpose: *(state reason for request)*. This authorization is signed with the under-standing that the information will not be passed onto anyone else without my

written permission and will not be used for any other purpose than that specified above. Authorization expires *(maximum of 90 days from date of signing).*
(Form should be signed and dated by both client and counselor.)

PROGRESS NOTES

In nearly all mental health treatment programs as well as in private practices, counselors are currently expected to maintain progress notes. Typically, progress notes are entries made in the client's chart or file each time the counselor has a session or other significant interaction with a client.

Progress notes are particularly useful in settings where several mental health professionals are working with a particular client. In a psychiatric hospital, for example, a nurse, a family counselor, a psychiatrist, and a case aide all may have contact with a client in a single day. Different schedules and other commitments typically make it impossible for the four helping professionals to meet daily to share their perceptions of the client's development. Progress notes provide the vehicle for that communication.

Progress notes also are a useful way for counselors to gauge client progress and plan the session-by-session direction of treatment. They serve as reminders to the counselor of important topics or plans for the client's treatment. Progress notes also document the nature of the counseling process and can help counselors to demonstrate that they have been providing appropriate treatment, should that be necessitated by a challenge to their competence.

Structured Formats for Progress Notes

Progress notes can be simply unstructured comments written into the client's record after each session. However, having a framework for writing progress notes can facilitate that process and make the notes more useful. Several formats are available for maintaining progress notes. Law, Moracco, and Wilmarth (1981) described a method that has been widely adopted. The acronym SOAP is used to identify four categories that are covered in the progress notes:

Subjective—In this section, counselors briefly summarize their impressions of a session, perhaps considering the degree of progress made, the client's mood level, the client-counselor interaction, and the pace of the session.

Objective—This includes specific and factual information on the client's progress and behavior and on the nature of the session itself.

Analysis—Next, counselors analyze the implications of the subjective and objective material. Particularly important are comments on the relationship of the session to overall treatment goals.

Plans—Finally, counselors focus on the future and list any tasks that clients have agreed to undertake, anything the counselor needs to do to prepare for the next meeting with the client, and areas to be explored or considered in the next session. Long-range plans also may be included in this section.

The following is an example of a progress note, written according to the SOAP format:

5/18/96—Third individual counseling session held with Carrie Carter. (S) Carrie seemed more animated and talkative than she had in previous sessions. She was more comfortable discussing her feelings about her relationship with George, but she still seemed afraid to talk about her family relationships. (O) For the first time, Carrie arrived on time for our appointment. She reported that she had revised her resumé and had begun an exercise program. She stated that she was feeling more cheerful but still felt stuck in her relationship with her boyfriend. (A) The behavioral approach to treatment, with some supportive interventions, seems to be effective. Carrie is mobilizing her own resources and is beginning to take constructive action. Homework assignments (e.g., rewriting her resumé) seem particularly useful. (P) Progress should be reinforced and continued in career and physical-fitness areas, with homework assignments suggested. Client also may be ready to role-play a discussion with George of some of her concerns.

Another format for progress notes is the TIPP format which includes the four categories illustrated in the following example:

9/20/96—Sixth individual counseling session with Debra Lee.

Themes/topics: Debra talked with pride about gaining more balance in her life and being more effective at using limit-setting and reinforcement with her children. She and her husband had gone out to dinner, but Debra reported feeling uncomfortable being alone with him. As planned, she wrote a letter to her mother-in-law about their last visit and felt a sense of relief that she had been able to express herself.

Interventions: Reflection and reinforcement were used to consolidate and strengthen gains. Progress since starting counseling was assessed using a 1–10 scale and was rated as follows: self-esteem—6, relationships with children—5, relationship with husband—2, mood—8. Examination of cognitions was used in an effort to modify Debra's all-or-nothing thinking about her family relationships.

Progress/Problems: Debra's depression has lifted and her energy has returned. She is having more positive interactions with her children but still needs help with her interaction with her husband. In addition, she continues to be other-directed with her sense of self coming from her ability to help others.

Plans:

1. Administer Beck Depression Inventory, compare with initial administration
2. Discuss assignment of writing descriptions of herself and her relationships with her husband and her mother-in-law, identifying both strengths and weaknesses
3. Teach relaxation to help her cope with tension resulting from family conflict

Progress notes tend to be fairly brief, often shorter than the examples presented here. Counselors with limited time may become perfunctory in their approach to such notes and may view them as burdensome. Such attitudes may result in notes like "Ms. Carter was seen for counseling today. Session dealt with career and interpersonal issues." While such notes may satisfy an agency requirement, they are not helpful to either the counselor or to others working with a client. Brief but informative progress notes can be written in a few minutes. Whenever possible, counselors should use progress notes as an opportunity to reflect on a session and refine treatment planning.

One caution must be raised about progress notes and other client reports. Such records may be subpoenaed by the courts and may be subject to review by the client. Counselors should bear this in mind; they should avoid labeling or judging clients and should avoid using terminology that may be stigmatizing or unprofessional. They should be specific and precise and provide quotations and details.

INTERIM EVALUATIONS

Thus far, this book has focused on diagnosis and treatment planning that takes place during the initial phase of the counselor–client interaction. However, counselors also use forms and reports to evaluate progress in an ongoing counseling relationship. A variety of circumstances may prompt a progress review:

1. The client may show little improvement or may express dissatisfaction with the counseling process.

2. New areas of importance may come to light as counselor and client develop rapport and the client becomes less guarded and defensive and as initial goals are achieved.

3. The insurance or managed care company providing third-party payments may request a progress report to determine whether continued mental health services are needed for a client.

4. The counselor working with a client may leave the agency, requiring the assignment of a new treatment provider to the client.

5. Counselor and client may want to assess whether it is time for the person to complete counseling.

6. A progress review can reinforce gains, encourage client motivation, and facilitate continued treatment planning.

All these are circumstances that can occur during counseling relationships and that call for an evaluation of progress and perhaps a reconceptualization of a client's diagnosis and treatment plan.

Informal Evaluations

Ideally, evaluation should be a continuous part of every counseling relationship, with the counselor reviewing the progress demonstrated at each session and counselor and client frequently discussing the client's growth. Such a process of informal evaluation is important to ensure that client and counselor are working together effectively and that the client is making satisfactory progress toward achieving established goals. Informal evaluations can facilitate the process of more formal interim evaluations.

A collaborative discussion of progress, built into a counseling session, can be a useful way to reinforce progress, to clarify goals and objectives, and to make changes in a treatment plan. Some counselors conduct such evaluations on a regular schedule, perhaps every two weeks, while others are spontaneous, waiting for appropriate times in the client's development. Particularly appropriate times for a re-evaluation might be a clear sign of progress (e.g., client's first social event as a single person); a setback (e.g., a perceptible increase in the client's level of anxiety); a noteworthy life event (e.g., the client's first day at college); calendar times such as the client's birthday, the start of a new year, the first anniversary of the client's divorce; or when the client expresses unusually positive or negative feelings about the counseling process.

One way to approach such an evaluation is to use the client's initial treatment objectives as a starting point and make *lists of accomplishments*, *additional objectives*, and *strategies for goal achievement*. This process seems to be most effective if the client takes the lead in developing the lists, with the counselor writing the items and helping the client to propose and clarify ideas. Items should be as specific and concrete as possible and should be written in such a way as to make the list a meaningful point of reference the next time such an evaluation is done.

The following is an example of such a formative evaluation, reflecting an assessment of progress after three months of counseling with Jane, a 58-year-old woman who sought counseling because of Agoraphobia and high anxiety:

INITIAL OBJECTIVES

1. Regain full mobility using car and subway.
   Baseline: No driving or use of subway.
   One month: Could drive in her neighborhood with another person.
   Three months: Can drive alone in neighborhood and can drive long distances with another person. Can take subway at times other than rush hours.
   Four-month goal: Drive alone to visit mother, take subway during morning rush hour.
2. Return to work on a full-time basis.
   Baseline: Has not been able to work in three months.
   One month: Client arranged with supervisor for her to do 10 hours of work a week at home. Has been to office weekly to pick up and drop off work.
   Three months: Is working at the office four hours a day, three days a week, while continuing to work at home.
   Four-month goal: Expand office hours to six hours a day, five days a week.
3. Develop at least two friends and two regular leisure activities.
   Baseline: Had no contact with friends and no leisure activities other than watching television.
   One month: Initiated contact with two former friends. Began taking a daily walk in the neighborhood.
   Three months: Signed up to take a course in genealogy and has been gathering information about singing groups she might join. Has been to church twice. Continues daily walking and contact with two friends.
   Four-month goal: Begin course in genealogy, go to church every week, have lunch with one friend, join a singing group.

Such lists can help both client and counselor see that progress has indeed been made, can clarify areas where change is still needed, and can provide the client with some encouragement to make those changes. Client and counselor should each retain a copy of the lists so they can be used as the basis for future discussion.

Structured Interim Reports

Sometimes, a more formal and extensive evaluation of a client's progress seems indicated, even though the person has not yet met his or her initial objectives. Such an evaluation may be requested by the client's insurance or managed care company, may be part of the agency's procedure for monitoring treatment effectiveness, may be indicated by the client's deterioration or failure to progress, or may result from a transfer of the client from one counselor to another.

In writing interim reports, counselors can usually assume that their readers have some knowledge of the intake report that was completed when the person entered treatment. While information on that report may be summarized, it need not be repeated. Typically, interim reports are fairly brief (longer than progress notes but shorter than intake reports). They are intended primarily to evaluate the client's progress in light of treatment objectives and to make recommendations for further treatment, if indicated. A combination of the intake report, the progress notes, and the interim report should provide a new counselor with all the information needed to begin working productively with a client.

If an interim report is being prepared according to agency policy or in response to a request from an insurance company, a format for writing such a report probably will be provided. The following example illustrates a typical format used by managed care companies. This report requests authorization for additional counseling sessions for Sharon Miles. The initial authorization request for this client was presented earlier in this chapter.

Client: Sharon Miles

Diagnosis:

> Axis I.   301.13 Cyclothymic Disorder, moderate
> Axis II. V71.09 No diagnosis on Axis II
> Axis III. Obesity, asthma, arthritis reported
> Axis IV. Marital conflict
> Axis V.   58

Date of initial assessment: May 15, 1996

Number of sessions since initial assessment: 9

> *Course of treatment to date, progress*: Individual cognitive-behavioral counseling has been the primary mode of treatment. In addition, two sessions were held with the client and her husband. Referral for medication was made and Prozac was

prescribed. Client's moods have stabilized and depression has been somewhat reduced. Ms. Miles has dealt effectively with the death of her mother.

Current symptoms and level of functioning: Client is functioning better at home; depressive symptoms and emotional outbursts have been reduced. However, she continues to experience low self-esteem, inertia, and weight gain.

Current goals and treatment plan: Ms. Miles now is ready to address her marital difficulties and to increase her activity level. Cognitive-behavioral counseling and systems family therapy will be used to help her locate part-time employment, increase her activity level, become involved in a weight control program, and improve marital communication and satisfaction.

Criteria for discharge: Ratings of self-esteem and marital satisfaction will be at least 6 on a 1–10 scale; client will be engaged in regular physical activity and will be participating in a weight control program. Mood will continue to be relatively stable.

Estimated number of sessions until termination of treatment: 10

TRANSFER SUMMARY

A transfer summary or report is designed to help a counselor continue the treatment of a client who has been in counseling with another therapist. It provides an overview of the client's treatment history, focusing on progress as well as continuing concerns, and gives information on how to work effectively with the client based on his or her reactions to the first part of treatment. Although some transition time probably will be needed for a client to develop trust and rapport with a new counselor and to work through any feelings of anger and grief connected with the departure of the first counselor, a transfer report can reduce the difficulties inherent in such a transition and pave the way for the establishment of a good counseling relationship.

EXAMPLE OF TRANSFER SUMMARY

Client: Aaron Rudderman   *Counselor*: Doris Lopez, M.Ed., LPC, NCC

Presenting Problems

Aaron Rudderman, a 51-year-old white Jewish male, sought counseling for help with depression, marital difficulties and career concerns, and in coping with his diagnosis of Parkinson's disease. Mr. Rudderman's physical health began deteriorating about three years ago. Soon after, Parkinson's disease was diagnosed and he was placed on medication to reduce the symptoms of the disease. However, he had to leave his job as a cab driver and could no longer engage in such physical activities as lawn care, car repair, and playing ball with his son, now 15. Depression and family conflict, probably present at a low level for many years, increased and led to suicidal ideation and talk of divorce. Mr. Rudderman was diagnosed as having a Major Depressive Disorder, late onset, with atypical features.

Nature of Treatment

The client has been seen for 17 sessions of individual counseling and five sessions of couples counseling. A multimodal approach to treatment was taken because of the pervasive impact of the client's medical condition, although brief psychodynamic psychotherapy was emphasized to address depression and guilt related to anticipated rejection. This approach also was helpful in clarifying Mr. Rudderman's ambivalent view of his present situation. Part of him longs to be the helpless invalid, cared for and pampered by his wife, while another side of him sees all symptoms of his Parkinson's disease as psychosomatic, denying the very real limitations he does have on his activities. Behavioral interventions also were an important part of treatment and served both to reduce depression and to increase goal-directed activities.

Progress

Mr. Rudderman's depression has been reduced and his marriage seems stronger, although both areas need continued attention. He has formulated some future goals, based on a long-standing interest in the stock market, and currently is taking courses to become a financial planner. He and his son have become closer and the client's self-esteem has shown some improvement. Sleeping and eating habits have improved and some appropriate weight gain has been reported.

Recommendations

The next six months may be difficult for Mr. Rudderman since he will complete his training in financial planning and expects to seek employment. He needs help in maximizing his use of his intellectual and physical abilities without setting unrealistic expectations for himself. Continued couples counseling can help to reduce his wife's tendency to be demanding and critical as well as the client's discouragement. Psychodynamic psychotherapy can continue to be helpful to this client, but his tendency to analyze and intellectualize excessively suggests that the psychodynamic approach needs to be balanced by some behavioral interventions. Behavioral counseling also can help him begin to develop some realistic leisure activities.

Although Mr. Rudderman is out of crisis, he needs continued help for at least the next six months to progress in his marriage and his career and try to establish a rewarding lifestyle in light of his physical limitations. He is expected to make the transfer to another counselor without much difficulty and has expressed enthusiasm about continuing his counseling.

CASE CONFERENCES

Some agencies have regularly scheduled case conferences in which staff members present cases and receive feedback from each other. These are not necessarily problem cases (although this can be a useful way to get help with an impasse in counseling) but may be a client with an unusual or interesting history or concern. Planning and writing notes in preparation for these meetings can increase their usefulness.

Case conferences generally are intended to be learning experiences for the presenter as well as for the other staff members, although they also can be intimidating or anxiety-provoking for the presenter. Case conferences should not be a place for mental health professionals to belittle each other's work or flaunt their own accomplishments. Rather, they should be a place where colleagues work together to help each other provide more effective client treatment. The counselor responsible for making a presentation at a case conference need not feel obligated to have all the answers about a client. In fact, the case conference probably will be more interesting and productive if the counselor has some specific questions about the dynamics, diagnosis, or treatment of the client to be presented.

Case conferences vary, depending on the nature of the mental health facility, the client being presented, and the style of the presenter. Some conferences involve the staff in observing the client and counselor engaged in counseling, while at others the client may attend part of the conference and speak directly to the participants about his or her concerns. Another approach to such conferences involves the counselor presenting an audiotape or videotape of part of a counseling session. Probably the most common format simply involves the counselor providing information about a client and their work together. Regardless of the particular format of a case conference, the presenting counselor generally should plan to cover the following areas in the information provided to the group:

1. *Identifying information*—client's name, age, education, occupation, family constellation, and other important demographic data
2. *Presenting and underlying concerns*
3. *Diagnosis*
4. *Brief overview of background*—development, physical and emotional characteristics, family history, educational and occupational history, relevant leisure activities, important relationships, significant events
5. *Treatment history*—previous treatment, duration and nature of present treatment, client attitude toward treatment, progress made
6. *Counselor's concerns/questions*—diagnostic questions, confusing dynamics, treatment impasses, client resistance, or questions about treatment planning

Considerable similarity exists between an assessment referral report and the sort of presentation counselors might make at case conferences. That is because both have the same purpose: providing others with enough information on a person so they can help the counselor answer questions about that client's development, diagnosis, and treatment plan. In both the written report and the oral presentation, counselors should be concise and should not undertake the impossible task of giving a full picture of a person's background and treatment. Only material that is relevant and essential to understanding either the client or the concerns of the counselor should be included. That process of selectivity should maximize counselors' chances of receiving the help they need with a case.

CLOSING REPORTS

The last reports to be reviewed here are closing or termination reports. These are prepared when a person discontinues counseling, regardless of whether the termination is a decision reached jointly by client and counselor or is a unilateral decision. Closing reports generally become part of clients' files at the mental health agency where they have been counseled so that if they return for treatment, information will be available on their difficulties, the nature of their treatment, and its impact. With the client's written permission, this information also can be released to medical or mental health personnel outside of the agency, should the client continue treatment elsewhere. Some counselors also prepare abbreviated versions of their closing reports to give to clients when they finish counseling. These may even be prepared in conjunction with clients and can serve as a means of reminding clients of the gains that have been made, reinforcing progress, and establishing some future goals and plans.

Closing reports typically are fairly brief, one to two pages at most. Although they usually include a short review of the client's history and development, these reports focus primarily on the current treatment, describing what progress was made, what interventions were especially effective, and what difficulties or goals the client continues to have.

Closing reports also can yield quantifiable information for an agency on the people who are being treated, their diagnoses, the type and length of treatment provided, and the progress made. This can substantiate treatment effectiveness and indicate areas of high need.

An example of a closing report follows. Counselors can adapt its structure in writing their own closing reports.

EXAMPLE OF A CLOSING REPORT

Client: Miranda Santiago   *Counselor:* Everett Fox, M.A., LPC
Dates of counseling: 8/13/96–12/15/96

Presenting Concerns

Miranda Santiago, a 42-year-old Latino woman, sought counseling to help her cope with her stressful family situation as well as her anxiety and depression. At the time she sought counseling, Ms. Santiago was living in a two-bedroom apartment with her second husband Carlos to whom she had been married for three years; her daughter Mindy, age 18; and her mother Julia, age 78, who was in the middle stage of Alzheimer's disease. Ms. Santiago was providing full-time care for her mother and had little time or energy for Carlos and Mindy. Both had complained of this situation and were spending as little time at home as possible. Ms. Santiago was very concerned about her marriage and her daughter's behavior, but felt it was her duty to care for her mother as her mother had cared for her. Ms. Santiago was diagnosed as having an Adjustment Disorder with Mixed Emotional Features.

Background

Ms. Santiago is an only child. Her father had been murdered during a robbery when she was three years old. Her mother took over her husband's bakery and, with little help, managed to support herself and her daughter. Ms. Santiago married for the first time at age 21. Her first husband was in the military and was killed in an accident when she was 27 and her daughter was 3. Her mother Julia helped Ms. Santiago until her own health began to deteriorate. Julia has been living with her daughter for the past two years. Ms. Santiago married Carlos after a long courtship. He was aware of her mother's condition but did not expect his wife to bring her mother into their home.

Treatment History

Ms. Santiago was in a crisis when she entered counseling. She felt immobilized by stress and believed that she was being forced to choose between her mother, on one hand, and her husband and daughter, on the other. Ms. Santiago was seen for seven sessions of individual counseling and three sessions of family counseling with her daughter and husband. A crisis counseling model was used to build on her strengths and develop feelings of optimism and empowerment. Cognitive distortions were explored and modified, and coping behaviors, including stress management, decision making, and increasing rewarding activities, were taught. Counseling was both supportive and structured in nature, promoting expression of feelings as well as behavioral change. Objectives of counseling included reducing stress, anxiety, and depression; improving family closeness and communication; and helping Ms. Santiago make decisions and take more control over her life.

Outcomes

Ms. Santiago responded very well to treatment. Depression and anxiety abated quickly as she began to take steps to improve her situation and realized that her husband remained committed to their marriage. She gathered information both on her mother's condition and on residential programs that could provide care for her mother, visited programs that seemed appropriate, and is now making arrangements to move her mother into a residential program that met Ms. Santiago's criteria. In order to give herself time to gather this information, she located and made good use of a day program for people with Dementia. She also began to use caregivers at home so that she could have more time with her husband and daughter. Family communication has improved, with family members using skills they were taught in the family counseling sessions.

Recommendations

Despite the marked progress made by this client, she will need time to build her self-confidence, to facilitate her mother's move to a residential program, and to improve her current family relationships. In addition, Ms. Santiago established future goals for herself including locating part-time employment, rebuilding friendships that she had neglected, and taking a college course. A timetable, along with specific steps, were delineated to help her move toward these goals. She felt she had the direction and motivation she needed and did not think she needed to continue counseling at present. However, a setback in her mother's condition or future family difficulties could necessitate additional short-term counseling. If she resumes counseling, a structured, behavioral approach is recommended. To be most successful in counseling this client, such an approach should allow for client self-expression but should not encourage extensive discussion of negative feelings or past difficulties.

From this report, another counselor working with Miranda Santiago would have some direction, some knowledge of the client's strengths and weaknesses, and information on the sort of counseling that is likely to be effective in helping her. Such information can ease the person's return to counseling and can facilitate the counseling process for both client and counselor.

FOLLOW-UP EVALUATIONS

A final procedure to be mentioned in this chapter on counseling reports is the follow-up evaluation. This involves contacting clients by mail or telephone some time after they have completed counseling in order to ascertain whether the gains made during counseling have been sustained (and perhaps even increased). A follow-up evaluation provides a way for counselors and agencies to monitor their level of effectiveness and is a vehicle for offering continued help to former clients who may be experiencing difficulties but who are reluctant to reestablish contact with their counselors.

Counselors who choose to conduct a follow-up evaluation of their clients are taking a risk. The counselors may learn that they have not helped clients as much as they thought they had. They may find that more work still needs to be done with people who seemed to be doing well a few months earlier. Another risk is that clients may misinterpret the contact and may try to transform a professional relationship into a social one. Counselors who make follow-up contact should make their goals very clear and should be prepared to offer further assistance to their clients.

On the other hand, learning that a client is doing well can be very rewarding to counselors. The follow-up process also can be reassuring to clients, whether or not further counseling is indicated, and can facilitate their seeking help if it is needed in the future.

Some agencies use written questionnaires for follow-up contact. These questionnaires are sent to clients after they have completed treatment. Other agencies have no policy on follow-up contact and leave it to the discretion and preference of the counselors. Therefore, no generally accepted guidelines for follow-up evaluations have been established. They should occur long enough after counseling to reflect persistence of change but not so long after that they seem out of place or overdue. A 3-month interval between termination and follow-up is common but both longer and shorter intervals are appropriate, depending on the nature of the client–counselor relationship, the client's concerns, and the guidelines of the mental health agency. Informing the client at termination that a follow-up contact will be done can pave the way for that contact as well as encourage the client's progress. No special format need be used for follow-up contact: an unstructured telephone call by the counselor is sufficient. However, some counselors and agencies use follow-up contacts as a vehicle for data gathering in order to demonstrate accountability. In such cases, a written questionnaire or structured interview might be preferable. Regardless of the format used, the follow-up evaluation can be an excellent way for counselors to show that they are genuinely concerned about and committed to helping their clients and are, indeed, advocates of the lifelong process of personal growth and development inherent in the philosophy of mental health counseling.

Future Trends and Projections

In the first edition of this book, published in 1986, I made nine projections about the future of the counseling profession (Seligman, 1986). This chapter will begin with a review and discussion of those projections, most of which have been fulfilled between the first and second editions of this book.

1. Changes are anticipated in counselor education programs in terms of both the students and the curriculum. Proportionately fewer students interested in school or college counseling will be enrolled while the mental health component of many programs will expand.... Counselor education programs are requiring more courses to enable students to meet state licensure requirements and function effectively in mental health settings. Some professionals believe that 60 semester hours should be the standard preparation for a master's degree in counseling. These changes will increase the number of qualified mental health counselors and should increase the visibility and credibility of the counseling profession.

As predicted, programs to train mental health counselors, including those to prepare marriage and family counselors, have grown more rapidly than other counseling specializations. While still the ideal rather than the norm, 60 semester hours has been gaining acceptance as the standard preparation for a master's degree in counseling. In addition, the credibility and visibility of the counseling profession have increased. These trends are expected to continue, with accelerated growth particularly evident in subspecialties of mental health counseling such as family counseling, substance abuse counseling, and counseling older people. The 60-semester-hour program will increasingly become the standard for excellence. The counseling profession will continue to gain in recognition and reputation, but probably require many years to achieve full parity with social work and psychology, professions with a much longer history. Both competition

and collaboration will escalate between counselors and other helping professionals, as counselors continue to gain employment and demonstrate their competence in a broad range of settings.

   2. Demographic and social trends will change and expand the com-
      position of mental health counselors' clientele, requiring counsel-
      ors to develop new skills. Examples of such trends are the growing
      number and percentage of people over 65 years of age in the
      population, the high divorce rate, the increasing number of mid-
      life career changers, and the growth in bilingual and foreign-born
      individuals in the United States.

Learning to counsel people from a diverse range of backgrounds who
present a broad range of concerns is essential to today's mental health counselor.
Not only has the client population become more varied, it also has become more
challenging. Counselors are dealing with such serious concerns as physical and
sexual abuse, drug and alcohol dependence, criminal behavior and suicidal
ideation in children and adolescents, and loss of contact with reality. Both the
diversity and the severity of the problems people bring into counseling are
expected to increase over the next 10 years. Approaches to counseling that
emphasize integration of skills and techniques and adaptation to special client
needs will become increasingly important.

   3. Greater emphasis will be placed on developmental and preventive
      approaches to counseling. This should enhance the counselors'
      role in working in non-medical settings and as consultants, train-
      ers, and human resource managers.

Certainly, counselors have gained greater acceptance in nonmedical and
nonclinical settings and are increasingly finding employment as consultants,
supervisors, trainers, and employee assistance and human resource professionals. However, while considerable attention has been paid to the developmental
and preventive aspects of counselors' roles in the literature, a gap seems to exist
between theory and practice. The work of most mental health counselors focuses
on remedial work. The counseling profession has not yet found effective ways
to integrate preventive and developmental aspects of counseling with remedial
ones. This is due to several factors, including the increasing severity of clients'
concerns, the emphasis of managed care on brief treatment, and the availablity
of third-party payments only for treatment of mental disorders. Unless counselors can find effective ways to integrate the preventive, developmental, and
remedial elements of their work, they probably will find that they are increas-

ingly focusing on treatment of pathology and will lose some the values and qualities that set mental health counselors apart from other helping professionals.

4. Increasing numbers of states will pass licensure laws for counselors. That trend also should increase counselors' visibility and credibility and open up new opportunities (e.g., private practice).

The trend toward licensure has indeed increased with over 40 states now offering licensure or certification for non-school counselors. Before another 10 years have passed, all states are expected to offer these credentials. Private practice, as well as a multitude of other settings, now offers employment to counselors, and counselors will continue to find employment in a broad and diverse array of settings. New and expanding settings for employment of mental health counselors will include public and private schools, hospitals and medical centers, community organizations, professional associations, and business and industry. However, the rapid growth of private practice for counselors is expected to diminish; in most areas, the number of private practitioners seems adequate to meet the demand and the restrictions and requirements of managed care are making private practice a less attractive option for counselors. Although many mental health counselors will continue to establish or find employment in private practices, the appeal of that option is expected to decline and, along with it, the number of new counselors successfully establishing private practices.

5. Shortages of both psychiatrists and psychologists are predicted with the gap being filled, at least in part, by mental health counselors. Cooperation among mental health professionals should increase and their distinctions decrease.

This projection, too, has come to pass. The limited number of psychiatrists are needed increasingly for medication management, necessitating counselors and other non-medical helping professionals to assume primary responsibility for psychotherapy and case management. Counselors in nearly all settings now maintain collaborative relationships with psychiatrists and sometimes with psychologists for medication evaluation and psychological testing. At the same time, distinctions among professionals are decreasing. Some psychiatric nurses and psychologists are receiving prescription privileges to offset the scarcity of psychiatrists; and the breadth of the counselor's role is increasing.

6. Federal funds, grants, and insurance reimbursements for mental health services all seem to be growing scarcer and more tightly controlled. In order to obtain a substantial share of those funds,

counselors will have to demonstrate their effectiveness and accountability."

Funds for mental health services have, indeed, become increasingly scarce. Although this trend is in many ways an unfortunate one, it probably has led counselors to provide more effective and efficient services. Goal setting, treatment planning, and regular evaluation of progress have become essential to the counseling process, and clients, as well as counselors, benefit from procedures that establish a clear direction to treatment and facilitate rapid improvement.

7. Acceptance of holistic health and the relationship of physical and emotional concerns seems to be increasing and should lead to a corresponding increase in the number and frequency of counselors working with physicians to ameliorate physical illness via stress management, mental imagery, and other approaches.

Emphasis on the mind–body connection has, indeed, increased. Research has demonstrated that counseling can not only help people cope more successfully with serious illness, but that counseling also can have a beneficial impact on a person's health. People who have been diagnosed with cancer, for example, who are helped through counseling to develop a fighting spirit and effective coping mechanisms, as well as cancer survivors who participate in support groups, have a longer average life expectancy and lower likelihood of recurrence of their disease than people who do not receive that help (Seligman, 1996). Research is expected to substantiate even further the close connection between the mind and the body and the importance of taking a holistic approach in counseling. These findings will lead to new opportunities for counselors in medical settings, working collaboratively with physicians to help people with chronic and life-threatening illnesses. In addition, counselors in other settings will make greater use of techniques such as relaxation and imagery that reflect the importance of the mind–body connection.

8. Improved computer technology and other research developments should bring counselors more efficient systems of record keeping, better time management, and new and more precise tests and inventories.

Computerized administration and scoring of many standardized tests and inventories now is available and is used by schools, community mental health centers, and other large counseling facilities. In addition, computerized systems for billing, diagnosis and treatment planning, and writing progress reports are available. Technology is expected to make an increasing contribution to counseling, although its function probably will be ancillary to the direct provision of counseling services. Efforts to develop computerized counseling programs have not proven successful and for the foreseeable future, technology will be used primarily to enhance the counselor's role and to relieve the counselor of some routine duties but will not be a replacement for the counselor.

9. The rapid change in counselors' roles and the increasing demand on counselors to work with a wide range of client groups often may be stressful and lead to feelings of frustration, apathy, cynicism, and anger. These feelings seem to be engendered in some counselors by the gap that they perceive between their ideal of what a counselor should be able to accomplish and what they actually can do. Attention will need to be paid to the professional and emotional development of counselors via peer support groups, peer counseling (already initiated by AMHCA), continuing education programs for counselors, and the further development of support services provided by professional associations for counselors.

Counselors, today, do seem to be under increasing pressure, not only because of the challenges presented by their clients, but also because of the requirements of managed care, the need to market their services and obtain funding, and the growing threat of malpractice claims. Continuing education programs for counselors have indeed grown dramatically, spearheaded by the Professional Development division of the American Counseling Association. In addition, many counselors have sought to combat the stress inherent in their work by forming peer support and supervision groups. However, a formal structure of peer support and peer counseling groups, to help both impaired professionals and well-functioning counselors cope with the rigors of their profession, has not yet been put into place. Such services probably are best provided on an agency or community level. Local and national professional organizations are encouraged to develop such support services to help counselors. State divisions of ACA already are helping by providing information on local trends and legislation, funding lobbying to promote the role of the counselor, and providing conferences to improve counselors' professional and self-help skills. Chi Sigma Iota has been formed to provide students in counseling with support and information as well as a source of representation. However, more services are needed to help counselors cope with stress, frustration, and burnout as they deal with the challenges of their profession.

TRENDS AND ISSUES IN COUNSELING ━━━━━━━━━━━━━━━━━━━━━━━━

The role of the mental health counselor is still in flux, ten years after the first edition of this book was written, and probably will continue that way for the foreseeable future. While it is impossible to predict with certainty what shape that role will take in the future, trends and patterns affecting the mental health counselor can be identified and hypotheses can be advanced as to the nature of their impact. These trends are organized here according to the ten chapters in this book, covering the roles and functions of the mental health counselors.

The Changing Role of the Counselor ━━━━━━━━━━━━━━━━━━━━━━━━

- Increased efforts will be made to develop a generally accepted definition of mental health counseling that encompasses developmental, preventive, rehabilitative, and remedial aspects. According to MacDonald (1991, p. 379), "Unless mental health counselors clarify their beliefs, they may doom themselves and the profession as a whole to sloppy, haphazard thinking and practice." Development of the profession will be slowed until consensus on the role of the mental health counselor is achieved.
- The Orlando Model Project is expected to yield important information on the roles and competencies of mental health counselors that will facilitate establishment of a clearer definition of the profession.
- The roles of the counselor will continue to expand and diversify, with counselors being found in a wide range of clinical, medical, academic, business, industry, government, leisure, and private practice settings. However, opportunities in private practice will decline while those in other settings will increase. Successful private practices will most often be group, multidisciplinary practices with emergency services and 24-hour coverage.
- Legislation will make licensure/certification for counselors available in all states and will increase the prevalence of Freedom of Choice legislation.
- Reciprocity of credentials between states will increase as will uniformity of standards for credentialing.
- CACREP will develop clear, integrated standards for accrediting training programs in community and mental health counseling. Once improved standards are developed, the number of CACREP-accredited programs to train mental health counselors will increase rapidly.

- Managed care will continue to be a powerful force, shaping the delivery of mental health services, although the greatest growth in managed care probably already has occurred. Managed care organizations will become somewhat more consistent and user-friendly in their requirements. If a National Health Insurance is established, it also will shape the counseling profession and the nature of services counselors provide.
- Health-care costs will continue to escalate and cost-effectiveness will continue to be an important concept for counselors.
- The 60-credit master's degree will become the norm.
- Graduate programs to train mental health counselors will place greater emphasis on providing coursework in psychopathology and the DSM, treatment planning, psychotropic medication, family dynamics and counseling, brief therapy, physical and sexual abuse, Substance Use Disorders, managed care, legal and ethical issues, supervision, consultation, program development and evaluation, and budget planning. Opportunities for specialization during graduate school will increase.
- As a result of these changes in training, graduates will have a more realistic understanding of the challenges and rewards of the counseling profession. Although the field may lose some of its mystique, counselors will be better prepared and less prone to disillusionment.
- The need for continuing education, CEUs, and postgraduate coursework will continue to increase as will the availability of professional development and home study programs.

Opportunities for the Mental Health Counselor

- Counselors will continue to study and strive to be sensitive to individual differences.
- Concepts of special populations and diversity will be broadened so that they no longer focus primarily on ethnic and cultural differences but pay greater attention to differences in age, gender, sexual orientation, background and experience, and other dimensions.
- Although attention will continue to be paid to learning about specific special populations, the focus will shift to broad-based models of understanding and counseling special populations. Especially important will be models that are systemic, holistic, epistemological, and phenomenological.
- Certain populations, including men, at-risk youth, people who have experienced traumas, people who are gay or lesbian, people with serious medical illnesses, people in nontraditional families, people in midlife, and the elderly will receive particular attention. Strategies developed to

work with these people effectively will broaden and diversify the counselors' repertoire of skills. For example, attention to counseling men has contributed the mythopoetic approach (e.g., ceremony, drumming) to the skills of the counselor.

- Greater attention will be paid to effecting change at the systemic level; community organization, marketing, grant writing, social activism, advocacy, and lobbying will increasingly become tools that counselors will use.

- Collaboration between counselors and other helping professionals will increase, and particularly strong alliances will be formed between school and mental health counselors and psychiatrists and mental health counselors.

Diagnostic Systems and Their Use

- Debate over the value of the *Diagnostic and Statistical Manual of Mental Disorders* is expected to decline as clinicians realize that the DSM is an essential ingredient of treatment planning and that it can be integrated into any theoretical framework and successfully combined with systemic and holistic approaches to assessment and treatment.

- Understanding of the complexity of depression will grow, leading to the development of new diagnoses such as Depressive Personality Disorder, Minor Depressive Disorder, Recurrent Brief Depressive Disorder, Mixed Anxiety and Depressive Disorder, Postpsychotic Depressive Disorder, and Dual Depression.

- Additional information will be obtained on the negative impact of caffeine and nicotine, leading to additional diagnoses describing use of those substances.

- Better criteria will be developed for distinguishing between genuine memories of abuse and false memories. The links among disorders such as the Dissociative Disorders, Borderline Personality Disorder, and Posttraumatic Stress Disorder, all often triggered by a history of abuse, will be clarified.

- The possibility of spectrum diagnoses, encompassing overlapping, superimposed, or otherwise related diagnoses, will be studied.

- Greater attention will continue to be paid to the impact of physical and medical conditions on emotional functioning.

- Training in diagnosis and treatment planning using the DSM will be required of all clinicians.

The Use of Assessment in Diagnosis

- The importance of assessment in the counseling process will continue to grow.
- Particular emphasis will be placed on the development of brief assessment tools that can be used to facilitate goal setting and provide a rapid measure of progress.
- Technology will play an increasing role in the administration, scoring and interpretation of tests and inventories, but paper-and-pencil inventories will continue to be used.
- The use of projective tests will decline as more reliable standardized instruments are developed.
- Greater sensitivity to and awareness of the potential for gender and cultural bias in assessment will develop but will lead to more cautious use rather than less use of assessment.
- Assessment will increasingly become multidimensional, drawing on many sources of information. Qualitative sources of information will receive particular emphasis, as assessment becomes more holistic, humanistic, and individualized; better integrated into the counseling process; and less judgmental.

Intake Interviews

- Intake interviews will continue to be an essential piece of diagnosis and treatment planning.
- The mental status examination will become a standard ingredient of diagnosis and treatment planning and will be required increasingly by managed care organizations.
- Additional training will be provided and tools will be developed to facilitate the interview process.
- Specific interview protocols will continue to be developed for the diagnosis of the major mental disorders.

The Nature and Importance of Treatment Planning

- New models for treatment planning will be developed.
- Criteria for inpatient treatment will become increasingly rigorous; inpatient treatment itself will become even briefer than it already is, with duration of treatment being determined by fixed schedules based on diagnostic-related groups.

- Despite the growing emphasis on brief treatment, clinicians will increasingly conceptualize their clients' difficulties in systemic and holistic terms, paying particular attention to the mind-body connection.
- Outpatient treatment will increasingly follow a brief, solution-focused model, with clearly specified goals and criteria for termination.
- Increasing attention will be paid to the nature, importance, and development of the therapeutic alliance and the personal attributes of the counselor.
- Scheduling of the counseling process will become more flexible and tailored to the needs of the individual client.
- The importance of medication in the treatment of mental disorders will grow, but emphasis will continue to be placed on the synergistic value of psychotherapy and medication.
- Appreciation will increase for the importance of adjunct services and between-session tasks and assignments.
- Treatment planning will become a mandatory ingredient of the counseling process.

Theories and Techniques of Individual Counseling

- Advances in the development of new theories of counseling will focus primarily on systematic, integrated, and eclectic approaches that facilitate prescriptive matching of interventions to diagnosis, problem, and person while also promoting growth and development.
- Greater attention will be paid to the empirical study of what treatments are effective in ameliorating what disorders, the study of differential therapeutics.
- Crisis intervention, solution-focused treatment, and other models of brief therapy will receive increasing attention.
- Research will shed more light on the common elements in approaches to counseling that determine their effectiveness.
- Use of cognitive and behavioral techniques such as skills training, *in vivo* exposure, problem-solving, and cognitive restructuring will increase.
- Use of interpretative techniques (e.g., analysis of transference, free association) and high risk techniques (e.g., flooding, catharsis, aversive conditioning, and paradoxical intervention) are likely to decrease (Prochaska & Norcross, 1994).
- Humanistic, psychoanalytic, existential, Gestalt, and transactional approaches to treatment are likely to decline in use while educational, cognitive, behavioral, psychobiological, systemic, and eclectic approaches are expected to increase in use.

- Transpersonal, shamanic, and other spiritual approaches to counseling will continue to receive attention and will influence but not replace more traditional models of counseling.
- Pluralism in counseling, encompassing a wide variety of clients and approaches to treatment, will continue, although increased emphasis on differential therapeutics will guide counselors' treatment plans.

Assessment and Treatment of Couples and Families

- Couples and family counseling will continue to grow in importance as an approach to treatment, a way of thinking, and an area of specialization for counselors.
- Nontraditional families will become more prevalent, and counselors will become more knowledgeable about the special needs of single-parent, gay and lesbian, combined, and other nontraditional families.
- Even if counselors are doing individual therapy, they will increasingly seek to understand and address systemic dynamics and concerns and will think in terms of complex and organismic rather than linear models of change and growth.
- Counselors will pay increasing attention to their place in a client's family and cultural system and world view.
- Narrative, contextual, constructivist, social learning, and epistemological approaches to treatment will receive increasing attention.
- Systems will be developed to diagnose disorders in families.

Assessment and Treatment Planning for Groups and Organizations

- Group counseling will grow in use, both because it is perceived as cost-effective and because it seems particularly useful in treatment of a broad range of disorders (e.g., Eating Disorders, Posttraumatic Stress Disorder, Substance Use Disorder).
- New models of group counseling that take an integrated and eclectic perspective will be developed, building on existing models.
- Greater attention will be paid to diagnosis and treatment planning in counseling groups.
- Research will provide greater clarification of when and when not to use group counseling.
- The use of counseling and support groups for prevention and maintenance will increase, especially in nontraditional settings such as business and industry.

Writing and Record Keeping in Counseling

- Documentation of their work, via reports and progress notes, will become increasingly important for counselors.
- New tools and models, most of which will be computerized, will facilitate counselors' record keeping.
- Counselors may shorten sessions or otherwise modify their schedules to allow more time for paperwork.
- Although some will find the increased paperwork burdensome, it also will provide a more solid basis for the work of the counselor, will facilitate treatment, and will be used to demonstrate effectiveness.

IMPORTANT AREAS OF INQUIRY

Whether the counseling profession will evolve in ways that have been predicted here or in other directions depends on many factors, including research and thinking on current professional issues and political, social, economic, and demographic developments. The field of counseling is rich with unresolved questions and issues such as the following:

The Changing Role of the Counselor

- How are counselors different from and similar to other mental health professionals? How can counselors be both unique and marketable? Are too many mental health counselors seeking to become psychotherapists and neglecting other aspects of their roles?
- What is the impact of the growing number of credentials available to counselors? Are counselors becoming too specialized and concerned with credentials or are the credentials beneficial to the profession?
- How can preventive and developmental orientations be integrated in light of the requirements of managed care?
- What impact is managed care really having on the counseling process and its effectiveness?
- How can counselors successfully manage managed care?

Opportunities for the Mental Health Counselor

- How can counselors realistically and effectively address issues of client diversity?
- Does training in counseling special populations really make a difference?

- Should counselors continue to expand their range of opportunities, or do they run the risk of blurring their distinct identity?

Diagnostic Systems and Their Use

- Are disorders such as Attention-Deficit/Hyperactivity Disorder and Dissociative Identity Disorder overdiagnosed?
- Some mental disorders, such as Dependent Personality Disorder and the Paraphilias, are diagnosed far more often in one gender than in the other. Does this reflect gender bias or the actual distribution of the disorder?
- How can diagnosis using the DSM be successfully integrated into systemic, holistic, preventive, and developmental models of counseling?
- What is the truth about the false memory syndrome? How should that impact counselors' work?

The Use of Assessment in Diagnosis

- Many new assessment tools have been developed in recent years. Which are effective and useful and which are not?
- Testing of intelligence declined in credibility and usage about 15 years ago but now seems to be having a resurgence. What is the appropriate use of intelligence tests?
- Are inventories of personality such as the MBTI sufficiently valid and reliable for use with individual clients, or should they be viewed primarily as tools for research?

Intake Interviews

- What impact do structured interviews have on accuracy of diagnosis, counselor–client rapport, and client attitude?
- What models for intake interviews are most likely to yield the information that is needed for sound diagnosis and treatment planning?

Treatment Planning

- Is treatment effectiveness dependent more on theoretical orientation or clinician characteristics?
- What guidelines should determine whether to use individual, group, or family counseling and which theoretical model to follow?

- What is the relative effectiveness of brief counseling compared to long-term counseling?
- Are techniques such as eye movement desensitization and reprocessing, hypnosis, and neuro-linguistic programming effective and, if so, how should they be integrated with conventional approaches to counseling?

Theories and Techniques of Individual Counseling

- What makes counseling effective?
- Which is more important in counseling, purity of technique or systematic eclecticism? Can an effective approach be developed that is eclectic and integrative?
- The effectiveness of several approaches to counseling including cognitive, behavioral, and brief psychodynamic approaches to treatment has been demonstrated while that of person-centered, existential, and other approaches has not. Are those approaches effective? If so, under what conditions? If not, should they continue to be used?

Assessment and Treatment of Couples and Families

- How does the effectiveness of new approaches to family counseling that emphasize phenomenology and narrative compare with that of earlier models?
- How can counselors best adapt treatment models to nontraditional families?

Assessment and Treatment Planning for Groups and Organizations

- What criteria should be used to determine a person's suitability for group counseling?
- How can group counseling follow the lead of individual and family counseling and develop eclectic, brief, and systemic models that are effective?
- Are peer support groups, such as Twelve Step programs really effective, and how should they best be combined with counseling?

Writing and Record Keeping in Counseling

- How can counselors most effectively maintain records without spending a great deal of time on record keeping?
- What access should clients have to their records?

Readers are encouraged to complete their study of the material in this book by thinking about, reading about, and perhaps even researching the answers to these questions. They also are encouraged to generate their own questions.

CONCLUSION

This chapter has reviewed the predictions made in the first edition of this book and whether and how they have been fulfilled. New predictions are made and questions of relevance to counselors are provided for discussion. This chapter, as well as the previous chapters, demonstrates the rich and evolving nature of the counseling profession, reflecting the rewards and challenges it offers to counselors.

Appendix

Using Key Questions to Facilitate Diagnosis

Table A1. Overview of Key Questions Applied to DSM-IV Categories

Category	Duration	Severity	Precipitant	Primary symptom
1. Adjustment disorders, other conditions (See Table A3, Sections I, II, III.)	Brief—usually 6 months or less	May be pervasive but not severe	Usually	Problems in coping with stressful situations
2. Behavior and impulse control disorders (See Table A3, Section II.)	Medium to long	At least moderate	Often for episodes but usually not for disorders	Poor impulse control in at least one area
3. Mood disorders (See Table A3, Section I.)	Varies	Pervasive; Severity varies	Sometimes for major depression, usually not for other forms	Depression and/or unusually elevated moods
4. Anxiety disorders (See Table A3, Section III.)	Medium to long	Varies	For some types (e.g., phobias)	Anxiety, avoidance, fear
5. Somatoform and Factitious disorders, Malingering (See Table A3, Section IV.)	Varies, often long	Usually moderate	Usually not	Medically unverified physical symptoms
6. Personality disorders (See Table A3, Section VI.)	Long	Pervasive, usually moderate in severity	No	Poor coping skills, poor self esteem, poor interpersonal skills, impairment in work and leisure
7. Cognitive, Dissociative and Psychotic disorders (See Table A3, Sections V and VII.)	Varies	Usually pervasive and severe	For some types	Loss of contact with reality, confusion

Table A2. Guide to Using the Tables to Make Diagnoses

Primary symptoms	See Table A3 section:
Depression	I
Unusually elevated mood	I
Maladaptive behavior in children, adolescents	IIa, IIe
Sexual/gender identity issues	IIb
Eating problems	IIa, IIc
Sleeping problems	IId
Problems of impulse control	IIa, IIe
Anxiety, not primarily in response to physical complaints	III
Medically unverified physical complaints	IV
Psychosis	V
Long-standing pervasive dysfunction	VI
Cognitive/memory impairment, dissociation	VII

Table A3. Using the Key Questions to Make a Diagnosis

A3.I. Disorders characterized by depressed or elevated mood

Primary symptoms	Duration	Severity	Precipitant	Diagnosis
Depression	Usually 2 weeks to 6 months	Moderately severe to severe	Often	MAJOR DEPRESSIVE DISORDER
Depression	At least 2 years—adults; 1 year for younger	Mild to moderate	Rarely	DYSTHYMIC DISORDER
Mania (may also have depressive episodes)	Episodes lasting weeks to months	Moderately severe to severe	Sometimes	BIPOLAR I DISORDER
Hypomania (may also have depressive episodes)	Episodes lasting weeks to months	Moderate	Sometimes	BIPOLAR II DISORDER
Numerous periods of mood instability	At least 2 years—adults; 1 year for younger.	Moderate	Rarely	CYCLOTHYMIC DISORDER
Depression	Brief; usually no more than 6 months	Mild to moderate	Always	ADJUSTMENT DISORDER
Depression stemming from drug/alcohol use	Varies	Mild to severe	Substance use	SUBSTANCE-INDUCED MOOD DISORDER

A3.II. Disorders characterized by maladaptive behavior, impulsivity

A3.IIa: First diagnosed in early years

Primary symptoms	Duration	Severity	Precipitant	Diagnosis
Subaverage intellectual functioning; poor adaptive functioning	Potentially lifelong	Varies: mild to profound	Sometimes (e.g., medical condition)	MENTAL RETARDATION
Abnormal or impaired social skills, communication, and behavior	Onset prior to age 3; continuous	Often severe	Sometimes, (e.g., may be associated with medical condition)	AUTISTIC DISORDER
Recurrent nonrhythmic motor movement or vocalization	At least 4 weeks	Varies	May be exacerbated by stress, some related to medical problems	TIC DISORDERS
Below expected school achievement in specific areas	Continuous	Mild to moderate	May be abnormalities in cognitive processing	LEARNING DISORDERS
Pervasive attention deficits	At least 6 months	Moderate	No	ATTENTION-DEFICIT/ HYPERACTIVITY DISORDERS
Multiple violations of rules, norms, laws	Generally at least 12 months	Moderate to severe	Sometimes	CONDUCT DISORDER
Defiant negativistic behavior	At least 6 months	Mild to moderate	Sometimes	OPPOSITIONAL DEFIANT DISORDER
Persistent eating of nonnutritive substances	At least 1 month	Mild to moderate	Occasionally	PICA
Regurgitation	At least 1 month	Usually moderate	Sometimes	RUMINATION DISORDER

(*continued*)

A3.IIa: First diagnosed in early years (continued)

Primary symptoms	Duration	Severity	Precipitant	Diagnosis
Inappropriate defecation	At least 3 months	Varies	Sometimes	ENCOPRESIS
Inappropriate urination	At least 3 months	Usually mild to moderate	Occasionally	ENURESIS
Refusal to speak in some or all settings	At least 1 month	Moderate	Sometimes	SELECTIVE MUTISM
Repetitive movements	At least 1 month	Moderate	Sometimes	STEREOTYPIC MOVEMENT DISORDER

A3.IIb: Sexual problems

Primary symptoms	Duration	Severity	Precipitant	Diagnosis
Lack of interest in sexual activity and/or problems in sexual arousal and/or response	Episodic or continuous; duration varies	Marked distress	Often	SEXUAL DYSFUNCTIONS
Primary source of sexual arousal dysfunctional	At least 6 months	Varies	Sometimes	PARAPHILIAS
Discomfort with own gender	Varies, usually prolonged	Mild to moderate	Sometimes	GENDER IDENTITY DISORDERS

A3.IIc: Eating problems[a]

Primary symptoms	Duration	Severity	Precipitant	Diagnosis
Dysfunctional eating and body weight less than 85% of expected weight	Varies; often long	Moderate to severe	Rarely	ANOREXIA NERVOSA
Recurrent binge eating, often with purging; weight at least at expected level	Varies; often long	Moderate to severe	Rarely	BULIMIA NERVOSA

[a]See also Table IIa

A3.IId: Sleeping problems

Primary symptoms	Duration	Severity	Precipitant	Diagnosis
Difficulty falling asleep; sustaining sleep	At least 1 month	Mild to moderate	Often	INSOMNIA
Oversleeping or feeling tired even though sleeping enough	At least 1 month	Mild to moderate	Rarely	HYPERSOMNIA
Sudden attacks of refreshing sleep	At least 3 months	Moderate	Rarely	NARCOLEPSY
Sleep walking	Recurrent	Mild to moderate	Sometimes	SLEEPWALKING DISORDER
Recurrent bad dreams recalled upon wakening	Varies; tends to remit with age	Mild to moderate	Sometimes	NIGHTMARE DISORDER
Recurrent bad dreams from which a person awakens in state of terror	Varies; tends to remit in children; chronic in adults	Moderate	Sometimes	SLEEP TERROR DISORDER

A3.IIe: Problems of impulse control[a]

Primary symptoms	Duration	Severity	Precipitant	Diagnosis
Impulsive theft of objects of little value	Recurrent	Varies	Sometimes	KLEPTOMANIA
Episodic emotional/physical outbursts	Recurrent	Moderate to severe	May have history of abuse	INTERMITTENT EXPLOSIVE DISORDER
Firesetting; interest in fire-related contexts	Episodic	Moderate to severe	Often	PYROMANIA
Excessive gambling	Episodic or chronic	Moderate to severe	Incidents often stress related	PATHOLOGICAL GAMBLING
Recurrent pulling out own head/body hairs	Recurrent	Mild to moderate	Sometimes	TRICHOTILLOMANIA
Acting out	Within 3 months of stressor; up to 6 months duration after stressor	Mild to moderate	Always	ADJUSTMENT DISORDER WITH DISTURBANCE OF CONDUCT
Acting out	Very brief	Mild	Usually	ANTISOCIAL BEHAVIOR
Dysfunctional use of drugs, alcohol	Hours to 12 months	Varies	Sometimes	SUBSTANCE USE DISORDER

[a]See also Table IIa.

A3.III. Disorders Characterized by Anxiety, Not Primarily in Response to Physical Complaints

Primary symptoms	Duration	Severity	Precipitant	Diagnosis
Panic with avoidance	Varies	Varies	May be internal or external	PANIC DISORDER WITH AGORAPHOBIA
Panic without avoidance	Varies	Varies	May be internal or external	PANIC DISORDER WITHOUT AGORAPHOBIA
Avoidance of clusters of situations without panic attacks	Varies	Moderate to severe	Sometimes	AGORAPHOBIA
Excessive fear of specific stimuli	Varies	Mild to moderate	Sometimes	SPECIFIC PHOBIA
Extreme fear of social situations	Frequently long-term	Mild to moderate	Sometimes	SOCIAL PHOBIA
Persistent unwanted thoughts and/or repeated behaviors	May wax and wane	Varies	Usually not. Stress may trigger	OBSESSIVE–COMPULSIVE DISORDER
Trauma-related fear; avoidance; reexperiencing	At least 1 month; maybe years	Moderate	Always (trauma)	POSTTRAUMATIC STRESS DISORDER
Trauma related fear; avoidance; reexperiencing	Less than 4 weeks	Mild to moderate	Always (trauma)	ACUTE STRESS DISORDER
Pervasive anxiety	At least 6 months	Moderate	Sometimes	GENERALIZED ANXIETY DISORDER
Anxiety stemming from drug/alcohol use	Varies	Mild to moderate	Always; use of substance	SUBSTANCE-INDUCED ANXIETY DISORDER
Anxiety, usually about specific situation	Within 3 months of stressor; up to 6 months duration after stressor	Mild to moderate	Always, not trauma	ADJUSTMENT DISORDER
Difficulty separating from caretakers; onset before age 18	At least 4 weeks	Moderate	Sometimes	SEPARATION ANXIETY DISORDER

A3.IV. Disorders Characterized by Physical Complaints[a]

Primary symptoms	Duration	Severity	Precipitant	Diagnosis
Multiple and diverse physical complaints	Usually long	Moderate to severe	Usually not	SOMATIZATION DISORDER
Worry about at least one physical complaint	At least 6 months	Mild to moderate	Sometimes	UNDIFFERENTIATED SOMATOFORM DISORDER
Motor or sensory dysfunction	Usually acute	Moderate to severe	Often	CONVERSION DISORDER
Experience of pain not adequately explained medically	Persistent	Varies	Sometimes	PAIN DISORDERS
Belief that one has serious illness	Varies	Moderate	Sometimes	HYPOCHONDRIASIS
Overfocusing on minor or nonexistent physical defect	Usually long-standing	Moderate	Sometimes	BODY DYSMORPHIC DISORDER
Deliberate feigning or inducing physical or psychological symptoms in self or others in order to assume sick role	Brief to chronic	Moderate to severe	Usually not	FACTITIOUS DISORDERS
Faking sick for external gains	Varies	Mild to moderate	Sometimes	MALINGERING
Having psychological symptoms that contribute to worsening of medical condition	Varies	Mild to moderate	Sometimes	PSYCHOLOGICAL FACTORS AFFECTING MEDICAL CONDITION

[a]Not fully explained by a general medical condition or a cognitive mental disorder.

A3.V. Disorders Characterized by Psychosis[a]

Primary symptoms	Duration	Severity	Precipitant	Diagnosis
Severe pervasive loss of contact with reality	At least 6 months	Severe	Usually not	SCHIZOPHRENIA
Severe, pervasive loss of contact with reality	1 to 6 months	Severe	Sometimes	SCHIZOPHRENIFORM DISORDER
Loss of contact with reality plus episodes of severe depression and/or mania not always related to psychosis	Varies	Severe	Usually not	SCHIZOAFFECTIVE DISORDER
Nonbizarre (possible) delusions inconsistent with reality	At least 1 month	Moderate	Often	DELUSIONAL DISORDER
Delusions and/or hallucinations	Less than 1 month	Moderate to severe	Usually	BRIEF PSYCHOTIC DISORDER
Delusions and/or hallucinations in context of close relationship	Usually long term	Moderate to severe	Usually not	SHARED PSYCHOTIC DISORDER
Psychosis stemming from drug or alcohol use	Varies	Moderate to severe	Substance use	SUBSTANCE-INDUCED PSYCHOTIC DISORDER +

[a]See also Table VII.

A3.VI. Disorders Characterized by Long-standing, Pervasive Dysfunction

Primary symptoms	Duration	Severity	Precipitant	Diagnosis
Pervasive suspiciousness, mistrust	Many years	Moderate	Usually not	PARANOID PERSONALITY DISORDER
Lack of interest in relationships	Many years	Mild to moderate	Usually not	SCHIZOID PERSONALITY DISORDER
Odd or eccentric behavior; thinking; poor social skills	Many years	Moderate to severe	Usually not	SCHIZOTYPAL PERSONALITY DISORDER
Breaking laws; violating social norms	Many years (age 18 or older)	Moderate to severe	Usually not	ANTISOCIAL PERSONALITY DISORDER
Low self-esteem; self-destructive behavior; impulsivity	Many years	Moderate to severe	Usually not	BORDERLINE PERSONALITY DISORDER
Egocentrism; overemotionalism	Many years	Mild to moderate	Usually not	HISTRIONIC PERSONALITY DISORDER
Egocentrism; grandiosity	Many years	Mild to moderate	Usually not	NARCISSISTIC PERSONALITY DISORDER
Extreme shyness; fear of rejection	Many years	Mild to moderate	Usually not	AVOIDANT PERSONALITY DISORDER
Sense of self comes from relationship with others; overinvestment in relationships; needy	Many years	Mild to moderate	Usually not	DEPENDENT PERSONALITY DISORDER
Perfectionism; overinvested in work; underinvested in interpersonal relations	Many years	Mild to moderate	Usually not	OBSESSIVE-COMPULSIVE PERSONALITY DISORDER

A3.VII. Disorders Characterized by Cognitive/Memory Impairment or Dissociation

Primary symptoms	Duration	Severity	Precipitant	Diagnosis
Partial memory loss of prominent aspects of life	Acute to chronic	Moderate to severe	Usually	DISSOCIATIVE AMNESIA
Total memory loss and relocation	Usually acute; may be chronic	Severe	Usually	DISSOCIATIVE FUGUE
Existence of 2 or more distinct identities	Chronic	Severe	Usually, in history	DISSOCIATIVE IDENTITY DISORDER
Episodes of feeling detached	Recurrent	Moderate	May accompany panic, stress, anxiety, depression	DEPERSONALIZATION DISORDER
Disturbed consciousness, change in cognition	Hours to days	Severe	May be medication, medical condition, substances	DELIRIUM
Multiple cognitive deficits	Progressive, static, or remitting	Mild to severe	General medical condition, substances, or multiple etiologies	DEMENTIA

References

Aiken, R. L. (1976). *Psychological testing and assessment.* Boston: Allyn & Bacon, Inc.

Alberding, B., Lauver, P., & Patnoe, J. (1993). Counselor awareness of the consequences of certification and licensure. *Journal of Counseling and Development, 72*(1), 33–38.

Altekruse, M. K. (1995). What mental health counselors do: A demographic analysis. In M. K. Altekruse & T. L. Sexton (Eds.), *Mental health counseling in the 90's* (pp. 13–24). Tampa, FL: National Commission for Mental Health Counseling.

Altekruse, M. K., & Sexton, T. L. (1995a). Mental health counseling in the 90's. In M. K. Altekruse & T. L. Sexton (Eds.), *Mental health counseling in the 90's* (pp. 7–12). Tampa, FL: National Commission for Mental Health Counseling.

Altekruse, M. K., & Sexton, T. L. (1995b). Implications for mental health counselors and counselor educators. In M. K. Altekruse & T. L. Sexton (Eds.), *Mental health counseling in the 90's* (pp. 61–66). Tampa, FL: National Commission for Mental Health Counseling.

Altman, K. P. (1992). Psychodramatic treatment of multiple personality disorder and dissociative disorders. *Dissociation Progress in the Dissociative Disorders, 5*(2), 104–108.

Amatea, E. S., & Sherrard, P. A. D. (1994). The ecosystemic view: A choice of lenses. *Journal of Mental Health Counseling, 16* (1), 6–21.

American Counseling Association Code of Ethics and Standards of Practice. (1995, June). *Counseling Today*, 33–40.

American Psychiatric Association. (1994). *Diagnostic and statistical manual of mental disorders* (4th ed.). Washington, DC: Author.

Amerikaner, M., Monks, G., Wolfe, P., & Thomas, S. (1994). Family interaction and individual psychological health. *Journal of Counseling and Development, 72*(6), 614–620.

Anastasi, A. (1992). What counselors should know about the use and interpretation of psychological tests. *Journal of Counseling and Development, 70*(5), 610–615.

Association for Specialists in Group Work (1989). *Ethical guidelines for group leaders.* Alexandria, VA: Author.

Aubrey, R. F., & D'Andrea, M. (1988). What counselors should know about high technology. In R. Hayes & R. Aubrey (Eds.), *New directions for counseling and human development* (pp. 261–274). Boston: Allyn & Bacon.

Battegay, R. (1990). New perspectives on acting out. *Journal of Group Psychotherapy, Psychodrama and Sociometry, 42*(4), 204–212.

Beck, A. T., Rush, A. J., Shaw, B. F., & Emery, G. (1979). *Cognitive therapy of depression.* New York: Guilford Press.

Beck, E. S. (1994). Mental health counselors in private practice: Reflections of a full-time practitioner (A commentary). *Journal of Mental Health Counseling, 16*(4), 497–505.

Becvar, D. S., & Becvar, R. J. (1993). *Family therapy.* Boston: Allyn & Bacon.

Becvar, R. J., & Becvar, D. S. (1994). The ecosystemic story: A story about stories. *Journal of Mental Health Counseling, 16*(1), 22–32.

Beer, M. & Spector, B. (1993). Organizational diagnosis: Its role in organizational learning. *Journal of Counseling and Development, 71*(6), 642–650.

Bender, K. J. (1990). *Psychiatric medications.* Newbury Park, CA: Sage Publications.

Betz, N. E., Fitzgerald, L. F., & Hill, R. E. (1989). Trait-factor theories: Traditional cornerstone of career theory. In M. B. Arthur, D. T. Hall & B. S. Lawrence (Eds.), *Handbook of career theory* (pp. 25–40). New York: Cambridge University Press.

Betz, N. E., & Hackett, G. (1981). The relationship of career-related self-efficacy expectations to perceived career options in college women and men. *Journal of Counseling Psychology, 28*(5), 339–410.

Beutler, L. E., Crago, M., & Arizmendi, T. G. (1986). Therapist variables in psychotherapy process. In S. L. Garfield & A. E. Bergin (Eds.), *Handbook of psychotherapy and behavior change* (3rd edition, pp. 257–310). New York: Wiley.

Blocher, D. H., & Biggs, D. A. (1983). *Counseling psychology in community settings.* New York: Springer.

Bloom, B. L. (1983). *Community mental health: A general introduction.* Monterey, CA: Brooks/Cole.

Bowen, M. (1974). Theory in the practice of psychotherapy. In P. J. Guerin, Jr. (Ed.), *Family therapy: Theory and practice.* New York: Gardner Press.

Bowman, S. L. (1993). Career intervention strategies for ethnic minorities. *The Career Development Quarterly, 42,* 14–25.

Brady, G. L. (1991). A group-work approach for sexually abused preschoolers. *Journal of Group Psychotherapy, Psychodrama and Sociometry, 43*(4), 174–183.

Braswell, L. (1993). Cognitive-behavioral groups for children manifesting ADHD and other disruptive behavior disorders. In J. E. Zins & M. J. Elias (Eds.), *Promoting student success through group interventions* (pp. 91–118). New York: Haworth Press.

Brill, A. A. (Ed.) (1938). *The basic writings of Sigmund Freud.* New York: Modern Library.

Brooks, D. K., Jr., & Gerstein, L. H. (1990). Counselor credentialing and interprofessional collaboration. *Journal of Counseling and Development, 68*(5), 477–484.

Brown, N.W. (1994). *Group counseling for elementary and middle school children.* Westport, CT: Praeger Publishers.

Bubenzer, D. I., Zimpfer, D. G., & Mahrle, C. L. (1990). Standardized individual appraisal in agency and private practice: A survey. *Journal of Mental Health Counseling, 12*(1), 51–66.

Cadbury, S., Childs-Clark, A., & Sandhu, S. (1990). Group anxiety management: Effectiveness, perceived helpfulness and follow-up. *British Journal of Clinical Psychology, 29*(2), 245–247.

Carter, B., & McGoldrick, M. (1988). Overview of the changing family life cycle: A framework for family therapy. In B. Carter & M. McGoldrick (Eds.), *The changing family life cycle* (pp. 3–28). New York: Gardner Press.

Carty, L. (1993). Group counseling and the promotion of mental health. *The Journal for Specialists in Group Work, 18*(1), 29–39.

Christensen, O. C. (Ed.). (1993). *Adlerian family counseling.* Minneapolis: Educational Media Corporation.

Clagett, A.F. (1992). Group-integrated reality therapy in a wilderness camp. *Journal of Offender Rehabilitation, 17,* 1–18.

Clance, P. R. & O'Toole, M.A. (1987). The impostor phenomenon: An internal barrier to empowerment and achievement. *Women and Therapy, 6,* 51–64.

Comiskey, P. E. (1993). Using reality therapy group training with at-risk high school freshmen. *Journal of Reality Therapy, 12*(2), 59–64.

Cook, E. P., Berman, E., Genco, K., Repka, F., & Shrider, J. (1986). Essential characteristics of master's level counselors: Perceptions of agency administrators. *Counselor Education and Supervision, 26*(2), 146–152.

Cooker, P. G. & Nero, R. S. (1987). Effects of videotaped feedback on self-concept of patients in group psychotherapy. *Journal for Specialists in Group Work, 12,* 112–117.

Corey, G. (1995). *Theory and practice of group counseling.* Pacific Grove, CA: Brooks/Cole.

Corey, G., Corey, M. S., & Callanan P. (1988). *Issues and ethics in the helping professions.* Pacific Grove, CA: Brooks/Cole.

Corey, M. S. & Corey, G. (1992). *Groups: Process and practice.* Pacific Grove, CA: Brooks/Cole.

Corsini, R. J. (1988). Adlerian groups. In S. Long (Ed.), *Six group therapies* (pp. 1–43). New York: Plenum Press.

Courtois, C. A. (1988). *Healing the incest wound.* New York: Norton.

Counselors in the world of work (1988, February). *AMHCA News,* pp. 9, 12.

Cowger, E. L., Jr., Hinkle, J. S., DeRidder, L. M., & Erk, R. R. (1991). CACREP community counseling programs: Present status and implications for the future. *Journal of Mental Health Counseling, 13*(2), 172–186.

Deffenbacher, J. L., McNamara, K., Stark, R. S., & Sabadell, P. M. (1990). A comparison of cognitive-behavioral and process-oriented group counseling for general anger reduction. *Journal of Counseling and Development, 69*(2), 167–172.

DeLeon, P. H., & VandenBos, G. R. (1991). Psychotherapy in managed health care: Integrating federal policy with clinical practice. In C. S. Austad & W. H. Berman (Eds.), *Psychotherapy in managed health care* (pp. 251–263). Washington, DC: American Psychological Association.

deShazer, S. (1991). *Putting difference to work.* New York: Norton.

Dinkmeyer, D., & Carlson, J. (1984). *Time for a better marriage.* Circle Pines, MN: American Guidance Service.

Donigian, J. & Malnati, R. (1987). *Critical incidents in group therapy.* Pacific Grove, CA: Brooks/Cole Publishing Company.

Dougherty, A. M. (1995). *Consultation.* Pacific Grove, CA: Brooks/Cole,

Drummond, R. J. (1988). *Appraisal procedures for counselors and helping professionals.* New York: Macmillan.

Duffy, T. K. (1990). Psychodrama in beginning recovery: An illustration of goals and methods. *Alcoholism Treatment Quarterly, 7*(2), 97–109.

Dushman, R. D. & Bressler, M. J. (1991). Psychodrama in an adolescent chemical dependency treatment program. *Individual Psychology Journal of Adlerian Theory, Research, and Practice, 47*(4), 515–520.

Ehly, S. (1993). Overview of group interventions for special services providers. In J. E. Zins & M. J. Elias (Eds.), *Promoting student success through group interventions* (pp. 9–38). New York: Haworth Press.

Ehly, S. & Dustin, R. (1989). *Individual and group counseling in schools.* New York: Guilford Press.

Endicott, J., & Spitzer, R. L. (1978). A diagnostic interview: The Schedule for Affective Disorders and Schizophrenia. *Archives of General Psychiatry, 35,* 837–844.

Erikson, E. H. (1963). *Childhood and society.* New York: Norton.

Falvey, J. E. (1992). From intake to intervention: Interdisciplinary perspectives on mental health treatment planning. *Journal of Mental Health Counseling, 14*(4), 471–489.

Fauman, M. A. (1994). *Study guide to DSM-IV.* Washington, DC: American Psychiatric Association.

Fischer, J., & Corcoran, K. (1994). *Measures for clinical practice* (vol. 1). New York: Macmillan.

Fong, M. L. (1990). Mental health counseling: The essence of professional counseling. *Counselor Education and Supervision, 30* (2), 106–113.

Foos, J. A., Ottens, A. J., & Hill, L. K. (1991). Managed mental health: A primer for counselors. *Journal of Counseling and Development, 69*(4), 332–336.

Frances, A., Clarkin, J., & Perry, S. (1984). *Differential therapeutics in psychiatry.* New York: Brunner/Mazel.

Fredman, N. Sherman, R. (1987). *Handbook of measurements for marriage and family therapy.* New York: Brunner/Mazel.

Friedman, R. M. (1994). Psychodynamic group therapy for male survivors of sexual abuse. *Group, 18*(4), 225–234.

Fry, P. S. (1992). Major social theories of aging and their importance for counseling concepts and practice: A critical review. *The Counseling Psychologist, 20*(2), 246–329.

Garvin, C. D. (1987). *Contemporary group work.* Englewood Cliffs, NJ: Prentice-Hall.

Gilliland, B. E., James, R. K., & Bowman, J. T. (1989). *Theories and strategies in counseling and psychotherapy.* Englewood Cliffs, NJ: Prentice Hall.

Gillis, H. L. & Bonney, W. C. (1989). Utilizing adventure activities with intact groups: A socio-dramatic systems approach to consultation. *Journal of Mental Health Counseling, 11*(4), 345–358.

Ginter, E. J. (1991). Mental health counselor preparation: Experts' preparation. *Journal of Mental Health Counseling, 13*(2), 187–203.

Ginter, G. G. (1995). *Systematic treatment planning with an overview of DSM-IV.* Workshop presented at the annual meeting of the American Counseling Association.

Ginzberg, E. (1972). Toward a theory of occupational choice: A restatement. *Vocational Guidance Quarterly, 20*(2), 169–176.

Gladding, S. T. (1995). *Group work: A counseling specialty.* Englewood Cliffs, NJ: Prentice-Hall.

Glosoff, H. L. (1992, May). Accrediting and certifying professional counselors. *Guidepost, 34*(12), 6–8.

Gottfredson, L. S. (1981). Circumscription and compromise: A developmental theory of occupational aspirations. *Journal of Counseling Psychology, 28*(6), 545–579.

Gresham, F. M. & Elliott, S. N. (1993). Social skills intervention guide: Systematic approaches to social skills training. In J. E. Zins & M. J. Elias (Eds.), *Promoting student success through group interventions* (pp. 137–158). New York: Haworth Press.

Gross, D. R., & Capuzzi, D. (1991). Counseling the older adult. In D. Capuzzi & D. R. Gross (Eds.), *Introduction to counseling: Perspectives for the 1990s.* Boston: Allyn & Bacon.

Groth-Marnat, G. (1990). *Handbook of psychological assessment.* New York: Wiley.

Guldner, C. A. & O'Connor, T. (1991). The ALF group: A model of group therapy with children. *Journal of Group Psychotherapy, Psychodrama and Sociometry, 43*(4), 184–190.

Gunderson, J. G. (1988). Personality disorders. In A. M. Nicholi, Jr. (Ed.), *The new Harvard guide to psychiatry* (337–357). Cambridge, MA: Harvard University Press.

Guterman, J. T. (1994). A social constructionist position for mental health counselors. *Journal of Mental Health Counselors, 16*(2), 226–244.

Haley, J. (1987). *Problem-solving therapy.* San Francisco: Jossey-Bass.

Havighurst, R. J. (1972). *Developmental tasks and education.* New York: McKay.

Hayes, R. L., & Hayes, B. A. (1988). Remarriage families: Counseling parents, stepparents, and their children. In R. Hayes & R. Aubrey (Eds.), *New directions for counseling and human development* (pp. 465–477). Denver: Love Publishing Company.

Healy-Romanello, M. A. (1993). The invisible griever: Support groups for bereaved children. In J. E. Zins & M. J. Elias (Eds.), *Promoting student success through group interventions* (pp. 67–90). New York: Haworth Press.

Herman, K. C. (1993). Reassessing predictors of therapist competence. *Journal of Counseling and Development, 72*(1), 29–32.

Hershenson, D. B. (1993). Healthy development as the basis for mental health counseling theory. *Journal of Mental Health Counseling, 15*(4), 430–437.

Hettler, B. (1984). Wellness: Encouraging a lifetime pursuit of excellence. *Health values: Achieving high level wellness, 8* (4), 13–17.

Hill, L. K. (1990). The future of mental health counseling in the new era of health care. In G. Seiler (Ed.), *The mental health counselors sourcebook* (pp. 105–138). New York: Human Sciences Press.

Hinkle, J. S. (1994a). Ecosystems and mental health counseling: Reaction to Becvar and Becvar. *Journal of Mental Health Counseling, 16*(1), 33–36.

Hinkle, J. S. (1994b). The *DSM-IV*: Prognosis and implications for mental health counselors. *Journal of Mental Health Counseling, 16*(2), 174–183.

Hipple, J., & Cimbolic, P. (1979). *The counselor and suicidal crisis.* Springfield, IL: Charles C. Thomas.

Hohenshil, T. H. (1993). Teaching the *DSM-III-R* in counselor education. *Counselor Education and Supervision, 32*(4), 267–275.

Hollis, J. W., & Wantz, R. A. (1994). *Counselor preparation: Status, trends, and implications* (vol. II). Muncie, IN: Accelerated Development.

Holman, A. M. (1983). *Family assessment.* Beverly Hills: Sage.

Honeyman, A. (1990). Perceptual changes in addicts as a consequence of reality therapy based group treatment. *Journal of Reality Therapy, 9*(2), 53–59.

Hood, A. B., & Johnson, R. W. (1991). *Assessment in counseling: A guide to the use of psychological assessment procedures.* Alexandria, VA: American Counseling Association.

Hosie, T. W., West, J. D., & Mackey, J. A. (1993). Employment and roles of counselors in employee assistance programs. *Journal of Counseling and Development, 71*(3), 355–359.

House, R. M. (1991). Counseling gay and lesbian clients. In D. Capuzzi & D. R. Gross (Eds.), *Introduction to counseling: Perspectives for the 1990s.* Boston: Allyn & Bacon.

Huddleston, R. (1989). Drama with elderly people. *British Journal of Occupational Therapy, 52*(8), 298–300.

Ivey, A. E. (1989). Mental health counseling: A developmental process and profession. *Journal of Mental Health Counseling, 11*(1), 26–35.

Ivey, A. E., & Rigazio-Digilio, S. A. (1991). Toward a developmental practice of mental health counseling: Strategies for training, practice, and political unity. *Journal of Mental Health Counseling, 13*(1), 21–36.

Johnsen, E. (1994). Utilization management and its impact on client well-being: The next frontier for mental health counseling. *Journal of Mental Health Counseling, 16*(2), 279–284.

Johnson, D. L. (1993). Toward a synthesis of theory: Adopting a new perspective to advance the field of mental health counseling. *Journal of Mental Health Counseling, 15*(3), 236–239.

Kalter, N. & Schreier, S. (1993). School-based support groups for children of divorce. In J. E. Zins & M. J. Elias (Eds.), *Promoting student success through group interventions* (pp. 39–66). New York: Haworth Press.

Kanas, N., Schoenfeld, F., Marmar, C. R., & Weiss, D. S. (1994). Process and content in a long-term PTSD therapy group for Vietnam veterans. *Group, 18*(2), 78–88.

Kane, R. (1992). The potential abuses, limitations, and negative effects of classical psychodramatic techniques in group counseling. *Journal of Group Psychotherapy, Psychodrama and Sociometry, 44*(4), 181–189.

Kaplan, H. I., & Sadock, B. J. (1994). *Synopsis of psychiatry* (7th ed.). Baltimore: Williams & Wilkins.

Kauff, P. F. (1993). The contribution of analytic group therapy to the psychoanalytic process. In A. Alonso & H. I. Swiller (Eds.), *Group therapy in clinical practice* (pp. 3–28). Washington, D.C.: American Psychiatric Press.

Kelly, K. R. (1991). Theoretical integration is the future for mental health counseling. *Journal of Mental Health Counseling, 13*(1), 106–111.

Kelly, K. R., & Hall, A. S. (1992). Toward a developmental model for counseling men. *Journal of Mental Health Counseling, 14* (3), 257–273.

Khantzian, E. J., Halliday, K. S., Golden, S., & McAuliffe, W. E. (1992). Modified group therapy for substance abusers: A psychodynamic approach to relapse prevention. *American Journal on Addictions, 1(*1), 67–76.

Kivlighan, D. M., Johnsen, B., & Fretz, B. (1987). Participant's perception of change mechanisms in career counseling groups: The role of emotional components in career problem solving. *Journal of Career Development, 14*(1), 35–44.

Klein, R. (1993). Short-term psychotherapy. In H. Kaplan & B. Sadock (Eds.), *Comprehensive group psychotherapy* (pp. 257–263). Baltimore: Williams and Wilkins.

Kobasa, S. C. (1979). Stressful life events, personality, and health. *Journal of Personality and Social Psychology, 37*(1), 1–11.

Kottler, J. A. (1994). *Advanced group leadership.* Pacific Grove, CA: Brooks/Cole.

Kormanski, C. (1988). Using group development theory in business and industry. *Journal for Specialists in Group Work, 13*(1), 30–43.

Kurpius, D. J. & Fuqua, D. R. (1993). Fundamental issues in defining consultation. *Journal of Counseling & Development, 71*(6), 598–600.

Law, J., Morocco, J., & Wilmarth, R. R. (1981). A problem-oriented record system for counselors. *AMHCA Journal, 3*(1), 7–16.

Lawson, D. M. (1995). Conceptualization and treatment for Vietnam veterans experiencing posttraumatic stress disorder. *Journal of Mental Health Counseling, 17*(1), 31–53.

Lazarus, A. A., & Beutler, L. E. (1993). On technical eclecticism. *Journal of Counseling and Development, 71*(4), 381–385.

Lee, T. (1991). The sociodramatist and sociometrist in the primary school. *Journal of Group Psychotherapy, Psychodrama and Sociometry, 43*(4), 191–196.

Levinson, D. J. (1986). A conception of adult development. *American Psychologist, 41*(1), 3–13.

Lewis, J. A., & Hayes, B. A. (1988). Options for counselors in business and industry. In R. Hayes & R. Aubrey (Eds.), *New directions for counseling and human development* (pp. 247–260). Denver: Love Publishing Company.

Lewis, V. J., Blair, A. J., & Booth, D. A. (1992). Outcome of group therapy for body-image emotionality and weight control self-efficacy. *Behavioural Psychotherapy, 20*(2), 155–165.

Livneh, H. (1991). Counseling clients with disabilities. In D. Capuzzi & D. R. Gross (Eds.), *Introduction to counseling: Perspectives for the 1990s* (416–443). Boston: Allyn & Bacon.

Lowman, R. L. (1993). *Counseling and psychotherapy of work dysfunctions.* Washington, D.C.: American Psychological Association.

McArthur, M. J. (1990). Reality therapy with rape victims. *Archives of Psychiatric Nursing, 4*(6), 360–365.

McCaulley, M. (1990). The Myers-Briggs Type Indicator: A measure for individuals and groups. *Measurement and evaluation in counseling and development, 22*(4), 181–195.

McCubbin, H. I., Patterson, J. M., Rossman, M. M., & Cooke, B. (1982). *SSI social support inventory.* Madison: University of Wisconsin.

MacDonald, D. (1991). Philosophies that underlie models of mental health counseling: More than meets the eye. *Journal of mental health counseling, 13*(3), 379–392.

McFarland, W. P. (1992). Counselors teaching peaceful conflict resolution. *Journal of Counseling and Development, 71* (1), 18–21.

McGoldrick, M., & Carter, B. (1988). Forming a remarried family. In B. Carter & M. McGoldrick (Eds.), *The changing family life cycle* (pp. 402–429). New York: Gardner Press.

McGoldrick, M., & Gerson, R. (1988). Genograms and the family life cycle. In B. Carter & M. McGoldrick (Eds.), *The changing family life cycle* (pp. 164–189). New York: Gardner Press.

MacKay, B. (1989). Drama therapy with female victims of assault. *Arts in Psychotherapy, 16*(4), 293–300.

MacLennan, B. W. & Dies, K. R. (1992). *Group counseling and psychotherapy with adolescents.* New York: Columbia University Press.

McNair, D. M., Lorr, M., & Droppleman, L. F. (1992). *POMS manual.* San Diego: EdITS.

McWhirter, J. J., & McWhirter, B. T. (1991). A framework for theories in counseling. In D. Capuzzi & D. R. Gross (Eds.), *Introduction to counseling: Perspectives for the 1990s* (pp. 69–88). Boston: Allyn and Bacon.

Madanes, C. (1981). *Strategic family therapy.* San Francisco: Jossey-Bass.

Magoon, T. M., Golan, S. E., & Freeman, R. W. (1969). *Mental health counselors at work.* New York: Pergamon Press.

Martin, R. B. & Stepath, S. A. (1993). Psychodrama and reminiscence for the geriatric psychiatric patient. *Journal of Group Psychotherapy, Psychodrama and Sociometry, 45*(4), 139–148.

Mawson, D. L. & Kahn, S. E. (1993). Group process in a women's career intervention. *Career Development Quarterly, 41*(3), 238–245.

Maxmen, J. S., & Ward, N. G. (1995). *Essential psychopathology and its treatment.* New York: Norton.

Messina, J. J. (1995). The historical context of the Orlando Model Project and the NCMHC. In M. K. Altekruse & T. L. Sexton (Eds.), *Mental health counseling in the 90s* (pp. 1–6). Tampa, FL: National Commission for Mental Health Counseling.

Millon, T. (1995). *Disorders of personality: DSM-IV and beyond.* New York: Wiley.

Minuchin, P. P. (1977). *The middle years of childhood.* Monterey, CA: Brooks/Cole.

Minuchin, S., & Fishman, H. C. (1981). *Family therapy techniques.* Cambridge, MA: Harvard University Press.

Montag, K. R. & Wilson, G. L. (1992). An empirical evaluation of behavioral and cognitive-behavioral group marital treatments with discordant couples. *Journal of Sex and Marital Therapy, 18*(4), 255–272.

Morran, D. K. (1992). History of group work. *The Journal for Specialists in Group Work, 17*(1), 5–9.

Morrison, J. (1995). *DSM-IV made easy.* New York: Guilford Press.

Morrissey, M. (1994, December). Counselors "helping the helpers" from becoming casualties. *Counseling Today, 37*(6), 1, 6–7, 12.

Morrissey, M. (1995, January). Executive coaching increases counselors' role in industry. *Counseling Today, 37*(7), 1–2.

Motto, J., Heilbron, D. C., & Juster, R. P. (1985). Development of a clinical instrument to estimate suicide risk. *American Journal of Psychiatry, 152,* 680–686.

Mueller, R. O., Dupuy, P. J., & Hutchins, D. E. (1994). A review of the TFA Counseling System: From theory construction to application. *Journal of Counseling and Development, 72*(6), 573–577.

Myers, J. (1989). *Adult children and aging parents.* Alexandria, VA: American Counseling Association.

Myers, J. E. (1990). Aging: An overview for mental health counselors. *Journal of Mental Health Counseling, 12*(3), 245–259.

Myers, J. E. (1992). Wellness, prevention, development: The cornerstones of the profession. *Journal of Counseling and Development, 71*(2), 136–139.

Nance, D. W., & Myers, P. (1991). Continuing the eclectic journey. *Journal of Mental Health Counseling, 13*(1), 119–130.

Nichols, M. (1984). *Family therapy.* New York: Gardner Press.

Nugent, F. A. (1990). *An introduction to the profession of counseling.* Columbus, OH: Merrill.

O'Donnell, J. M. (1988). The holistic health movement: Implications for counseling theory and practice. In R. Hayes & R. Aubrey (Eds.), *New directions for counseling and human development* (pp. 365–383). Denver: Love Publishing Company.

Olson, D. H. (1986). Circumplex model VII: Validation studies and FACES-III. *Family Process, 25,* 337–351.

Paradise, L. V. (1990). Consumer rights in counseling: Duty to disclose. *Journal of Mental Health Counseling, 12*(2), 225–227.

Parsons, F. (1909). *Choosing a vocation.* Boston: Houghton Mifflin.

Patterson, J. M. & McCubbin, H. S. (1987). *A-COPE: Adolescent-coping orientation for problem experiences.* Madison, WI: University of Wisconsin.

Pedersen, P. (1990). The multicultural perspective as a fourth force in counseling. *Journal of Mental Health Counseling, 12*(1), 93–95.

Perry, J. C., & Cooper, S. H. (1989). An empirical study of defense mechanisms. *Archives of General Psychiatry, 46,* 444–452.

Pfeiffer, S. M. (Spring, 1995). Editor's corner. *Advance, 2* & 16.

Piaget, J. (1963). *The child's conception of the world.* Patterson, NJ: Littlefield, Adans.

Pietrofesa, J. J., Hoffman, A., & Splete, H. H. (1984). *Counseling: An introduction.* Boston: Houghton Mifflin.

Powell, S. R. (1993). The power of positive peer influence: Leadership training for today's teens. In J. E. Zins & M. J. Elias (Eds.), *Promoting student success through group interventions* (pp. 119–136). New York: Haworth Press.

Prochaska, J. O., & Norcross, J. C. (1994). *Systems of psychotherapy.* Pacific Grove, CA: Brooks/Cole.

Puig-Antich, J., & Chambers, W. (1978). *The schedule for affective disorders and schizophrenia for school-aged children.* New York: New York State Psychiatric Institute.

Rajendran, R., & Kaliappan, K. V. (1990). Efficacy of behavioural programme in managing the academic stress and improving academic performance. *Journal of Personality and Clinical Studies, 6,* 193–196.

Ratican, K. L. (1992). Sexual abuse survivors: Identifying symptoms and special treatment considerations. *Journal of Counseling & Development, 71*(1), 33–38.

Remer, R., Morse, H. B., Popma, J., & Jones, S. M. (1993). Spontaneity training and psychodrama with Alzheimer's patients. *Journal of Group Psychotherapy, Psychodrama and Sociometry, 45*(4), 131–138.

Riess, H. & Rutan, J. S. (1992). Group therapy for eating disorders: A step-wise approach. *Group, 16*(2), 79–83.

Rigazio-Digilio, S. A. (1994). A co-constructive-developmental approach to ecosystemic treatment. *Journal of Mental Health Counseling, 16*(1), 43–74.

Ritchie, M. H., Piazza, N. J., & Lewton, J. C. (1991). Current use of the *DSM-III-R* in counselor education. *Counselor Education and Supervision, 30*(3), 205–211.

Robins, L. N., Helzer, J. E., Croughan, J., & Ratcliffe, K. S. (1981). National Institute of Mental Health Diagnostic Interview Schedule: Its history, characteristics, and validity. *Archives of General Psychiatry, 10,* 41–61.

Rockwell, P. J., Jr. (1991). The counseling profession: A historical prespective. In D. Capuzzi & D. R. Gross (Eds.), *Introduction to counseling: Perspectives for the 1990s* (pp. 5–24). Boston: Allyn & Bacon.

Rogers, C. R. (1942). *Counseling and psychotherapy.* Boston: Houghton Mifflin.

Rutan, J. S. & Stone, W. N. (1993). *Psychodynamic group psychotherapy.* New York: Guilford Press.

Sasson, F. (1990). Psychodrama with adolescents: Management techniques that work. *Journal of Group Psychotherapy, Psychodrama and Sociometry, 43*(4), 121–127.

Satir, V. (1967). *Conjoint family therapy.* Palo Alto, CA: Science and Behavior Books.

Satir, V. (1983). *Conjoint family therapy.* Palo Alto, CA: Science and Behavior Books.

Satir, V., Banmen, J., Gerber, J., & Gomori, M. (1991). *The Satir model.* Palo Alto, CA: Science and Behavior Books.

Scholssberg, N. K. (1992). Adult development theories: Ways to illuminate the adult experience. In H. D. Lea & Z. B. Leibowitz (Eds.), *Adult career development* (pp. 2–16). Alexandria, VA: American Counseling Association.

Schwiebert, V. L., & Myers, J. E. (1994). Midlife care givers: Effectiveness of a psychoeducational intervention for midlife adults with parent-care responsibilities. *Journal of Counseling and Development, 72*(6), 627–639.

Seiler, G., & Messina, J. (1979). Toward professional identity: The dimensions of mental health counseling in perspective. *AMHCA Journal, 1*(1), 3–8.

Seligman, L. (1986). *Diagnosis and treatment planning in counseling.* New York: Human Sciences Press.

Seligman, L. (1990). *Selecting effective treatments.* San Francisco: Jossey-Bass.

Seligman, L. (1991). Diagnosis in counseling. In D. Capuzzi & D. R. Gross (Eds.), *Introduction to counseling: Perspectives for the 1990s* (pp. 181–204). Boston: Allyn & Bacon.

Seligman, L. (1993). Teaching treatment planning. *Counselor Education and Supervision, 33*(4), 287–297.

Seligman, L. (1994). *Developmental career counseling and assessment.* Thousand Oaks, CA: Sage.

Seligman, L. (1995). *DSM-IV: Diagnosis and treatment planning home study.* Alexandria, VA: American Counseling Association.

Seligman, L. (1996). *Promoting a fighting spirit: Psychotherapy for cancer patients, survivors, and their families.* San Francisco: Jossey-Bass.

Seligman, L., & Ceo, M. N. (1986). Multidisciplinary mental health treatment teams. In A. J. Palmo & W. J. Weikel (Eds.), *Foundations of mental health counseling* (pp. 145–165). Springfield, IL: Charles C. Thomas.

Selvini Palazzoli, M. (1988). *The work of Mara Selvini Palazzoli.* New York: Jason Aronson.

Sexton, T. L. (1995). Outcome research perspective on mental health counselor competencies. In M. K. Altekruse & T. L. Sexton (Eds.), *Mental health counseling in the the 90's* (51–60). Tampa, FL: National Commission for Mental Health Counseling.

Sexton, T. L., & Whiston, S. C. (1991). A review of the empirical basis for counseling: Implications for practice and training. *Counselor Education and Supervision, 30*(4), 330–354.

Shaffer, J. & Galinsky, M. D. (1989). *Models of group therapy.* Englewood Cliffs, NJ: Prentice-Hall.

Shea, C. S. (1990). Contemporary psychiatric interviewing: Integration of *DSM-III-R*, psychodynamic concerns, and mental status. In G. Goldstein & M. Hersen (Eds.), *Handbook of psychological assessment* (pp. 283–307). New York: Pergamon Press.

Shertzer, B., & Linden, J. D. (1979). *Fundamentals of individual appraisal.* Boston: Houghton Mifflin.

Shertzer, B., & Stone, S. C. (1980). *Fundamentals of counseling.* Boston: Houghton Mifflin.

Shulman, L. & Gitterman, A. (1986). The life model, mutual aid, and the mediating function. In A. Gitterman & L. Shulman (Eds.), *Mutual aid groups and the life cycle.* (pp. 3–22). Itasca, IL: Peacock.

Smith, M. L., Glass, G. V., & Miller, T. I. (1980). *The benefits of psychotherapy.* Baltimore: Johns Hopkins University Press.

Snyderman, M., & Rothman, S. (1987). Survey of expert opinion on intelligence and aptitude testing. *American Psychologist, 42*(2), 137–144.

Spiegel, D. (1990). Can psychotherapy prolong cancer survival? *Psychosomatics, 31,* 361–366.

Spitzer, R. L., Gibbon, M., Skodol, A. E., Williams, J. B. W., & First, M. B. (1994). *DSM-IV casebook.* Washington, DC: American Psychiatric Association.

Splete, J. J. (1988). Consultation by the counselor. In R. Hayes & R. Aubrey (Eds.), *New directions for counseling and human development* (pp. 275–285). Denver: Love Publishing Company.

Spruill, D. A., & Fong, M. L. (1990). Defining the domain of mental health counseling: From identity confusion to consensus. *Journal of Mental Health Counseling, 12*(1), 12–23.

Standards for the clinical practice of mental health counseling. (1994, June 8). *The Advocate*, p. II.D-1.

Steenbarger, B. N. (1991). All the world is not a stage: Emerging contextualist themes in counseling and development. *Journal of Counseling and Development, 70*(2), 288–296.

Steinberg, J. A. (1986). Clinical interventions with women experiencing the impostor phenomenon. *Women and Therapy, 5,* 19–26.

Stoltenberg, C. D. (1993). Supervising consultants in training: An application of a model of supervision. *Journal of Counseling and Development, 72*(2), 131–138.

Stuart, R. B. (1980). *Helping couples change.* New York: Guilford Press.

Sue, D. W., Arredondo, P., & McDavis, R. J. (1992). Multicultural counseling competencies and standards: A call to the profession. *Journal of Counseling and Development, 70*(4), 477–486.

Sue, D. W. & Sue, D. (1990). *Counseling the culturally different: Theory and practice.* New York: Wiley.

Sundberg, N. D. (1976). *Assessment of persons.* Englewood Cliffs, NJ: Prentice-Hall.

Sundel, M., & Bernstein, B. E. (1995). Legal and financial aspects of midlife review and their implications for mental health counselors. *Journal of Mental Health Counseling, 17*(1), 114–123.

Super, D. E. (1957). *Vocational development: A framework for research.* New York: Teachers College Press.

Tart, C. T. (1992). *Transpersonal psychologies.* San Francisco: HarperCollins.

Terry, A., Burden, C. A., & Pedersen, M. M. (1991). The helping relationship. In D. Capuzzi & D. R. Gross (Eds.), *Introduction to counseling: Perspectives for the 1990s* (pp. 44–68). Boston: Allyn and Bacon.

Three-year strategic plan: July 1, 1992-June 30, 1995. (1992, June). *Guidepost, 34*(14), 22–26.

Thomas, M. B. (1992). *An introduction to marital and family therapy.* New York: Macmillan Publishing.

Thompson, C. E., & Atkinson, D. R. (1991). Counseling visible racial/ethnic group (VREG) men and women. In D. Capuzzi & D. R. Gross (Eds.), *Introduction to counseling: Perspectives for the 1990s* (pp. 388–415). Boston: Allyn and Bacon.

Throckmorton, E. W. (1992, March). *State licensure and third party reimbursement: Which states permit professional counselors to provide reimbursable clinical services?* Paper presented at the national convention of the American Association for Counseling and Development, Baltimore, MD.

Towl, G. (1994). Anger control groupwork in practice. *Issues in Criminological and Legal Psychology, 20,* 75–77.

Twohey, D., & Ewing, M. (1995). The male voice of emotional intimacy. *Journal of Mental Health Counseling, 17*(1), 54–62.

Vacc, N. A., & Loesch, L. C. (1987). *Counseling as a profession.* Muncie, IN: Accelerated Development, Inc.

Vaillant, G. E., Bond, M., & Vaillant, C. O. (1986). An empirically validated hierarchy of defense mechanisms. *Archives of General Psychiatry, 43,* 786–794.

Walker, D. E. (1981). *Clinical practice of psychology.* New York: Pergamon Press.

Wantz, R. A., & Scherman, A. (1982). Trends in counselor preparation: Courses, program emphases, philosophical orientation, and experimental components. *Counselor Education and Supervision, 21,* 258–268.

Waterman, R. H., Peters, T. J., & Phillips, J. R. (1980). Structure is not organization. *Business Horizon*, *23*, 14–26.

Watson, R. J. & Stermac, L. E. (1994). Cognitive group counseling for sexual offenders. *International Journal of Offender Therapy and Comparative Criminology*, *38*(3), 259–270.

Weikel, W. J., & Palmo, A. J. (1989). The evolution and practice of mental health counseling. *Journal of Mental Health Counseling*, *11*(1), 7–25.

Weinrach, S. G., & Thomas, K. R. (1993). The National Board for Certified Counselors: The good, the bad, and the ugly. *Journal of Counseling and Development*, *72*(1), 105–109.

Welner, Z., Reich, W., Herjanic, B., Jung, K., & Armado, H. (1987). Reliability, validity, and parent-child agreement studies of the Diagnostic Interview for Children and Adolescents (DICA). *Journal of the American Academy of Child Psychiatry*, *26*, 649–653.

West, J. D., Hosie, T. W., & Mackey, J. A. (1987). Employment and roles of counselors in mental health agencies. *Journal of Counseling and Development*, *66*(3), 135–138.

White, J., Keenan, M., & Brooks, N. (1992). Stress control: A controlled comparative investigation of large group therapy for generalized anxiety disorder. *Behavioural Psychotherapy*, *20*(2), 97–113.

Williamson, R. S. (1992). Using group reality therapy to raise self-esteem in adolescent girls. *Journal of Reality Therapy*, *11* (2), 3–11.

Witmer, J. M., & Sweeney, T. J. (1992). A holistic model for wellness and prevention over the life span. *Journal of Counseling and Development*, *71*(2), 140–148.

Wolber, G. J., & Carne, W. F. (1993). *Writing psychological reports: A guide for clinicians*. Sarasota, FL: Professional Resource Press.

World Health Organization. (1992). *ICD-10 classification of mental and behavioural disorders*. Geneva: Author.

Wubbolding, R. E. (1990). *Expanding reality therapy: Group counseling and multicultural dimensions*. Cincinnati, OH: Real World Publications.

Yalom, I. D. (1995). *The theory and practice of group psychotherapy*. New York: Basic Books.

Zimpfer, D. G. (1995). Third-party reimbursement experience of licensed clinical counselors in Ohio. *Journal of Mental Health Counseling*, *17*(1), 105–113.

Zimpfer, D. G., & DeTrude, J. C. (1990). Follow-up of doctoral graduates in counseling. *Journal of Counseling and Development*, *69*(1), 51–56.

Zinker, J. (1991). Creative process in Gestalt therapy: The therapist as artist. *Gestalt Journal*, *14*(2), 71–88.

About the Author

LINDA SELIGMAN received the Ph.D. degree in Counseling Psychology from Columbia University. She is a full professor at George Mason University in Fairfax, Virginia, where she is in charge of the graduate program in Community Agency Counseling.

Dr. Seligman is a licensed psychologist and licensed professional counselor. She has experience in a variety of clinical settings, including psychiatric hospitals, community mental health centers, substance abuse treatment programs, foster care, corrections, and private practice. She is currently the Director of the Center for Counseling and Consultation, a private practice with offices in Fairfax, Virginia, and Bethesda, Maryland.

Dr. Seligman's research interests include diagnosis and treatment planning, counseling people who are coping with cancer, and career counseling. She has completed five books, including *Promoting a Fighting Spirit: Psychotherapy for Cancer Patients, Survivors, and Their Families*; *Developmental Career Counseling and Assessment*; and *Selecting Effective Treatments*, and has authored over 40 professional articles and book chapters. In addition, she has lectured throughout the United States and Canada on diagnosis and treatment planning.

Dr. Seligman has been the editor of *The Journal of Mental Health Counseling* and has served as president of the Virginia Association of Mental Health Counselors. In 1986, she was selected as a Distinguished Professor by George Mason University, and in 1990, she was selected as Researcher of the Year by the American Mental Health Counselors Association.

Index